An Ecumenical Theology of the Heart:

The Theology of Count Nicholas Ludwig von Zinzendorf

To Marcia

May grace, peace, and joy be yours,

Arthur J. Freeman

Arthur Freeman
Dec 1998

The Moravian Church in America
1021 Center St., Bethlehem, PA 18018
459 S. Church St., Winston-Salem, NC 27101

Copyright © 1998 by Arthur J. Freeman

Library of Congress Catalog Card Number: 98-65184

ISBN: 1-878422-36-7 hardcover
       1-878422-38-3 paperback

The cover painting, "The Resurrected Christ with His Wounds," by the Moravian painter John Valentine Haidt (1700-1780), is used courtesy of the Moravian Archives, Bethlehem, Pa. In Zinzendorf's theology there is no other God than the wounded God.

The author is grateful to the University of Iowa Press for permission to reprint extension quotations from *Nine Public Lectures on Important Subjects in Religion* by Count Zinzendorf, translated and edited by George W. Forell, copyright 1973 by the University of Iowa Press.

Cover designer: Ron Tinsley

Published by
Board of Communications
Moravian Church in America
P.O. Box 1245
Bethlehem, PA 18016-1245
        telephone 800-732-0591
        fax 610-866-9223
        e-mail <pubs@mcnp.org>

Printed in the United States of America

Contents

Preface

The intent of this book is to bring to the English-speaking reader resources ordinarily available only in German regarding Nicholas Ludwig von Zinzendorf, to discuss Zinzendorf's theology not only for the Moravian reader but an ecumenical audience, and to integrate his insights with the voices of Scripture and spirituality. Though Zinzendorf's views are treated with historical respect, they are seen as part of a longer tradition of theological reflection within the Moravian Church and as resource, critically appraised, for the present and future. The fact that his theology was a response to the issues of the eighteenth century which shaped our modern world makes his views of contemporary value.

The painting on the cover is "The Resurrected Christ with His Wounds" by John Valentine Haidt (1700-1780). Born in Danzig, he was received into the Moravian Church in London. From 1754 until his death his primary place of residence was Bethlehem in Pennsylvania. Though he served in many offices, his primary contribution was the painting not only of important persons within the Moravian Church but of biblical scenes and an artistic recording of the "First Fruits" of the Moravian missions. He was the first colonial American painter to treat religious subjects. Central to Zinzendorf's theology are the wounds of Christ with which he appeared to his disciples after his resurrection, according to Zinzendorf's interpretation of John 20. This meant that the significance of the incarnation was continued in Christ's post-resurrection existence. He takes his wounds and his humanity with him to heaven, where he remains the one wounded for us, the one who loves us with a gentle and patient love. There is no other God than the wounded one. God never leaves the wounds behind. This portrayal of Christ also symbolizes Zinzendorf's Christocentric understanding of God.

This book has been the product of over forty years of work on Zinzendorf. Because my primary teaching responsibility has been New Testament and my second has been Spiritual Formation, Zinzendorf often came in last because of limitations on my time, though I owe much of my own theology to his insights. I explain this merely to indicate why this work took almost a lifetime. There is much more that I would like to do in research, but one has to stop somewhere. And this is the time, especially as the 300th anniversary of Zinzendorf's birth approaches.

I express appreciation to Otto and Elisabeth Piper, who are no longer with us, for their encouragement and his directing me to the hermeneutics of Zinzendorf while I was at Princeton Theological Seminary working on my Th.D. I express appreciation to my students over the years, who responded insightfully to the presentation of Zinzendorf's theology, and to the Moravian Church and the Moravian Theological Seminary, which gave me the opportunity for teaching and research. I realize that if I had stayed in the parish as an organizer of new congregations, my initial responsibility, this study might never have been written. I express appreciation to the pastors of the Moravian Church whose ministries made possible my specialization and so in some way share in this.

I thank Dr. Albert Frank, assistant archivist of the Moravian Church, Northern Province, whose reading of the manuscript and advice helped give consistency to materials that had been written over the years; Peter Vogt, former student and friend, a number of whose suggestions have been incorporated; Dr. Hermann Weinlick, Director of the Moravian Interprovincial Board of Publications and Communications, for encouragement and extensive editorial involvement; Dr. Thomas Haupert for valuable assistance with the footnoting of sources; Nena Asquith for many hours at the computer to compose and prepare this book for the printer, and Barbara Stout, friend and former student, whose insistence kept me attentive to goals and deadlines.

Extensive quotation has been used due to the lack of availability of English translations of the materials. The quotations will provide the reader with the opportunity of becoming acquainted with Zinzendorf's thought and language in the original sources. At times I allow the quotations to speak for themselves rather than also describing or summarizing their content. Hopefully those able to work with eighteenth-century German will make some of Zinzendorf's works available in English in the future. Zinzendorf, as did many of the educated of his time, frequently used words from languages other than German. For him this also had the special purpose of using words he felt more appropriate to the Christian experience than some of the equivalent German words. In the quotations, words in languages other than German are retained, placed in italics (even the English words that are in the German text), and their translation, where necessary, is placed in brackets. Thus his use of these words will be apparent to the reader. There are also words derived from other languages which have been germanized by the addition of appropriate endings, and these I have not indicated. I have translated titles of German works where mentioned in the text. The reader will want to consult the footnotes for the German titles. Footnotes are used rather than endnotes, since they often include not only references but comments on issues in the text.

Footnotes, and the bibliography provided, will enable those who can read German to refer to the sources. In the footnote for each quotation from Zinzendorf the date of the origin of the material is listed in parentheses. Since the dates of publication are not usually the same as the date of origin, this will help the reader to see Zinzendorf's statements in the context of his life. Bibliographical references in the footnotes contain full information in the first mention of a source within a chapter. Thereafter they are abbreviated in the notes of the chapter according to the pattern indicated in the first and full treatment of the source.

I believe that inclusive language is crucial, not only to meet contemporary standards, but to preserve the dignity and equality of persons, realizing how language unconsciously affects attitudes and perceptions. However, there are two exceptions. I have not always been able to use inclusive language with regard to God without making the text very awkward. I do understand God inclusively, as expressed in the poem near the end of chapter 2. The other exception is the problem of translating eighteenth-century texts which were not sensitive to this issue in modern terms. I have tried to be inclusive where the language allows. At times I have omitted masculine pronouns where they did not seem necessary for translation. Otherwise, I needed to be responsible to the text as it was.

I dedicate this to my wife Carole, with whom I have shared my life in the last fourteen years and who has patiently allowed me to have my nose in the books and my hands on the computer, and sometimes to have my mind in the eighteenth century.

Introduction

Though I was raised in the Moravian Church, it was only while pursuing my Th.D. at Princeton Theological Seminary that I was urged to explore Zinzendorf's theology by Otto Piper, then Professor of New Testament.[1] Piper had a deep interest in hermeneutics and urged his graduate students to pursue the hermeneutics of significant persons in their theological tradition. He came from Germany, had a working knowledge of Zinzendorf, and daily used for his devotions *Die Losungen*, the *Moravian Daily Texts*. I have been forever grateful to Piper, for Zinzendorf has decisively shaped my own theology. Though I differ with him in some respects, I have found myself strangely drifting towards his views even in areas in which I differ.

From the time of my graduate studies it has been my hope that in some way I might contribute to the recovery of this significant theological heritage within the Moravian Church and make others more aware of the person whom Karl Barth has called "a church father who is important and fruitful for the whole church."[2] Especially in the North American Moravian Church I have frequently discovered an anti-Zinzendorf attitude which identifies him with the conservative period following his death which severely limited the development of the Moravian Church in North America until the mid-nineteenth century. Since the ability of pastors to use German declined here and disappeared by the mid twentieth century, the Zinzendorf sources could no longer be explored. With the exception of a translation of nine sermons, the only English translations of a limited body of his work, not

---

[1] Arthur James Freeman, "The Hermeneutics of Count Nicolaus Ludwig von Zinzendorf" (Th.D. diss., Princeton Theological Seminary, 1962). Quotations are mostly in German.

[2] H. Schmidt, H. Bintz, and W. Günther, eds., "Protokoll des Gesprächs zwischen Professor Dr. Karl Barth und Vertretern der Brüdergemeine am 12. Oktober 1960 in Basel," *Civitas Praesens*, no. 13, special issue (May 1961): p. 3. (Abbreviated in subsequent notes as Schmidt, Bintz, and Günther, eds., "Protokoll des Gesprächs.")

now easily available, were made in the eighteenth century.[3]

Because of the dearth of material available on Zinzendorf in English, this work will be important if it does nothing more than make available some of the sources, and I include a significant number. Since my primary training is in New Testament and I have a special interest in Spiritual Formation, the reader should understand that these interests and perspectives will appear in the book. Hopefully they will make their contribution. The chapters end with reflection which seeks to bring the insights of Zinzendorf critically into the present.

My purpose in writing is

1. to make available a systematic treatment of Zinzendorf's theology, along with sources;
2. to place Zinzendorf's theology within the context of his time and the stream of Moravian theological reflection since the fifteenth century;
3. to reflect on its contribution and possibilities for contemporary theological reflection and formation;
4. to clarify that in practice and formulation his theology is really ecumenical, providing a common foundation and inclusive perspective for the theological work of other traditions;
5. to join theological reflection to spiritual formation on personal and communal levels, to regard theological reflection itself as a formative process, so that doing theology may become or facilitate experience of its subject.

The last point has been important to me. The study of Bible, theology, and the formulation of theology has challenged and changed

---

[3] The only modern translation into English of one volume of his sermons was made by George W. Forell: *Nine Public Lectures on Important Subjects in Religion Preached in Fetter Lane Chapel in London in the Year 1746* (Iowa City: University of Iowa Press, 1973). This is a translation of *Neun Oeffentliche Reden über wichtige in die Religion einschlagende Materien, Gehalten zu London in Fetterlane-Capelle Anno 1746* (n.p., Zu finden in den Brüder-Gemeinen, n.d.). Eighteenth-century translation: *Nine Publick Discourses Upon Important Subjects in Religion, Preached in Fetter-Lane-Chapel at London in the Year 1746.* Translated from the German (London: James Hutton, 1748).

The other eighteenth-century English-language publications or translations (titles abbreviated) include:

Sixteen Discourses on the Redemption of Man, 1740 (Berlin sermons to the men, 1738).

A Manual of Doctrine, 1742 (*Probe eines Lehrbüchelgens,* 1740).

Seven Sermons on the Godhead of the Lamb, 1742 (*Sieben Letzte Reden,* 1742).

Twenty-one Discourses or Dissertations upon the Augsburg Confession, 1753 (*Ein und zwanzig Discurse über die Augspurgische Confession,* 1747-48, n.d.).

An Account of the Doctrine, Manners, Liturgy, and Idiom of the Unitas Fratrum, 1749.

Maxims, Theological Ideas and Sentences out of the Present Ordinary, extracted by John Gambold, *1738-47,* 1751.

An Exposition, or True State, of the Matters Objected in England to the People known by the Name of Unitas Fratrum, 1755.

me, drawing me beyond itself to the realities about which it speaks and forming not only my theology but my life in the process. The experience of the realities to which theological language refers has in turn informed and challenged the concepts with which I was working. The process was dialogical, and so it should be: concepts interpreting and affecting life, and life distinguishing the intention and referents of the concepts. Poetry has become very important to me as a style of theological expression which embraces the spiritual realities of life without seeking to hold them captive. I suggest that poetry may be the best way to do theology. For Zinzendorf, poetry was important because it took the experienced realities of faith seriously rather than understanding religious truth as intellectual and conceptual formulation. At the end of a chapter I will frequently use poetry as a way of expressing its concerns.

An excursion into Moravian terminology for the church

The name "Moravian" was not used by the Moravian Church prior to the eighteenth century and was not even used at the beginning by those who gathered on Zinzendorf's estate. It has become a name of convenience, rather than using different names for different historical periods. For the Moravian Church from 1457 to 1621 we use the name "Ancient Moravian Church." The Ancient Moravian Church initially called itself "Brethren of the Law of Christ," affirming its special allegiance to Jesus' Sermon on the Mount as an expression of Christian life. It later gave itself the name *Unitas Fratrum,* which means "Unity of the Brethren." Since the Thirty Years War eliminated the right of the Moravian Church to legally exist in its home areas of Bohemia and Moravia, it continued to exist during the period 1621-1721 primarily as a "Hidden Seed" (a technical term by which this period is known) in its homelands and in several congregations in Poland. In 1722 a group of refugees from Moravia was given permission to settle on the estate of Count Zinzendorf in Saxony and formed the beginning of what historians call the Renewed Moravian Church. This fact was later to give the name Moravian to this church, which initially was intended to be a society within the Lutheran Church. Three *Tropi* (indicating different "ways of teaching") were formed in the 1740s within the Moravian Church: Reformed, Lutheran and Moravian (those from Moravia who preserved the tradition of the Ancient Moravian Church). Sometimes when Moravian Brethren are referred to, it means the Moravian *Tropus* within the Moravian Church, not the whole church. Diaspora Society is a name given the societies formed within the state or regional churches according to the Pietistic principle of *ecclesiolae in ecclesia* (little churches within the church). In Europe membership in Diaspora Societies was always much larger than that of the Moravian settlements and congregations.

Religion was a term often used by Zinzendorf for denominations or the confessional churches, but never used for the Moravian Church, which understood itself not to be primarily constituted by a confession or historical tradition, but by its living relationship with the Savior. The first bishops of the Renewed Church were ordained by the last remaining bishops of the Ancient Moravian Church, and thus the continuity of ministerial orders was preserved. Though such terms as Moravian Brethren and Herrnhuters (from Herrnhut, the village on Zinzendorf's estate where the Church was renewed) were applied to the Renewed Moravian Church, it preferred the name *Brüdergemeine*, which was in a sense a translation of the name of the Ancient Church, *Unitas Fratrum*. *Brüder* means "brothers" and in its religious sense could be understood to include both men and women. *Gemein* means "common, public, general," and in its religious usage is similar to *Unitas*. *Gemeine* was used in the eighteenth century as *Gemeinde* later came to be used, meaning community or congregation. Luther use this for "church" in his translation of the New Testament, and Zinzendorf also used this for the universal church. *Brüdergemeine* was used by Zinzendorf both for a congregation and for the whole Moravian Church, since both the congregation and the whole church were constituted by the same reality: fellowship with Christ and each other. Thus *Brüdergemeine* means "community, congregation, or Church of the Brethren," but usually is rendered in English as "Moravian Church." Because of the experience of separation of the Continental Province from other Moravian provinces during the Second World War, and expressing a conscious decision of the international synod of 1957, the term "Unity" became the term of preference for the international Moravian Church.

A Tradition of Moravian Theology?

As to whether there is really a tradition of Moravian theology, the Moravian Interprovincial Faith and Order Commission in 1990 stated in a position paper developed for guiding its own theological tasks:

> Although it has often been said that the Moravian Church does not have a theology or is not theologically inclined, it is our understanding that it has a very definite theology. In its long history it has variously had its unique stance, also being influenced by the

theological expressions of the other theological traditions: in the late sixteenth and early seventeenth century the Ancient Church was decidedly affected by the Reformed tradition, while in eighteenth-century Germany the Renewed Church was quite Lutheran, affirming the special role of the Augsburg Confession.

Generally, sometimes more and sometimes less consciously, there has been an awareness of epistemological issues which has decidedly affected the position of the Moravian Church on theology. It is well expressed in the statement on theology in 1979 by the Joint Theological Commission of the Northern and Southern Provinces, U.S.A.:

> Theological reflection in the Moravian tradition is not to be understood as an attempt to arrive at final answers but is a way of thinking about God and His relationship to us so that He can, through His Spirit, draw us to Himself, and to His Son, and we can know Him as the Source of our living. Such reflection should lead to sharing of ideas and experiences, articulation of our faith, new levels of trust toward each other as persons through whom God partially discloses Himself in various ways, stimulation of the Christian life and our attentive waiting upon God for His clarification of our understanding.[4]

One may say that the theological views which are particular to the Moravian Church were formed by an awareness that Christianity at its heart is relational and devotional, not conceptual; that the fostering of relationship with God and Christian life are central, without which concepts have no "coinage." Conceptual, liturgical, and institutional expressions, while sharing the foundational experience of faith and life,

---

[4] "The Theological Task As Understood Within the Moravian Tradition," was revised and accepted for use by the Interprovincial Faith and Order Commission of the Northern and Southern American Moravian provinces on July 13, 1990. This paper was intended as a statement of theological method which was to be foundational for the future work of the Commission. The mentioned Joint Theological Commission was formed before the Faith and Order Commission and was given the responsibility of examining the theology of the Moravian heritage to see if theological differences contributed to the failure of an attempted merger of the two provinces. The 1979 statement indicated the sharing of a common theology between the two provinces and that theological differences were not contributive to the failed merger.

are always shaped by historical and cultural contexts.[5] The theological understanding of the Ancient Moravian Church was particularly formed by its dividing all theological and ecclesial matters into *essentials, ministerials, and incidentals.* For it the essential was the relationship with the Triune God expressed in the threefold response of faith, love, and hope. In the Zinzendorfian period we have the emphasis on basic truths or fundamentals, and Heart *Religion* (the heart relationship with the Savior) — somewhat equivalent to the essential of the Ancient Church. This is a very explicit theology, though it is not a systematic theology. Zinzendorf, for example, did not write a systematic theology because he theologically believed that it was not possible — one cannot know and express God that way.[6] Any attempt to systematize understanding of God will always have gaps because of human limitations. One needs to

[5] Wilhelm Bettermann, formerly director of the Archives in Herrnhut, published an article on "Grundlinien der Theologie Zinzendorfs," *Zeitschrift für Systematische Theologie* 11 (1934): pp. 3-18. He uses the German word *erbaulich* to describe the character of Zinzendorf's theology. This word may be translated as "edifying" or "devotional." He asserts that in Zinzendorf, "devotional and theological expressions cannot be separated from one another: his devotional language, in sermons as in hymns, is theological and his theology is devotional. He has undertaken, and that is a great thrust of his theology, to close the chasm which has been erected between theology and devotional language." Moreover, "Zinzendorf in his practical activity had to do with a lay theology; and through engagement with this theology, and at the same time also with scientific theology, his own theology arose" (pp. 3-4). Bettermann also asserts that Zinzendorf recognized that "theology and doctrine change with the times" (p. 5).

[6] The closest expression of a systematic treatment of theology is his *Ein und Zwanzig Discurse über die Augspurgische Confession,* where his subject matter committed him to a topical treatment (Full citation: Nikolaus Ludwig von Zinzendorf, *Ein und zwanzig Discurse über die Augspurgische Confession gehalten vom 15. Dec. 1747. bis zum 3. Mart. 1748. denen Seminariis Theologicis Fratrum zum Besten aufgefaßt und bis zur nochmaligen Revision des Auctoris einstweilen privatim mitgetheilet* [n.p., n.d.]; translated under the title *Twenty One Discourses Or Dissertations Upon The Augsburg Confession, Which is also the Brethren's Confession of Faith: Deliver'd by the Ordinary Of the Brethren's Churches before the Seminary. To which is prefixed, A Synodal Writing Relating to the same Subject. Translated from the High Dutch, By F. Okeley, B.A.* [London: J. Beecroft, 1753].) However, even here Zinzendorf as the poet is evident, for he made primary use of a poem/hymn of 161 stanzas he composed on the Confession. The extensive body of poetry and hymns which he produced indicates that poetry was for him an important way of doing theology. For Zinzendorf the *Augsburg Confession* was "uncontestably the best from the time of the apostles until now." (I can no longer locate the source of this quotation, but the first discourse on the Confession clearly supports this. AJF) In early 1741 Zinzendorf with some forty others (a Pilgrim Congregation) visited Geneva and here he came across the resolutions of the Synod of Bern (1532). He understood these as "pastoral instruction" about homiletical methodology: instruction for the proclamation of doctrine. He adopted the first eighteen articles and, as with the *Augsburg Confession,* composed a hymn of 198 stanzas as an appropriate way of sharing the Bern resolutions with the Moravian Church. From this time on it is the first twenty-one articles of the Augsburg Confession and the first eighteen articles of the Bern Synod that Zinzendorf regards as normative for his theology (Mary B. Havens, "Zinzendorf and the Augsburg Confession:

accept that the only Christian system is Christ, the historical expression of the Person of God. As Zinzendorf has God say in a poem that expresses his epistemology, "My nature, which no one sees, has built itself a body."[7] Zinzendorf's belief that Heart Religion[8] was the basis of all Christian *religion* allowed him to recognize that different creeds and theologies may be adhered to in different contexts as legitimate cultural incarnations of Christianity, each valid for its context. Thus Moravians of the Renewed Church in different countries adhered to different confessions, yet all belonged to the same religious community. In the eighteenth-century Moravian Church separate membership lists were even preserved for Moravians, Reformed, and Lutherans so that the treasures of each would not be lost. The Moravian Church initiated relationships with the Lutheran Church, the Anglican Church, and the Reformed Church, was in contact with the early developments of the Methodist movement, provided harbor for the Schwenkfelders. It helped to initiate the Pennsylvania Synods, which Zinzendorf intended would create a German-speaking ecumenical community of churches, a Church of God in the Spirit. Moravians are members of local and regional councils of churches and the World Council of Churches and have recently participated in formal theological dialogue with the

An Ecumenical Vision?" [Ph.D. diss., Princeton Theological Seminary, 1989], pp. 300-301). Zinzendorf argued that "the Bern Synod, with its Christological emphases, is written 'in one and the same spirit' as the unaltered *Augsburg Confession*; there is no contradiction between the two" (ibid., p. 528). This is commented on in the *Apologetische Schluß-Schrift* of Spangenberg (*M. Avgvst. Gottl. Spangenbergs Apologetische Schluß-Schrift, Worinn über tausend Beschuldigungen gegen die Brüder-Gemeinen und Ihren zeitherigen Ordinarium nach der Wahrheit beantwortet werden, Nebst einigen wichtigen Beylagen* [Leipzig and Görlitz: In der Marcheschen Buchhandlung, 1752]; reprinted in Nikolaus Ludwig von Zinzendorf, *Ergänzungsbände zu den Hauptschriften*, ed. Erich Beyreuther and Gerhard Meyer [Hildesheim: Georg Olms, 1964-85], 3:33. The page cited is p. 33 of vol. 3, of the reprint edition. [Citation of the reprint edition will be abbreviated in subsequent notes as Zinzendorf, *Ergänzungsbände*.]) I also call attention to an article by Martin Schmidt, "Zinzendorf und die Confessio Augustana," *Theologische Literaturzeitung* (Leipzig), no. 11 (Nov. 1968): pp. 802-24.

[7] "Allgegenwart," in *Graf Ludwigs von Zinzendorff Teutscher Gedichte Erster Theil* (Herrnhut: Zu finden im Waisenhause, 1735), pp. 106-8.

[8] Zinzendorf defined "Heart" as the inner person which had five senses as did the outer person. The "Heart," especially when it has been brought to life by the Holy Spirit, can perceive the Savior objectively and directly. In modern terms we might speak of this as "intuition" or "extrasensory perception." Zinzendorf's approach is very similar to Teresa of Avila's "intellectual vision." One knows one has seen and experienced, but this is not dependent on images or emotions. The best evidence for the Heart relationship with the Savior is changed life. There are several biblical examples of "Heart *Religion*" which Zinzendorf liked to cite. One was that of John and Jesus' mother gathered at the cross. Another was the objective perception of Jesus by John the Baptist while he was still in his mother's womb (Luke 1). See *Einiger seit 1751. von dem Ordinario Fratrum zu London gehaltenen Predigten in Dreyen Haupt-Abtheilungen edirter Erster Band* (London and Barby: Zu finden bey dem Seminario Theologico, 1756), pp. 153-56 (17 Jan. 1753).

Lutheran and Anglican Churches, among others.[9]

The Moravian Church, then, is inheritor of a particular approach to theology and a particular understanding of Christianity about which it has not always been adequately conscious or articulate. It is also inheritor of a variegated 500-year heritage, which means that it inherits within its history the debate and process by which differing perspectives are resolved or held in creative tension. Its ability to work in this way indicates that there is an implicit supposition that the sustaining of relationship is a divine imperative. *The greatest heresy in the Moravian Church is to break relationship.* It is not a church without creeds or a theology. The Ancient Church had its creeds.[10] The Renewed Church accepted the ecumenical creeds of early Christianity and the Reforma- tion confessions as indigenous expressions of faith while affirming that Christianity was not primarily conceptual/creedal. It also produced several significant formulations of faith.[11] The Easter Morning Liturgy

[9] The March 1997 issue of *TMDK: Transatlantic Moravian Dialogue–Correspondence,* English[-language] edition (Bethlehem, Pa.) deals with twentieth-century dialogues in which the North American Moravian Church has been involved and also includes the Anglican-Moravian Dialogue in Great Britain which resulted in the following docu- ment: Church of England and Moravian Church in Great Britain and Ireland, *Anglican- Moravian Conversations: The Fetter Lane Common Statement with Essays in Moravian and Anglican History,* Occasional Paper No. 5 (London: The Council for Christian Unity of the General Synod of the Church of England, 1996). *TMDK* is published bilingually in Karlsruhe, Germany, and Bethlehem, Pa., and serves international theological dialogue in the Moravian Church.

[10] Miloš Strupl, *Confessional Theology of the Unitas Fratrum* (Ph.D. diss., Vanderbilt University, 1964). (Abbreviated in subsequent notes as Strupl, *Confessional Theology.*) Also, Miloš Strupl, "The Confessional Theology of the Unitas Fratrum," *Church History* 33 (1964): pp. 279-93.

[11] Shortly after Zinzendorf's death August Gottlieb Spangenberg published *Idea fidei Fratrum, oder Kurzer begrif der Christlichen lehre in den evangelischen Brüdergemeinen* (Barby, 1779); translated under the title *An Exposition of Christian Doctrine, as Taught in the Protestant Church of the United Brethren or Unitas Fratrum,* 3rd ed. (Winston-Salem, N.C.: The Board of Christian Education of the Southern Province of the Moravian Church, 1959). Spangenberg states in his preface that the Augsburg Confession remains the confession of the Moravian Church, and that this publication is only a laying before the public, in a free, clear and unconstrained connection, the Moravian insight into the gospel. In the latter half of the nineteenth century there were the significant works of Hermann Plitt: *Die Gemeine Gottes in ihrem Geist und ihren Formen* (The Church of God in Its Spirit and Forms) (Gotha: F. A. Perthes, 1859); *Evangelische Glaubenslehre nach Schrift und Erfahrung* (Evangelical Doctrine According to Scripture and Experience), 2 vols. (Gotha, 1863-64); *Zinzendorfs Theologie* (Zinzendorf's Theology), 3 volumes, Gotha: F. A. Perthes, 1869-74); and *Die Gnade und Wahrheit in Christo Jesu: Kurze Darstellung der christlichen Lehre in der evangelischen Brüdergemeine* (Grace and Truth in Jesus Christ: A Short Presentation of Christian Teaching in the Evangelical Moravian Church) (Niesky, 1883). In the North American context there was produced: Augustus Schultze, *Christian Doctrine and Systematic Theology,* 2nd ed., rev. (Bethlehem, Pa.: Bethlehem Printing Co., 1914).

came to be regarded as a creed.[12] The Renewed Church's exploration of doctrinal issues was contained in the minutes of its international (then called General) Synods, and in 1957 *The Ground of the Unity*,[13] a simple yet profound doctrinal statement, was worked out as an expression of the unity of the church following the Second World War.

I hope that this *Ecumenical Theology of the Heart* will share with an ecumenical audience, as well as Moravian, the values and insights of the Zinzendorfian segment of the Moravian heritage.

Recovering Our Heritage

The church is faced with the task of living, maintaining its faith, and speaking in a relevant way in a developing global society with its economic, political, ecological, and population concerns. It must also speak to a potentially global society still limited by self-interest and conflict. The world is pluralistic in politics, economics, and *religion*, which introduces complexity into attempted solutions to issues. The church is faced with this task at a time when culture no longer supports *religion*, economic resources are diminishing, other religions are competing to answer spiritual longing, and the authority of religious institutions and traditions has diminished.

The churches are becoming cognizant of the need to respond and to deal with the political, economic, social, and religious movements of the time. They are becoming cognizant of the importance of rethinking bases of authority, involving laity in the church's ministry (necessitated economically and theologically), and helping laity and clergy alike reach deep into the experiential realities of the faith so that Christian values may be interiorized and transcendent resources for living may be provided in a secular and pluralistic society where they are called into question.

The issues of contemporary society are not really all that new. The European Enlightenment, at its height in the eighteenth century, posed many of the questions which today affect our understanding of the authority of religious traditions and institutions. The Ancient and Renewed Moravian Churches, as did others, struggled with the issue of

---

[12] The Easter Morning Liturgy, developed originally in the eighteenth-century German context of the Moravian Church used much of Luther's Shorter Catechism. It was modified over the years. Many Moravians regard it as a confession of faith. Certainly Easter morning is a wonderful time to rehearse faith, and to do this in a liturgical context expresses the Moravian marriage of worship and theology.

[13] *The Ground of the Unity* was first developed by the European Continental Province and then brought to the General Synod in Bethlehem, Pa., in 1957 where it was revised and accepted. The Unity Synod of 1995 in Tanzania made further revisions. Appendix B contains *The Ground of the Unity* as revised in 1995.

what it is essential to believe within the tradition. The Ancient Moravian Church, in changing historical circumstances and concern for Christian integrity, formulated different views about its relationship with society and politics. Zinzendorf called the Renewed Church to think seriously about the issues posed for faith by nascent biblical criticism and the philosophies of the time, and sought to fill the experiential emptiness of the established churches with the reality of the risen and wounded Savior. Ecclesiastes reminds one that "there is nothing new under the sun" (1:9). What may seem new has likely in some fashion been dealt with before.

In our individual lives we deal with challenges out of the accumulated wisdom, or foolishness, of our life experience. Perhaps we also have absorbed the wisdom of others, contemporaries or ancestors. If we have not, then we must live only out of the limitations of our own experience, conducting the same experiments to which others may have already formulated solutions. Life is too short to seek wisdom only within the confines of individual existence.

Whatever problems the church and Christians must cope with today, the Christian community stands within a three-thousand-year stream of living experience. One thousand years of this represents the history of life and experience with God embodied within the biblical material, and two thousand years represents the history of the church. The Moravian Church has over five hundred years of experience, and the Reformation churches have over four hundred. What a wealth of insight, if it is appropriated. To adequately envision our future and deal with today's issues we need to recover our heritage in ways that do not merely transmit the past, but allow its spirit to inform, and perhaps transform, the present.

The Traditioning of Our Heritage

There are helpful precedents for the handling of tradition in the New Testament materials. After all, the writers of the New Testament were handling traditions in their use of both the Old Testament and the tradition of Jesus' sayings and deeds. Jesus' critical and selective use of the Old Testament (e.g., his opposition to certain Old Testament concepts in Matthew 5 and his preference for Isaiah to inform his self-understanding) and Paul's reinterpretation of the Law as a stopgap measure in salvation history (Galatians 3) are illuminating. Both Jesus and Paul struggled with the Pharisaic position that all truth had been given by God in the Law,[14] if it only could be interpreted, a type of ancient fundamentalism. Both Jesus' and Paul's approaches provided for ongoing revelation, revelation beyond "Scripture." Paul theologically developed this in his description of the role of the Spirit, who provides ongoing guidance to the church, helping it to interpret the tradition and to discern answers to issues where the tradition is not helpful. 1 Corinthians 7 makes an interesting case study as Paul provides answers to various practical questions, citing a saying of Jesus when he has one (on divorce - 7:10), giving his own opinion ("I say, not the Lord" - 7:12), and in conclusion to his advice remarking, "And I think that I have the Spirit of God" (his way of indicating both that he has sought God's guidance and that there are subjectivities involved about which he is not absolutely sure - 7:40).

The Johannine tradition provides for the "creative" handling of tradition in an even more striking fashion, a process that some commentators call "creative remembrance." In the Farewell Discourses (John 14-16) Jesus comments on the function of the Spirit. The most complete treatment of this is in John 16:12-15. The implications of Jesus' words are: "I could not tell you everything while I was with you. Therefore the Spirit of truth will *guide you into all truth*. His truth, however, is not merely new, but has continuity with my truth, which in turn has continuity with the truth of the Father."[15] In 14:25ff. the Spirit "will teach you all things, and bring to remembrance all that I have said to you." Thus the function of the Spirit is to help the church to creatively remember the traditions of Jesus, so that these traditions come alive in new historical circumstances, and also to lead the church into truth that could not be dealt with or anticipated in the historical circumstances of Jesus' life. That this would lead the Johannine Church into problems related to subjectivity is not to be denied. The author of 1 John wrestles with this. The group that broke away from the Johannine community under the impetus of inspiration had gone too far. But he never rejects believing that God and Christ function in a contemporary way to help the church to discern truth in the present.

[14] Matthew presents Jesus as coming not to destroy but fulfill the Law (5:17). Jesus is a new Moses bringing a new law in the form of the Sermon on the Mount. The Great Commission indicates that discipling is teaching converts to observe what Jesus has commanded (28:20). But Matthew's position does not seem to be generally supported in the tradition of Jesus' sayings nor is it supported by Paul. The passage equivalent in Luke (16:16-17) to Matthew 5:17 has Jesus saying something quite different. Here the Law was only until the time of John the Baptist. Now something else is here: the good news of the kingdom. But the new is entered with difficulty because it is hard for the Law to be set aside.

[15] Author's paraphrase.

It is important to note that the whole of the biblical tradition can be seen in terms of the reinterpretation of tradition. The Exodus event was reinterpreted in a number of ways throughout Jewish history and reinterpreted again in the New Testament. There are several creation accounts in the Old Testament. These are reinterpreted in the Old Testament (for example in Psalm 8 and 2 Isaiah) and are also reinterpreted in the New (John 1, Colossians 1, Hebrews 1 and in the use of the First Adam - Second Adam antithesis). Some New Testament authors prefer the Genesis 1 account (e.g., John 1, which interprets Genesis 1 without reference to Genesis 2-3) and others prefer the Genesis 2-3 account (e.g., 1 Timothy 2:13ff.). The New Testament reinterpretation, of course, interjects Christ into the creative process as had been done with Wisdom in the Jewish Wisdom tradition (see Proverbs 8 for the earliest evidence of this in Judaism).

If one takes the biblically described process of transmission of traditions seriously, it becomes difficult to think that all truth is tied to any historical period or any written expression. While we must stand within our traditions, God leads us to an ever-growing understanding of them and to new expressions of truth not yet stated or anticipated in them. That this happens does not deny the value of the traditions for the past nor that they do provide roots and wisdom within the present. But God is an ever-present God who engages us in the present and calls us to deal with life that is constantly changing, presenting issues often not adequately anticipated within the tradition.

Forgiveness and freedom from legalism are essential for the transmission and reinterpretation of tradition, for they provide the freedom that one needs to work creatively and responsibly. Paul called upon Christians in Galatia, tempted to return to legalism, to "stand fast" in their freedom, because "for freedom Christ has set us free" (Galatians 5:1). It is only in freedom that we are able to make the mistakes which are possible in seeking to be responsible to God, mistakes inherent in the limited nature of knowledge and prophecy and the limits of our humanity. All those who express themselves on theological and ethical issues should note Paul's comments on the limitations of prophecy and knowledge in 1 Corinthians 13:8-13. Only when seeing God face to face will we fully understand.

In examining the value and nature of the Moravian tradition, it is helpful to be aware of the above process in the formation and transmission of tradition. Each theological tradition of a particular historical period takes previously existing tradition and reworks it in the light of new experiences and understandings and under the pressures of various external cultural forces, seeking to re-form the tradition and make it relevant. The Moravian Church clearly has faced this challenge numerous times. To name a few significant moments: the transition from the anti-world and anti-society attitudes of its beginnings to the transformations under Lukáš of Prague, the transitions in coming to terms with the Lutheran and Reformed Reformations, the transition represented by Comenius when most of the Moravian Church was destroyed by the Thirty Years War, the transition in the reestablishment of the Moravian Church on the estate of Zinzendorf and the resolution of differences between Zinzendorf's vision and that of his Moravian refugees, the transition after the death of Zinzendorf, the nineteenth-century transition when the North American provinces gained autonomy, and the transition after the Second World War which resulted in the formulation of the doctrinal statement *Ground of the Unity* and the evolution of former mission fields into provinces so that the Unity is now strongly influenced by its provinces in the developing world.

There are those historical periods when the forces of greatest creativity break through, but there are also those times when creativity diminishes or other powerful influences present themselves and accommodation to cultural forces or practical needs occurs. The periods of greatest creativity and new insights frequently posed greater problems (e.g., the Sifting Period[16] in the 1740s) as well as offering significant contributions. The accommodations to cultural influences may also interject new life and ideas besides calling for modification in a conservative direction. What is especially intriguing about the examination of the theology of the Ancient Moravian Church is that often Moravians did not merely intend to accommodate their unique traditions to the developing views of the Second Reformation, but approached them with a conscious desire to be open to new truth. Amedeo Molnár, once dean of the Comenius Faculty in Prague, commented:

> The Unitas Fratrum never proclaimed the unchangeability of the dogmatic expression. The Unitas was convinced that the continu-

---

[16] The Sifting Period is the name given to a time, lasting from 1743 to 1750 (though it continued in North America somewhat longer), when the language of the wounds of Christ and the image of mystical marriage, along with a concern for inspiration, child-like simplicity, creativity and religious experience, were carried to excess to the neglect of other responsibilities. One might compare this to the excesses of the modern charismatic movement. However, the development of excess should not deny the legitimacy of more balanced expression of the same insights. See Hans-Walter Erbe, "Herrnhaag: Eine religiöse Kommunität im 18. Jahrhundert," *Unitas Fratrum* (Hamburg: Friedrich Wittig), nos. 23, 24 (1988): pp. 8ff.; Hans-Walter Erbe, "Herrnhaag — Tiefpunkt oder Höhepunkt der Brüdergeschichte?" *Unitas Fratrum* (Hamburg: Friedrich Wittig), no. 26(1989): pp. 37ff. (Abbreviated in subsequent notes as Erbe, "Herrnhaag —Tiefpunkt oder Höhepunkt?")

ity of its theology was given primarily by its attachment to the essential tenets of the Christian faith, as they are attested in the midst of Christ's confessors by the Holy Scriptures.[17]

Barriers

There are natural barriers to the recovery of heritage besides the passing of time. One is our attitude to the past. Does this history, or in fact any history, have value for the present? Another is the work involved in understanding the past – not merely its forms, but its essence – and finding ways to use it and express it in the present. For the American Moravian Church primary barriers to the reading of its traditions have been the linguistic barriers of the Czech and German languages and its exposure, within the American cultural scene, to indigenous religious forces, e.g., American fundamentalism and conservatism. Whereas the revival of interest in Zinzendorf on the European scene began towards the end of the last century and flowered in the period after the First World War, only a few books on Zinzendorf are available in English.[18] Some materials on the Hussite movements have been written in English by Czech scholars in the U.S. and Canada.[19]

[17] Strupl, "Confessional Theology" [Ph.D. diss.], p. 134.

[18] A very valuable aid for research is Dietrich Meyer's, *Bibliographisches Handbuch zur Zinzendorf-Forschung* (Düsseldorf, Published by the compiler, 1987), though one still needs to be able to use German. Most English-language works and translations are included.

[19] English-language bibliography on Zinzendorf:

Nikolaus Ludwig von Zinzendorf. *Nine Public Lectures on Important Subjects in Religion, Preached in Fetter Lane Chapel in London in the Year 1746.* Edited and translated by George W. Forell. Iowa City: University of Iowa Press, 1973.

J. Taylor Hamilton and Kenneth G. Hamilton. *History of the Moravian Church: The Renewed Unitas Fratrum 1722-1957.* Bethlehem, Pa.: Interprovincial Board of Christian Education, Moravian Church in America, 1967.

Gary S. Kinkel. *Our Dear Mother The Spirit: An Investigation of Count Zinzendorf's Theology and Praxis.* Lanham, Md.: University Press of America, 1990.

Arthur James Lewis. *Zinzendorf, the Ecumenical Pioneer: A Study in the Moravian Contribution to Christian Mission and Unity.* Philadelphia: Westminster Press, 1962; reprint, Bethlehem, Pa., and Winston-Salem, N.C.: Moravian Church in America, 1998.

Henry H. Meyer. *Child Nature and Nurture According to Nicolaus Ludwig von Zinzendorf.* Chicago: Abingdon, 1928.

John R. Weinlick. *Count Zinzendorf.* Nashville: Abingdon, 1955; reprint, Bethlehem, Pa., and Winston-Salem, N.C.: Moravian Church in America, 1989.

See footnote 3, above, for eighteenth-century English-language materials.

English-language works on the Ancient Moravian Church:

Rudolf Říčan. *The History of the Unity of the Brethren.* Translated by C. Daniel Crews. Bethlehem, Pa., and Winston-Salem, N.C.: Moravian Church in America, 1992. (Abbreviated in subsequent notes as Říčan, *History.*)

Jarold K. Zeman. *The Hussite Movement and the Reformation in Bohemia, Moravia and*

One interesting additional barrier to the American appropriation of the European Moravian tradition was the negative reaction to things European as the American Moravian provinces gained their autonomy in the mid-nineteenth century after a century of centralized European dominance. Their reaction to the conservatism of the post-Zinzendorfian period deprived them of an adequate appreciation for the creativity of the Zinzendorfian period.

The Moravian tradition

The process of the formation and transmission of the Moravian tradition could be outlined as follows:

ANCIENT MORAVIAN CHURCH

I The Old Brethren 1457-95

The Old Brethren were inheritors of more radical (Taborite) forms of the Hussite Reformation and the teaching of Petr Chelčický. This was the era of Gregory (Řehoř), who sought a "true" Christianity in separation from society and obedience to the Sermon on the Mount. They first called themselves Brethren of the Law of Christ. By a decree in 1495 this period was consciously brought to an end. One of the distinctive elements of the theology of the Ancient Moravian Church was division of the elements of Christian faith and life into *essentials, ministerials* (that which served the *essentials*), and *incidentals* (the way things were done). John Taborsky, a priest during this period, commented:

> Such, we hold, is the difference between things essential or basic, and [things] ministrative, and again incidental. All the members of the Holy Church should keep themselves always, without ceasing, in every place, at all times, by every reason, in the essential things. For as a man comes quickly by God's grace to the knowledge of the Lord God and by that to the true faith and love while holding on to God, in the light of that knowledge he uses judgment while differentiating between the good and the bad. By the power of faith he ought to shun evil and by grace do good and from this have hope of eternal reward. He ought always to live in this and never depart from it. Then what things ministrate to such, as is the ministry of the Word of God and the sacraments; with such, people

Slovakia (1350-1650): A Bibliographical Study Guide with Particular Reference to Resources in North America. Reformation in Europe, no. 1. Ann Arbor: Published under the auspices of the Center for Reformation Research by Michigan Slavic Publications, 1977.

should occupy themselves. All this should take place as the officials of the church recognize the need for the growth of the essential things; and they should use the incidental things for edification and betterment.

Therefore the people who do not employ this differentiation and, accordingly, consider things ministrative or incidental as essential, judging them to be faith and truth, place themselves in great jeopardy with regard to the work of their salvation.[20]

II Era of Brother Lukáš 1495-1531

Lukáš helped the church move from a rural sect into its society and cities and encouraged opening the door of the church to the nobility. He formulated a theology which affirmed the distinction of *essentials* from *ministerials,* and his theology continued to play a significant role throughout the Ancient Moravian Church's history.[21] The *essentials* are in the hand of God and cannot be within the power of people, church or sacraments. However, his expressions were scholastic and he still believed in seven sacraments. He began the contacts with the "Second Reformation" of Luther and Calvin, though he maintained his independence.

III Period of Lutheran Orientation 1531-46

Under the leadership of John Roh and John Augusta the Moravian Church was strongly influenced by the Lutheran Reformation, establishing contacts with Luther and producing a Confession of 1535 informed by Lutheranism. During this time it was decided that the writings of Lukáš were not to be binding.

IV Era of Matthias Cervenka and John Blahoslav 1546-71

Pupils of Melanchthon advocated a return to Lukáš and a less passive attitude to society. At this time members of the church moved into Poland and East Prussia because of persecution. Greater contacts developed with the Reformed tradition. The Sendomir Consensus between the Moravians, Reformed, and Lutherans was developed in Poland in 1570.

---

[20] Strupl, "Confessional Theology" [Ph.D. diss.], p. 134.

[21] I call attention to a treatment of his theology by C. Daniel Crews, "Luke of Prague, Theologian of the Unity," presented as the W. V. Moses Lecture at Moravian Theological Seminary on April 24, 1997.

V The Last Fifty Years in Bohemia and Moravia 1571-1620

The nobility was influential in leadership. There was a stronger turn to Calvinism, greater appreciation of the Old Testament, publishing of Kralice Bible (equivalent in the Czech language to Luther's translation into German), relaxing of ascetic attitudes to life. The Thirty Years War brought the institutional existence of the Ancient Church to an end, though it continued to some extent in Poland almost to the time of its renewal by Zinzendorf.

VI The Exile and Comenius 1620-1721

This is often called the "time of the hidden seed," when the Moravian traditions were maintained in secret. Bishop John Amos Comenius (died 1670) dedicated much of his life to keeping the heritage of the Ancient Church alive, preserving it for such as Zinzendorf who would rediscover it in the future. Comenius worked on improving education as a theologian. He sought to bring together Scripture, reason, and emotion to solve the questions of his time. For him faith in Christ as king was central, and he saw this as soon to be expressed in the near end of time. Because of the nearness of Christ's second coming, he saw no period of church history as standard for all. Only the age to come provided the paradigm of the church. In 1662 Comenius published the last Confession of the Unity.

It is important to note that theology in the Ancient Moravian Church was more of a communal than an individual enterprise:

> Whether or not the Unity of Brethren in the course of its history, as we have indicated, had enough theological leaders with creative powers of thought, it still had in all periods of its development a unique quality in that it appreciated theology as a congregational, communal function of the whole church. It was properly a function of all servants of the Word. Because of this, their theological statements time and again are for the most part those of synods and sessions of the Inner Council rather than the result of individual speculative effort.[22]

RENEWED MORAVIAN CHURCH

VII Era of Zinzendorf 1722-60

The beginnings of the Renewed Moravian Church in Herrnhut are portrayed in detail in chapter 6 on the church. At first it was best

---

[22] Říčan, *History*, p. 400.

described as a fellowship of committed persons from Berthelsdorf and Herrnhut, under the guidance of the Lutheran pastor and under the oversight of Zinzendorf, which came to include persons from Lutheran, Moravian, and Reformed traditions. Zinzendorf was a Lutheran Pietist who sought to forge creative answers to the Enlightenment. He used the developing Moravian Church as a lab in which to experiment with his theological understandings and Pietistic concerns for the creation of a true Christian community, what he came to call "Gemeine of God in the Spirit." The Moravian elements of this community, who began their migrations to Zinzendorf's estate in 1722, insisted on the revival of their ancient traditions, which Zinzendorf, with great hesitation, ultimately came to feel was God's will. The Renewed Church needed to sensitively relate itself to the existing creeds and catechisms of the state churches. Though it is unclear how much Zinzendorf's thought was affected by his growing awareness of the Ancient Church, it is clear that many of his ideas are strikingly similar. Consecration of Moravian bishops was received through the last remaining bishops of the Ancient Church. This was an extremely creative period, seeing the spread of the Moravian Church to many lands. Zinzendorf's ideas, his own blend of Pietism, Luther, and Mysticism, are formative for this period, though not always fully understood or accepted.

VIII Reorganization, Stabilization, Expanding Influence 1760-1857

The Synods of the first two decades after Zinzendorf both preserved and modified his insights in "more acceptable" directions, and reorganized and centralized the church. A. G. Spangenberg published his *Idea Fidei Fratrum* and *Life of Zinzendorf*, Gregor's Tune Book was published in 1784. Moravian schools flourished. There were pressures to modernize, and the great settlement congregations, the communal form of church life, gradually declined. Such a person as Schleiermacher, who called himself a "Moravian of a higher order" and attended Moravian schools, expressed a critical reaction to this period. Hans-Walther Erbe describes the transition to the post-Zinzendorfian period:

> The Moravians, who previously had spread abroad so much noise, so much excitement and unrest, the Church which had been like a volcano, now became – it is scarcely to be believed – the "Welt der Stillen im Lande" (the world of the quiet in the land), a piece of German Biedermeier, middle class and noble, closed in upon itself in its settlement congregations, these quiet and proper villages, simple and distinguished, separate from the greater world, at the

same time intimate and worldwide, with its culture in lifestyle and the arts worthy of respect, in constantly new realizations of community (*Gemeine*) shaped by its focus upon itself.[23]

IX The Modern Period From 1857 to the Present

There were decentralization of church government and attempts to update doctrine, including new interest in Zinzendorf in the last quarter of the nineteenth century, exemplified in Hermann Plitt's *Zinzendorfs Theologie*. The interest in Zinzendorf has greatly grown on the continent in this century and the North American Moravian Church is now developing its own cadre of Zinzendorf scholars. Significant matters with which the church has had to deal are the development of liberal theology, the ecumenical movement, two world wars, developing secularism and pluralism, the decline of the position and influence of established Christianity, and the development of modern technology. Decentralization and the barriers of language have frequently allowed the provinces to undergo indigenous theological developments only vaguely in touch with the heritage of the Ancient Church or Zinzendorf. Since the Second World War the former mission provinces have been granted status equal to those in Europe, England, and North America, and the majority of Moravians are now in the developing world. Unity Synods, the governing body of the international Moravian Church, are strongly influenced by this developing world. The church in Tanzania alone is much larger than the Moravian Church in North America, Europe, and Great Britain put together.

As is evident from the above outline, Zinzendorf stood at a crucial juncture in the transmission of the Moravian tradition. Not discounting the refugees from Moravia that settled on his estate, it is through his instrumentality that the tradition of the Ancient Church was preserved, and it was in him that it took new shape. It is true that his discovery of the Moravian tradition happened in his twenties, long after the impact of Lutheran Pietism upon him. And yet the characteristics of his religious approach were not fully developed until his thirties, when he described himself as being converted to Luther and rejected the presuppositions of Halle Pietism. Thus the Moravian tradition and the Moravians influenced him at a crucial period. The extent to which Zinzendorf was aware of the thought of the Ancient Moravian Church

[23] H.-W. Erbe, "Herrnhaag — Tiefpunkt oder Höhepunkt?" pp. 45-46.

is debated, but it must be said that his ideas are strikingly similar to the approach to *religion* of the Ancient Church.[24]

Zinzendorf is perhaps "*the* creative theologian" of which the Renewed Moravian Church can boast. Our exploration of his thought in this volume is clearly legitimized in the estimation of him by Karl Barth:

> Reverend Sirs. Brethren! Let me begin with a beatitude: Be happy and thankful that you have the Brethren's Church. In Zinzendorf you have a church father who is important and fruitful for the whole church. I would like to resolutely reject the matter of giving up the Brethren's Church. Remain what you are.
>
> It is neither accidental or arbitrary, but a necessity, that in the course of the years I have worked my way closer to Zinzendorf. Earlier I have said a few unpleasant things about Zinzendorf. . . .
>
> If Zinzendorf is right in the main matter — not only in the form — with regard to his central point: Jesus Christ and he alone; with respect to the relation of creation and salvation; with respect to his view about the already completely accomplished reconciliation of God with the world; with respect to the relation of Law and Gospel; with respect to his view of the church as the congregation of the Lamb, the living Christ — if he is right, then I may say in all modesty: then I also am right. On this my whole theological thinking hinges and over this I am attacked. If he is right, then Zinzendorf and I stand and fall together.[25]

---

[24] Dr. Amedeo Molnar wrote to me about this issue: "The affinities of thought between Zinzendorf and the Unity of Brethren are often striking. They are all the more surprising in that Zinzendorf seems not to have studied in depth the origins of the Ancient Brethren. In connection with this, it is useful to read the work of J. Th. Müller, *Zinzendorf als Erneuerer der alten Brüderunität* [actually *Brüderkirche*]. Much more reserved, but pertinent, is the study of F.M. Bartos, 'Komensky a Zinzendorf,' unfortunately published in the Czech language in *Reformacni sbornik*, Prague, 1929. Müller's book was published in Leipzig in 1900. In reference to *essentialia* and *ministerialia* in the view of Comenius, I have written a few pages in the *Revue d'histoire etude philosophie religieuses*, Strasbourg, 1949, pp. 107-31: 'Esquisse de la theologie de Comenius' (letter in French, Nov. 18, 1974).

[25] Schmidt, Bintz, and Günther, eds., "Protokoll des Gesprächs," p. 3.

Chapter 1

Zinzendorf and His Context

The Man

Greatness and genius are a flower that must grow in a fertile field. The potential of a person will show itself to some extent in whatever situation that person is found. However, it takes the challenge of some particular moment in time, some particular situation in history, to bring possibilities to full flower. In Count Nikolaus Ludwig von Zinzendorf capacity and context joined to produce a person whose religious insights, ecumenical fervor, poetic productivity, missionary dedication, and understanding of human psychology mark him as one of the great men of his day.

As one might imagine, the reactions to Zinzendorf were as varied as the individuality of the persons and communities that encountered him. That a vast body of *Streitschriften*,[1] apologetic literature, developed clearly indicates not only the debate which he created, but his significance. A person of no significance creates little response.

Ludwig von Schrautenbach, a contemporary and friend of Zinzendorf, described him in appreciative and idealistic terms:

> The Count was large in appearance, and after his return from Pennsylvania (1743) somewhat corpulent; but his mien was noble, full of energy, and highly distinguished aside of other men. You are greatly struck with his air, when you see him moving in the society of the great and noble of the highest rank; or if you follow him at a distance as he calmly passes through the crowded streets of a great

[1] Dietrich Meyer's *Bibliographisches Handbuch zur Zinzendorf-Forschung* (Bibliographical Handbook for Zinzendorf Research) (Düsseldorf: Published by the compiler, 1987) has a list of apologetic literature covering 218 pages (pp. 281-499).

city like London or Amsterdam, and notice how the people bow to him, step out of his way, or gladly render him any service. His dress was simple and unstudied. His lodgings were plain. He was quite indifferent as to the style of his furniture. Upon the whole, he never thought of deriving pleasure from external things, and set no value on earth's glittering trifles. He had few personal wants as to clothing and food. In all these respects he was peculiar — and incorrigible. His countenance was sublime and capable of great expression. His forehead was broad and ample; his eyes dark-blue, full of fire and in constant motion; his nose well-shaped and slightly Roman; his lips well-formed and calmly-closed, and his glance quick and penetrating. He was of middle stature; his gait lively; his step firm, and his head erect and well-poised between his shoulders. His deportment was graceful and grave, and free from all affectation of grand and solemn airs. His manners were dignified but modest. He was respectful towards every one with whom he had to do; although all felt and acknowledged his superiority. It has happened to more than one who sought the Count's chamber in order to say certain things to him (perhaps disagreeable ones), that he found, after leaving the room, he had entirely forgotten what he wanted to say to the Count; and then dismissed the whole subject from his mind. The peculiar influence of the mere presence of great men has, however, the unavoidable effect that they seldom hear the warning voice of a true friend. When we come into contact with men who are really great, and who combine good-nature and *bonhommie* with the dignity of their rank and station, we involuntarily become guilty of a refined kind of sycophancy. An ordinary man (even the rich American) takes pleasure in offering a little incense to the great and noble.[2]

Johann Gottfried von Herder, the Weimar poet, said of Zinzendorf after his death:

Nicolas Louis, Count and Lord of Zinzendorf and Pottendorf, born 1700, departed as a conqueror from this world in 1760. Moreover, there were few like him, and in the past century, none. He could claim he had congregations or disciples "in Herrnhut, Herrenhaag, Herrendijk, Pilgerruh, Ebersdorf, Jena, Amsterdam, Rotterdam, London, Oxford, Berlin, in Greenland, St. Croix, St.

---

[2] Ludwig Carl Freiherr von Schrautenbach, *Der Graf von Zinzendorf und die Brüdergemeine seiner Zeit*, ed. F. W. Kölbing (Gnadau: H.L. Menz, 1851), pp.65-67 (Abbreviated in subsequent notes as Schrautenbach, *Zinzendorf und die Brüdergemeine.*)

Thomas, St. John, Barbados, Palestine, Surinam, Savannah in Georgia, Carolina, Pennsylvania, Guiana, Liefland, Esthonia, Lithuania, Russia, on the White Sea, in Lappland, Norway, in Switzerland, on the Isle of Man, in Ethiopia, Persia, among the messengers to the heathen on land and sea."[3]

Friedrich Christoph Oetinger, a famous Tübingen theologian who had worked on a biblical project with Zinzendorf, said that he considered the Count "a riddle above all riddles," but also said, "I have observed the Count to the present [1737] and cannot deny that a divine hand leads him."[4]

Conrad Weiser, also his contemporary, commented on him in his Journal. Weiser, who represented the governor of Pennsylvania to the Indians and could speak their languages, once a monk at the mystical community of Ephrata, Lutheran, father-in-law of Henry Melchior Mühlenberg, and first president judge of Berks County, was an amazing man whose career embraced much of colonial history. He worked with Zinzendorf, Spangenberg, and others in the developing mission to the North American Indians.

Four years after Zinzendorf left Pennsylvania, Weiser was asked by a Philadelphia Lutheran pastor who came from Halle to characterize Zinzendorf. Weiser, after indicating that he did not wish to get mixed up in a church row, responded:

I take him to be a man who in his youth had the great misfortune never to have had his strong will broken: in his college years, to be sure, he was diligent, and sought the truth, and he was visited in his time by the light of God's grace, for which he, being a high-born count, was much admired and praised. But . . . he never had his fingers properly rapped, instead he was always treated as the high-born count, and in short seems to have come out of the oven with too little baking to make a Reformer of the Church of Christ. He likes to command and dictate. . . . His ideas came in flashes, and were often good, he confirmed them by drawing lots. His flock had to swallow them. They called submission to his dictates "Giving up one's will." . . . In attaining his ends, the Count was bounded by no

[3] Johann Gottfried von Herder, *Adrastra*, vol. 4 of *Herders Sämmtliche Werke*, ed. Bernhard Suphan (Berlin, 1886), quoted in Ernst Benz and Heinz Renkewitz, eds., *Zinzendorf-Gedenkbuch* (Stuttgart: Evangelisches Verlagswerk, 1951), p. 46. The section within the quotation marks is taken from a biographer which Herder does not identify.

[4] Erich Beyreuther, *Zinzendorf und die Christenheit* (Marburg: Francke, 1961), p. 60. (Abbreviated in subsequent notes as Beyreuther, *Zinzendorf und die Christenheit*.)

law, human or divine. He held that whatever served his flock was right, however much falsehood might be involved in it. . . . He is very hot but soon cools again. He holds no grudges . . . I cannot separate his qualities, I mean the good from the bad. Certainly both are intermixed in him. And I doubt if he by himself, however much he tried, could ever get free from this tangle without the help of God's strong hand: for it is his very life. I hope his enemies, who bombard him without cause, or out of sectarian jealousy, may not read these words.[5]

When one reads Weiser's journal, it is clear not only that Weiser had a better understanding of the Indians to whom he and Zinzendorf went, but that Zinzendorf had little understanding of how to relate to persons of so different a culture, notwithstanding his passion for this mission and his theoretical understanding of the role of culture. The biographer of Weiser is critical of both these men and their growing difficulties which spilled over into Lutheran - Moravian relationships in Pennsylvania. He comments: "To a man of such enthusiastic loyalty and combativeness as Weiser possessed, Ludwig von Thürnstein, Count Zinzendorf, was a man whom it was inevitable he should both follow and fight. Zinzendorf was a kind of Christian mastodon, trampling ruthlessly over all obstacles that stood between him and the Lamb of God." But he ends with: "Count Zinzendorf, like Conrad Weiser, was an original, and one of the best and most lovable men who ever set foot on American soil."[6]

Two events which have influenced understanding of Zinzendorf and his relations with others are his conflicts with John Wesley and Henry Mühlenberg. It is interesting that the Moravians evidently did not consider it important enough to record these encounters and so we hear of them "from the other side." The Zinzendorf - Wesley dialogue,

----

[5] Conrad Weiser to Peter Brunnholtz, 16 Feb. 1747, quoted in Paul A. W. Wallace, *Conrad Weiser (1696-1760): Friend of Colonist and Mohawk* (Philadelphia: University of Pennsylvania Press, 1945), p. 242. (Abbreviated in subsequent notes as Wallace, *Conrad Weiser.*) Quoted also in Charles H. Glatfelter, *Pastors and People: German Lutheran and Reformed Churches in the Pennsylvania Field, 1717-1793* (Breinigsville, Pa.: Pennsylvania German Society, 1981), 2: 80.

[6] Wallace, *Conrad Weiser*, pp. 135-37. One can follow the growing misunderstandings between Weiser and the Moravians in this biography, which included his involvement with taking the Moravian lock off the disputed Rieth's church in Philadelphia so that it might be taken over by a Lutheran contingent. His rejection of the mysticism of the monks at Ephrata seemed to make him suspicious of Moravian piety, though they were quite different. The misunderstandings had grown to the point where in 1748, during an illness, word got around that the Moravians were trying to pray him to death. The appearance of a comet presented a sign. Mühlenberg asked him if he got better whether he would not "join with other Christians in full communion with Jesus Christ." Weiser asked for baptism, receiving the same and Holy Communion, thus being received back into the Lutheran Church (p. 257).

as recorded by Wesley in his journal, was later published by the Moravians in the *Büdingen Collection*.[7] Mühlenberg's journal is also the primary account of his encounter. It is important to remember that the conflicts involved real issues: with Wesley they were theological, and with Mühlenberg they concerned hostilities between Zinzendorf and Halle along with Zinzendorf's advocacy of possible new forms of church and mission in the unique context of North America.[8] The Bilateral Dialogue of the Moravian Church in North America and the Evangelical Lutheran Church in America worked extensively on the issues of the Mühlenberg-Zinzendorf encounter, and there are a number of helpful papers available.[9]

To understand Zinzendorf and his interpersonal encounters, it is important to recognize that he was raised as part of the nobility and so belonged to a different world from that of middle-class crafts persons or

[7] John Wesley, Journal, 1 Nov. 1739 to 3 Sept. 1741, selected portions quoted in *Büdingische Sammlung Einiger In die Kirchen-Historie Einschlagender Sonderlich neuerer Schrifften Erster Band. Nebst darzu gehörigen Registern. Sind wir doch ererbtes gut.* (Büdingen: Korte, 1744), 3:1027f. (Abbreviated in subsequent notes as *Büdingische Sammlung*.)

[8] The differences between Zinzendorf and Wesley were regarding sanctification. Zinzendorf, in Lutheran fashion, saw holiness purely as a gift while Wesley saw it as a process in the Christian life. Regarding Mühlenberg, he was sent by Halle. Gotthilf Francke, the son of A. H. Francke, who attended Halle at the same time as Zinzendorf, did not get along with him personally or theologically. The request for a pastor in Pennsylvania had lain on Francke's desk for some years until he heard that Zinzendorf had gone to Pennsylvania. Also, Mühlenberg had worked for Zinzendorf's aunt Henriette, who was not sympathetic to Zinzendorf. Thus the scene was set for conflict, each also thinking they were representing Lutheran interests. Zinzendorf wanted to move beyond the European church traditions to the creation of a Church of God in the Spirit, an ecumenical German-speaking Protestant church, while Mühlenberg in his Journal indicates: "I was sent [by the Lutheran ecclesiastical authorities in Halle and London] to investigate conditions here and to see whether order cannot be established ... I have been called, sent, and accepted ... My call has been signed, and I shall trouble myself no further, but just follow the instructions of my superiors in Europe." (See George W. Forell, trans. and introduction to *Nine Public Lectures on Important Subjects in Religion, Preached in Fetter Lane Chapel in London in the Year 1746* by Nikolaus Ludwig von Zinzendorf, [Iowa City: University of Iowa Press, 1973]. [Abbreviated in subsequent notes as Zinzendorf, *Nine Public Lectures* (1973).] Pages ix-xxix of the Introduction contain the text of these two encounters. The quotation in the paragraph above is from p. xxiv.) It is important not to see either of these two meetings as merely a clash of egos.

[9] Unpublished papers include: Samuel Zeiser, "A History of Lutheran-Moravian Interaction in America," with a Moravian response by Arthur Freeman (Dec. 1992); Samuel Zeiser, "The Henry Melchior Mühlenberg Who Met Count Nicholas Ludwig von Zinzendorf in 1742" (June 1993); Otto Dreydoppel, Jr., "The Incident at Philadelphia: A Moravian Perspective on the Mühlenberg-Zinzendorf Encounter" (June 1993). Papers are available from offices of the Northern Province, P.O. Box 1245, Bethlehem, PA 18016, and the Southern Province, Drawer O, Winston-Salem, NC 27108. The convenor of the Lutheran team in the Dialogue, Walter H. Wagner, wrote an article in the spring 1998 issue of the *Concordia Historical Quarterly* (St. Louis, Mo.) titled "A Key Episode in American Lutheranism: Muhlenberg's and Zinzendorf's Encounter."

farmers. He was educated for leadership and to exercise authority. Erich Beyreuther argues strongly that to understand Zinzendorf you must become acquainted with the world of the nobility in pre-industrial Europe.[10]   He also would have been affected by the personal losses, isolation, and nature of socialization in his childhood: the deaths of his father and grandfather, the remarriage of his mother, and his primary association with adults rather than children.

Each person bears the marks of family, education and experience. One does not become less human if dedicated to God. It is worthy of note that even the Apostle Paul spoke of his struggles with his humanity (flesh), his "messenger of Satan," his "thorn in the flesh," which accompanied his deepening spiritual experiences (2 Corinthians 12:7).[11] We live through our humanity, and it is the medium of whatever greatness we manifest and the vehicle of our accomplishments. In fact, deepening spirituality frequently heightens the human struggle. More-over, Zinzendorf's approach to ethics and the Christian life, the spon-taneous expression of one's inner nature ("heart"), would have pro-duced some of his difficulties. To disclose the heart is to express not only the inner presence of the Savior, but also the realities of one's humanity. The Christian life is always this paradoxical incarnation, and the disclo-sure of inner life bears witness to its complexity. But if one hides one's humanity and imperfections, one hides all, including the Savior. It is like closing one's eyes to the external world because it contains pain, conflict, and imperfection. Then one sees nothing.

There are clear comments from Zinzendorf regarding situations in which he considered himself as conciliatory in conflict. How much he actually was so we cannot know merely from his own reflections. But particularly worthy of consideration is the memoir which Zinzendorf wrote on Christian David, another strong personality and the key figure in leading persons from Moravia to Herrnhut.[12] Christian David and his Moravian refugees became the basis for the renewal of the Ancient

[10] Erich Beyreuther, *Die große Zinzendorf-Trilogie* (Marburg: Francke, 1988), 1:9ff. (Abbreviated in subsequent notes as Beyreuther, *Trilogie.*)

[11] For Paul this language represents Rabbinic analysis of human existence. Each person had a *yetzer ha-ra* and a *yetzer ha-tob*, an evil and a good impulse. The evil impulse was particularly connected with the "flesh" and was the equivalent of Freud's "libido," the human drive which was necessary for life in the world. The *yetzer ha-ra* was the "location" in human existence where Satan could attack. For Judaism the Torah which informed the *yetzer ha-tob* was remedy for the *yetzer ha-ra*, while in Christianity it was primarily the Spirit and the understanding of life in Christ provided in baptism.

[12] Count Nikolaus Ludwig von Zinzendorf and others, *Christian David, Servant of the Lord, Being a Translation of the Memoir of Christian David as Written by Zinzendorf and Translations of Selected Letters and Reports Written by Christian David or Pertaining to Him*, trans. Carl John Fliegel and ed. Vernon H. Nelson, publication no. 2 (Bethlehem, Pa.: Archives of the Moravian Church, Northern Province, n.d.). (Abbreviated in subse-quent notes as Zinzendorf, *Memoir of Christian David.*)

Moravian Church on Zinzendorf's estate. The Ancient Moravian Church in its latest historical period had been under Reformed influence. Christian David and the Moravians seem to have brought this orientation to Herrnhut. There were decided differences between Christian David and Zinzendorf, often over an inadequate appreciation of grace as advocated by Luther. But the two also had different opinions on other matters, and at one time David withdrew from Herrnhut to be absent when he believed God would judge and destroy it, even calling Zinzendorf the beast of the book of Revelation. When they were reconciled in Zinzendorf's pastoral work at Herrnhut in 1727, Zinzendorf offered him leadership within the Herrnhut congregation. David went on to become a significant leader in Europe and in the Moravian mission in Greenland. There were times he embarrassed the Moravian Church because he let out secrets about the Danish royal house which had befriended him and to which Zinzendorf was related. Yet Zinzendorf never repudiated this man, who had given so much of his life to the Moravian mission. At the conclusion of the memoir Zinzendorf said:

I can say about him what I once said to the late Prof. Mischke (of Halle) when he was passing away. "You for your part have done well. Go, brother, go now, sleep, commit the sheep to the Lamb who keeps eternal watch."

He will shine brightly, where he now is, as soon as he stands before that seat of judgment which does not have to conform to anyone. The verdict of the Brethren, as we all know, is relative. We cannot speak and judge as we would like to. We cannot act as masters but at all times have to declare ourselves according to the circumstances of a case. In difficult and ambiguous situations the best we can do is keep silence. But where he [Christian David] now is, there is sovereign, unrestrained freedom in passing judgment, even as his creatures were known to the Savior before he placed them under the modifications of this physical body. And here I am firmly assured that in the character of our Christian David there is something precious, which, if he had lived twenty years longer, would have developed more and more and certainly is being appreciated where he now is. I myself have seen this at all times, through all intervening instances, and have always traced this in him and have often thought: "Now is the happy moment when his vision will be enlarged to the fullest extent." But it never came to that. The retort is broken, and the Savior has removed his child to his throne.[13]

[13] Ibid., p. 30.

Also interesting is Zinzendorf's assumption of leadership over the Moravian Church. He was often criticized for this and, as he himself indicated, accused of being archbishop, patriarch and pope. He commented on this at the celebration of the tenth anniversary of the declaration of Christ as Chief Elder in London in 1751, for his leadership role at various times seemed to contradict the importance he and other Moravians gave to Christ's rule of the church. His explanations make rather good sense.[14] He indicated that he assumed leadership to care for the church which had come under his protection, to preserve its character in a way which was necessary for it to survive in relationship to governmental authorities, and to deal with failures such as excesses of the Sifting Period in which he played a major role. He also desired to hold the Moravian Church to his intended design. For the latter some might criticize him, but is it really fair to fault his vision, though it might have been somewhat different from that of the exiles from Moravia, who continuously fought for re-establishment of their Ancient Church? At least his explanations of the need for an authoritative role should be heard, and his natural role as nobleman and lord of the estate needs to be respected.

He watched through the conflicts of 1724-26 at Herrnhut to see if they would settle themselves and form a peculiar society. When he saw they were serious, in 1726 he took hold of the helm without anyone's invitation to help them avoid difficulty with governments. This included a trip in 1726 to Moravia, where he negotiated with government officials about the Moravian exiles who settled on his property. He installed himself as Advocate of the Brethren's Church in 1726 and became Ordinary (teacher) in 1727 when the Moravians on his estate were having difficulty with the Berthelsdorf minister.[15]

He said that he laid down this office on March 15, 1730, and then again in July 1741 (before his departure to America), but declared each time that "in case of necessity I would resume it again, but it would then be a token that the congregation was not in a good condition; as on the other hand when I had neither that spiritual nor temporal service to do, it would be a token that matters went very well."[16]

[14] His comments are contained in a periodical found in the Dublin Archives by the Rt. Rev. Joseph H. Cooper, probably an issue (marked No. 71, 45th Week, 1751) of *Weekly Leaves*. I have not indicated page numbers in this *Weekly Leaves* since I do not have the original. Often I follow the terminology of the original without placing words within quotation marks unless the quotation is extensive.

[15] Johann Andreas Rothe, pastor of Berthelsdorf, sought to keep the developments in Berthelsdorf-Herrnhut within the Lutheran Church.

[16] See note 14.

The realization that Christ wished the office of Chief Elder occurred on September 16, 1741, announced in the European congregations on November 13.[17] On Zinzendorf's return from North America in 1743, because of his concern about developments during his one and a half year absence, he again stepped to the helm.[18] Here he asked the Savior to suspend his office, though he did not inform the congregation about this. He stepped between the Savior and the congregation in matters of religious office, but not in a spiritual sense. His purpose was to control the future direction of the church, but he also explained this as a way of keeping the Savior from receiving the blame for some things that happened. He expressed concern to limit church growth (the making of converts with an atheistical heart and the building of churches at a time when love was cold) and the loaning of money. There were also the problems of the Sifting Period (for which he accepted responsibility[19]) and the need to leave the Wetteravian congregations because of opposition from local rulers.

It grieved Zinzendorf that he was criticized for his role. "But still what should I do? I hoped every year it would be at an end, but

[17] The doctrine of Christ's Chief Eldership was initially not understood as applying to North America, to which it was extended in 1748 (J. Taylor Hamilton and Kenneth G. Hamilton, *History of the Moravian Church: The Renewed Unitas Fratrum 1722-1957* [Bethlehem, Pa. and Winston-Salem, N. C.: Interprovincial Board of Christian Education, Moravian Church in America, 1967], p. 74). It is important to remember that the Chief Eldership was related to the government of the Church. It was not until the summer of 1742 that the Moravian Church in North America began to become organized and it was not until 1748 that it was clear that the attempt to create the Church of God in the Spirit in Pennsylvania had failed.

[18] What had happened in Zinzendorf's absence involved the negotiation of the General Conference responsible for Europe with the Prussian sovereign for recognition, the founding of new churches, actions of the Count of Promnitz who joined the Church and seemed to be vying for leadership, the development of a group of "strict Moravians" who not only wanted to restore the Ancient Moravian Church but to restore its moral austerity, tensions between the younger generation (expressing joy, enthusiasm, and developing a language which used diminutives to express endearment and dwelt upon the wounds of Jesus) and the older. When one understands this complex state of affairs, it becomes clear that Zinzendorf's action was not arbitrary, but legitimate. For a discussion of this, see Hans-Walter Erbe, "Herrnhaag: Eine religiöse Kommunität im 18. Jahrhundert," *Unitas Fratrum* (Hamburg: Friedrich Wittig) nos. 23/24 (1988) (Abbreviated in subsequent notes as H. - W. Erbe, "Herrnhaag: Eine religiöse Kommunität"). This is really a book rather than an article and occupies the whole double issue. Note particularly the section on "Mährische Opposition." Though this article is about Herrnhaag, it provides important insight into the life of the Moravian Church from 1738 to 1750. As in all issues of *Unitas Fratrum*, there is an English-language summary of the article. See also Hans-Walter Erbe, "Herrnhaag – Tiefpunkt oder Höhepunkt der Brüdergeschichte?" *Unitas Fratrum* (Hamburg: Friedrich Wittig) no. 26 (1989): pp. 37ff.

[19] At the Synod of Barby in 1750 he accepted responsibility for the Sifting Time, placed his resignation as Ordinary before the Synod and requested to be called "Disciple."

continually something fresh dropped in" so that he needed to "supply the Saviour's place in the Congregation, so that if things ended ill, this man might bear the reproach and not the Watchman of Israel Himself, who cannot help it; since He however still reigns as yet in Cross's Figure, and when his Cross's people make blunders upon his name, He can't so presently shake off the blame of it." However, Christ has a patient love and treats us with tenderness.

He also stated that his involvement in the government of the church was necessary to provide "fortresses" for its future. If the Brethren were oppressed they could subsist in another denomination (this seems to refer to the recognition of the Moravian Church by the English Parlament in 1749), if expelled they could remain in their original inheritance, and if this was spoiled they could retreat into "the Fellowship of that Name, which none knows save he that receiveth it." He indicated he was in a constant waiting and preparation after 1748, standing as it were with one foot already set forward for the putting off this garment and resigning the staff of command into the Lamb's hands, but the needs of the church did not seem to allow it. However, "on the 16th of September this year your Bishop has been introduced, and there is nothing more in the way, that could disturb his proper post, or bring reproach upon his Office."[20]

His Life and Significant Influences

Zinzendorf was born on May 26, 1700, in Dresden, Saxony, heir to a long and noble line.[21] His father's family traces back to the duchy of Austria. In 1662 Emperor Leopold conferred upon its head the office of count of the Holy Roman Empire. When the Reformation came, part of the family embraced it. Because of the Counter-Reformation Zinzendorf's grandfather moved to Oberbürg in Franconia. His two sons entered the service of the elector of Saxony. The younger, who served as privy councilor at Dresden, was the father of Zinzendorf. Both his father's and mother's families were Lutheran, strongly influenced by

[20] *Weekly Leaves*, periodical found in the Dublin Archives by the Rt. Rev. Joseph Cooper. See note 12, above.

[21] The life of Zinzendorf is presented in outline form in Appendix A, together with the publications that belong to each major period. What is presented here is a brief summation of his life and a discussion of the influences on his life. Attention is called to two works in English on his life:

Arthur James Lewis, *Zinzendorf, the Ecumenical Pioneer* (Philadelphia: Westminster Press, 1962; reprint, Bethlehem, Pa., and Winston-Salem, N.C.: Moravian Church in America, 1998).

John R. Weinlick, *Count Zinzendorf* (Nashville: Abingdon, 1955; reprint, Bethlehem, Pa., and Winston-Salem, N. C.: Moravian Church in America, 1989). (Abbreviated in subsequent notes as Weinlick, *Count Zinzendorf*.)

Pietism. He was born into an exciting period in history. Europe was still recovering from the Thirty Years War of the previous century. The cultural and philosophical developments known as the Enlightenment were in full bloom, including the beginnings of modern science and historical critical methodology. It was a time of change, which also in Zinzendorf's century gave rise to such political phenomena as the American and French Revolutions. It was a crucial time for the church, whose authority was being challenged by new thought and methods.

Zinzendorf's life can be divided into several periods:[22]

1700-21   Childhood and Education
1721-27   Service in the Dresden Court and Beginning of
           Herrnhut
1727-36   The Building Up of Herrnhut
1736-55   The Pilgrim Count
1755-60   Final Residence in Herrnhut

His early years were marked by significant losses in his family. His father, Georg Ludwig von Zinzendorf, died the year that he was born. He and his mother, Charlotte Justine von Gersdorf, then moved to the home of his maternal grandparents at Gross-Hennersdorf, Upper Lusatia. Two years later his grandfather died. Zinzendorf had lost all parental male figures in his immediate family. In 1704 his mother married Prussian Fieldmarshal von Natzmer and moved away, leaving Zinzendorf to be raised by his grandmother, Henriette Catharine von Gersdorf. His mother continued to involve herself in his life through correspondence and visits. His grandmother, a cultured, gifted woman, deeply related to the Pietistic movement, was so influential that he later said of her:

> I received my principles from her. If she would not have been, so would all in which we were involved not have come about. She was a person who applied herself to everything in the world which interested the Savior.[23]

When he was ten he was uprooted from his grandmother's home and for the next six years sent to the Halle Pädagogium, center of the Pietism of August Hermann Francke. Even though he was granted the privileges of nobility, his early years there and his relationship with his tutor were not happy. However, he did receive an education which was rooted in the principles of Pietism. He was later to differ with Halle,

---

[22] Beyreuther includes an "*Itinerarium Zinzendorfs*" in the second and third volumes of his *Trilogie*: pp. 289-90 in volume two for the years 1700-1732 (containing an itinerary for the first two volumes) and pp. 291-94 in volume three for the years 1732-60.

[23] Zinzendorf, *Memoir of Christian David*, p. 54.

particularly as he rediscovered the thought of Luther. From 1716 to 1718 he studied law at the orthodox Lutheran University of Wittenberg, but also pursued his theological interests. Here he became more familiar with the Lutheran thought which was characteristic of his time, more focused in correct theology than in the concerns of Pietism. Having experienced both Halle and Wittenberg he attempted a project he was never able to implement: the reconciliation of the two. From 1719 to 1721 Zinzendorf took his *Bildungsreise*, his educational trip or Grand Tour, which was intended to round off and enrich his educational development. He studied for a time at the University of Utrecht in Holland, stayed in Paris for about a year, and spent some time in Switzerland. This experience brought him into contact with other religious traditions, particularly Calvinism and Roman Catholicism. His stay in France enabled a significant friendship with Roman Catholic Cardinal Noailles, a Jansenist with whom he discovered many common concerns and continued to correspond. He said, "From this time on I sought to discover the best in all Confessions."[24]

It was during this time that he visited Ebersdorf, the home of his wife-to-be, Erdmuthe Dorothea von Reuss, and experienced the *Schlossgemeine* (castle church), an ecumenical community in the Reuss castle which probably laid the foundation for the *Jüngerhaus* (Disciples' House) congregation which later traveled with Zinzendorf. This visit also profoundly affected the form of his piety. Beyreuther indicates that the time he spent in Ebersdorf was "of decisive significance for his inner development."[25]

During his residence in Dresden, 1721-27, Zinzendorf served as aulic and judicial councilor in the electoral government of Saxony. However, his heart was still in his religious interests. He held many gatherings in his home to discuss religious matters and, in the fashion of the times, published weekly papers to share his ideas, such as the *German Socrates*.

[24] Zinzendorf, quoted in Beyreuther, *Trilogie*, 2:8.

[25] Ibid., 2:220. Beyreuther gives eleven pages to this visit. Erdmuthe's sister Benigna also profoundly affected him. Benigna not only led the young Count to the cross, but opened his eyes to the whole life of Jesus and joy in the person of Jesus, a type of piety which Beyreuther indicates came from the mystics of the Ancient and Medieval Church, but to which was now added a new, individually styled private relationship with the living Savior which was not completely new to Zinzendorf (2:222-23). Here his longing for the fellowship of all the children of God was also encouraged: "So I have had the fortune that I . . . have come to Ebersdorf and have seen such a Gemeine for the first time in my life. I met in Ebersdorf a group of souls who gathered together without distinction of *Religionen* (denominational allegiance), without the distinction of the private ideas which each had, without distinction (separation) because of external constitution" (2:226).

In 1722 he bought Berthelsdorf as his estate and married Erdmuthe Dorothea von Reuss. In 1724 his first son was born, Christian Ernst, who died soon after his birth. Zinzendorf and his wife were to have twelve children, only four living to maturity and three daughters outliving them. Most significant in this period was the arrival of refugees from the old Kingdom of Moravia who claimed as their heritage the Ancient Moravian Church and were committed to reviving this tradition. Given refuge on the Berthelsdorf estate, they, along with other Reformed and Lutheran refugees, became the basis for the developing community of Herrnhut (a word meaning "under the care of the Lord" or "on watch for the Lord"). The development of this community was to give Zinzendorf the laboratory for his religious ideas. His theology was to be tested and formed in the context of praxis. An important expression of his thought of this period is his poem *Allgegenwart* (Omnipresence), which presents his reflections upon how God can be known — his answer to the issues of the Enlightenment. The tenth stanza reads:

> O! Come here and see
> the concealed Abyss,
> the hidden Majesty.
> In Jesus, the humble child, see
> whether humanity exists in grace;
> see whether He your praise deserves,
> for whom love grows in the heart
> who believes, from all care becomes free.[26]

In the winter of 1726 Zinzendorf returned to Herrnhut, still technically in the service of the Saxon court. The community at Herrnhut had come upon difficult times because of the variety of peoples and viewpoints that it now contained. Zinzendorf, as lord of this estate, needed to give attention to healing divisions and setting things in order. He therefore began visiting within the community, functioning as both pastor and manorial lord. On May 12, 1727, he brought together the members of the community to express allegiance to the "Manorial Prohibitions and Injunctions," rules by which the community should live. To this on July 4 was added the "Brotherly Agreement" expressing the spiritual life of the community. By August 1727, a new spirit had begun within the community, and a profound spiritual experience occurred at a Communion service held on August 13 in the parish

---

[26] "Allgegenwart," in *Graf Ludwigs von Zinzendorff Teutscher Gedichte Erster Theil,* Herrnhut: Zu finden in Waisenhause, 1735, pp. 106-8. The translation is the author's. The whole poem is included in chapter 2.

church at Berthelsdorf.[27] This has often been regarded as the Moravian Pentecost, touching even those who were not at the service. Herrnhut was ready for mission, and it developed rapidly.[28]

The years 1727 to 1736 were the period of the building up of Herrnhut. Amazing things took place within these few years. This small congregation began the establishment of "societies" within the state church. In 1732 the first Moravian missionaries were sent to the Danish West Indies, and by 1735 Moravians arrived in Savannah, Georgia. In 1731 there was the first printing of the "Daily Texts" devotional book and the first edition of a hymnal for the Renewed Moravian Church.

For Zinzendorf this period was personally important. It was not only an exciting time within Herrnhut, but new insights came to him. In 1734 he was converted to Luther and the centrality of grace. Formative factors included the biblical studies of the *Collegium Biblicum* (biblical college or guild) in 1734 and his growing frustration with Halle Pietism.

The developing differences between himself and Halle focused on their understanding of sanctification and Halle's accusation that Zinzendorf could not describe a valid conversion experience. Moreover, the animosity of Gotthilf Francke, A.H. Francke's son, and Halle's dismissal of Augustus Spangenberg, who then came to Herrnhut, provided additional fuel for the fire.

Zinzendorf was long familiar with Luther's writings. He had heard Luther's works read at home and he had read them during his educational process, but now the meaning of Luther came home — not of Lutheran Orthodoxy but of Luther himself. He came to realize that all was of grace. From this time grace was a central focus of this theology. His controversy with Wesley must be understood in this light, as should his concerns about some forms of mysticism and his opposition to Halle Pietism. Concerned about having an official validation of his theology and still convinced that he was called to the ordained ministry, he satisfied church and royal officials in Denmark, Sweden, and Germany

---

[27] This experience is often remembered as completing the resolution of differences within the Herrnhut congregation. This was true for a while. With Zinzendorf's return from North America in 1743 it was evident that many differences had again developed and he had to deal with these. Thus it became clear that the church must always deal creatively with differences rather than seeking an idyllic freedom from what is natural to the normal human social context.

[28] Wollstadt, Hanns-Joachim, *Geordnetes Dienen in der christlichen Gemeinde: Dargestellt an den Lebensformen der Herrnhuter Brüdergemeine in ihren Anfängen.* Arbeiten zur Pastoraltheologie, vol. 4 (Göttingen: Vandenhoeck and Ruprecht, 1966), pp. 282ff. Wollstadt describes not only ministry within the Herrnhut community, but also "Mission as Ministry Beyond the Area of the Congregation," the title of a chapter. A first preaching mission occurred in August of 1727, and by 1732 Moravians were in the West Indies.

about his theological training. In 1734 the Pastoral College of Stralsund certified his orthodoxy and the Theological Faculty of Tübingen University issued an affidavit that Zinzendorf was a man in good standing and had all the knowledge of Christian faith in a manner which was fully acceptable for Lutheran orthodoxy, and indicated that they could see no objection as to why a man of high nobility should not also preach the Gospel. With this certification he publically entered ministry in the *Stiftskirche* in Tübingen in 1735 without formal ordination.

The years 1736 to 1755 may be regarded as the period of the pilgrim Count. The external occasion was his banishment from Saxony in 1736. He traveled about Germany, Switzerland, Holland, England and even journeyed to the West Indies and North America. During his visit to Pennsylvania he helped to initiate the Pennsylvania Synods, drawing together German-speaking religious groups, and engaged in three exploratory journeys into Indian country. The Moravian Diaspora in Livonia, some seven thousand members, was coming under pressure from the government, and so in 1743 he journeyed into Russia, getting as far as Riga, and then after house arrest was ordered to leave. He continued to travel long after the rescinding of his banishment in 1747. The year 1749 saw the Moravian Church recognized in Saxony and an act of Parliament in England "for Encouraging the People Known by the name of Unitas Fratrum . . . to Settle in His Majesties Colonies in America." From 1749 to March 1755 for all but 13 months Zinzendorf and his associates had their headquarters in London. In 1750 a ninety-nine year lease was taken on Lindsey House on the Thames.

In 1737 he was ordained a Moravian bishop. It is to the period around 1738 that he assigned his realization of the nature of the work of the Holy Spirit, something that he believed was an emphasis in Luther neglected by contemporary Lutherans. Zinzendorf's theology seems to have progressed experientially. In the *Catechism for the Heathen* he advised those to whom the Gospel was preached to start with the Savior and then allow the Savior to teach them about the Father and the Spirit, a process which reflected his own experience. As a child he knew the Savior and became aware that it was only in the concreteness of the Savior that the Father is known. Then in the late 1730s he became more experientially aware of the role and activity of the Spirit. His understanding of theology was that the Savior would lead one to comprehend what it was necessary to know. That which the Savior did not lead one to know was not necessary for one's salvation. One might theologically reflect on more, but such reflections were unsure matters until their truth was revealed in human experience.

The years 1743 to 1750 are called the Sifting Period, though it continued into the early 1750s in such places as Bethlehem. Here Zinzendorf's focus on experiential *religion* and the intimate relationship with Christ was carried to excess. There was neglect of practical responsibilities, excessive involvement in religious experience and ceremonies, excessive experiential language focusing on the blood and wounds of Christ and spiritual marriage. This was particularly true in the Wetteravian congregations and seems to have been more the religious expression of the younger generation. Zinzendorf's son, Christian Renatus, was deeply involved in this. An "Order of Little Fools" was established among younger members. Zinzendorf later explained its intent:

> The Order of Little Fools of 1743 had as its intent simplicity and joy in order to move us beyond the difficult *negotia* [matters] at hand and frightening circumstances and save us from perplexity, so that we can regard all matters as not being overwhelming but also not regard them too philosophically and not be inclined to make them too important nor diminish their significance too much. A few then resolved before the Savior: to become a little animal, a child in arms, to want to let our elders take charge and thus be concerned about everything, but for us to depend on him and in all circumstances preserve for ourselves the rest, peace, joy, and blessedness of our heart.[29]

Zinzendorf finally modified these extremes in 1749 and recalled his son to London. At the same time it became necessary for the Wetteravian congregations to close because local rulers forbade their relationship with the Moravian Church. In 1752 Christian Renatus died. Though these matters will be discussed again, it should be said that the excesses of this period were an outgrowth of a legitimate concern to deal with *religion* experientially, for *religion* was at its heart the relationship with and experience of the Savior, dependence upon him, and joy in him. Much wisdom that came out of this noble exploration of experiential *religion* needs to be heard, for it relates to the contemporary concern for the appropriate role of religious experience. Zinzendorf commented on the Sifting Period with the following:

> The test we have gone through has been brief but fearful. I probably occasioned it by giving utterance to an idea which I have never been able to lay aside, and which I still hold, namely, that in

[29] Diarium des Jüngerhauses, pp. 836f., 839, Synod at Barby, 26 Sept. 1750, quoted in H.-W. Erbe, "Herrnhaag: Eine religiöse Kommunität," pp. 62-63.

order to enjoy all the blessings purchased by the death of Jesus, we must become children in the bottom of our hearts. I have been powerfully impressed by this idea, and when I came back from America I sought to inculcate it in my brethren. It found acceptance and was immediately carried into effect. But what was at first a small circle of men, who really had the spirit of children, soon grew into a large society and in a few years greatly degenerated.[30]

The publications of this period are extensive, including many sermons, a number of catechisms, two attempts at translating the New Testament, and a start on creating an "Enchiridion" of the Bible, a Handbook eliminating unnecessary, repetitious or confusing materials. Seven hymnals were published from 1743 to 1754.

The time 1755 to 1760 is the period of Zinzendorf's final residence in Herrnhut. He still traveled, but his life was centered in Herrnhut. His wife, Erdmuthe Dorothea, died in 1756 and on June 27, 1757, he secretly married Anna Nitschmann, who was not of the nobility. For a long time she had held significant offices within the church and was frequently involved with his traveling "Pilgrim Congregation." Some questions have been raised about the nature of their relationship, but here one must remember Zinzendorf's views on marriage and life. All was subordinate to the service of the Savior. Thus his marriage with Erdmuthe Dorothea was a "Warrior-Marriage." Though he must be regarded as human as others, it is difficult to think that his relationship with Anna would not have been subjected to the same ideals.[31] It is also important to recognize that in the history of spirituality there are numerous male and female partners who complement each other: Abelard and Eloise, Teresa and John of the Cross, Francis de Sales and Jane de Chantal. While Erdmuthe Dorothea managed the household and fulfilled her very significant role within the Moravian community and the life of Zinzendorf, he early became aware of the spiritual gifts of Anna and undoubtedly discovered a resonance between them. Zinzendorf died on May 9, 1760. The day before his death he said to David Nitschmann:

[30] Zinzendorf, quoted in Felix Bovet, *The Banished Count, or, the Life of Nicholas Louis Zinzendorf*, trans. John Gill (London: Nisbet, 1865), p. 251, quoted in Weinlick, *Count Zinzendorf*, p. 205.

[31] In the primary biography of Erdmuthe Dorothea there is also a discussion of the role of Anna Nitschmann in the life of the Church and the life of Zinzendorf: Lic. Wilhelm Jannasch, *Erdmuthe Dorothea, Gräfin von Zinzendorf, geborene Gräfin Reuss zu Plauen: Ihr Leben als Beitrag zur Geschichte des Pietismus und der Brüdergemeine dargestellt* (Herrnhut: Im Verlag des Vereins für Brüdergeschichte, In Kommission der Unitätsbuchhandlung in Gnadus, 1915). Published in *Zeitschrift für Brüdergeschichte* (1914), pp. 399-406. Note that the date 1915 does appear on the title page in the issue of *Zeitschrift für Brüdergeschichte* for 1914.

Did you suppose, in the beginning, that the Saviour would do as much as we now really see, in the various Moravian settlements, amongst the children of God in other denominations, and amongst the heathen? I only entreated of him a few of the firstfruits of the latter, but there are now thousands of them. Nitschmann, what a formidable caravan from our church already stands around the Lamb.[32]

The Enlightenment

The century into which Zinzendorf was born was one of those pivotal times in the history of humanity when everything was in flux. Finding its roots in the Renaissance and the Reformation, the Enlightenment, the name by which this period of change was labeled, extended not only to *religion* and philosophy but to science, economics, and politics as well.

Such as René Descartes (1596-1650) and John Locke (1632-1704) had supplied tools for the change. Descartes approached the world he experienced and reflected upon it with radical doubt, and thus began his quest for certainty. His Archimedean point was "I think, therefore I am." Reality differs from the way that it appears to the senses. The properties of things are those that can be quantified. The world can be explained by mechanistic physics. His work placed epistemology in the center of philosophical thought.

Reason was no longer used to show the truth of the Christian faith, as had been done by St. Thomas Aquinas, but now challenged the basic tenets of *religion* itself and the methods by which *religion* approached knowledge of truth. Only that is truth which will fit into a harmonious, rational system and subject itself to the logicality and objectivity of the mathematical sciences. The attitude of the Enlightenment was well expressed in Descartes' *Discourse on Method*: "There can be nothing so remote that we cannot reach to it, nor so recondite that we cannot discover it."[33] Actually, however, Descartes did postulate the existence of an infinite God because of the existence of the idea in the human mind.

In the eighteenth century the understanding of reason moved beyond a body of "knowledge, principles, and truths" to "a kind of energy, a force which is fully comprehensible only in its agency and

---

[32] Zinzendorf, quoted in Spangenberg, *Leben* [full bibliographical details at n. 59, below], quoted in Weinlick, *Count Zinzendorf*, pp. 231-32.

[33] R. M. Easton, *Discourse on Method, Descartes Selections* (New York: Scribner, 1927), p. 17.

effects."³⁴ It analyzed all things, dissolved the old structures, and constructed the new. The physics of Newton (1643-1727), while presuming universal law and order in the material world, went beyond Descartes in believing that one cannot start there. One must start with phenomena, observation, and analysis.

Locke's essay *Concerning Human Understanding* rejected that there were some ideas which were an innate part of the natural mind. Knowledge came rather through the senses and human reflection upon this. Thus the mind of the child inherited nothing. Everything that was to belong to the mind in the future was to come from the environment in which the person developed. This view, emphasizing human experience as a source of knowledge, came to be known as Empiricism, a seemingly mild concept which overthrew empires. It not only denied the Christian concept of the effect of original sin upon the human race (freeing persons from the need for church rites which dealt with human sin), but also denied the inherent rights of the religious, political, social, and economic institutions, helping give birth to the American and French revolutions. It was a time of optimism and confidence. Humans could reform society and its institutions into harmony with a universal order and overcome the mistakes of the institutions of the past.

D'Alembert's essay on "The Elements of Philosophy" begins with a helpful portrait of the spirit of the mid-eighteenth century:

> If one examines carefully the mid-point of the century in which we live, the events which excite us or at any rate occupy our minds, our customs, our achievements, and even our diversions, it is difficult not to see that in some respects a very remarkable change in our ideas is taking place, a change whose rapidity seems to promise an even greater transformation to come. Time alone will tell what will be the goal, the nature and the limits of this revolution whose shortcomings and merits will be better known to posterity than to us. . . . Our century is called, accordingly, the century of philosophy par excellence. . . . If one considers without bias the present state of our knowledge, one cannot deny that philosophy among us has shown progress. Natural science from day to day accumulates new riches, Geometry, by extending its limits, has borne its torch into the regions of physical science which lie nearest at hand. The true system of the world has been recognized, developed, and perfected. . . . In short, from the earth to Saturn, from the history of the heavens to that of insects, natural philosophy has been revolu-

³⁴ Ernst Cassirer, *The Philosophy of the Enlightenment*, trans. Fritz Koelln and James Pettegrove (Boston: Beacon Press, 1951), pp. 13-14. (Abbreviated in subsequent notes as Cassirer, *Philosophy of the Enlightenment*.)

tionized; and nearly all other fields of knowledge have assumed new forms. . . .

The study of nature seems in itself to be cold and dull because the satisfaction derived from it consists in a uniform, continued, and uninterrupted feeling, and its pleasures, to be intense, must be intermittent and spasmodic. . . . Nevertheless, the discovery and application of a new method of philosophizing, the kind of enthusiasm which accompanies discoveries, a certain exaltation of ideas which the spectacle of the universe produces in us — all these causes have brought about a lively fermentation of minds. Spreading through nature in all directions like a river which has burst its dams, this fermentation has swept with a sort of violence everything along with it which stood in its way. . . . Thus, from the principles of the secular sciences to the foundations of religious revelation, from metaphysics to matters of taste, from music to morals, from the scholastic disputes of theologians to matters of trade, from the laws of princes to those of peoples, from natural law to the arbitrary laws of nations . . . everything has been discussed and analyzed, or at least mentioned. The fruit or sequel of this general effervescence of minds had been to cast new light on some matters and new shadows on others, just as the effect of the ebb and flow of the tides is to leave some things on the shore and to wash others away.[35]

Zinzendorf was drawn to the Enlightenment and its issues. In his earlier life he read widely in its literature. In the latter part of his residence in Halle he gave a talk on "*de causis quibus inductus Cartesius vulgarem philosophandi viam desererit*" ("Concerning the causes by which Descartes was influenced to desire a common life of philosophizing").[36] He read Spinoza and wondered "that there are persons who consider as philosophy such dry straw,"[37] though he showed a deep appreciation for Leibniz's *Theodicy*.[38] His reading of the *philosophes* of his time came to serve his own apologetic purposes:

[35] Cassirer, *Philosophy of the Enlightenment*, pp. 3-4.

[36] Bernhard Becker, *Zinzendorf im Verhältnis zu Philosophie und Kirchentum seiner Zeit: Geschichtliche Studien* (Leipzig: Hinrich, 1886), p. 37. (Abbreviated in subsequent notes as Becker, *Zinzendorf.*)

[37] Zinzendorf, Tagebuch, 19 Mar. 1731, quoted in Becker, *Zinzendorf*, p. 38.

[38] Nikolaus Ludwig von Zinzendorf, *Der Teutsche Socrates. Das ist: Aufrichtige Anzeige verschiedener nicht so wohl unbekannter als vielmehr in Abfall gerathener Haupt-Wahrheiten, in den Jahren 1725 und 1726* (Leipzig: Samuel Benjamin Walthern, 1732), annotation concerning article no. 1 of the table of contents [Anm. zu Stück 1 der Inhaltsangabe], cited in Otto Uttendörfer, *Zinzendorf und die Mystik* (Berlin: Christlicher Zeitschriften, Verlag, [1952]), p. 81. (The Uttendörfer work will be abbreviated in subsequent notes as Uttendörfer, *Zinzendorf und die Mystik.*)

There are no stronger arguments and demonstrations of the divine truths than the writings of those who are avoided because they scorn [the faith]. Therefore I never read theologians, but rather the writings of the "scorners." They have been my preceptors. For if I read only two pages, I see several arguments which I can use, on which they had not reflected.[39]

A number of issues of the Enlightenment need to be understood so that the issues with which Zinzendorf was confronted will become clear.

Concern for the human.

This was a time when (over against the traditional focus on God, the other world, and the established institutions which ordered human life) there was a deep desire to assert the significance of this world, the autonomy and value of humanity, and to break through the traditions and institutions (religious and political) which prevented this. Humanity was coming of age, asserting its ability to understand and handle the world by use of mind and science.

The struggle between the heart and the mind

It was a struggle of bravery. Freedom from past traditions did not come suddenly, and it did not come without anxiety and doubt, for the hearts of many *philosophes* were still rooted in the old culture and institutions. Peter Gay well described the struggle in *The Enlightenment: An Interpretation: The Rise of Modern Paganism.* Speaking of the *philosophes* he wrote:

> Their Christian inheritance sometimes lay heavily upon them. It was not merely that the philosophes were less cheerful than they appeared in public — most men are; not that they experienced private upheavals — many philosophers, especially young philosophers, do. There was more to their moods of discontent than that. Christianity had dominated their childhood; its teaching had saturated their formative years and had been reinforced by glowing promises and grim warnings. Many philosophes had a brother who was a priest or a sister who was a nun; many philosophes had seriously weighed a clerical career. Christianity did not retain possession of their intellects, but often it haunted them. When they turned against *religion*, they did so not from ignorance or indifference: their anticlerical humor has all the bitter intimacy of a family joke; their anti-Christian passion has the specificity and

[39] Zinzendorf, Herrnhut Archives, R2A15,1,p. 33 (13 July 1745), quoted in Uttendörfer, *Zinzendorf und die Mystik,* p. 12.

42 An Ecumenical Theology of the Heart

precision available only to men of long, close experience. They knew their Bible, their catechism, their articles of faith, their apologetics; and they knew, too, because it had been drummed into them early and without pause, that heretics and unbelievers suffer in hell forever. "He had to change his *religion*," Voltaire writes about Henri IV before Paris, "that always costs an honest man something."[40]

Gay went on to give several examples. Lessing grew up in a Lutheranism both conservative and humane, with a father who was a learned and tolerant pastor.

> Toward the end of his life, in the midst of his most intense religious speculations, he confessed that he was uncertain whether it was a good or a bad thing that he should have lived in a time when theological controversy was fashionable. He describes himself as swallowing one book after the other, astonished at the scorn of each cleric for the rest and the dogmatic certainty of all. "I was pulled from one side to the other; none wholly satisfied me." The latest polemicist was always the most insistent, the most sarcastic, and in consequence, all polemics had unintended effects: "The more conclusively the one tried to prove Christianity to me, the more doubtful I became. The more petulantly and triumphantly another tried to trample it into the ground, the more inclined I was to preserve it at least in my heart."[41]

Though many worked through their struggles, some clung tenaciously to aspects of their previous faith. Rousseau (1712-78), who became a Deist, in reply to Voltaire's poem on the Lisbon earthquake (which dashed the belief of many in the goodness of the world and God's order), wrote:

> All the subtleties of metaphysics will not make me doubt for a moment the immortality of the soul or a beneficent Providence. I feel it, I believe it, I want it, I hope for it, and I shall defend it to my last breath.[42]

This struggle between what is known and felt in the heart and what is reasoned and perceived by the mind was very much a part of Zinzendorf's own life. He was troubled by doubt from childhood and

[40] Peter Gay, *The Enlightenment: An Interpretation: The Rise of Modern Paganism* (New York: Alfred A. Knopf, 1976), pp. 59-60.
[41] Ibid., pp. 60-61.
[42] Ibid., p. 68.

ultimately decided for what he knew in his heart. There will be extended discussion of this in chapter 2.

Two seventeenth-century French scholars contributed much to understanding the struggle with doubt: Blaise Pascal (1623-62) and Pierre Bayle (1647-1706). Though Zinzendorf does not say much about Pascal, his and Pascal's thoughts moved in similar directions. Pascal moved beyond mathematical reasoning to intuition, the knowledge of the heart, for him fueled by a revelatory experience he could only describe as "fire."[43] "The heart has its reasons, which reason does not know."[44] Pascal also affirmed the centrality of grace, struggled with the nature and freedom of the will, and understood the heart as an organ of perception: "The heart is the place in us in which God acts, makes himself perceived, as well as felt or loved, and in short operates our salvation."[45]

Pierre Bayle, herald of the radical French Enlightenment, was a person to whom Zinzendorf was greatly attracted, whose name he mentions, and to whose works he alludes. Bayle experienced the persecutions of Protestants in France and the opposition of narrow Calvinism in Holland, where he was for some time a professor of philosophy. He was author of the *Critical and Historical Dictionary*, in which he attacked the Bible and institutional *religion*, but not *religion* itself. He distinguished between *religion* as church and *religion* as the gift of God's grace.

Bayle was not anti-religious, but sought to establish tolerance on the basis of skepticism, and the primacy of reason in all matters, with the exception of the non-institutional religious area. Reason as the rationalists used it or as the orthodox used it was inadequate to the religious task. The object of the Christian faith is a paradox, and Christianity must retain the tension between reason and revelation. Reason is only the servant of theology, and to use it to create theology is to create God in our own image. Bayle believed that belief and religious life are only the gift of God and God's Spirit along lines that seem to be influenced by

[43] On Nov. 23, 1654, Pascal wrote, "From about half past ten in the evening until about half past twelve, FIRE. God of Abraham, God of Isaac, God of Jacob, not of the philosophers and scholars. Certitude. Certitude. Feeling. Joy. Peace. God of Jesus Christ. *Deum meum et Deum vestrum*" (Emile Cailliet, *Pascal: Genius in the Light of Scripture* [Philadelphia: Westminster Press, 1945], p. 131 [Abbreviated in subsequent notes as Caillet, *Pascal*]).

[44] Blaise Pascal, *Pensées*, Section iv, quoted in Caillet *Pascal*, p. 101.

[45] Jan Miel, *Pascal and Theology* (Baltimore: Johns Hopkins Press, 1969), p. 158. The quotation is Miel's description of Pascal, not Pascal's words.

mysticism.[46] There was a conflict between Jurieux (a leading Dutch Calvinist) and Bayle, and Zinzendorf commented:

> On the other hand, that has made me thankful to certain writers on whose condemnation theologians of the most diverse religions seem to be in agreement: and I have often thought, I would rather be taken for a follower of Bayle by the followers of Jurieux, than among the followers of Bayle pass for a follower of Jurieux.[47]

As Zinzendorf settled his understanding of *religion* and his struggle with the issues of the Enlightenment, he read less widely and came to live primarily out of Scripture. This was even true of theological writings which he said were "too much cooked in the head."[48]

Epistemology

This was a major issue of the times: how can one know and what can be known? The object of knowledge was no longer primarily God and ultimate realities, but humankind and the world. Fostered by critical methods developed since the Renaissance, furthered by developing science, at times using reason and at times the senses as points of departure, the Enlightenment began to explore even the nature of the person who knows. It dealt with such issues as the significance of reason and sensory information, the effect of reflection on sensory information, the inner relationship of the different fields of sensation, and the role of imagination and emotions in perception. Zinzendorf was intensely interested in such "psychological" issues from the perspective of what they said both about individuals and about the variety of peoples and cultures with which he dealt.

[46] Erich Beyreuther, "Die Paradoxie des Glaubens: Zinzendorfs Verhältnis zu Bayle und der Aufklärung," *Studien zur Theologie Zinzendorfs: Gesammelte Aufsätze* (Neukirchen-Vluyn: Kreis Moers, 1962), p. 215.

[47] *Ludwigs von Zinzendorf Peri Eautou. Das ist: Naturelle Reflexiones über allerhand Materien, Nach der Art, wie Er bey sich selbst zu denken gewohnt ist: Denenjenigen Verständigen Lesern, Welche sich nicht entbrechen können, über Ihn zu denken, in einigen Send-Schreiben, bescheidentlich dargelegt* (n.p., n.d.), pp. 5f. A weekly, published Dec. 1746-Dec. 1748, and gathered into various collections. There were three editions of *Naturelle Reflexiones*, which were not dated. The one quoted in this book is the largest of these editions, containing twelve issues and nine supplements, and is the reprint edition found in Nikolaus Ludwig von Zinzendorf, *Ergänzungsbände zu den Hauptschriften*, ed. Erich Beyreuther and Gerhard Meyer, vol. 4 (Hildesheim: Georg Olms, 1964-85). (The citation for this edition will be abbreviated in subsequent notes as Zinzendorf, *Naturelle Reflexiones*.)

[48] Nikolaus Ludwig von Zinzendorf, Minutes of the 1750 Synod, quoted in *M. Avgvst. Gottl. Spangenbergs Apologetische Schluß-Schrift, Worinn über tausend Beschuldigungen gegen die Brüder-Gemeinen und Ihren zeitherigen Ordinarium nach der Wahrheit beantwortet werden, Nebst einigen wichtigen Beylagen* (Leipzig and Görlitz: In der Marcheschen Buchhandlung, 1752), p. 456-57. Here Zinzendorf describes his attitude towards various types of literature.

Original sin

The Augustinian doctrine of the corruption of human nature, based upon the story of the Fall, was foreign to the new optimism about humanity. Original Sin and God's judgment had passed a sentence upon humans that could only be modified by proper religious authorities. Fallenness questioned human capability and motivation. Humanity could not rise to maturity and responsibility bound with such chains. And yet there is a truth in the biblical description of the danger which resides in human nature. Zinzendorf not only came to terms with the new assertion of the value and possibilities of human life, but also preserved the legitimate insights about the limitations of human nature contained in the idea of the Fall. It was not the Enlightenment which freed humanity from the chains of this negative perspective, but it was God in Christ who freed humanity from sin by restoring the world to its potential. The cross freed the world from Original Sin and released the Spirit into the world to facilitate new human potential and counteract the power of Satan. The effects were cosmic. It was not knowledge but grace which created the new situation. Thus one may regard children as born good and humanity as having potential because of God's grace, if only persons do not relapse into the conditions from which God gave freedom and if they deal with the difficult tendencies of human nature.

Theodicy

Theodicy, the justification of God's (or the world's) moral order, was a deep concern of the eighteenth century. People had become aware of the tragic nature of life and were freed to question why. Voltaire (1694-1778) in *Candide* parodied Leibniz in the form of Dr. Pangloss, who went around proclaiming that this is the best of all possible worlds. After all his tragic experiences and wanderings, Candide winds up on a farm with his Cunegonde who by now "was decidedly ugly, but she soon made excellent pastry." Dr. Pangloss still argues:

> There is a chain of events in this best of all possible worlds; for if you had not been turned out of a beautiful mansion at the point of a jackboot for the love of Lady Cunegonde, and if you had not been involved in the Inquisition, and had not wandered over America on foot, and had not struck the Baron with your sword, and lost all those sheep you brought from Eldorado, you would not be here eating candied fruit and pistachio nuts.

To this Candide perceptively replies, "That's true enough, but we must go and work in the garden."[49]

The Lisbon earthquake of 1755 profoundly affected people. And there were still memories of the tragic Thirty Years War of the previous century. The literature on this problem is immense, for many felt that the fate of *religion* and metaphysics hinged upon this issue. When not dealt with as a matter of God's order, theodicy was dealt with by the philosophes as a matter of the world's order. For Zinzendorf, his theology of the cross and the suffering Savior was the answer.

Toleration

The Enlightenment felt that the most serious obstacle to truth was not the lack of knowledge. Given time, this can frequently be dealt with. More dangerous is perverted knowledge which pretends to be truth — dogma and superstition. It was philosophy alone, says Voltaire in his *Treatise on Tolerance*, that "has disarmed the hands of superstition which have so long been reddened with gore; the human spirit awakened from its intoxication is astonished at the excesses it committed under the influence of fanaticism."[50]

Along with advocacy of tolerance, there was an awareness of a natural *religion* beyond the historical religions which was not only universal but enduring. Diderot, in his essay *On the Sufficiency of Natural Religion*, commented:

Everything that has a beginning will sometime have an end, and, vice versa, that which has never had a beginning can never perish. Now the Jewish and Christian religions have had beginnings, and there is no *religion* on earth the date of whose origin is not known with the exception of natural *religion*. This *religion* alone then will never end, while all the others will perish.[51]

In his contrast between natural and revealed religions he said:

The former testimony I find within myself inscribed by the hand of God; the latter has been written on parchment and marble by superstitious people. The former I bear within myself, and I find it always the same; the latter lies outside myself and differs with every country and clime. The former brings together and unites

---

[49] Voltaire, *Candide, Or Optimism*, trans. John Butt (New York: Penguin Books, 1947), p. 144.

[50] Voltaire, quoted in Cassirer, *Philosophy of the Enlightenment*, p. 169.

[51] Denis Diderot, "On the Sufficiency of Natural *Religion*," quoted in Cassirer, *Philosophy of the Enlightenment*, p. 170.

civilized man and barbarian, Christian and heathen, philosopher and people, scholar and uneducated, old man and child; the latter estranges father and son, arms man against man, and exposes the wise to the hatred and persecution of the ignorant and fanatic.[52]

Zinzendorf also advocated tolerance through understanding the forms of *religion* as historically and culturally conditioned, finding their commonality in a more fundamental religious experience — but not that of natural *religion*. We find what we share through the universal experience of the Creator who is Savior. And the Savior/Creator is tolerant, gentle, and patient, working out his plan for all his souls according to their peculiarities.

Historical criticism

The Enlightenment, with its scientific and rationalistic developments, became very consciously aware of history and the historically conditioned nature of culture and institutions. This then was directed towards religious institutions and the Bible.

Richard Simon, a Catholic, in his *Histoire critique du vieux Testament* (1678) tried to show the error of the Protestant reliance on Scripture and rejection of all other religious authority. The Bible needs the support of the concurring testimony of Christian tradition. Spinoza is considered the "originator of the idea of the historicity of the Bible, and the first to develop it with sober precision and clarity,"[53] though his views were not popular in the eighteenth century. Spinoza believed that the ultimate source of certainty was being, not becoming, not that which is temporal and historical. Therefore he attacked the Bible as historical to reduce its role as an authority. Spinoza commented in his *Theologico-Political Treatise*:

> I may sum up the matter by saying that the method of interpreting Scripture does not widely differ from the method of interpreting nature — in fact, it is almost the same. For as the interpretation of nature consists in the examination of the history of nature, and therefrom deducing definitions of natural phenomena on certain fixed axioms, so Scriptural interpretation proceeds by the examination of Scripture, and inferring the intention of its authors as a legitimate conclusion from its fundamental principles. By working in this manner everyone will always advance without danger of error — that is, if they admit no principles for interpreting Scrip-

---

[52] Denis Diderot, quoted in Cassirer, *Philosophy of the Enlightenment*, p. 170.
[53] Cassirer, *Philosophy of the Enlightenment*, p. 185.

ture, and discussing its contents save such as they find in Scripture itself — and will be able with equal security to discuss what surpasses our understanding, and what is known by the natural light of reason.[54]

Very influential on Zinzendorf's century was Hugo Grotius, who, influenced by the great humanist Erasmus, presented his plan for the scientific criticism of the Bible in his *Annotations* on the Old and New Testaments. Diderot's article on the Bible in the French *Encyclopaedia* presents an almost complete sketch of the tasks and criteria of biblical criticism.

Lessing utilized and transformed Spinoza's philosophy. History and time are a part of being, for it is only in the process of history that being reveals itself. Lessing viewed God as the force which permeates and shapes the world from within, not as one who is separate and intervenes. Authentic *religion* is expressed in the historical spiritual process and not in the historical religions. Cassirer comments:

> The authentic, the only absolute *religion* is simply the *religion* which comprehends within itself the totality of the historical manifestations of the religious spirit. Within this *religion* no detail is completely lost; there is no opinion, however, eccentric, and no error which does not indirectly serve and belong to truth.[55]

Consequently Lessing, in his *Education of Humanity*, developed the idea of *religion* as a divine plan for the education of humanity. Because of his views, he could not accept contingent historical truths as proof for the necessary truths of reason.

> If I have no grounds historically on which I can object to the statement that Christ resurrected a dead man, must I therefore consider it true that God has a son in His own image? . . . If I have no grounds historically on which I can deny that Christ rose from the dead, must I therefore consider it true that this resurrected Christ was the son of God? . . . To jump from that historical truth to an entirely different class of truths, and to ask me to alter all my metaphysical and moral concepts accordingly . . . if that is not a 'transformation to another kind', then I do not know what else Aristotle meant by this term. . . . This is the ugly, wide ditch over which I cannot leap, however often and earnestly I try. If anyone

---

[54] Baruch Spinoza, *Theologico-Political Treatise*, quoted in Cassirer, *Philosophy of the Enlightenment*, pp. 185-86.

[55] Cassirer, *Philosophy of the Enlightenment*, p. 192.

can help me over, I pray, I conjure him to do so. God will recompense him.[56]

What one sees in the above developments is a twofold attack on the religious institutions. On the one hand their historically bound nature is perceived, and on the other hand the philosophical developments find ultimate truth in what is beyond the particulars of history. Zinzendorf was impressed with the Enlightenment's historical sensitivity. However, as in so many cases, he used its arguments for his own purposes. For him revelation was always *ökonomisch*, bound to the particular history in which it is given. That is the way that God works, for God works in a way relevant for each time. Each time, then, has its sense of the numinous and its own theological system. Each person in each period has the faith which is right for them.[57] It is, however, true that *religion* transcends historical institutional forms. But true *religion* is not the impersonal spiritual process of history, as with Lessing, but the personal heart relationship with the Savior which extends through all time and cultures.

Pietism

In Zinzendorf's time the authorities by which the church existed and supported its truth were coming into question. Reason and historical method were the arbiters of truth, rather than revelation and Scripture. Part of the church entrenched itself defensively within the walls of its traditions, but there were those who sought to respond to the Enlightenment and to bring new life into the church, seeking a conscious return to the ideals of the original Christian community reflected in the New Testament. Philip Jacob Spener and August Hermann Francke were the leaders of this movement, called Pietism, which in its most influential aspects found a home at Halle. Spener's *Pia Desideria* (Pious Desires) was the programmatic writing of the movement.[58] Zinzendorf's parents on both sides were under the sway of this movement.

[56] Gotthold Ephraim Lessing, *Über den Beweis des Geistes und der Kraft*, quoted in Cassirer, *Philosophy of the Enlightenment*, pp. 193-94.

[57] Nikolaus Ludwig von Zinzendorf, *Der Predigten die der Ordinarius Fratrum von Anno 1751. bis 1755. zu London gehalten hat, Zweyter Band, Nebst Einem Anhange einiger an Englische Brüder-Gemeinen gehaltenen Homilien*, sec. 4 (London and Barby: Zu finden bey dem Seminario Theologico, 1757), pp. 35ff. (Abbreviated in subsequent notes as Zinzendorf, *Der Predigten zu London gehalten* [Londoner Predigten, vol. 2].)

[58] See Peter C. Erb, ed., *Pietists: Selected Writings*, The Classics of Western Spirituality (New York: Paulist Press, 1983), pp. 31ff.

Under the influence of Pietism lay participation in the church was renewed; a more practical emphasis was placed upon the preparation for ministry; the study of the Bible was encouraged; small religious groups, *ecclesiolae in ecclesia,* were formed for the furtherance of study and the pious life; and interest in foreign missions was encouraged. Most importantly, a way of knowing was advocated in response to the Enlightenment's emphasis on reason and the orthodox Lutheran emphasis on the church's tradition. Experience was seen as revealing religious reality, and this revelation was often cast into the form of a standardized conversion experience. Many of these emphases found fruition in Zinzendorf, although Zinzendorf was to affirm them in ways particular to him.

There were really several Pietistic movements in German Lutheranism. One could divide Pietism into the movement identified with Halle, where Zinzendorf was educated and with which he later came to disagree; the movement identified with Zinzendorf and the Moravian Church; the radical Pietists, who would separate from the established churches; and then Württemberg Pietism, of which the great biblical scholar Albrecht Bengel was representative. He produced the Greek New Testament text which Zinzendorf later used. Zinzendorf's first contact with Bengel was probably when he traveled to Tübingen in 1733, attempting to secure a member of the Tübingen faculty as pastor of the Herrnhut congregation. Bengel lived in nearby Denkendorf. Spangenberg says that during their visit Bengel explained his views of the prophetical writings of Scripture.[59] In his *Remarks on the So-called Brethren's Church,* published in 1744, Bengel was appreciative of some aspects of the Moravian Church, but on the whole was highly critical.[60] In this and later writings he criticized Zinzendorf's emphasis on the cross, his understanding of the Trinity, and his interpretation of eschatology. Regarding eschatology, Zinzendorf focused on the present

---

[59] *Leben des Herrn Nicolaus Ludwig Grafen und Herrn von Zinzendorf und Pottendorf. Beschrieben von August Gottlieb Spangenberg* ([Barby]: Zu finden in dem Brüder-Gemeinen, 1773-75), p. 791. (Abbreviated in subsequent notes as Spangenberg, *Leben.*)

[60] Bengel published several works that were critical of Moravian and Zinzendorfian views. Besides his "Anmerckungen von der sogenannten Brüder-Gemeine" mentioned in the text (to be found in *Büdingische Sammlung,* 3:734-55, which also contains Zinzendorf's answers to Bengel), Bengel in 1751 published *Abriß der so genannten Brüdergemeine in welchem die Lehre und die ganze Sache geprüfet, das Gute und Böse dabey unterschieden, und insonderheit die Spangenbergische Declaration erläutert wird durch Johann Albrecht Bengel. Erster Theil [Zweyter Theil]* (Stuttgart: Johann Benedict Metzler, 1751). Erich Beyreuther in his *Zinzendorf und die Christenheit,* pp. 37ff. (third volume of a trilogy on the life of Zinzendorf), discusses Bengel's relationship with Zinzendorf. (Full bibliographical details at n. 4, above.)

realization of the relationship with the Savior and heaven, while trusting the future to Christ and refusing to speculate on it. Bengel saw the Apocalyptic materials of the Bible as predicting the future and believed he knew the stages by which it would happen. It should be noted that in 1734 Zinzendorf was examined and passed for ordination by the faculty at Tübingen, located in Württemberg. The same year Oetinger, a member of the Tübingen faculty, participated in a *Collegium Biblicum* at Herrnhut. However, during the 1740s the relationship of Zinzendorf with the Tübingen faculty worsened, probably because of the excesses of the Sifting Period. Plitt notes that the Tübingen faculty was much more critical of Zinzendorf than was the Württemberg consistory.[61]

Zinzendorf gradually grew away from Halle Pietism as well as experiencing its opposition, particularly in the person of A. H. Francke's son, Gotthilf. As Zinzendorf turned more to the insights of Luther regarding the centrality of grace, he rejected the Pietistic striving for holiness, something he believed to be the gift of God.

> Children of God don't go so far in morality as people of the world; they have no heroic striving for virtue nor aspiring to a higher humanity. But what is to be seen in them is what is in the heart. They want to be nothing more than they are, and they are graced sinners.[62]

And thus he could use the interesting metaphor regarding the rapidity with which grace settles the matters of the Christian life, "We ride on horseback, and the Pietists go on foot."[63]

In connection with his 1744 reply to Bengel's *Remarks On the So-called Brethren's Church*, Zinzendorf commented on the Pietist attempt to standardize the conversion experience:

> As far as the so-called *Buss-Kampf* [a term describing the conversion experience as including a penitential struggle] is concerned, that seems to me like Law-righteousness as expressed in Paul. I am able to endure a rigorous examination over the matter, and who knows whether several defenders of the *Buss-Kampf* have ever reflected as much on it as I have experience of it. However, I am not so taken in that I should not strongly believe that the attacks which still persist are merely spiritual pedantry. I value those saints who in the great matter of salvation have come so close to Christ's own way of

---

[61] Hermann Plitt, *Zinzendorfs Theologie* (Gotha: F.A. Perthes, 1869-74), 2:32.

[62] Zinzendorf, quoted in Beyreuther, *Trilogie*, 1:25 (Beyreuther does not place footnotes within the text of this first volume, but lists sources for each chapter at the end of the volume).

[63] Zinzendorf, quoted in Beyreuther, *Trilogie*, 1:24.

teaching that they have not known what "struggle" is until they looked it up in a spiritual lexicon.[64]

Lutheranism

The Lutheran Church of Zinzendorf's time was the expression not merely of Luther's thought, but of almost a century and a half of theological and institutional development. Lutheran scholasticism came to regard correct theology as the essence of Christian faith. Zinzendorf was brought up within the Lutheran Church, but in a way strongly influenced by Pietism. Many Lutherans were strongly suspicious of Pietism. In his stay at Wittenberg, where he formed a close relationship with Professor Gottlieb Wernsdorf, Zinzendorf had a more extensive introduction to orthodox Lutheranism.

Zinzendorf must have struggled a good deal with the implications of traditional Lutheran thought and the concerns of Pietism. His personal process gradually led him to an awareness that Luther and the scholastic Lutheranism of his time were not at one. By 1734-35 he spoke of a conversion to Luther, which he qualifies by saying, "I do not speak of the *religion*, but what I admire is the teaching."[65]

From what Zinzendorf said on a number of occasions, he seemed to feel that he was recapturing the insights of Luther. In an apologetic work Zinzendorf replied to more than three hundred accusations that were directed against him, the questions being formulated by Spangenberg.

Question 101
Is your struggle with the teaching of the Evangelical Lutheran Church? Or do you differ with many of the present teachers?
Answer
I differ with those present teachers who no longer teach that which is Lutheran.
Question 102
You say in vol. III of the *Büdingen Collection*, p. 613, that you do more for Lutheran teaching and order than your opponents, and that you live and die by the same.[66]

---

[64] Zinzendorf, quoted in *Büdingische Sammlung*, 3:743.
[65] Zinzendorf, quoted in Uttendörfer, *Zinzendorf und die Mystik*, p. 18.
[66] M. Aug. Gottl. Spangenbergs Darlegung richtiger Antworten auf mehr als dreyhundert Beschuldigungen gegen den Ordinarivm Fratrvm nebst verschiedenen wichtigen Beylagen (Leipzig and Görlitz: In der Marcheschen Buchhandlung, 1751), pp. 128f.

The answer to question 102 was an invitation to compare his writings with those of Luther and of the Lutheran theologians. Question 103 concerned Zinzendorf's reproach of the Lutheran theologians for their neglect of Luther's teaching on the Holy Spirit.

In the foreword to a new edition of his *Bedenken*, he commented, "Luther has no greater lover far and wide: his writings, his hymns, his divine style of writing, his Little Catechism, his expressions in many writings are my daily admiration and satisfaction."[67]

Zinzendorf also expressed a deep loyalty to the Augsburg Confession, "In short, the Augsburg Confession remains my system for teaching. It is the best which we have; and since I have near what satisfies me, I don't need to seek it at a distance."[68]

His journey towards Luther had been underway since childhood.

If people observe how precisely Lutheran I have spoken, they could think that I read Luther's writings day and night and that I enjoyed teaching *paradoxa* [in Greek this may mean "incredible matters" or "matters contrary to opinion"], because I knew where they were in his writings and I could show where to look them up. Who knows me knows that I have none of Luther's writings. The origin of this is that in my childhood, before I even went to Halle, I had heard many of the best products of Luther. Mrs. von Meisbach [his great-aunt, 1650-1733] always told at the table what good things about the Savior she read in Luther; and in the evening I often listened while she read. Along with my meditation on the Savior, that has been important to me from childhood on, so that I can easily speak about a hundred matters in the very words of Luther without being aware of their source.... On the other hand I have retained nothing out of Arndt and Spener whose writings I had to read in my childhood, for they were not to my taste. I can not understand how Arndt can be seen as a Lutheran theologian.[69]

From Zinzendorf's description above one assumes there was a great deal of Luther implanted in his subconscious and that this was to be raw material for his later development. We have already mentioned his education at Wittenberg and his association with Professor Wernsdorf. His attraction to Pierre Bayle and Bayle's emphasis on grace would have been further support for the move to Luther. In the early thirties the rupture with Halle took place, and Spangenberg, who had been dis-

---

[67] Zinzendorf, quoted in *Büdingische Sammlung*, 1:299.
[68] Zinzendorf, *Naturelle Reflexiones*, p. 23.
[69] Zinzendorf, quoted in Uttendörfer, *Zinzendorf und die Mystik*, p. 19.

missed by Halle, joined Zinzendorf. In 1732 a commission from Dresden investigated Herrnhut's orthodoxy. Then in 1733-34 Friedrich Christoph Oetinger, Tübingen theologian, spent a year at Herrnhut, where he, along with Zinzendorf and others, began preliminary studies and attempts at a revised German translation of the Bible. This careful biblical study must have had its affect on Zinzendorf. In 1734 Zinzendorf was examined at Stralsund in March and at Tübingen in December. Before this, on Sunday, February 14, 1734, Zinzendorf spoke of the impact upon him of the hymn verse associated with the Daily Text:

> The old verse: "Let us in your nail mark see our election" out of the hymn by Martin Behm: "O Jesus Christ, My Life's Light" of 1644, which belonged to the Daily Text, became for us as new as if we had heard it for the first time. . . . So we then entered into the matter for which zeal has grown all year long.[70]

The consequence of turning to Luther was the cessation of the Pietistic struggle for salvation and sanctification, and a finding of the solution to the problems of life in God's grace alone, as revealed in Christ. Both Zinzendorf and Herrnhut turned away from legalism and the idea that a personal struggle must lead to conversion. Joy is characteristic of this newfound orientation and there is confidence in God's forgiveness over against the uncertainty and anxiety fostered by Halle's approach. Beyreuther notes the changed tone in the correspondence of Zinzendorf after this change. The difference between joy and confidence in the Savior and the struggled life and legalism was to continue to characterize the separation between Herrnhut and Halle.[71] Zinzendorf's adherence to Luther's theological emphases, viewing sanctification as a gift of God's grace and not a process, was to be a dividing point between him and the Wesleys, and it also helps explain the ways in which he appropriated and opposed mysticism.

There are now extensive materials on the relationship of the Moravian tradition to the Lutheran from the Bilateral Dialogue concluded in 1996 in North America. The Dialogue and its results are described in the Consensus Paper, "Following Our Shepherd to Full Communion."[72]

---

[70] Zinzendorf, quoted in Beyreuther, *Trilogie*, 3:63.

[71] Beyreuther, *Trilogie*, 3:64-65.

[72] Evangelical Lutheran Church in America and Moravian Church in America, Northern and Southern Provinces, *Following Our Shepherd to Full Communion: Report of the Lutheran-Moravian Dialogue with Recommendations for Full Communion, Worship, Fellowship and Mission* (Evangelical Lutheran Church in America, 1997).

Mysticism

There was a natural kinship between mysticism and Pietism. Both sought to move beyond traditional theological and institutional forms of *religion* and to allow religion's reality to be experienced and expressed. It was natural that Zinzendorf would have been in some way affected by mysticism.

Uttendörfer, in his *Zinzendorf und die Mystik*, which is the culmination of a life of study of Zinzendorf, gives an excellent summary of the streams of mystical thought that impinged upon Zinzendorf's period.[73] There was the continuing influence of Bernard's Christ-mysticism in Lutheran hymnody, particularly in Johann Scheffler (1624-77). But there is much more.

German mysticism reached a high point in the theosophical system of Jacob Böhme (1575-1623), whose idea that God was to be grasped by faith in Christ supported Lutheran emphases. Böhme's ideas were developed by Johann Georg Gichtel (1638-1710). Christ must live in us so that we can become little gods in the great God. We must experience Christ, taste, smell, become like him. Self-denial was central, even to poverty and celibacy. A sect arose which followed Gichtel and deserted the church of "Babel."

Johann Arndt (1555-1621) was a Lutheran who through his four books on *True Christianity* called for a piety expressed in life. He followed a somewhat traditional pattern for spiritual development in three stages: purification or repentance - childhood; illumination - youth; and union with God - maturity. This was not a process of divine grace, but a striving of the soul and an imitation of Christ independent of justification which led to union. If at the stage of union one lets God effect what God will, one receives again the nobility of one's soul and experiences God in inexpressible ways. He also asserted that the soul should live in contemplation of its white and red (i.e., wounded) bridegroom, especially his suffering, and unite itself with him in inexpressible love. Lutheran orthodoxy fought his views because of his emphasis on human striving rather than divine grace. Although Zinzendorf in 1725 caused Arndt's True Christianity to be translated into French, dedicating it to Cardinal Noailles, later in 1753 he re-

---

[73] Uttendörfer, *Zinzendorf und die Mystik*, pp. 3-11. See also Dietrich Meyer, "'Christus mein ander Ich': Zu Zinzendorfs Verhältnis zur Mystik," *Zeitwende* 54 (1983): pp. 87-101 (Abbreviated in subsequent notes as Dietrich Meyer, "'Christus mein ander Ich.'"); Wilhelm Bettermann, "Vorläufiges über Zinzendorfs Stellung zur Mystik," *Zeitschrift für Kirchengeschichte* (Stuttgart) 52 (1933): pp. 599-609.

marked, "I cannot understand how Arndt can have been regarded as a Lutheran theologian."[74]

Gottfried Arnold (1666-1714) was very influential in the Lutheran Church. He published some of his own mystical writings, but made a significant contribution in his translations of the works of other mystics: e.g., John of the Cross, Catherine of Genoa, and such French mystics as Madame Guyon. There are some interesting features to his views. By new birth, the overcoming of the world, one enters into the holy "Nothing" and finds union with God. This is effected through one's relation with Christ, especially his suffering and cross. There is some treatment of a special reverence for the wounds and side-hole of Christ. The Spirit draws its strength out of the wounds of Christ. Knowledge of Christ through reason and history is not sufficient. Christ must mystically take form in us. Physiognomy (an attempt to discern the inner life of a person from outward appearance) becomes important for this reason. The true church consists of those who are born again and exist both inside and outside of the confessional churches. In his famous *History of the Undivided Church and the History of Heresy* Arnold attempts to identify the true mystical theology in all ages. The end of history is the disappearance of all divisions so that Christ becomes all in all.

One of the mystics whom Arnold brought to Germany in his translations was Peter Poiret (1646-1719). Though he wrote relatively few mystical writings of his own, he edited a number of the older mystics such as Guyon and Fenelon, with whose writings Zinzendorf was acquainted. One of his main contributions was in his opposition of mysticism to philosophy. Originally a follower of Descartes, he rejected the Cartesian position that God could be proved mathematically or logically. Reason and philosophy rather lead only to partial knowledge and finally to atheism. True knowledge is secured through the receptive capabilities of the soul, i.e., the mind, experience and the passive intellect. True theology then is not a matter of the head, but the heart. It is simple (trusting, uncomplicated), naive souls, surrendered to God, that are illumined. Such illumined souls turn from the conflicts of the theologians, do not think in confessional terms, and are united in their religious experience. The similarity with some of Zinzendorf's views is striking.

One of the mystics that Poiret edited was Madame Guyon (1648-1717). Guyon held that God is motionless, self-contained perfection. Humanity was created to be united with him. For this to happen, repentance and mortification are necessary so that the soul becomes

---

[74] Zinzendorf, quoted in Uttendörfer, *Zinzendorf und die Mystik*, p. 19.

completely empty and perceives the inner word. After that, illumination follows, and the soul lives in complete surrender to God, in quiet delight, without striving or self-interest.

In 1731 several individuals introduced Zinzendorf to the works of Madame Guyon. He selectively summarized the contents of some of her spiritual discourses and spoke on them at some meetings in Herrnhut.[75] Spangenberg thought Zinzendorf did this primarily to turn the church members away from her writings.[76] In 1744 Zinzendorf commented:

> In mysticism there is a spirit, for which no design is proper and nothing is clear, but entirely prefers what is dark, even if it does not understand it. Madame Guyon [L. (that is Ludwig, i.e., Zinzendorf) does not hold her views] has many errors. The creature can never become God.[77]

Konrad Dippel (1673-1734) called true believers out of the Babel of the historic churches. Righteousness came through Christ alone. God is a God of love, and the teaching of the wrath of God is false. Christ died in order that we should die to sin and grow to perfection, inasmuch as Christ lives in us. The way to God's blessing is also possible for the heathen, for Christ is eternally working among them. Dippel was in contact with Zinzendorf, who was attracted to his view of the atonement. Zinzendorf came to reject him and particularly his separatist views with regard to the church.

Franz Buddaeus (1667-1729) carried on influential work at Jena. He understood *religion* as *aisthesis*, a tasting and feeling of God, which can be better experienced than described. Personal experience then provides stronger proof than all rational proof. One comes to know God through effected changes in life. He believed that the historical revelation (Scripture) was significant authority along with experience. In contrast to dogma, which is understood by few, history is easily understood. Here one finds interesting similarities to Zinzendorf. Buddaeus was especially close to the Moravians. Schrautenbach tells of a visit the Count made in August 1728 to Jena, where he had been invited to the meeting of a learned society which met under Buddaeus.[78] Later

---

[75] Zinzendorf's selection of some materials out of her discourses and some comments on them are contained in *Inhalt der Geistlichen Reden der Madame Guion*, in *Der Freywilligen Nachlese, Bey den bißherigen Gelehrten und erbaulichen Monaths-Schrifften* (Frankfurt and Leipzig: Marche, [n.d.], *1. Sammlung. Etiam inter manipulos colligat, et pudore non afficiatis eam. Ruth. c. II. v. 15*, collection [Sammlung] 3, pp. 97ff.

[76] Spangenberg, *Leben*, p. 658ff.

[77] Zinzendorf, quoted in Wilhelm Bettermann, *Theologie und Sprache bei Zinzendorf* (Gotha: Klots, 1935), p. 34.

[78] Schrautenbach, *Zinzendorf und die Brüdergemeine*, p. 129.

Zinzendorf attempted to form a *Collegium pastorale practicum* (College for Practical Pastoral Work) at Jena and offered Buddaeus the superintendency, which Buddaeus was willing to accept. However, the project did not materialize.[79]

It would seem that Zinzendorf's ongoing experience of relationship with the Savior and his location of the essence of the Christian *religion* in the experience of the heart would necessitate some relationship to or sympathy with mysticism. Dietrich Meyer provides a perspective on Zinzendorf's mysticism in "Christ My Other I." He suggests stages in the development of Zinzendorf's mysticism: Lutheran-Halle Pietism; Philadelphian Longing (for restoration of the ideal Philadelphian church, related to the Philadelphian movement); the Turn to Luther and the Rejection of Mysticism; and the Playful Blood and Wounds Cult. Most helpful is his exploration of the Christ mysticism of the mature Zinzendorf and Zinzendorf's terminology.

The phrase "my other I" he traces back to Zeno and Diogenes Laertius, meaning "a best friend." However, Zinzendorf seemed to use this in a stronger way which expresses Christ's formation of the identity of the Christian. Meyer indicates that important in the loving relationship with Christ is the "sinner-shame" which makes one aware that there is nothing one can do. All is of grace. "*Umgang mit Christus*" ("living with Christ"), which receives more extended treatment in the chapter on Christian Life and Ethics, goes beyond *Imitatio Christi*, for the stress is on connection with the "Man of Pain," not on doing or imitation. Christ is also spoken of as present in all daily matters and as the source of the life hidden in us. "I am from moment to moment *absolut* dependent on him who has given me life, no detached, isolated life, but an eternally hidden life which is from his life." Zinzendorf's expressions concerning *Umgang mit Christus* must be understood as representing community piety rather than merely individual piety.[80]

When one speaks of Zinzendorf as a mystic, there is need to note that he stamped his mysticism with a very definite character, as implied in the terminology Meyer discussed. One might summarize his approach as follows:

1. His turn to Luther and grace, away from the striving of Halle Pietism or mysticism, gave his mysticism a particular character. All that mattered was of grace, not the result of a process of human struggle.

2. The predicament in which human existence was immersed meant

[79] Spangenberg, *Leben*, p. 493.
[80] Zinzendorf, *Der Predigten zu London gehalten* [Londoner Predigten, vol. 2], p. 355, quoted in Dietrich Meyer, "'Christus mein ander Ich,'" p. 98.

that humans could not extricate themselves. This took God's grace and the atonement.

3. The goal of the human transformation and growth process was not divinization or absorption into the divine. Humans cannot become God.

4. Zinzendorf's mysticism was a Christ mysticism. The Father could not even be known until one was in relationship with Christ.

5. In terms of "visions," Zinzendorf seems to opt for what Teresa of Avila called the "intellectual vision," a vision grasped by the soul and not necessarily in the mind/imagination. He did speak of painting Christ before the eyes of the soul and therefore making use of the imagination; but what was needed for salvation was not a vision that could be seen, but an objective seeing of Christ by the soul, which might not be apparent in the imagination but would only be known by its after-effects.[81]

6. Zinzendorf was always careful not to be separatist and affirmed not only that the experience of Christ united one with other Christians throughout the world, but that the historic churches were witnesses to the faith in Christ worth treasuring.

7. Zinzendorf's approach to *religion* was relational. The heart relationship was with the person of Christ and with all those joined together by him. Through the relationship with Christ the relationship with the Father and the Spirit developed. Relationship and identity never disappeared within "something greater."

8. Zinzendorf's use of the mystical idea that God dwelt in darkness, and that knowledge of God was "dark" knowledge, was only in regard to the Father. Ontologically one was separate from God, so one could not know the Father. However, God has always revealed God's self experientially in the Son, and now the Son has become flesh. Thus the knowledge of God in Christ is not dark, but clear and plain. It is historical. When one gets to know the Son, the Son then reveals the Father, who otherwise is hidden in mystery. This revelation of the Father is a "personal" revelation, not a revelation of divine information.

9. Zinzendorf reversed the usual mystical process, which starts with mortification, the receiving of illumination, and then goes on to mystical union, frequently using the imagery of the mystical marriage. Zinzendorf started with union. As a gift of God's grace we receive union with the Savior at the outset of the Christian life. This was often treated by Zinzendorf in terms of marriage with the Bridegroom. Though we grow in our perception and living of relationship with the Savior, the relationship of the Savior with us does not grow. It is all there in its

[81] See particularly lecture 7 in Zinzendorf, *Nine Public Lectures* [1973].

totality at the beginning of the Christian life. Union is at the beginning, not the end, providing the basis and resource for all that follows. In the second Discourse on the Augsburg Confession Zinzendorf said:

This quasi-deification which was necessary to make us a bride of Jesus Christ, and without which no one can be a bride of God, which we do not regard as the final degree of perfection that a bit surpasses eternity (as do the mystics in their order of salvation), but on the contrary with this our soul has its beginning. Our true Father, the Father of our Lord Jesus Christ, has begotten us of incorruptible seed; the only Mother has borne us out of her womb; and the God (that out of a clod of earth had formed us into human figures, and breathed the breath of life in this statue, to make natural humans, propagating themselves bodily, but not spiritually) who so gently redeemed us again after the Fall, who became a holy human for our sake, that we might be made holy, that the Holy Spirit might be acquired by us; the same is our Bridegroom, our future Husband.[82]

Zinzendorf's Reflections on His Development

It is interesting to listen to Zinzendorf's own reflections on his development. Uttendörfer in *Zinzendorf and Mysticism* refers to rich resources.[83]

---

[82] Nikolaus Ludwig von Zinzendorf, *Ein und zwanzig Discurse über die Augspurgische Confession gehalten vom 15. Dec. 1747. bis zum 3. Mart. 1748. denen Seminariis Theologicis Fratrum zum Besten aufgefaßt und bis zur nochmaligen Revision des Auctoris einstweilen mitgetheilet* (n.p., n.d.), p. 70 (16 Dec. 1747). N.B.: There are two eighteenth-century German-language printings of this work. Both are undated, and have very different page-numbering schemes. They can be distinguished by title page spellings of two words: one edition, *Discourse . . . Autoris*; the other, *Discurse . . . Auctoris*. All quotations in this book are from the latter. Citation of the printing used in this book will be abbreviated in subsequent notes as Zinzendorf, *Ein und zwanzig Discurse* [Title page: *Discurse . . . Auctoris*].

The "Mother" who bears us in her womb is the Holy Spirit. Zinzendorf's understanding of the Spirit as Mother will be treated in the next chapter. To the word "quasi-deification" Zinzendorf adds the following footnote: "To be transformed into a heavenly being, to be made participant in the divine nature, to be transformed in Christ: these are equivalent ways of speaking. The old hymn expresses it thus: He takes our place wonderfully, flesh and blood he assumes, and thus in his Father's kingdom, grants us simple divinity."

[83] Uttendörfer, *Zinzendorf und die Mystik*, pp. 16-22. Beyreuther makes a remark in his *Trilogie*, 1:218, which perhaps should be mentioned. It does seem that Zinzendorf's memory of historical events is not always precise and may occasionally present different perspectives on the same event. Beyreuther's remark deals particularly with Zinzendorf's interpretation of his attempted engagement with a woman named Theodore of Castell. She then became engaged to his friend, Heinrich von Reuss, an event which was, of course, filled with sensitive issues. "To remember faithfully in historical matters is a gift

His grandmother, with whom he lived, was the person to whom he gave credit for much of his personal and spiritual formation:

My intimate acquaintance with the Savior came from my being educated for ten years in my grandmother's, the Countess von Gersdorf's, own room in Hennersdorf. There I have heard her speak about matters with the Savior which I did not completely understand, but I concluded from this that the communal worship outside and at home did not have at all to do with the person with whom I lived, but that it had more and more to do with her Lord.[84]

When asked what she was best at, he replied: "Praying, believing, being still and not avoiding either cross or work when God beckons."[85]

When Zinzendorf was three, his mother told him how his father, while dying, had directed his gaze to the "*Martyrman*" and was comforted by the hymn "O Sacred Head Once Wounded." He then began to seek God earnestly as much as his childish ideas allowed. "I spoke as gladly of the dear Savior as I heard from him, and when I was alone, so I spoke to the chairs which I gathered as part of my play. My mouth spoke of what my heart was full."[86]

As real as the Savior was to him, real doubts also assailed him even in his early years. He felt that God had given him a goodly measure of reason and imagination, strong doubts assailed his mind, and he had the unforgettable experience as a child of eight of being overwhelmed with doubt, laying awake the whole night.

When thirty-four he wrote, "I have been severely burdened by strong spiritual testings from my eighth year to the present. Who has no experience of this, I congratulate."[87]

His heart gave him an understanding of things that his reason could not grasp and his temptations and doubts could not assail.

I have always been a simple sheep in theology. I did not know what my heart did not understand. I still don't understand twenty texts. ... If the Savior gives me understanding of something, it becomes as sweet as honey to me and I rejoice greatly over that. But theologians have the mistake, or the prejudice, that they must understand everything at the same time.[88]

which simply escapes him. So there often exists a profound difference between earlier and later reports by Zinzendorf regarding events of his life which each biographer helplessly faces who does not recognize the breadth of all the attestations."

[84] Zinzendorf, quoted in Beyreuther, *Trilogie*, 1:63.

[85] Zinzendorf, quoted in Beyreuther, *Trilogie*, 1:63.

[86] Zinzendorf, quoted in Beyreuther, *Trilogie*, 1:71-72.

[87] Zinzendorf, quoted in Beyreuther, *Trilogie*, 1:80.

[88] Zinzendorf, Tagebuch, 25 July 1718, quoted in Uttendörfer, *Zinzendorf und die Mystik*, p. 16.

His going to Halle as a ten year old suddenly wrenched him away from the security of his relationship with his grandmother and her home and subjected him to the pedagogy of those who did not know him well. The pedagogy of his time assumed that the will of a child needed to be broken and that pride in oneself was bad. This was reinforced by religious understanding of pride as a basis for sin. Zinzendorf told of his mother's instructions to Halle:

> The faithful soul [his mother] on the first day of my arrival said to Professor Francke in my presence that they must thoroughly humble me, for I was inclined to pride, to great undertakings, and imagined myself to be something because of my gifts. . . . I was not wholly free from pride. Unfortunately this presentation of me was listened to. From that moment on I had to struggle with the thought that I must be something special when it was necessary to keep me so sharply bridled.[89]

Zinzendorf remembered his first experience of the Lord's Supper as a decisive moment in his life:

> Then God grasped me in my heart: Do you see now how foolish your imagination has been! On what do you depend for glory? How vain! You want to convert people — for that was my serious wish and request — and you make such great mistakes against Christianity. What have you accomplished, except for the state, by your study, and in what have you taken pride, except in being a member of your select class? All then came to me that I had done wrongly in my life. I earnestly made the decision that I wanted to seek my future honor in the cross of Christ, I wanted to become another person with God's help, I wanted to be in continual prayer; then I became in my mind more at peace, my soul became established and still, and from that hour on the faithful God has dug deeper and deeper, has laid a better foundation.[90]

In spite of his difficulties at Halle, eventually he gained the admiration of the elder Francke and developed there the beginnings of his vision of a mission for Christ and a society committed to it (his Order of the Mustard Seed). Later, on his sixteenth birthday, his grandmother presented him with a medallion for this society. In his diary he wrote:

> Blessed Grandmother presented me with the first medallion of my Society on that day. It was a gold piece the size of a Taler, with the

[89] Zinzendorf, quoted in Beyreuther, *Trilogie,* 1:89.
[90] Zinzendorf, quoted in Beyreuther, *Trilogie,* 1:116. Written in 1722.

portrayal of the thorn-crowned Jesus on one side with the inscription "Vulnera Christi" [wounds of Christ], on the other a mourning person with wings lying under his heavy cross with the inscription: "Nostra Medela" [our healing].[91]

While at Wittenberg he formed a "Society of the Confessors of Christ," patterned after the English Society for the Propagation of Christian Knowledge. When later asked why this society did not succeed, Zinzendorf said that they confused Law and Gospel in concern for Christian morality.[92] It is interesting that when one vision did not work, Zinzendorf dreamed a new one. "God has given me, be he thanked, a tireless spirit to further his honor and fame, a spirit which can never rest."[93]

A painting in an art gallery in Düsseldorf, seen at the beginning of his educational journey, made a lasting impression. On May 22, a few days before his nineteenth birthday, he wrote in his diary:

Düsseldorf interrupted these thoughts [about eternity] for a moment. A beautiful brick residence of the previous Prince! Among many hundreds of the most splendid portraits in the gallery, the only *Ecce homo* drew my eyes and mind to itself. Its meaning was incomparably expressed in the subscript: *Ego pro te haec passus sum; Tu vero, quid fecisti pro me?* . . . I was embarrassed that I here would not even have been able to give much of an answer and asked my Savior to forcibly bring me into the community of his suffering if my mind did not wish it.[94]

Zinzendorf's educational journey brought him into contact with many other Christian traditions and from that time on he "made the effort to discover the best in all confessions."[95]

But nothing so affected him as his half-year series of conversations with the French Cardinal Noailles. When each gave up any attempt to convert the other, they found that each shared "the Universal *Religion* of the Savior." We "were together for a half year with hearts filled with heavenly joy and did not reflect on what church one or the other

---

[91] Zinzendorf, quoted in Beyreuther, *Trilogie*, 1:123.
[92] Zinzendorf, quoted in Beyreuther, *Trilogie*, 1:151-53.
[93] Zinzendorf, quoted in Beyreuther, *Trilogie*, 1:153.
[94] Zinzendorf, quoted in Beyreuther, *Trilogie*, 1:169. The Latin translated is: "I for you have suffered this; truly, what have you done for me?" This painting by Domenico Feti shows Christ as a man of suffering. His head with the crown of thorns is inclined to the side. A rough cord is hung around the neck of the Savior. His tender hands are chained. Zinzendorf also associated this painting with the painting with which his father identified on his deathbed.
[95] Zinzendorf, quoted in Beyreuther, *Trilogie*, 2:8.

belonged to." Their theme became entering more deeply "into the bottomless sea of the suffering and merit of Jesus and the grace received through that to become blessed and holy."[96]

His description of his interaction with the Moravians who settled on his estate is interesting.

> I left the court and the office I had for no other reason than that I wanted to convert from the error of their ways my recently arrived guests from Moravia and other places who were described to me as crypto-Calvinists and Separatists; and if I was confident of any place where I might have my say and not get into arguments, it was there. But that was quite wrong. My friends were hotter in the beginning than I, for they came out of persecution and I came from the court. That gave me a little advantage over them. Accordingly they learned from me in a short while to speak and think with more effect, and I also learned something new. I had to busy myself with much in treatises in which I reflected on how to get "unstuck," and in a half year I learned more church history and received more data for a solid criticism of heresy than I would have gathered from Arnold's *History of Churches and Heresies,* yes, even from Bayle. Never has the providence which cares for me preserved me from a more real danger than on this occasion, and when I see what can occur from a little dose of impartiality for a tested specific, I give thanks. The human mind does not have the ability to go from one extreme to the middle. It commonly makes its way over to the other extreme. And so for several years I have pursued the course of careful testing, step by step, of the many ways, interpretations, and understandings of Christian persons, who either sought me or to whom my calling directly or indirectly had led. But I rejected partially or wholly none of the particulars which I had not pondered for a long while previously. As this has applied for me in reference to things, so does it much more come into play with respect to persons. It is not unusual that I have listened for an extended time to a person with respect, whom my companions at first considered confused, and was scarcely able to convince myself not to gain any profit from it other than what I myself discovered in a few minutes.[97]

Zinzendorf provided a number of reflections on his developmental process.

---

[96] Zinzendorf, quoted in Beyreuther, *Trilogie,* 1:194.
[97] Zinzendorf, *Naturelle Reflexiones,* pp. 13f. (15 Dec. 1746), quoted in Uttendörfer, *Zinzendorf und die Mystik,* p. 20.

It was about 1730 when I first experienced the first deep drawings of grace which arose from the preaching of the cross. All can be related to my calling as a servant: the longing to bring souls to Jesus entered my heart and my plan in my heart became the Lamb, though I thought of different methods of arriving at this plan: in Halle, directly; in Wittenberg, through morality; in Dresden, through philosophy; since then through the imitation of Christ, not earlier than the founding of Herrnhut in 1727, an approach which agreed with Dippel's emphasis on the simple teaching of his death and dying.[98]

As Uttendörfer summarized some of Zinzendorf's reflections,

when he was still a young man, he was still partially enchanted with the world, a free spirit, a half Hallensian and an eclectic.[99] Another time he described the periods of his life as follows: since the second year of his residence in Wittenberg, a pious orthodox; from his majority on through Graf Henckel (Erdmann Heinrich 1681-1752) he became a Pietist until 1727 when he became a Moravian brother; since his acquaintance with Dippel, a "Räsonneur" (a person who uses reason or argumentation), until 1734 and the hymn "Thou our chosen Head."[100] After that not many changes occurred with him, except that after his exile he became more Lutheran. He did not consider himself unfortunate to have passed through all these changes.[101]

His turn to Luther is presented in various ways. He once commented that he originally had a "house-idea" and did not want to have any "*religion*" (established church), and so his wife continued to think. That

[98] Zinzendorf, Herrnhut Archives, R20A1,1, 20 Jan. 1740, quoted in Uttendörfer, *Zinzendorf und die Mystik*, p. 17.

[99] Zinzendorf, Herrnhut Archives, R2A3a,1, p. 108, 14 June 1740, cited in Uttendörfer, *Zinzendorf und die Mystik*, p.17.

[100] Hymn 973 in *Berthelsdorfer Gesangbuch*, published as *Sammlung Geistlicher und lieblicher Lieder, Eine große Anzahl der Kernvollesten alter und erwecklichsten Neuen Gesänge enthaltend* (Leipzig: August Martini, n.d.), cited in Uttendörfer, *Zinzendorf und die Mystik*, p. 17. The hymn, remembered by the Moravian community as connected with this new orientation, was:
Thou our chosen Head,
in whom our soul believes,
let us in your nail mark
discover our election.
And through your pierced side
our souls go in and out.

[101] Herrnhut Archives, R2A17,1, pp. 141f., 12 Aug. 1745, cited in Uttendörfer, *Zinzendorf und die Mystik*, p. 17. This whole paragraph is a quotation from Uttendörfer in which he alludes to a number of statements of Zinzendorf.

meant that he would have founded a more radical Pietistic community similar to that of her home in Ebersdorf and did not want to belong to a confessional church. Then he continued:

> I was converted as a Lutheran since 1734-5. The teaching did not bring that about. . . . In Halle they should have focused their theology on D. Anton instead of their Pietism. He had the true Lutheran teaching within. D. Anton (1661-1730) is my spiritual father. He made me into a Lutheran through his little writings, and I simply believed that whatever D. Anton said was Lutheran teaching. Afterwards I read Rambach's (1693-1735) excerpts from Luther and they agreed with what Anton said. I do not speak of the *Religion* (denomination or church), but what I admire is the teaching. Since then I have been a "sectarian" (a devotee to a certain teaching), and it is ridiculous if theologians don't want to allow that I am a Lutheran.[102]

In a sermon of 1751 he expressed how his growing awareness of human need was one of the motives for his turning to Luther:

> I don't think differently now than in 1706. It is said that I had then experienced a conviction, which I still have, which accompanied me even through my whole life. . . . The conviction, which I experienced forty-five and more years ago, arose in a wounding of the heart over the suffering form of Jesus, over love for the martyr of God. Then I still did not know that one is and remains a sinner, nor had I seriously considered that all suffering happened for the sake of sin, but I believed the Gospels as a little dumb sheep: that God died for us that we might live eternally. . . . The feeling of misery and need out of which one cries to the Savior and gains personal participation in his suffering and merit, I first learned in 1732 as a great wisdom . . . on the occasion of the controversy with Dippel. Then I really knew what it meant to fall in love with the martyr-person of the Savior without knowing the greatness of one's own need and hereafter was convinced of the greatness of the necessity of his suffering. Mine is a praeternatural method, which is not well esteemed by many and probably would not have worked out well for me if I had not chosen to be what I am, without understanding whatever might be argued for or against. I have wholeheartedly considered the suffering of the Savior the main matter and said nothing else to my fellow students in the

---

[102] Zinzendorf, Herrnhut Archives, R2A39b, pp. 60f., 9 June 1756, quoted in Uttendörfer, *Zinzendorf und die Mystik*, pp. 17-18.

Paedagogium, but I had no understanding of human corruption. Rather I had the wonderful opinion of the high nobility of the soul and the consequences of this,[103] and believed that if one rightly preached to people about their Creator, they would fall to their knees; if they heard that their Creator died for them, they would at the same time want to follow him. I selected the spiritual position which made it possible to preach such to thousands. At the time I never preached without thinking that I and my hearers were of one mind. It was fairly so, but actually I also noticed that in two or three days it was again past and forgotten. Out of the unfaithfulness of so many persons called with me, whereby they lost their calling and election to a certain degree, I first rightly became acquainted with the human race and in other ways even got to know myself. So it went from one thing to another, and now we understand that we know ourselves as sinners and we learned to understand the reality and seriousness of the wrath of God out of Jesus' suffering. Especially had the Holy Spirit during the last years (during the time of the "heresy") brought about the faith which comes out of a little crowd of holy persons gathering together who greatly rejoice over the Savior and forget who they are and what it cost him to redeem them.[104]

Reflections

Zinzendorf was an incomparable person. His time, his culture and its issues, his noble heritage, but, above all, his Lord, seem to have called him to his role. One will not find in Zinzendorf all that is modern. He could not have anticipated all of the modern questions and the issues related to them. Yet he responded to a world which was giving birth to our world; so often we find ourselves resonating with his solutions to significant religious issues.

His response to his times was a response for God, for his Savior, in his times. One of his most significant contributions was his discovery that the heart may know what the mind cannot understand. And he knew that *religion* was not primarily conceptual and institutional, but

---

[103] Uttendörfer, *Zinzendorf und die Mystik*, p. 18, comments that Zinzendorf expressed the same thoughts in *Des Ordinarii Fratrum Berlinische Reden, nach dem vollständigen und von ihm selbst eigenhändig revidirten Exemplar, in Druk gegeben von Gottfried Clemens, des Seminarii Theol. Decano und Schloss Prediger zu Barby*. Tom. 1 (London and Barby: Zu finden bey dem Seminario Theologico, 1758), p. 138, note.

[104] Zinzendorf, in Diarium des Jüngerhauses, 21 Dec. 1751, quoted in Uttendörfer, *Zinzendorf und die Mystik*, p. 19.

involves the reality of a God who is personal and relational. He took
seriously the historical nature of all religious experience, and saw God's
working within history and culture as part of God's taking seriously the
times and nature of human existence. He listened to the sciences and
movements of his time, but he also listened to his heart and affirmed
that ultimately the issues of life are resolved in relationship to the God
of the wounds, an understanding of God which turns upside down the
marriage of *religion* and power.

His response to his times was mission. This mission encompassed
the world, but this mission was God's, not his. As there can be no *religion*
without community, so there can be no *religion* or religious community
without mission. This mission was to share in the process that was
already underway in the heart of God: to bring souls to their Creator/
Savior. It did not have all of the social, economic, and political aspects
that might accompany modern missions, but it was a mission for the
world as it was for the Savior. The stories of those who, with minimal
resources, were sent out by the Moravian Church into the dangers of
primitive areas are moving indeed.[105]

To imitate Christ is to heed the call of God, of Christ, within our
times, responding to the issues of our times. It is not primarily to do what
Christ did in the first century. Moreover, Christ no longer belongs only
to the first century, but to all time — and so we must ask what he himself
would do in our time. It is also true that to be responsible to the insights
of Zinzendorf one should not seek the literal repetition of his ideas or
faith forms in our time. We must be inspired by his desire to be for Christ
in his world and his time, so that we can be for Christ in ours. We need
to allow his insights to find their own form in our time.

Ode to Christ

Had you not been
I could not be.
Had you not lived,
I could not find the way
to live a life
    in truth.

---

[105] Hartmut Beck, ed., *Wege in die Welt: Reiseberichte aus 250 Jahren Brüdermission* (Erlangen:Verlag der Ev.-Luth. Mission, 1992).

Truth's not
to be and live
in some unfleshed
unwordly way,
but
to be true
to times and God
— together —
with single passion.

Truth's not
apart from life.
Life, history, times,
the things
as well as God
do call.

To be
apart from life,
silent,
bespeaks
both death and sin.

Had you not been
I could not be,

And so I give
my thanks.[106]

---

[106] By the author.

Chapter 2

The Knowledge of God

How and what can be known about God, and whether there is a God to be known, are age-old questions. We are born into a world that is mystery to us, and as we mature, observe, and reflect, we push back the walls of this mystery. We may take advantage of the great religious and philosophical traditions which in themselves are the result of attempts to understand. But whatever wisdom we gain, the mystery remains, and we know that we know in very limited ways. To understand this mystery is not just a general and philosophical concern, but is driven by very intimate and personal concerns to understand life, relate to its powers, and discover our identity, source, and destiny.

Creation has often been understood as reflecting something of its Creator. During the eighteenth century this natural knowledge of God was very important. Emphasis was often upon the ordered nature of creation, especially as perceived by the developing sciences and human reason. Of course, the encounter with creation is also an encounter with transcendence and beauty which calls attention to that which is beyond the human. Its aesthetic appeal also touches the heart and insists upon some reality beyond comprehension and analysis. And yet creation is at times disordered, ugly, and frightening.

Beyond creation one may philosophize about existence. Perhaps the very idea of God attests to the reality of God. Or one may make Pascal's wager, that if one bets on God and God is real, then one has gained everything; and if God is not real, one has not really lost anything. But if one does not bet on God, and God is real, then one has lost everything.[1]

---

[1] The wager is contained in sec. 343 of *Pascal's Pensées*, trans. Martin Turnell (New York: Harper and Brothers, 1962), p. 201-5. It must be said that for Pascal this was not merely a wager for the reality of God, but a way of moving beyond reason, in response to a "reasonable" appeal, into the reality of God by which the wager is then legitimized in experience. One then moves from the idea of God to the reality of God.

Another possibility is that, given our theological traditions, one may argue from within them, developing their assumed truths into a coherent system of truth without challenging the truthfulness of the assumptions themselves. Christianity has often taken this approach, as have other religions, based upon the authority of special revelation, though general or natural knowledge of God also has played various roles. It is often taken for granted that the biblical witness to God's actions in the past and the theological traditions derived from this are complete and adequate for the present. Though recognizing that this witness was initially based upon revelation *as experienced,* some Christians assert that one should now work from the witnessing tradition and not contemporary revelation and experience, which are now regarded as dubious because they do not arise directly out of the tradition. Sometimes the special revelations and experiences during the apostolic age were understood as having the special purpose of initiating Christianity. They were necessary at that time. But now this is no longer needed or given. Experience now would be misleading, while it was not so during the apostolic period. The church has often felt that this perspective avoids the dangers of subjectivity, forgetting that this gives ultimate authority to institutionalized subjectivities.

The challenge to the authority of the Bible and religious institutions presented by the Enlightenment, along with the declining cultural support of religious institutions and beliefs, return us to the need to deal with experience, for if we cannot find experience which is in some sense the experiential referent of our God words, then it is really questionable whether our God words are about anything that is real and true.

Moreover, the failure to deal with experience assumes that Christian truth is about matters which can easily bypass the question of religious experience: ethics, philosophical or theological concepts worked into some sort of system, historical descriptions, and various human processes initiated by taking God language seriously. But when one reads the New Testament materials, Jesus' instruction to call God "Abba, Father" (Luke 11:2, Galatians 4:6, Romans 8:15) is an invitation to devotional and obedient relationship, and the gift of the Spirit is the gift of God's self in relationship. From this relationship life of a unique quality emerges.

Religion is not about thought systems, institutions, or human possibilities, but about God. God enters into relationship with humanity and reconciles estranged humans to God's self. It is then a question of whether one can really have *religion* without having the reality of God as a central question for oneself. Of course, this does not argue for any particular type of God experience or root the reality of God in mere feelings. It indicates that the foundational human need is more than thinking about God. Rather it is relationship with God; and God provides this relationship, however awareness of it emerges in a person's experiences.

The mystics have been helpful in calling our attention to the centrality of the knowing of God, which is "all knowledge transcending." John of the Cross expresses this well:

> I entered — where — I did not know,
> Yet when I found that I was there,
> Though where I was I did not know,
> Profound and subtle things I learned;
> Nor can I say what I discerned,
> For I remained uncomprehending,
> All knowledge transcending.
>
> . . . .
>
> And if you wish to hear,
> This highest knowledge is conceived
> In a sense, sublime and clear
> Of the essence of the Deity;
> It is an act of His great Clemency
> That keeps us there uncomprehending,
> All knowledge transcending.[2]

The way of the mystic is the way of intellectual "unknowing," the *via negativa*, the way of laying aside all of the expressions of *religion* to discover the Great Reality which lies behind them. It is ultimately the love of God which calls forth our love beyond all thoughts of reward or reason. The relationship comes to exist for its own sake as the foundational constituent of human existence. As expressed in a sonnet by an unknown author (sometimes ascribed to Teresa of Avila):

> Thou movest me, my Lord; my heart does glow
> To see Thee nailed upon that shameful tree;
> To see Thy body wounded piteously,
> To see Thee die, with agonizing throe;
>
> Thy love, in sooth, doth move me in such wise,
> That if there were no Heaven, my love would burn
> And, if there were no Hell, my will would bow;

[2] John of the Cross, quoted in Gerald Brenan, *St. John of the Cross: His Life and Poetry* (Cambridge: Cambridge University Press, 1973), p. 179.

I love Thee not for hopes beyond the skies,
For did my every hope to nothing turn,
I'd love Thee still, as I do love Thee now.[3]

The Struggle Between Heart and Head

How one might know God was very much an issue during Zinzendorf's life, and he was affected by it on both a philosophical and an experiential level. Though Carl Jung was born more than a century after Zinzendorf's death, his struggle with the knowledge of God was so much like Zinzendorf's that to examine Jung's experience provides understanding and legitimization of Zinzendorf's description of his.

In *Memories, Dreams, Reflections* Carl Jung described his own struggle with the knowledge of God.[4] As a young boy he experienced sleepless nights feeling that God was forcing him to think some unthinkable thought. Finally he surrendered, and grace broke upon him. He commented:

I felt an enormous, and indescribable relief, Instead of the expected damnation, grace had come upon me, and with it an unutterable bliss such as I had never known. I wept for happiness and gratitude. The wisdom and goodness of God had been revealed to me now that I had yielded to His inexorable command. It was as though I had experienced an illumination. A great many things I had not previously understood became clear to me. That was what my father (a Reformed Pastor) had not understood, I thought; he had failed to experience the will of God, had opposed it for the best reasons and out of the deepest faith. And that was why he had never experienced the miracle of grace which heals all and makes all comprehensible. He had taken the Bible's commandments as his guide; he believed in God as the Bible prescribed and as his forefathers had taught him. But he did not know the immediate living God who stands, omnipotent and free, above His Bible and His Church, who calls upon man to partake of His freedom, and can force him to renounce his own views and convictions in order to fulfill without reserve the command of God. In His trial of human courage God refuses to abide by traditions, no matter how sacred. . . .

[3] Quoted in Helmut A. Hatzfeld, *Santa Teresa de Avila* (New York: Twayne Publishers, 1969), p. 27.
[4] Carl G. Jung, *Memories, Dreams, Reflections*, recorded and edited by Aniela Jaffe, trans. R. Winston and C. Winston, rev. ed. (New York: Vintage Books, Random House, 1965), pp. 36ff.

From the beginning I had a sense of destiny, as though my life was assigned to me by fate and had to be fulfilled. This gave me an inner security, and, though I could never prove it to myself, it proved itself to me. I did not have this certainty, it had me. Nobody could rob me of the conviction that it was enjoined upon me to do what God wanted and not what I wanted. That gave me the strength to go my own way. Often I had the feeling that in all decisive matters I was no longer among men, but was alone with God. And when I was "there," where I was no longer alone, I was outside time; I belonged to the centuries; and He who then gave answer was He who had always been, who had been before my birth. He who always is was there. These talks with the "Other" were my profoundest experiences: on the one hand a bloody struggle, on the other supreme ecstasy.[5]

Jung then searched the theological books in his father's library and seeking philosophical works finally came upon Krug's *General Dictionary of the Philosophical Sciences*, second edition, 1832 (his father actually had no philosophers in his library). Krug defined *God* as derived from *good*. The existence of God could not be proved. Krug ventured that the idea of God exists innately in humanity and that if our intellectual powers are adequately developed, they may be "capable of engendering so sublime an idea." Jung continued:

This explanation astounded me beyond measure. What is wrong with these "philosophers"? I wondered. Evidently they know of God only by hearsay. The theologians are different in this respect, at any rate; at least they are sure that God exists, even though they make contradictory statements about Him. This lexicographer Krug expressed himself in so involved a manner that it is easy to see he would like to assert that he is already sufficiently convinced of God's existence. Then why doesn't he say so outright? Why does he pretend — as if he really thought that we "engender" the idea of God, and to do so must first have reached a certain level of development? So far as I knew, even the savages wandering naked in their jungles had such ideas. And they were certainly not "philosophers" who sat down to "engender an idea of God." I never engendered any idea of God, either. Of course God cannot be proved, for how could, say, a clothes moth that eats Australian wool prove to other moths that Australia exists. God's existence does not depend on our proofs. How had I arrived at my certainty about

[5] Ibid., pp. 40, 48.

God? I was told all sorts of things about Him, yet I could believe nothing. None of it convinced me. That was not where my idea came from. In fact it was not an idea at all — that is, not something thought out. . . . Why do these philosophers pretend that God is an idea, a kind of arbitrary assumption which they can engender or not, when it is perfectly plain that He exists, as plain as a brick that falls on your head.[6]

The parallel to Zinzendorf is striking, though the form of faith that each developed was different. Jung's was theocentric while Zinzendorf's was Christocentric. Both were confronted with religious experience in times of doubt and religious uncertainty and found little help in the theological institutions or philosophical thought of their time. Each was led eventually to decide for the validity of their experience. Zinzendorf described this in terms of the real and objective perceptions of the heart (in contrast to the mind). Jung described it in terms of the perceptions of his "personality number 2."[7]

In the foreword to the *Büdingen Collection*, Zinzendorf commented:

When I was eight years old, I lay a whole night without sleep and through an old song which my grandmother sang before she went to sleep (O Eternity, Thou Word of Thunder), I entered into meditation and deep speculation. This went so far that at the last I lost my powers of hearing and sight. The clever ideas of the atheists began in my mind, and I was so affected by this and deeply involved in it that everything which I have heard and read since then seemed to me very shallow and insignificant and made little impression on me. But because my heart is sincerely devoted to the Savior and many times I had wondered whether it were possible that there could be another God than he — I would rather be damned with the Savior than be blessed with another God — so had speculation and rational deductions, which returned again and again, no power with me other than to make me anxious and

---

[6] Ibid., pp. 61-62.

[7] Jung comments: "Although we human beings have our own personal life, we are yet in large measure the representatives, the victims and promoters of a collective spirit whose years are counted in centuries. We can well think all our lives long that we are following our own noses, and may never discover that we are, for the most part, supernumeraries on the stage of the world theater. There are factors which, although we do not know them, nevertheless influence our lives, the more so if they are unconscious. Thus at least a part of our being lives in the centuries — the part which, for my private use, I have designated 'No. 2'" (Carl G. Jung, *On The Nature of the Psyche*, trans. R. F. C. Hull, Bollingen Series 20, vol. 8 [Princeton: Princeton University Press, 1960], p. 91).

destroy my sleep. But in my heart they had not the least effect. What I believed, that I wanted; what I thought, that was odious to me. I then arrived at the firm conclusion to use reason (*Verstand*[8]) in human matters so far as it suffices and to let it explain and delineate these matters so far as it can be driven; but in spiritual matters to remain so simply with heart-grasped truth and the cross and blood theology of the Lamb of God that I lay it as the ground of all other truths and what I could not deduce from it I wanted to reject at once. And that has stayed with me even to the present.[9]

In a letter to Liborius Zimmermann, 1728, Zinzendorf remarked:

When I was eight years old I already had the most serious temptations and thought. I was sufficiently protected against all dangerous books and discourses in my grandmother's house, still the atheistic arguments were well arranged in my head. I had invincible doubts and can indeed say that what afterwards I heard presented of the most hostile and malicious arguments about existence gave me no satisfaction, because still none touched my argument which no one had contradicted although I investigated the strongest writings. . . .

[8] Zinzendorf distinguished between *Verstand* and *Vernunft*. *Verstand* is practical wisdom, a knowing how to do things in life. *Vernunft* is the critical spirit which was part of the Enlightenment. It is reason thinking that it is the standard of all things. In the *Londoner Predigten* Zinzendorf says: "With us Germans there is a clear distinction between the words *Verstand* and *Vernunft*, as much as these are not distinguished in common usage. *Verstand* is the *bon sens* which God has given all humans so that they might make judgments about matters which they need to know. That which is read, experienced, aptly treated and answered with the *Verstand* is called *sophia*, Wisdom. A philosopher is a person who gladly uses his *Verstand* in a right way and uses it as far as it is necessary. Then, when he dies, he can say to his Savior: I have used the *Verstand* which you have given me as well as I could. Who will oppose *sophia* and philosophers who study from the heart with *Verstand?* That would be to reject God's gift.

"*Vernunft* is, according to my knowledge, a use of *Verstand* for finding out difficulties, of which one solves a hundred and makes fifty new ones, of which one solves twenty-five while thirty new ones arise. And, if one dies, so one is involved in fifty difficulties of which there are several that could not be solved. And if of these only two remain, then these are the unfortunate cause for the soul not believing" (Nikolaus Ludwig von Zinzendorf, *Einiger seit 1751. von dem Ordinario Fratrum zu London gehaltenen Predigten in Dreyen Haupt-Abtheilungen editer Erster Band* [London and Barby: Zu finden bey dem Seminario Theologico, 1756], sec. 3, p. 335f. [12 Jan. 1755]. [Abbreviated in subsequent notes as Zinzendorf, *Einiger zu London gehaltenen Predigten* {Londoner Predigten, vol. 1}]).

[9] *Büdingische Sammlung Einiger In die Kirchen-Historie Einschlagender Sonderlich neuerer Schrifften. Erster Band. Nebst darzu gehörigen Registern. Sind wir doch sein ererbtes gut* (Büdingen: Joh. Chr. Stöhr [vol. 1], Korte [vols. 2, 3], 1742-44), vol. 1, foreword [Vorrede], pages not numbered. (Abbreviated in subsequent notes as *Büdingische Sammlung.*)

As strongly as skepticism struggled with my thoughts in my tender youth, so long Jesus remained mine in my heart, which was full of love for him. I relegated all doubts about the existence of the Father because, as among the flowers, a Son was known before the Father according to human perception (the *Herbstzeitlose*— whose fruits and leaves appear in the spring and whose flowers appear in the fall). That the Son of God was my Lord, that I knew as certainly as I knew my five fingers. So many years had I loved him, so often had I besought him; so many sweet, so many bitter experiences; so many blessed, so many serious remembrances; so much praise, so much punishment, so much prayer, so much exaltation has always been mine. I have been clearly aware of that — which agrees with the word that I first learned to read after my sixth year, but previously knew to express mostly by heart and to test inwardly.[10]

It is interesting that the struggle between heart and head began so early in life for both Jung and Zinzendorf. Yet they knew the reality of God. For Zinzendorf, Christ was as real to him as the air he breathed. He experienced a depth of fellowship with him which others mistook for spiritual pride. Throughout all his doubt and difficulty in attaining certainty about the existence of the Father, he never doubted the reality of the Son. But the Son who became real to Zinzendorf was not the resurrected and ascended Christ, but the Savior who died on the cross. It was at the foot of the cross that he knew his Savior. In whatever varied circumstances of life the Savior comes into the heart, the form in which he comes is in his suffering form.[11] In answer to Bengel's accusation that "the Brethren rest everything upon the blood of the Lord," Zinzendorf answered:

If I prove from the suffering of God that he again has risen, then I have all rational persons on my side, for Sheol and God don't long suit each other. I do not prove out of his resurrection that he died for my sins nor that he is God, for already many have risen, but none

[10] Nikolaus Ludwig von Zinzendorf to Liborius Zimmermann, 1728, quoted in Otto Uttendörfer, *Zinzendorf und die Mystik* (Berlin: Christlicher Zeitschriften Verlag, [1952]), p. 75. (Abbreviated in subsequent notes as Uttendörfer, *Zinzendorf und die Mystik*.)

[11] *Auszüge aus des Seligen Ordinarii der Evangelischen Brüder-Kirche Herrn Nicolaus Ludwig Grafens und Herrn von Zinzendorf und Pottendorf sowol ungedrukten als gedrukten Reden über die vier Evangelisten, gefertiget und herausgegeben von Gottfried Clemens* (Barby: Gottfried Clemens, 1766-90 [vols.5 and 6 have the notation: H{eraus} g{egeben} von J{akob} C{hristoph} Düvernoy, 1781 and 1790, respectively]), 6:18-19 (18 Sept. 1746). (Abbreviated in subsequent notes as Zinzendorf, *Auszüge über die vier Evangelisten.*)

has died for me. For him who is on the cross, who remains my God, would I scorn the whole world.[12]

The God We Never Knew by Marcus Borg, one of the scholars involved in contemporary research on the historical Jesus, was published in 1997. In his book Borg paralleled the Enlightenment with his personal journey from childhood faith in a small Lutheran church in North Dakota to the discovery of a new understanding of God fueled by the challenges of our culture. Without knowing it, he was "reliving the history of modern thought" in his own experience.[13] Jung, Zinzendorf, and Borg all really experienced the "reliving of the history of modern thought." Borg discovered *The God We Never Knew*, a God described by the term Panentheism, present within history and experience, answering to a relational model of the Christian life rather than a monarchical one. Spirituality is for the "hatching of the heart." The fruit of the Christian life is compassion. "The Christian life as life in the Spirit involves a process of transformation quickened within us by the Spirit of God." Also included is the "dream of God" for the world, informed by a "politics of compassion."[14] For Borg this meant an unexpected perspective on the Jesus and other biblical traditions which, if viewed properly, actually offered these alternative perspectives.

It was also true of Zinzendorf that his understanding of God was transformed by his experience and his exploration of the biblical tradition in the context of his times. He emerged with a relational and Christocentric model. This model was incarnational, understanding God not in terms of power but in terms of suffering. God joins us in our world and life, submitting to their conditions. The remote God of deism and natural *religion* suited neither experience nor the central emphases of the New Testament traditions.

Many of those brought up within the church even today will relive the history of modern thought in their own experience and discover the God they did not previously know.

Christ and the Hidden God

When only in his early twenties (1722 according to the 1766 edition of *German Poetry,* or 1725 according to the 1735 edition) Zinzendorf

---

[12] Johann Albrecht Bengel, "Anmerckungen von der sogenannten Brüder-Gemeine" [with responses by Nikolaus Ludwig von Zinzendorf], in *Büdingische Sammlung,* 3:746.
[13] Marcus J. Borg, *The God We Never Knew: Beyond Dogmatic Religion to a More Authentic Contemporary Faith* (San Francisco: HarperSanFrancisco, 1997), p. 23.
[14] Ibid., pp. 128-29, 133.

composed a poem, *"Allgegenwart"* ("Omnipresence"), in which he described the resolution of the human search for God. Becker comments: "This composition surpasses in depth of content and beauty of form all that his contemporaries have produced with similar concerns."[15]

In the first seven stanzas the poet portrayed a search for an understanding of God whose marks upon creation can be observed, but remains the hidden One. It is important to note that the one who would speak of God is a poet and that what he seeks to express is a song of praise, a doxology. This is very much Zinzendorf's approach to theology, which was best expressed in poetic and doxological language. "How dare the tongue venture . . . where eye and sense stand still?"

The next three stanzas are God's answer. "Cease to seek what flees you! . . . My nature, which no eye sees, has built itself a body. . . . O come and see the concealed Abyss, the hidden Majesty in Jesus." The last stanza is the doxology of the soul: "Here I find myself. . . . Now I love you, believe and rest."

The poem is quoted and translated from the 1735 edition of *German Poetry*. A number of changes were made in the poem in the 1766 new edition of *German Poetry* published after Zinzendorf's death.[16] Several of the 1766 changes are in the footnotes. The changes are interesting. Those introduced into stanza nine diminish the intense personal nature of God's revelation and sound like the words of the poet about God rather than the words of God (which stanzas eight to ten are intended to be). The emphasis on incarnation is also diminished by changing the word "body" to "something visible." The changes introduced into stanza eleven identify the ultimate mystery of God (Eternity) with the "Word of God," probably in terms of John 1, thus presenting God before incarnation in more Christocentric terms. In both the 1766 and 1735 editions this poem bears the heading: "Completion of an continuous five-year contemplation of God." In the 1766 edition there is added to the heading: "O Being of Beings, Have mercy!" (*O Ens Entium, Miserere*).

[15] Bernhard Becker, *Zinzendorf im Verhältnis zu Philosophie und Kirchentum seiner Zeit: Geschichtliche Studien* (Leipzig: Hinrich, 1886), p. 28.

[16] *Graf Ludwigs von Zinzendorff Teutscher Gedichte*, Erster Theil (Herrnhut: Zu finden im Waisenhause, 1735), pp. 106-8. Edition of 1766: *Graf Ludwigs von Zinzendorf Teutscher Gedichte Neue Auflage* (Barby: Heinrich Detlef Ebers, 1766), pp. 59-61. (The first edition, 1735, will be abbreviated in subsequent notes as Zinzendorf, *Teutscher Gedichte*, [1735].) The preface for the second edition indicates that Zinzendorf had looked through a copy and here and there corrected it, though I am not aware if all of the corrections in the 1766 edition were his. A few of the changes seem editorial. There is a corrected copy in the Zeist Moravian Library now held in the State Archives in Utrecht.

Completion of a five-year continuous contemplation of God.

Vollendung einer fünfjährig-fortgewährten Betrachtung Gottes.

1. Omnipresence! I must confess
you inexpressibly the deep height
fill without being seen.
Yet everywhere I go and stand
the trace of your almighty path,
never to be fathomed,
still overall is found,
as far as mind can wander.

1. Allgegenwart! ich muß gestehn,
Du unaussprechlich tiefe Höhe
Erfüllest, ohne Dich zu sehn,
Doch alles, wo ich geh' und stehe.
Die Spur von Deinem Allmachts-Pfad,
Die ewiglich nicht auszugründen,
Ist dennoch überall zu finden,
So weit man Raum zu denken hat.

2. So can it not be otherwise,
because I note you everywhere.
So with earnestness I venture,
the greatness of your might and
        power
your blinding bright majesty
before which the dark deeps shrink,
to grasp with a song
that which surpasses all song.

2. So kan es ja nicht anders seyn,
Weil ich Dich allerwegen merke;
So geb ich mich mit Ernst darein,
Die Grösse Deiner Macht und Stärke,
Die blendend-helle Majestät,
Vor der die finstren Tieffen weichen,
Mit einem Liede zu erreichen,
Das über alle Lieder geht.

3. Only, you indescribable Husband,
where do I sing my thoughts of praise
to lay the foundation stone?
Where should I place your limits?
In what time of life was
my understanding first so illumined
that it should travel high and low
and not completely go astray.

3.Allein du unbeschriebner Mann,
Wo sing ich meinen Lobs-Gedancken
Den ersten Stein zu setzen an?
Wohin versetzt ich ihre Schrancken?
In welchem Lebens-Jahre wird
Erst mein Verstand so aufgekläret,
Dass er hinauf und niederfähret,
Und sich nicht überall verirrt.

4. Here speaks, O hidden God,
one who is your creature.
Be s/he not scorned for this
by all who herein read.
S/he will in proper fashion
the saying need to prove
that all know nothing more
than what you have revealed.

4. Es spreche, du verborgner Gott,
Ein Mensch, was eigentlich dein Wesen
Und werde nicht dabey zu Spott
Vor allen, die den Ausspruch lesen;
Er wird, mit ausgesuchter Art,
Die Sprache also führen müssen,
Dass er und alle nichts mehr wissen,
Als was du längst geoffenbahrt.

5. How dare the tongue venture
into your deep attributes,
which individually and together
precisely belong to your Being,
and scorn the wonder of your Name
which refuses to be named.
yet gives itself only to be experienced
where eye and sense stand still?

6. Who leads me to your source,
Unendlessness, Astonishment of the
    mind!
Where do I find liberty
to trumpet forth your wonders.
To all creatures I give warning,
from princes to intellectuals,
even to the wise ruler
of your awesome presence.

7. I allow, you are too high,
too deep, O God, too great and
    bright
for a mind in body's yoke,
or vision incorporeal!
How did creation come to mind?
There lacked a prince of creatures
to give you, Creator, direction
for the rest of creation.

Divine Answer

8. Cease to seek what is so far,
cease to seek what flees you;
you have the Kernel which matters,
don't trouble with externals.
Torment not your soul's light
to reach what is eternal.
You might capture Darkness
and still find me nowhere.

5. Wie wagte sich die Zung hinein
In deine tiefe Eigenschaften?
Die sonderlich und insgemein
Genau an deinem Wesen haften?
Und zu des Nahmens-Wunder-Höhn,
Der sich zu nennen nicht beliebet,
Sich auch nur zu erfahren giebet,
Wo Aug und Sinne stille stehn.

6. Wer führet mich zu deiner Quell,
Unendlichkeit! des Geists Erstaunen!
Wo find ich eine freye Stell
Von deinen Wundern zu possaunen,
Ich warnte alle Creatur
Vom Fürsten an der Reinen Geister,
Bliss zu der Weisen Obermeister,
Vor deiner fürchterlichen Spur.

7. Ich lasse dich, du bist zu hoch,
Zu tief, O Gott! zu gross und lichte,
Vor einen Geist im Leibes-Joch,
Vor ein umcörpertes Gesichte:
Wie kam das Schaffen dir im Sinn?
Verfehlt ein Fürst der Creaturen
Zu dir, dem Schöpfer, Bahn und
    Spuren,
Wo will die andre Schöpfung hin.

Göttliche Antwort

8. Hör auf zu suchen, was so fern,
Hör auf zu forschen, was dich fliehet;
Du hast den ausgemachten Kern,
Sey nicht ums Aussen-Werck
    bemühet
Verücke nicht dein Seelen-Licht
Biss zu dem Kreis der Ewigkeiten,
Du möchtest Finsterniss erbeuten,
Und fändest mich doch nirgends
    nicht.

9. Why, you foolish child,
will you fetch me from the depths?
Where do you think I can be found?
Do you seek me at heaven's poles?
Do you seek me in the creature?
My nature, which no eye can see,
has built itself a body
and still you miss my sign.[17]

10. O! Come here and see
the concealed Abyss,
the hidden Majesty.
In Jesus, the humble child, see
whether humanity exists in grace;
see whether He your praise de
    serves,
for whom love grows in the heart;
who believes, from all care becomes
    free.

The Soul

11. O Eternity! Beauteous Light!
Reflection of the glorious King![19]
O love, which pierces heaven
to dwell in my small inn!
Here I find myself, here I lay hold.
Of course I have not seen you,
yet that will one day be.
Now I love you, believe and rest.

9. Wie so? du unverständigs Kind!
Wilt du mich aus der Tiefe hohlen?
Wo meynest du, dass man mich findt?
Suchst du mich bey den Himmels-
    Polen?
Suchst du mich in der Creatur?
Mein Wesen, das kein Auge schauet,
Hat sich ja einen Leib erbauet,
Und du verfehlst doch meine Spur.[18]

10. Ihr Menschen! kommt herbey,
    und seht
Die zugedeckte Abgrunds-Schlünde,
Die eingehullte Majestät,
In Jesu, dem geringen Kinde!
Seht obs der Mensch in Gnaden sey,
Seht, ob er euer Lob verdienet,
Wem dessen Lieb im Hertzen grünet;
Wer glaubt, wird aller Sorgen frey.

Die Seele

11. O Ewigkeit! du schönes Licht!
Des Königs Abglantz aller Ehren![20]
O Liebe! die den Himmel bricht,
In meiner Hütten einzukehren,
Hie find ich mich, hie greif ich zu.
Zwar hab ich dich noch nicht gesehen,
Jedoch Das wird einmal geschehen.
Itzt lieb ich dich, und gläub, und ruh.

---

[17] The last three lines in the version of 1766, translated, are:
God, whom no physical eye sees,
has built something visible,
sign of the whole fullness of God.
    [18] The last three lines in the version of 1766 are:
Gott, den kein leiblich Auge schauet,
Hat etwas sichbarlich erbauet,
Der ganzen Gottes-Fülle Spur.
    [19] The first two lines in the version of 1766, translated, are:
O Word of God, you true light,
you splendor of the glorious King!
    [20] The first two lines in the version of 1766 are:
Ach Gottes Wort, du wahres Licht,
Du Glanz des Königs aller Ehren!

Though one may see the traces of God in creation, the great Darkness of God, the concealed Abyss, is beyond human reach and comprehension. It is important to note that Zinzendorf used the terminology of mysticism here. The God who cannot be seen, was described as Darkness, Nothing, Source, Unendlessness, hidden Majesty. For many mystics this mysterious Darkness, Nothing in the sense of not-like-any-thing, may be related to as the culmination of mystical experience; but for Zinzendorf the mystery of God's self could only be related to in Christ, where God's nature has built itself a body. Christ has always been and always will be "the Character τῆς ὑποστάσεως *Patris* ὁ λόγος καὶ τὸ σῶμα τῆς θεότητος [the character of the substance of the Father, the logos and the body of the deity], and will remain so eternally."[21] He is the "concentrated God,"[22] "the κεφάλαιον [principle part, sum] and epitome" of the Trinity.[23]

The Savior Is also the Creator

In commenting upon the Prologue to the Gospel of John, Zinzendorf said:

But how does John call this God who was with God, and by whom all exists? Here I must bring a word from the original text. Just as *logikos* more than once in Scripture signifies *raisonable*, it seems to me - related to rational principles; so *logos* here *consequenter* does not signify a word or speech, but *ratio, causa,* cause, *causa prima,* the cause of all things: as those who concerned themselves about the causes of things were accustomed from ancient times to call God. And as Jesus afterwards (Hebrews 5:9) is expressly called the cause of salvation.

[21] Nikolaus Ludwig von Zinzendorf, *Ein und zwanzig Discurse über die Augspurgische Confession gehalten vom 15. Dec. 1747. bis zum 3. Mart. 1748. denen Seminariis Theologiscis Fratrum zum Besten aufgefaßt und bis zur nochmaligen Revision des Auctoris einstweilen nitgetheilet* (n.p., n.d.), p. 101 (23 Dec. 1747). (Abbreviated in subsequent notes as Zinzendorf, *Ein und zwanzig Discurse* [Title page: *Discurse . . . Auctoris*]. For information about the two different printings of this work, see chapter 1, note 82.

[22] M. Avgvst. Gottl. *Spangenbergs Apologetische Schluß-Schrift, Worinn über tausend Beschuldigungen gegen die Brüder-Gemeinen und Ihren zeitherigen Ordinarium nach der Wahrheit beantwortet werden, Nebst einigen wichtigen Beylagen* (Leipzig and Görlitz: In der Marcheschen Buchhandlung, 1752), p. 219. (Abbreviated in subsequent notes as *Spangenbergs Apologetische Schluß-Schrift.)*

[23] M. Aug. Gottl. *Spangenbergs Darlegung richtiger Antworten auf mehr als dreyhundert Beschuldigungen gegen den Ordinarivm Fratrvm nebst verschiedenen wichtigen Beylagen* (Leipzig and Görlitz, In der Marcheschen Buchhandlung, 1751), p. 56. (Abbreviated in subsequent notes as *Spangenbergs Darlegung richtiger Antworten.)*

So then should the words of John exactly, clearly, and especially mean: the cause of all things was from the beginning, i.e., always, and this cause of all things was with God, and this cause of all things was himself God, and through him all things were made.

One may easily make a mistake in explaining such deep things of God; but to say this simply and naturally produces this result: therefore the cause of all things is God over all, because the whole creation, all worlds, all spirits, and all creatures came into being through him.

He is the cause as well of a leaf upon the tree as of a human.

He is the cause that there is a star in heaven, or a drop of water in the sea.

Because he has brought all into being, so he stands even before all: because he wished the happiness, well-being, and pleasure of these little creatures, so he made them all. All had been created from him and through him and to him: from the smallest worm to the highest archangel, all exists for his sake.[24]

From the reference to Hebrews included in the above quotation it is apparent that Zinzendorf drew not only on John, but a broader New Testament tradition, including Hebrews and Paul's letter to the Colossians, which presented Christ as related to creation. In a reply in Spangenberg's *Answers* Zinzendorf asserted that the New Testament supports his view of Christ as Creator, rather than the Father. Of course, he read the Old Testament statements about the Creator in the light of the New. He commented that if the Holy Spirit would really have wanted to say that the Father was creator,

he would have only needed to say one time: "The Father of Jesus has really created the world, and not the Son." Then theology would be on another foundation ("foot") and the Athanasian Creed could be done without. That would be very reasonable. But because creation is expressly assigned to the Son, and is nowhere clearly assigned to the Father, so I will wait until another Bible is published by God. Now I remain with Jesus Christ.[25]

[24] *Des Herrn Grafen Ludwig von Zinzendorff Sieben Letzte Reden So Er In der Gemeine, Vor seiner am 7. Aug. erfolgten abermahligen Abreise nach America, gehalten. Denen noch beygefügt sind zwey in Gelnhausen von demselben gehaltene und ehmals einzeln gedruckte Predigten* (Büdingen: Johann Christoph Stöhr, 1743), pp. 8-9 (11 June 1741). (Abbreviated in subsequent notes as Zinzendorf, *Sieben Letzte Reden* [1743 edition].)

[25] *Spangenbergs Darlegung richtiger Antworten*, p. 51.

Christ Always the Mediator of God to the World

Christ is also the person of the Godhead who has been universally experienced. "Natural persons neither have the Father nor are able to know him."[26] Thus Christ is the one who has been experienced as "Father." The Savior is "the direct Father of humanity, and everything which they have in his (Christ's) Father, they must get from him."[27]

Consequently, *the Father is the new revelation in the New Testament, not the Son*:

> The reason why we thought that in the Old Testament God the Father is treated (from which the *idee* arose that the theology of the Savior was the new revelation while it was the other way around and the revelation of the Father is a new theology which was not previously known, for the Savior said: I have told these men that I have a Father, I have first named your name to them)— the reason, I say, for this misunderstanding is because the prophets have treated the matter in two ways: namely one without revelation and the other with a very dark, incomplete revelation. Of the Godhead, for example, they had no more revelation other than he is One — and now and then it is said that the God who made us is also our Husband.[28]

The prophets had no understanding "that there was more than one person in the Godhead, for the theology of that time spoke only of one."

> In the New Testament, however, it is positively stated that the divine being in himself dwells in a light into which no one can come, which no one has seen or can see (1 Timothy 6:16). No one has rightly understood that before the Son came from the bosom of the Father and preached it to us (John 1:18). If one puts these matters together, then it is clear that the Old Testament actually treats only of the God who in the New Testament is called Jesus Christ.

[26] Minutes of the 1750 Synod, quoted in *Spangenbergs Apologetische Schluß-Schrift*, p. 488. In the *Nine Public Lectures on Important Subjects in Religion* Zinzendorf discusses his preference not to use the Lord's Prayer in public gatherings because one cannot pray to the Father without the Son (Nikolaus Ludwig von Zinzendorf, *Nine Public Lectures on Important Subjects in Religion Preached in Fetter Lane Chapel in London in the Year 1746*, trans. and ed. George W. Forell [Iowa City: University of Iowa Press, 1973], pp. 3ff. [28 Aug. 1746]. [Abbreviated in subsequent notes as Zinzendorf, *Nine Public Lectures* {1973}]).

[27] *Spangenbergs Darlegung richtiger Antworten*, p. 60.

[28] Nikolaus Ludwig von Zinzendorf, *Der Öffentlichen Gemein-Reden im Jahr 1747. Erster Theil. Mit einem Anhang einiger zu Ende des Jahres 1746. gehaltenen Homilien* (n.p.: Zu finden in den Brüder-Gemeinen, 1748), pp. 240-41 (12 Mar. 1747). (Abbreviated in subsequent notes as *Zinzendorf, Öffentlichen Gemein-Reden, 1747, pt. 1.*)

The Bible, which all Christians have, treats of him. And he himself, whose mouth does not lie, says: "It is true, eternal life is there to be sought: for it is the book which treats of me" (John 5:39).[29]

Zinzendorf saw intimations of the Trinity in the term *Elohim* in Genesis 2, but this does not appear later in the Old Testament.[30] In the 1746 translation of the New Testament he assigned the Old Testament Law to Christ, while the Father is the legislator of the New Testament.[31]

Zinzendorf also asserted that Christ will always remain the mediatorial person between God and the world. In the fourth discourse on the Augsburg Confession he argued against Paul's idea (1 Corinthians 15:28) that Christ in the end hands over sovereignty to the Father. Rather, Christ after the ascension rests while the Father assumes responsibility for the subjection of all to Christ. But when this is done, "then will the man Jesus Christ get up from his couch of rest, and will be again the only mediatorial person, who will eternally keep the creature in familiarity with the Holy Trinity."[32] Here Zinzendorf followed Hebrews 10:12, which better fits his Christocentrism.

Atheism Without Christ

Since the knowledge of God comes only through Christ, what of religious experience in general and philosophical reflection? Without Christ one is an atheist, without God. Following directions indicated in the Prologue to John, Zinzendorf acknowledged universal religious experience, but identified all religious experience with experience of Christ, who even before and after the incarnation was the only Mediator of God to humanity. As he commented in one of his *Berlin Sermons* in 1738:

And we Christians call him: Immanuel, our God, who gave himself for us so that the Godhead might become visible, understandable

[29] Nikolaus Ludwig von Zinzendorf, *Auszüge aus des Seligen Ordinarii der Evangelischen Brüder-Kirche sowol ungedruckten als gedruckten Reden über biblische Texte, nach Ordnung der Bücher heiliger Schrift gefertiget und herausgegeben von Gottfried Clemens* [Drei Bände über die Bücher Mose] (Barby: n.p., 1763-65), 1:3-5 (2 Jan. 1755).

[30] Zinzendorf, *Sieben Letzte Reden* [1743 edition], p. 32 (9 July 1741).

[31] Nikolaus Ludwig von Zinzendorf, *Eines Abermahligen Versuchs zur Übersetzung Der Lehr- und Prophetischen Bücher Neuen Testaments unsers Herrn Jesu Christi aus dem Original Erste Probe zweyte Edition Worinnen die meisten besagter Lehr-Bücher befindlich sind, Von den vorigen Schreib- Druck- und andern Fehlern gebessert* (Büdingen: Joh. Christoph Stöhr, 1746), note on Heb. 12:26.

[32] Zinzendorf, *Ein und zwanzig Discurse* [Title page: *Discurse . . . Auctoris*], pp. 100-101 (23 Dec. 1747).

and physical for us. . . .

Therefore, if one knows nothing of the high nature of God and knows only Christ, one can be saved through that alone. For God's name is in him: in him dwells all the fullness (of God).

But who knows nothing of Christ, and is not acquainted with the God of the New Testament, whom all tongues should confess as their Lord, he is an atheist, a person who is without God in this world, and is lost in spite of all his wisdom and God's care.

For who sees the Son sees the Father.

In him will the Father be glorified.

He who does not have the Son has no God.

Therefore one must above all things get to know Christ, who is as much God the Lord as the Father and the Holy Spirit. He is our Special-Lord, since he became human for us and has taken on himself a nature which binds us to him.[33]

This revelation of God in Christ has changed the role of philosophy in religious knowledge.

As long as the Savior had not yet appeared in the flesh, as long as the Creator had not yet become the carpenter of Nazareth, as long as he was not betrayed by his own religious contemporaries, crucified and buried . . . so long were philosophy and *religion* quite compatible. A person who has the true *religion* could be a philosopher and without any difficulty a philosopher could go to school with a person of the right *religion* and could learn something and have his light increased out of that.

But that has astonishingly changed.[34]

Now that the Creator/Savior has become physical and visible for us, we cannot pretend that this has not happened. The human religious and philosophical predicament (and opportunity) is best expressed in the fact that our hard-gained and mature wisdom must now be laid *at the feet of a child*:

I cannot fault the high and wise of this world that they are troubled that they need to bind all their insights to a child, turn all their understanding to a child, sacrifice all their powers to a child, direct

[33] *Des Grafens von Zinzendorff Inhalt dererjenigen Reden, Welche zu Berlin vom 1ten Januar. 1738. bis 27ten Aprilis in denen Abend-Stunden sonderlich für die Manns-Personen gehalten worden.* Dritte Auflage [3rd ed.] (Flensburg and Altona: Gebrüder Korte, 1743), p. 257-58 (12 Feb. 1738). (Abbreviated in subsequent notes as Zinzendorf, *Reden zu Berlin für die Manns-Personen* [3rd ed., 1743].)

[34] Zinzendorf, *Öffentlichen Gemein-Reden 1747*, pt. 1, p. 146 (12 Feb. 1747).

all their thoughts to a child, and expect all their weal and woe from a child.[35]

The Trinity

Zinzendorf is often accused of neglecting the first and third persons of the Trinity in favor of the second, Christ. It becomes clear that this is not really so when one realizes that his understanding of God necessitates the approach to the hidden God (the Father) through the revealed God, Christ, who is both Savior and Creator. One must begin there, and so the preaching of the Gospel to those outside the church must begin with Christ. When persons know Christ, then one may speak with them about the Father and the Spirit, to whom the Savior will gradually introduce them in their experience. Language about the Trinity is only for the Christian community, which is engaged in the process of becoming acquainted with the totality of God.

Though Zinzendorf never neglected to deal with the Trinity with those who knew Christ, in the last twenty years of his life there seems to have been an increased discussion of the Trinity within the church. In his second discourse on the Augsburg Confession (1747) Zinzendorf mentioned that in the last two years there was an unusual frequency of treatment of the Father and the Holy Spirit.[36] Beyreuther indicated that Zinzendorf's "speculation" about the Trinity seems to have been at a high point between 1742 and 1748, with a series of sermons at each end of this period.[37] At the beginning of this period we have the *Seven Last Sermons of Count L von Zinzendorf Before His Aug. 7 Departure to America*[38] and at the end of the period we have the *Twenty-one Discourses on the Augsburg Confession*. The "Conversation (of Moravians) with Karl Barth" also calls attention to the giving of more space to the veneration of the Father in the hymns of 1757.[39] Moreover, during the last twenty years of Zinzendorf's life there was a growing realization of the importance of the Spirit as the Mother of the church, something to which most

[35] Zinzendorf, *Reden zu Berlin für die Manns-Personen* [3rd ed., 1743], p. 239 (2 Feb. 1738).

[36] Ibid., p. 23 (16 Dec. 1747).

[37] Erich Beyreuther, *Studien zur Theologie Zinzendorfs: Gesammelte Aufsätze* (Neukirchen-Vluyn: Kreis Moers, 1962), p. 28.

[38] Zinzendorf, *Sieben Letzte Reden* [1743 edition]. Translated in the eighteenth century under the title *Seven Sermons On The Godhead of the Lamb; Or The Divinity of Jesus Christ. By the Right Reverend and most Illustrious Count Zinzendorf, Bishop of the Moravian Church. Preached in the Congregation, just before his second Voyage to the West-Indies: And translated from the German Manuscript* (London: James Hutton, 1742).

[39] H. Schmidt, H. Bintz, and W. Günther, eds., "Protokoll des Gesprächs zwischen Professor Dr. Karl Barth und Vertretern der Brüdergemeine am 12. Oktober 1960 in Basel," *Civitas Praesens* (Königsfeld), no. 13, special issue (May 1961): p. 7.

contemporary Moravians pay little attention. The greater discussion of the Trinity does not seem to indicate any basic change in approach, but rather, "*ne ignoretur quid sentiamus, in tanta Doctrinarum Confusione, ad futuram Rei Memoriam* [so that there might not be ignorance of what we think, amongst so much confusion of doctrines, for the sake of knowledge of the matter in the future]."[40]

The liturgical life of the congregations also seems well balanced in its address to the three persons of the Trinity, though even liturgies not directed to Christ would have many Christological references. The Bethlehem Diary records that in April 1747 it was decided to assign the following liturgies for congregational worship:

Sunday a.m.	*Te Matrem* (We praise you, O Mother)	
p.m.	*Anbeten with Te Agnum* (Prostate prayer with We praise you, O Lamb)	
Monday	*Kirchen-Gebet zum Vater* (Church's prayer to the Father)	
Tuesday	*Kirchen-Gebet zur Mutter* (Church's prayer to the Mother)	
Wednesday	*Kirchen-Gebet zum Manne* (Church's prayer to the Husband)	
Thursday	*Te Jehovah* (We praise you, O Jehovah [Christ])	
Friday	*Wunden Litaney* (Litany of the Wounds of the Husband)	
Saturday	*Singstunde - Gemein Litaney* (based on Luther's Great Litany) and the *Te Patrem* (We praise you, O Father)[41]	

[40] Zinzendorf, *Ein und zwanzig Discurse* [Title page: *Discurse . . . Auctoris*], p. 64 (16 Dec. 1747).

[41] Craig D. Atwood, "Blood, Sex, and Death: Life and Liturgy in Zinzendorf's Bethlehem" (Ph.D. diss., Princeton Theological Seminary, 1995), p. 147. (Abbreviated in subsequent notes as Atwood, "Blood, Sex, and Death.") Some of the content of the thesis was written into a published article: Craig D. Atwood, "Zinzendorf's 'Litany of the Wounds,'" *Lutheran Quarterly* 9 (1977): pp. 189-214. This weekly rhythm of devotion was modified from time to time. Atwood's thesis provides very helpful insight into the worship life of the Bethlehem community and includes many of the liturgies in appendices. After 1753 the names of some of the liturgies were changed. The Litany of the Wounds (*Die Wunden-Litaney*) was divided into *Litaney des Leben, Leidens und Tod des Mannes* and the *Hymno von dem Wunden* (the Hymn to the Wounds previously at the end of the Litany of the Wounds was made into a separate liturgy). The *Te Jehova* became the *Te Logos*. The *Te Patrem* became referred to as the *Te Abba*. This followed the return of Spangenberg to the Bethlehem congregation in 1752. See Atwood, "Blood, Sex, and Death," p. 151.

Understanding God as Trinity makes the affirmation that *God in God's nature is relational,* and Zinzendorf was well aware of this. Thus the Trinity in its inner relationship is the prototype and model for the Christian community.[42] Spirituality in its origin is communal.

The Heart Relationship with the Savior: The Essence of *Religion*

The life and activity of the Savior and the giving of the Spirit, which proceeded from his sufferings, his side-wound,[43] "began a new 'economy' and *religion,* the *religion* of the heart."[44] This term *heart* Zinzendorf uses to describe "the whole inner person,"[45] which then becomes the locus of religious knowledge instead of the rational mind. This "inner person" possesses all the senses which the outer person does and by these senses, in a way that we might talk of today as "intuition" or "extrasensory perception," perceives the reality of the living Christ. The heart smells, sees, tastes, feels, and hears.[46]

All that it takes to constitute one as Christian is to have seen the Savior. One needs to

> have caught sight of the Savior when the Savior looked into his heart for the first time. This is the order. First the Savior looks at us, and we perceive him, at that moment we have the matter in hand, and the Christian is ready. . . .
>
> I do not pretend that we see a body with our corporeal eyes; I do not desire that the mind try to imagine a body or try to conceive a representation of it, or that the mind look into itself or turn its thoughts in toward itself until it sees a form standing before it. But I do ask for the essential in this, and that is that a person who has seen abstractly and purely must in the next moment realize that he has actually seen; that a person must know as certainly that his spirit has seen, that his heart has seen and felt, as when in ordinary human life one can be certain that he has seen or touched something. In the moment when this happens, he does not need to have a sense-experience or see something visible (this cannot be excluded with any certainty, but neither is it essential): it is only necessary that afterward the essential effect remain, that one can

---

[42] Peter Zimmerling, *Gott in Gemeinschaft: Zinzendorfs Trinitätslehre,* Giessen and Basel: Brunnen, 1991.

[43] Zinzendorf, *Ein und zwanzig Discurse* [Title page: *Discurse . . . Auctoris*], pp. 160-61 (18 Feb. 1748).

[44] Ibid., p. 99 (23 Dec. 1747).

[45] Minutes of the 1750 Synod, quoted in *Spangenbergs Apologetische Schluß-Schrift,* p. 452.

[46] Minutes of the 1750 Synod, quoted in *Spangenbergs Apologetische Schluß-Schrift,* p. 451.

say not only, "I have seen, I have heard"; but rather, "Thus have I seen it, and thus have I heard." [47]

There are several terms which Zinzendorf used to describe this inner perception of religious reality. "Feeling" (*Gefühl*) is a term often used to describe one's awareness of the heart-relationship with the Savior.[48] This is not to be confused with feelings.

He also used "My heart tells me," which he said is the only "evangelical proof."[49] At the Synod of 1750 he discussed his use of the expression "It is thus to me" (*Es ist mir so*). He said, "It is thus to me — is the only reality." All else is subject to doubt and self-deception. Take away "It is thus to me" and one becomes skeptical and does not even know whether one exists. Scripture verifies this by saying, "I have given him that in the heart, written on the mind"; and the effect of that is: "*Es ist mir so*," "*ita sentio*."[50] In his poetry he intentionally avoided mere artistry and technique. His primary concern was: "As it is to me, so I write. I am not obligated to use higher and deeper words than that related to my meaning. I put out of my view the rules for the sake of the emphasis."[51]

Though Zinzendorf at times seemed to equate "feeling" and "It is thus to me," there is an important distinction. "Feeling" expresses the experience of the new person in Christ, who through the action of the Spirit has received a "heart." "It is thus to me" is applicable on a broader scale. It seems to describe an immediate and intuitive awareness of one's inner reality according to which one then acts and speaks without letting extensive reflection intrude. This is valid for both the Christian and the natural human being.

"It is thus to me" does not support any examination, but the minute when it is so to one, one must so express it. If it again is otherwise to one, one must express it otherwise. As soon as one begins to study, so one brings several days' ideas together, and out of these weeks' ideas and out of these a year's ideas, and finally customs, and then comes a false modesty which results in correcting.[52]

When natural persons act out of what one is, then out of the manner of acts and speech they become aware of the real nature of their existence and are convinced of their disjointedness. This then may be

[47] Zinzendorf, *Nine Public Lectures* [1973], pp. 80-81 (25 Sept. 1746).

[48] Zinzendorf, *Auszüge über die vier Evangelisten*, 4:97ff. (19 May 1757).

[49] Zinzendorf, *Öffentlichen Gemein-Reden, 1747*, pt. 1, pp. 18f. (25 Dec. 1746).

[50] Minutes of the 1750 Synod, quoted in *Spangenbergs Apologetische Schluß-Schrift*, pp. 629ff.

[51] Zinzendorf, *Teutscher Gedichte* [1735], from the foreword [Vorrede] (pages not numbered).

[52] Ibid., p. 630.

a means of coming to the Savior. However, it is only when one has received a heart through the Spirit that this approach gives one valid religious knowledge. As will be seen when Zinzendorf's approach to ethics is treated, Christian living in its best sense is spontaneous interaction with situations out of one's inner reality and thus is characterized by simplicity rather than complexity.

Language, Concepts, Systems, and Argumentation

Religion has to do with the reality of God communicated through the Creator/Savior. Because of the human difficulties in attaining knowledge of God and understanding the experience of God, God has expressed historically all that is needed in the person of Christ. The giving of the Spirit enables the restoration of the heart in each person willing to receive it, so that what God gives can also be inwardly perceived. Moreover, the Spirit exercises the role of Mother towards the church and communicates the reality of the ascended Christ within and outside the church until that time, at the end of time, when Christ again assumes his direct mediatorial role.[53]

What has been given and what is inwardly perceived is not some information about salvation, but the Creator/Savior and the possibility of fellowship with him, the "Man of Pain." *Religion* is not about God, it is God. The primary concern is not its explication or argumentation. The primary question has to do with whether we want, come to, find, approach God. This is the only *religion* against which no arguments can be argued. In its essence it only needs the Savior and a human being in relationship, though this immediately creates community with those who share it.

> Therefore the holding of hourly fellowship with the "Man of Pain" is all that one can do until body and soul separate. That is also one of the greatest arguments for personal relationship with him. For where that is not put at the basis of *religion*, no single *religion* stands on its feet, but there is always something more plausible to show and *argumenta* [arguments] are found which destroy one's supposed foundation. And if one thinks, "I have laid down this and that," then there comes a third and one lays it again down. That is the fate of all religions and sects, not only in the rest of the world

[53] See the discussion of the Spirit in this chapter. Zinzendorf's view of the ascension is taken from Heb. 10:12-18, where Christ as high priest now sits at the right hand of God after having offered his single sacrifice for sin, until his enemies should be made a stool for his feet. Until then the Holy Spirit bears witness. This is discussed at several points in this chapter.

but also in Christianity. The only *religion* against which no arguments can be driven nor means found to destroy them is the heart-*religion* which needs no more people than the Creator and a human creature. This church consists of one person who is mortal and another who alone has immortality but who in his resurrection body still shows the marks that it once was changed into sinful flesh and therefore always has its passion for the children of humanity. This person and each human individual constitute the *religion*; and if no one is added, where two or three are gathered in my name, there is he in the midst of them. Matthew 18:20. That is the oldest *religion*, far older than Peter's throne at Rome and long before all patriarchates and institutions of Christianity. I reduce it to two persons. John and Jesus, both in their mothers' wombs, and their mothers, constitute together in any case a Christian *religion*. There begins the "feeling," the experience and (inner) movement which today in Christianity people regard as dream and imagination. "When I heard the voice of your greeting, the child in my womb leapt for joy" (Luke 1:44). If John would never have come into the world, but would have been called again to his Creator in his mother's womb, so would he have left his body in the true *religion*, in faith in Jesus Christ. On such *principia* [principles] must we establish *religion*, which makes it all superior to that which human understanding thinks out, which Satan suggests, what one's own mind imagines, and the attacks and arguments that mere flesh can make into stumbling blocks. "He is the vine. I am the branch." "Near wounds of Jesus, I would not wish to be more than a hair's breadth from your odor."

To implement the love of God and the connection of the soul with him poses, as mentioned, no difficulty. No great effort is needed, no running and running, but a glance from the Creator as he did to Peter. "Jesus looked at Peter, and he went out and wept bitterly" (Luke 22:61-62). The blessed moment when the Creator works in his creature through the Holy Spirit is the conversion about which there is so much talk: the remorse over one's previous condition, the knowledge of one's misery, the sinner-tears over the separation from one's Creator and Savior, and the faithful acceptance of his merit — how near together all that is! For it happens between the Creator and his creation, no third matter intervenes, no human can produce or hinder it. . . . The criterion for salvation, on which it depends, is to want or not to want, to come or not to come, to find in the Savior what is *gusto* [pleasurable] or *degusto* [displeasurable], to remain distant in heart or to approach. The

Savior lets us prove with our example the way one has to be saved
here in time and there in eternity: concise, near at hand, and
depending on no one other than the Savior and us ourselves.[54]

In this approach to *religion*, language and concepts are secondary
and there is a particular understanding of the function of language.
Language is not an end in itself which may be approached as part of a
system of thought having an exact correspondence to truth. Concepts
are not precise descriptions of reality. Language and concepts refer to
a reality which transcends them and by its very nature cannot be
completely captured.

Linguistic analysis makes the helpful distinction between primary
and secondary language. Primary language makes use of the language
which is available within the culture to describe. Because it already has
usage and a tradition of meaning, when one borrows it for use, its
traditional meaning may not be precisely related to the use to which one
puts it. One's use of it always carries along linguistic baggage related to
prior use.[55] This imprecision in language is not so troublesome if the
primary concern is to communicate a reality experienced and the
ultimate concern is not the precise descriptiveness of the language itself.
In fact, when dealing with spiritual realities one would expect the reality
to transcend the language. Language then may be intended to bring us
close to and to mediate the reality encountered, much as Paul in
Romans 1:16 speaks of the Gospel as "the power of God." For Paul the
language of the Gospel mediated the reality about which it spoke.
Though not *precise*, it was *faithful* language and thus became an occasion
for God's presence and action. This mediative function is more
important than precision in description. Precision is not itself the
means by which the religious reality is communicated. Crucial is
whether the language is *functionally adequate*, faithful to the reality
described, that it communicate rather than block the reality.

Secondary language is language which is concerned for precision
and arises out of reflection on how to improve description of that to
which the language refers. Such further refinement is helpful, but one

[54] Zinzendorf, *Einiger zu London gehaltenen Predigten* [Londoner Predigten, vol.1],
sec. [Abtheilung] 2, pp. 153-56 (17 Jan. 1753). These, and a second volume containing
sections [Abtheilungen] 4 through 6, are known as the *Londoner Predigten.*

[55] Of course, language in the process of its use gradually loses its baggage from prior
use until it comes to mean what we make it mean in its new context of use. And yet when
we as historians study texts from the past, the issue of the meaning of language prior to
its use in a text again recurs. For example, when studying the New Testament texts the
prior use of its language in Judaism and the Greco-Roman world cannot be ignored.
Such historical study of language keeps us humble about language in which we have
invested a type of infallibility when we separate it from its roots and context.

must always keep in mind whether that which one seeks to describe can be described with precision. Here again the nature of religious reality would seem to indicate that it will always transcend description. As Paul indicates in 1 Corinthians 13, "our knowledge is imperfect" and we now see as "in a mirror dimly." Thus while in describing spiritual reality one may improve the descriptions, the descriptions will remain limited though, we hope, becoming functionally more adequate. The danger in refining the language is that we may draw away from the reality described and invest ourselves in the language itself. This could be particularly true when we try to put our descriptions together into a type of system of knowledge. Systems may be constructed wherein we recognize their limitations and emphasize their functional value rather than expecting of them ontological precision. But systems may also be constructed in which the concern is coherence within the system itself and in which the hope is to capture the described reality in some final way. When this happens, we have left behind our concern to stay responsibly close to the reality described and to grant it the freedom to be what it is rather than seeking to capture it within our descriptions. When we seek to capture it all, the human desire to control has probably taken over. There is a different approach to systems of knowledge, and this will be suggested shortly.

Traditions of religious language and description have been developed to speak of religious matters. In the minutes of the Synod of 1750 Zinzendorf, where engaged in a discussion on the use of theological terminology, stated that in so far as a *Tropus* is concerned (a *Tropus* is a "way of teaching," such as Lutheran or Reformed), he had no objection to the *Tropus* learning to speak theologically in a way which was suitable to its own people. Neither did he object if his German writings were later corrected in their wording according to Lutheran teaching. However, the usefulness of religious traditions in providing ways to speak about religious matters should not cause us to forget that there is a reality which religious language seeks to communicate. When speaking of this reality Zinzendorf indicated he could not beforehand, a priori, determine to speak in certain terminology; nor must a "free church of Jesus" even if it could. To do so would result in quarreling over terms. But even more, there is no power in this approach because then "one thinks about the words and does not need to speak and think out of the fullness of the heart."[56] One must speak out of the reality about which one would speak, and the words themselves are secondary.

When one speaks out of the reality about which one would speak, this is *Gemeintheologie* rather than theology out of a particular tradition

[56] Minutes of the 1750 Synod, quoted in *Spangenbergs Apologetische Schluß-Schrift*, pp. 549ff.

or with a view to constructing a precise system of description. *Gemeintheologie* arises out of a religious community which seeks to express the reality which lives within it. Within this community various languages or systems of description can be utilized without being inappropriate.

> That is the miracle of community theology (*Gemeintheologie*) which humans cannot understand, i.e., how such a countless number of opinions can be under one hat and be brought into a system and still people, who have their origin in a particular understanding, do not therefore need to change all their opinions and styles of speaking, but perhaps to present the matter in various ways, yet to believe, feel, and have the same thing. We know from experience that all people whose ideas are gathered in their heart, think out of one principle and speak from one mouth.[57]

Wilhelm Bettermann's *Theology and Language in Zinzendorf*[58] discusses Zinzendorf's concern for language. He used the technical terms which were natural to theological discussion in his time, especially in his more learned discourses such as those on the *Augsburg Confession*.[59] His education prepared him to use several languages, including Greek and Latin, and the inclusion of words other than German in his discourse represented common practice among the educated.

But one finds in him also a seeking for words adequate to expression of the Christian reality. He felt that there was a dearth of words in German for communicating experience, and Christianity is an experience of the heart.[60] Poetry and hymns are also of special value, for in them experience rises to expression.[61] Zinzendorf held the darkest

---

[57] Nikolaus Ludwig von Zinzendorf, *Vier und Dreyßig Homiliae über die Wunden-Litaney der Brüder, Gehalten auf dem Herrnhaag in den Sommer-Monathen 1747. von dem Ordinario Fratrum* (n.p.: Zu finden in den Brüder-Gemeinen, n.d.), pp. 110ff. (11 June 1747) (Abbreviated in subsequent notes as Zinzendorf, *Vier und Dreyßig Homiliae*), quoted in *Nikolaus Ludwig Graf von Zinzendorf: Evangelische Gedanken: Gewißheit, Freude, Kraft*, ed. Otto Uttendörfer. Hilfe für's Amt, vol. 14 (Berlin: Christlicher Zeitschriftenverlag, 1948), p. 172.

[58] Wilhelm Bettermann, *Theologie und Sprache bei Zinzendorf* (Gotha: Klotz, 1935).

[59] *Spangenbergs Darlegung richtiger Antworten*, pp. 105f.

[60] Nikolaus Ludwig von Zinzendorf, *Die an den Synodum der Brüder, in Zeyst vom 11. May bis den 21. Junii 1746. gehaltene Reden, Nebst noch einigen andern zu gleicher Zeit in Holland geschehenen Vorträgen* (n.p.: Zu finden in den Brüder-Gemeinen, n.d.), p. 152 (16 May 1746).

[61] Zinzendorf, *Ein und zwanzig Discurse* [Title page: *Discurse . . . Auctoris*], pp. 242ff. (18 Feb. 1748). His comments here on the composition of the hymn on the Augsburg Confession and the Synod of Bern are interesting. For an extended discussion of his use of poetry see Gerhard Meyer's introduction to Zinzendorf's *Teutscher Gedichte*, 1766, 2nd ed., in Nikolaus Ludwig von Zinzendorf, *Ergänzungsbände zu den Hauptschriften*, ed. Erich Beyreuther and Gerhard Meyer (Hildesheim: Georg Olms, 1964-85), 2:vii-xlvii.

expressions in hymns to be clearer than the clearest in prose.[62] He produced a prodigious amount of hymnody and poetry and influenced the Moravian Church in the extensive use of hymns in its liturgical materials.

Zinzendorf also turned to *Bilder-Reden*, pictorial speech, such as the use of Father, Bridegroom/Husband, and Mother for the persons of the Trinity, and extensive use of the imagery of the wounds and language of mystical marriage. The Christian, he said, is like a painter, but with words, who paints "cross-pictures" before the eyes of persons until they realize by their originality and vividness that the painter has seen and experienced something and until they see in the Spirit the events of the cross.[63] This is a seeing and not seeing. It is not a matter of one's external senses, but a matter of the senses of the heart. It is known after it has occurred but may not be noticed in the imagination or feelings.[64] The Bible, rich in pictorial and concrete images, simple in its approach to the reflection of religious experience, akin to the minutes of a meeting where the reader has what the writer had,[65] provided the model for Christian language.

Though it is clear that his understanding of language derives from his understanding of religious reality, there is also indication that it fulfilled a compensatory function for personal characteristics. His inclinations were at first in the direction of abstract thinking,[66] and he had difficulty with creating images in his imagination. His images were more thought than seen. Regarding this he said:

> I cannot create images. When I close my eyes, I get no image, but it is black to me. And I have already thought a great deal about whether it were not a wisdom of the Savior that he has been able to make a brother so astonishingly abstract who has so much to do with salvation and experiences.[67]

There is another issue related to the role of language in *religion*. To understand *religion* conceptually creates the possibility of an elitism

---

[62] Nikolaus Ludwig von Zinzendorf, Confession to the King of Sweden (8 July 1734), published in *Büdingische Sammlung*, 1:118.

[63] Zinzendorf, *Vier und Dreyßig Homiliae*, pp. 304ff. (8 Aug. 1747).

[64] Zinzendorf, *Nine Public Lectures* [1973], pp. 82-84 (25 Sept. 1746).

[65] See the chapter on Scripture.

[66] Arthur James Freeman, "The Hermeneutics of Count Nicolaus Ludwig von Zinzendorf" (Th.D. diss., Princeton Theological Seminary, 1962), p. 221.

[67] Herrnhuter Synodalrede of 1747, quoted in Hans-Günther Huober, *Zinzendorfs Kirchenliederdichtung: Untersuchung über das Verhältnis von Erlebnis und Sprachform*, Germanistische Studien, no. 150 (Berlin, 1934; reprint Nendeln/Liechtenstein: Kraus Reprint Limited, 1967), pp. 25ff.

where religiosity depends on the accumulation of knowledge or under-standing. Zinzendorf felt this was contrary to the fact that Christian existence depended on God's gift of relationship and that the most spiritual persons were not always those with the highest education. Relationship with God is similar to the relationship of parent and child, where there is much that is unspoken and unconceptualized. One of the great divisions in Christianity has been over Baptism as to whether understanding and the ability to articulate faith were necessary prereq-uisites. So for some Christians Baptism was possible only for believers. If Baptism rather signifies relationship with the Savior, then all who are in relationship may be baptized, even though understanding may not yet exist, may be inadequate, or may no longer exist. Thus Baptism of both infants and the senile is legitimate.

In his *German Socrates* Zinzendorf described how understanding *religion* as a matter of experience, rather than concepts, makes *religion* available to all.

1. *Religion* can be grasped without conclusions drawn by reason, otherwise no one could have a *religion* except the one who has an enlightened mind, and they would be the best students of God who had the greatest rational capacity; however, that is not believable and wars against our experience.

2. *Religion* must be something which is obtained without any concepts, through mere experience; otherwise no one deaf, or still less someone born blind, or even less an insane person, or a child, could have the *religion* which is necessary for salvation. The first could not hear the truth, the second lacks the sensual perception which would awake his mind and incite his thoughts, and the third type lacks the ability to understand concepts, relate and test them.

3) Truth in concepts is less important than truth in experience, errors in teaching are not as bad as in essence, an ignorant person is not as badly off as one impervious (to God).

4. The conceptual meanings vary with age, education, and other conditions. The experienced meanings are not so much subject to these variations; they remain firmly established in the face of time and circumstances.[68]

In the experience of God the *sensus numinis* (sense of the numinous) is proper for the historical period of those who have the experience, and

---

[68] Nikolaus Ludwig von Zinzendorf, "Gedancken vor gelehrte und doch gutwillige Schüler der Wahrheit," in *Der Teutsche Socrates. Das ist: Aufrichtige Anzeige verschiedener nicht so wohl unbekannter als vielmehr in Abfall gerathener Haupt-Wahrheiten, in den Jahren 1725 und 1726. Anfänglich in der Konigl. Residentz-Stadt Dreßden, Hernach aber dem gesamten lieben Vaterland teutscher Nation zu einer guten Nachricht nach und nach ausgefertiget, und von*

the *systema theologicum* (theological system) developed on the basis of this is also proper to the time. The experience and theology of the next historical period cannot occur until the new period exists, but when the time comes, the experience and thought will also be relevant to this new time. What is expected of a person is neither complete experience nor complete knowledge, but the proper response to what God has given as right for the time. As stated in the *London Sermons*:

> When one believes, one is afforded an inner experience and feeling of God, a little *sensus numinis* as it is proper for the time in which one lives. Each time has its own *sensus numinis*, which never contradicts that of the previous time but from generation to generation increases and becomes clearer. This is apparent in the great historical periods before and under the Law and under Christ where the sense of the divine in each was appropriate for its own time. Accordingly each time has its own *systema theologicum* which already leads to the following period (as 1 Peter 1:11 indicates). However, the theology of the following period cannot be learned before the time is fulfilled, and still each person of this historical period has the faith which is right for them. That which is of primary concern then is not so much the completeness of knowledge, but the faithful faith-obedience which a person expresses in their historical period towards the content and object of faith which is presented to the heart's and mind's eyes. Each soul is evaluated in God's heart according to whether or not it is willing to do that.[69]

It is in the heart-experience that one finds the *only possible theological system*. The system may be viewed from the perspective of the spiritual reality itself or of the personal or communal reality which it brings into being.

In terms of the spiritual reality itself, the varying aspects of theology are held together in the system of *the person of Christ* rather than in a conceptual theological system. Conceptual knowledge is always limited by the way the reality described transcends its description. It is also conditioned by the needs and circumstances of history and the under-

dem Autore selbst mit einem kurtzen Inhalt jedes Stücks, nunmehro auch mit verschiedenen Erläuterungen, die sich in der ersten Auflage nicht befinden, und einem Anhange versehen. (Leipzig: Samuel Benjamin Walther, 1732), pp. 35f.

[69] Nikolaus Ludwig von Zinzendorf, *Der Predigten die der Ordinarius Fratrum von Anno 1751. bis 1755. zu London gehalten hat, Zweyter Band, Nebst Einem Anhange einiger an Englische Brüder-Gemeinen gehaltenen Homilien* (London and Barby: Zu finden bey dem Seminario Theologico, 1757), sec. [Abtheilung] 4, pp. 35ff. (Abbreviated in subsequent notes as Zinzendorf, *Der Predigten zu London gehalten* [Londoner Predigten, vol.2].)

standings already embodied within the language tradition used for description. To say this in no way diminishes the importance of conceptualization or denies the fact that some conceptualizations are better than others, but recognizes their character and limitation. Because differing conceptualizations describe and share in a common reality, they can exist together even though they would not be able to live well together apart from this reality, the person of Christ. Because they partake of and fit together within this reality, they mediate it rather than merely mediating themselves, rather than providing mere description. A good example of this is the great variety of Christological language in the New Testament which only coheres in the person it describes and most properly mediates him whom it describes. Apart from Christ, the concepts of Messiah, Son of Man, Wisdom, New Moses, Virgin Birth, Incarnation cannot logically coexist together.

The second type of system exists in the heart of the believer in which all of the ideas and experience of Christian life are gathered. But this also is not a conceptual system. It is more a *system of the heart* in which all hangs together which might not hang together if it were isolated outside the heart. It also exists as a *system within congregational life,* a lived and living system and a communal reality which embraces the many ways it may be named and the individual ways in which it is experienced.

There is a passage in the *Sermons on the Litany of the Wounds* which expresses this. Zinzendorf observed how a child seems to learn naturally within the environment of home, and that this way of learning and education through daily contact and observation seems to leave the child with knowledge which it would take a great deal of study to acquire. Children should learn their theology through their daily activity in the congregation. In this way their heart becomes a "cone" wherein what they learn is collected into a true theological system:

> Therefore children also would learn their whole theology through the daily fellowship in the congregation. Indeed it is certainly to be wished that they not be able to bring it together before that, but that the reality be spread out as something to be seen and that they get their ideas of it only by and by until their heart becomes a cone which is set up and wherein the numerous ideas that lie separate can be collected into a true theological plan and system. This finds its fulfillment in all persons, in whose heart the combination of ideas exists, thinking out of common principles and speaking out of one mouth.[70]

Fundamental truths cannot be proved or argued. They are rather stated on the basis of their experienced authority, and persons must

---

[70] Zinzendorf, *Vier und Dreyßig Homiliae,* p. 111 (11 June 1747).

respond to them as they are able: either by intuitively perceiving their authority or by receiving them through trusted others who have perceived their authority. This is extensively discussed in Discourse XIII on the *Augsburg Confession.*

> Demonstrations are fine, they cannot be accurate enough, the more critical the better: but to want to demonstrate fundamental truths a priori, and without laying 'Αυτὸς ἔφα [I myself have spoken] for the basis, or indeed to want to grasp thoughts, fundamental truths, i.e., *prima principia* [first principles] to expose them to reason's *petitorio* [claim], is a sign of a spiritual pendant. . . .
>
> It is the *maxim stantis et cadentis theologiae apostolicae, primaevae, reformationi proximae* [by which theology stands or falls that is apostolic, early, faithful to the Reformation], that one must not demonstrate foundational truths, but *nude et crude* [nakedly and crudely] maintain them and let whoever will, and can, believe. This is the *crinomenon* [criterion] of true theology, this is the highest wisdom, such a wisdom as comes out of the heart of God. Therefore the Apostles, and our Savior himself, did not always make use of arguments, as were to be *soutenable* [warranted] upon the strictest rules of logic, but perhaps only demonstrated *rhetorice and ad hominem* [for the sake of public presentation and on the level of human needs]; and as soon as they engaged in demonstrating, they did a foreign work out of condescension. . . .
>
> In this simplicity there is a similarity to Scripture, which sanctifies and anoints the productions of men, and that gives to their productions what they call in French and Italian, with *Johanne Apostolo* [John the Apostle], the *unctionem* [unction, anointing]; about which it is not usual to speak much in German universities. That means to speak from a whole, full heart, with full conviction to be oneself, "so it is, so do I think: if you have the good fortune to believe it, it is well for you!" Does any one say, I cannot believe; one answers, "I am sorry that you are so unfortunate, but that does not change my conviction."[71]

The Humanity of Jesus

To understand Zinzendorf's theology it is necessary to recognize the importance of Jesus' real humanity. The church, in its concern to affirm the Virgin Birth (which separated Jesus from humanity on his father's side) and the view which developed into the Immaculate Conception (which separated Jesus from humanity on his mother's side), had in

[71] Zinzendorf, *Ein und zwanzig Discurse* [Title page: *Discurse . . . Auctoris*], pp. 232-35 (18 Feb. 1748).

reality separated Jesus from the human experience as we know it. Carl
Jung perceived this and believed that the incarnation of God in Jesus was
not a real and full incarnation. Jung felt that the incarnation only fully
occurred in the coming of the Spirit upon real human beings.[72] But for
Zinzendorf, God in Christ had really assumed the fullness of human
existence.

> It is a primary concern that our Savior be presented not only as
> divine but as truly human, that one speak humanly when one
> wishes to speak of his birth and life on earth. When in some
> denominations they have been talking to me so much of the
> Godlike Savior, and have as it were deified his humanity, I have
> listened to it *indignabundus* [with indignation], because I thought,
> there is an intention to degrade or take away from his Godhead
> behind this Godlike honor, which at the same time hides his
> humanity.
>
> It does not harm the divinity of the Savior in the least when one
> lets his humanity be quite human and small: for, as we know once
> for all, he is *unione hypostatica* (by union of his natures) one Christ,
> God and human; therefore the limited circumstances of his hu-
> manity do not hinder the immeasurability of his Godhead. And
> this incomprehensible divine majesty took pleasure in that very
> mean and abject form, in the quite *extraordinair* humbled *modifica-
> tion* of its humanity.[73]

Though his divinity continued in union with his humanity, it did not
help him in the course of his human life. His human struggles were real,
though his divinity continued to exercise a controlling or governing
effect on the world — but without this entering consciously into his
humanity.[74]

His humanity extended even to his being a male. We know

> that he was a child, as other children also are, that he was a poor
> needy child; that he was even a little male, and was under an
> obligation to undergo the same discipline on his distinguishing
> member, the covenant discipline, which had been expressly im-
> posed for a certain period of time on his own special people,
> although it had also been transformed into a covenant-grace. . . .
> And this *factum* was to be carefully noted and preserved, even to

[72] Carl G. Jung, *Answer to Job*, trans. R. F. C. Hull, Bollingen Series (Princeton: Princeton University Press, 1973), pp. 67-70.
[73] Zinzendorf, *Ein und zwanzig Discurse* [Title page: *Discurse . . . Auctoris*], pp. 94-95 (23 Dec. 1747).
[74] Ibid., pp. 97-98.

these last days; that no human creature need reflect long about this divine entry into one of the human sexes. A man must either deny his own male-form, or be obliged to let Jesus' male-form pass for certain as naturally, as entirely, as simply as his own which constitutes him.[75]

The humanity of Christ remains eternally with him. The risen Christ continues to be a man.

Concerning our dear Savior, we know moreover that he is a human as we are, that he bears our members, that he ascended as human into heaven, that he sits as human at the right hand of God his heavenly Father, that he will abide so in the παλιγγενεσία [rebirth] of the whole of nature, that he will judge as a human, and appear as the Son of Man in the clouds. Thus, to be sure, he is very well known to us, and fellowship with him is easy to us.[76]

As well as remaining human, he is always the one who was known in his life and sufferings. This avoids spiritualizing him in any way,[77] and roots faith in history. We believe historically.

Be that as it will, my brothers and sisters, the great main plan of our *religion* in general is that we believe historically that the creator of the whole world, that the Father of eternity, was born of a pure maid whom never a man knew, and who, being overshadowed by the Holy Spirit, actually brought forth the salvation of the world out of her body; and that her child, not mystically or hieroglyphically, but truly, grew and increased in the powers of body and mind, and afterwards in diverse kinds of outward employments, labor, and difficulties, and in a very simple, uniform way, passed his life till he was thirty years of age; and then for a short time, in character of a teacher, a witness, a benefactor of the whole human race, still dignified the world with his presence; but at last concluded his life and his teaching as a martyr.[78]

"To believe historically" is a phrase which Zinzendorf uses a number of times, stressing the rootage of truth in history and in the historical and human person of Christ.

[75] Ibid., pp. 146-47 (2 Jan. 1748).

[76] Ibid., p. 156 (6 Jan. 1748).

[77] Compare Zinzendorf, *Einiger zu London gehaltenen Predigten* [Londoner Predigten, vol. 1], pp. 141f. (15 Apr. 1754) and p. 208 (2 Sept. 1754). Also *Ludwigs von Zinzendorf Peri Eautou. Das ist: Naturelle Reflexiones über allerhand Materien, Nach der Art, wie Er bey sich selbst zu denken gewohnt ist: Denenjenigen Verständigen Lesern, Welche sich nicht entbrechen können, über Ihn zu denken, in einigen Send-Schreiben, bescheidentlich dargelegt* (n.p., n.d.), p. 355 (See note concerning editions and modern reprint at chapter 1, footnote 47).

[78] Zinzendorf, *Ein und zwanzig Discurse* [Title page: *Discurse . . . Auctoris*], pp. 113-14 (26 Dec. 1747).

A primary aspect of Jesus' incarnation and humanity is "the blood-theology, the teaching of Jesus' cross and martyrdom."[79] Jesus' sufferings are an essential part of his human identity. In the Litany of the Wounds, central to the worship life of Moravian congregations during the Sifting Period, his whole life is treated in terms of his suffering: his painful birth, his holy first wound of circumcision, his labor sweat, his weakness, and ultimately the sufferings connected with his death. After the petition "Anoint us, you red wounds!" there is the concluding hymn verse:

> Till in my faith I see
> His body bruised for me
> Whereon so steadfastly
> We here trust and rely
> And close to Him can greet
> The prints in hands and feet.[80]

In the *Sermons on the Litany of the Wounds* Zinzendorf said:

If we speak of the cross in the congregation, so we mean a certain form, a certain style and fashion, in which the Savior, the God over all, the Creator of all things, has appeared in this present time. He rules and does what he wants; he gives us life and breath, he makes us healthy, he keeps us, he preserves us, he conquers sin and every earthly need for us, he carries out his decree for our salvation as it was foreknown by him from eternity: but all that, my sisters and brothers, he does for now in the cross-form. One must not try to present that as a way of power, a kingly method, a despotism striking to the eyes: he is a despot, but in the cross-form. Everything appears according to the fact that he is a Lamb who endures, who is so patient, lamblike, open, contented, self-composed, gentle if it does not go his way.[81]

In the fourth discourse on the *Augsburg Confession* Zinzendorf poetically concluded:

[79] Zinzendorf, *Auszüge über die vier Evangelisten*, 6:32 (12 Dec. 1756).

[80] From Albert H. Frank, "The Litany of the Wounds: A Commentary on Zinzendorf's Liturgical Bilder-Rede," paper for course, Theology of Zinzendorf, Moravian Theological Seminary, Dec. 1970. This translation is from the British hymnal of 1745. This litany was developed about 1744 and soon became a centerpiece for Moravian worship, translated even into Indian languages in North America. The reader can find a translation of a highly modified version of this litany in Peter C. Erb, ed., *Pietists: Selected Writings*, The Classics of Western Spirituality (New York: Paulist Press, 1983), pp. 296ff. A better representation of the original litany can be found in Atwood, "Blood, Sex, and Death," App. 3, pp. 270 ff.

[81] Zinzendorf, *Vier und dreyßig Homiliae*, pp. 60f. (14 May 1747).

It is all for his sake. When we have walked a mile in time, we have been walking towards him; when we have walked a hundred miles, we are walking towards him; when we have walked a thousand years, we are walking still towards him; and when we have been flying for a million ages, as quick as the swiftest dove, yet we always say, "We are flying to our window.".... And what is that? How is it called? The through-pierced Side. And that is for us ever new. He will be your Lord, and with all your longings you will constantly want to come to him. Genesis 3, compare Psalm 45.[82]

The humanity of the Savior provided the model for human life and development at its various stages, from infancy to adulthood. The exaltation of his humanity in the ascension provides continuity between the historical Jesus and the resurrected Christ and expresses the possibilities of our humanity. The cross-form and woundedness of Jesus' existence (even into eternity) speaks the love and redemptive gentleness of God and sets the pattern for the life and ministry of the church. Jesus' humanity points the way for the character of the existence of both religious persons and their community.

The Holy Spirit

The Holy Spirit was very important to Zinzendorf's approach to *religion*. Though *religion* is a matter of relationship with the Savior, the Savior has ascended to take his rest, and so both the Savior and the will of the Father need to be communicated through the active participation of the third person of the Trinity.[83]

One of the difficulties one encounters in translating into English what Zinzendorf says about the Spirit is the gender one should assign to the Spirit. *Geist* in German means "spirit" or "mind" and is masculine in gender. Pronouns and possessive adjectives must agree in gender with the noun to which they refer, and so they must also be masculine. Thus in German the Spirit is a "he" or "him." In Greek the noun for "spirit" is neuter, and in translations of the New Testament text it would be referred to as an "it." This has been carried over into English where the Spirit is usually referred to as "it." To call the Spirit "it" has often created

---

[82] Zinzendorf, *Ein und zwanzig Discurse* [Title page: *Discurse . . . Auctoris*], pp. 105-6 (23 Dec. 1747).

[83] Zinzendorf based his view of Christ's ascension, sitting down at the right hand of God, and taking his rest after his earthly ministry, on Heb. 10:12-13, a passage which for him better supported the continuing role of Christ as mediator of the Godhead. Here it is not Christ who subjects the cosmic powers so that all might be given to God (as in 1 Cor. 15:28), but the powers are subjected to Christ.

a misunderstanding that the "Spirit" is some sort of spiritual substance or power or mere expression of the dynamics of the other two persons, rather than a person having unique identity both within the oneness of God and in relationship to the world. Though the New Testament does not always clearly speak of the Spirit as person, the Nicene-Constantinopolitan Creed affirmed the doctrine of "one Being, three persons" with greater attention to the Spirit than in the original Nicene Creed. And thus the Spirit was fully person with the others.[84] However pronouns relating to the Spirit are translated, we need to preserve the dignity of the Spirit being fully person. The question then is whether one should use masculine or feminine pronouns when referring to the Spirit. Consideration should also be given to Zinzendorf's preferred name for the Spirit after 1738: Mother. Yet Zinzendorf chose this name because the Spirit functioned as Mother of the church, not because he wanted to argue that the Spirit was feminine, a more modern concern. This meant that in German Zinzendorf spoke of the Spirit who is Mother as a "he," for the noun *Geist* was masculine. In some of the translations I have followed this practice, not wishing to use the pronoun "it."

Zinzendorf described a development in his understanding of the Spirit. A new stage began in 1738: "I did not know what I should make out of the Holy Spirit and I was very happy when the Savior in 1738 gave me the first conclusion about that. . . . It happened to me as to Basilius. I had not understood the Holy Spirit's divinity, and whoever knew me, knew that I never spoke of it." He said that he had believed that the Spirit was the third person of the Godhead, "But I was not able to say how that was so, but only thought of him *abstracte.*"[85] As he explained in the *London Sermons,* he did not know what he should make of the Holy Spirit at first until the Savior gave him the first explanation in 1738 in the hymn, "O, Pray God the Holy Spirit." Before he came to his understanding of the Spirit, he desired to give the Spirit a place in the church so that the members might "get a feeling of him." Thus he gave him the title *Heger* ("protector, preserver") and later *Kämmerer* (meaning "servant in a chamber," which Zinzendorf said is derived from the idea of the "friend of the Bridegroom"). However, these two terms were "liturgical," and when he knew the Spirit as "Mother,"[86] then it was *naturell* (natural) to him. The full explanation of the Spirit came to him while he was on the ship *Torbay* on his second trip to America in 1741. In the term "Mother" one has an "economical" (from *ökonomisch,* i.e., related to the

[84] See discussion in Thomas F. Torrance, *The Trinitarian Faith: The Evangelical Theology of the Ancient Catholic Church* (Edinburgh: T. and T. Clark, 1988), p. 336.
[85] *Spangenbergs Apologetische Schluß-Schrift,* p. 576.
[86] For a discussion of Zinzendorf's understanding of the Spirit as Mother, his sources for this understanding, and his debate with his contemporaries over this, see

times) word which would be good for the heart as *Abba* is for the heavenly Father and *Mann*(Husband) for the Savior.[87] When Zinzendorf arrived in Philadelphia, his first sermon in Germantown, December 1741, presented this as a well-developed understanding. He divided history into three spiritual "economies": in the first, God was Father of his house, a time characterized by the fear of God. The second period was that of a kingdom or theocracy. The third period is

> the blood-friendship with Jesus or the divine family on earth, since we have in heaven a Father, a Mother, and a Husband: here the Father of our Lord Jesus Christ is our true Father and the Spirit of Jesus Christ is our true Mother; because the Son of the living God, his only begotten Son, is our true Brother and Husband. . . .
> The Father must have love for us and can not do otherwise; the Mother must guide us through the world, and can not do otherwise; the Son/Brother/Husband must love our souls as his own soul, our body as his own body, because we are flesh of his flesh and bone of his bone, and he cannot do otherwise.[88]

That Zinzendorf should grow in his understanding of Christian realities was perfectly natural, for he was not dealing with conceptual understanding which could be formed apart from experience, but with a reality to which description would be applied as it was experienced. He said, "Theologians make the mistake or have the prejudice that they are able to understand everything at the same time. Therefore they have no new blessings, for they are quite complete when they finish their education." He then went on to say:

> The Holy Spirit has known me well, but I have not known him before 1738. Therefore I carefully avoided entering into the matter until I so clearly understood the Mother-Office of the Holy Spirit. Since I have known him as Mother, it is natural to me.[89]

Gary S. Kinkel, *Our Dear Mother the Spirit: An Investigation of Count Zinzendorf's Theology and Praxis* (Lanham, Md.: University Press of America, 1990). This was originally a doctoral dissertation at the University of Iowa.

[87] Zinzendorf, *Der Predigten zu London gehalten* [Londoner Predigten, vol. 2], sec. [Abtheilung] 6, pp. 39-40 (24 May 1752).

[88] Nikolaus Ludwig von Zinzendorf, *Eine Sammlung Offentlicher Reden, Von Dem Herrn der unsere Seligkeit ist, und über die Materie von seiner Marter. In dem Jahr 1742. Mehrentheils In den Nordlichen Theil von America der das Englische Canada ausmachet vor allerley Christlichen Religions-Meetings gehalten, von Dem damaligen Evangelischen Lutherischen Inspectore und Past. zu Philadelphia Erster Theil. [Zweyter Theil.] Zweyte Edition* [2nd ed.] (Büdingen: Johann Christoph Stöhr, 1746), 1: 38. This sermon was not included in the edition of 1760.

[89] *Spangenbergs Apologetische Schluß-Schrift*, p. 576.

In the *Augsburg Confession Discourses* of 1747-48 he expressed criticism of the Apostles' Creed and Lutheran theology contemporary to him for limited treatment of the Spirit. Of those (not the apostles) responsible for the very brief statement about the Spirit in the Apostles' Creed he said that they "were not very well acquainted with the Holy Spirit, as may be seen by their very concise line of treating him."[90] In Spangenberg's *Answers to More Than 300 Accusations* he reproached Lutheran theologians for their neglect of Luther's teaching on the Holy Spirit.[91]

The Spirit is primarily a Christian experience, although there was some experience of him before Christ made the unique Christian experience of him possible. However, before the time of Christ, to be filled with the Holy Spirit was "an extraordinary state, one of the strangest and most unusual things."[92]

> Indeed the Holy Ghost is the Nurse of Mankind, and they always had some dark Notion of it; for this Divine Person, in his Energy at least, was not so properly unknown under the Old Testament, like the Father, as inaccessible by reason of Man's Offence. They knew of one who *moved* (or brooded) *upon the Face of the Waters,* Gen. 1, as the spiritual *Chavah,* the Mother of all living. Among the Heathens Satan described a Minerva, who educated and form'd young Heroes; and thus when Wisdom must appear too divine a thing for Man to ascribe to himself, the Acknowledgement was however turn'd from the true Mother and Nurse.[93]

The most singular manifestation of the Spirit of God is in the person of Christ.[94] Christians receive the Spirit from Jesus, but there is no single way of receiving the Spirit. The first communication of the Spirit to Jesus' disciples was in the upper room, when Jesus breathed upon them in a special act of consecration (John 20). At Pentecost the 120 received the Spirit (Acts 2). However, Thomas, who was not present when Jesus breathed out the Spirit in the upper room, would have missed the

---

[90] Zinzendorf, *Ein und zwanzig Discurse* [Title page: *Discurse . . . Auctoris*], pp. 91f. (23 Dec. 1747).

[91] *Spangenbergs Darlegung richtiger Antworten,* pp. 128f.

[92] Zinzendorf, *Ein und zwanzig Discurse* [Title page: *Discurse . . . Auctoris*], p. 159 (6 Jan. 1748).

[93] Discourses at Marienborn and Herrnhaag, 1747, published in Nikolaus Ludwig von Zinzendorf, *Maxims, Theological Ideas And Sentences, Out Of The Present Ordinary Of The Brethren's Churches His Dissertations And Discourses From the Year 1738. till 1747. Extracted by J. Gambold, M.A. With a Letter from the Author annex'd.* (London: J. Beecroft, 1751), pp. 275-76.

[94] Ibid., p. 276.

special act of consecration by Jesus if he had been able to receive the Spirit only at Pentecost. Thus "upon him our Savior does not breath, but agrees to another Ritual he himself had pitch'd upon, ver. 25.27. tho' still the Spirit flows from the human Body of JESUS." When Thomas laid his hand in the Savior's side, he received the Spirit. Noted Zinzendorf, "This makes the manner of Thomas's Ordination so important to us."[95]

Of course, the reason Jesus' way with Thomas is important is because Zinzendorf felt the experience of Thomas was close to that of the Moravians. The side wound of Jesus then becomes the place from which the Spirit issues forth into the world, bringing all of the little spirits which are the seeds of the spiritual life of persons.

> Who sees him (Jesus) sees the Father and the Holy Spirit who constituted himself out of the matrix of his holy side wound, as it were, who previously was not *en vogue*, who did not yet exist in human thoughts and knowledge, who first when the spear entered the dear Lamb, at the same time gushed out with the incorruptible blood and life of the dear lamb and with the source of every little spirit to be distributed to human individuals during this time, and has taken along the whole host of souls in his πληρώματι [*pleroma*, fullness]. As now all souls come from God, all human souls, so will, *ut ita dicam* [if I may speak thus], the little spirits, the imperceptible, invisible, uncomprehensible gracious and Jesus-like spirits which came out of the side of the Savior. These are preserved, sealed, and locked-up in the Holy Spirit and distributed one by one among human *individua* [individuals]; so that if one wants to describe himself, he says, I know him, I know that I belong to him.[96]

It is interesting to note that as Zinzendorf understood Christ's Atonement to deal with original sin and remove all humankind from its guilt and influence (if sin again occurs, it occurs because of human relapse), so he understood the Spirit to have been poured out on all humankind and to be working among all peoples in appropriate times and seasons. Thus the absence of the Spirit occurs only by a forfeiture of the times of grace.

> When the dear Savior died and poured out his blood, when his side was opened, then the Holy Spirit as a pent-up stream broke out again; he burst his way through, he made the whole earth his bed, as a part of its surface is covered with water, the whole world has, at

[95] Ibid., pp. 284-85.

[96] Zinzendorf, *Ein und zwanzig Discurse* [Title page: *Discurse . . . Auctoris*], pp. 76-77 (16 Dec. 1747).

least little by little, been covered with the Holy Spirit. He once more brooded over the whole earth as at the time of creation and has afterwards continually worked on human minds: sometimes he caused himself to be perceived here, sometimes there.[97]

The difference between such working of the Spirit in the world and his working in the believer is that whoever believes in Jesus through the activity of the Spirit and is "brought through the washing of the church into the death of Jesus, into his blood and wounds, in such a one he will formally dwell anew; such should by this means be exempted from the lamentable *Casu* [situation] of living without the conversation of the Holy Spirit, as the rest of the world did."[98] The Spirit does not just work on the believer, but abides in her or him and becomes the source of faith and life.

In his eighth discourse on the *Augsburg Confession* Zinzendorf discussed the "procession" of the Holy Spirit. He acknowledged the controversy between the Western and the Orthodox churches over procession from the Son, and indicated that such passages as John 15:26 and 16:7 do not indicate a procession from the Son in regard to *essence*, but in regard to *mission*. Moreover, to talk about procession in terms of essence is to move beyond what can be said about the mystery of God, which one cannot describe.

That the sending and procession out of his essence are not the same thing, nobody can deny. But because the Holy Trinity for wise reasons causes it to happen that humankind, when it soars into the divine essence, and *definitiones hypermetaphysicas* [hypermetaphysical definitions] thereof, never learns to define satisfactorily about it; therefore we also shall without scruple pass by such theoretic discussions, and hold ourselves to the heart-truth, viz., that the Savior has entrusted the Holy Spirit to speak and act in his name, to repeat what he has said, and to take his people very specially under his care, in the same manner as he himself would do if he dwelt among us bodily.[99]

To further illustrate his understanding of the Spirit's mission as proceeding from the Son, he uses the analogy of a father who goes on a journey and entrusts the care of the family to the mother. While the father is gone, the mother refreshes the family's memory of the father

[97] Ibid., pp. 160-61 (6 Jan. 1748).
[98] Ibid., p. 160 (6 Jan. 1748).
[99] Ibid., p. 155 (6 Jan. 1748).

so they will know him when he returns. So the Spirit cares for the Savior's children and reminds them of him until he returns.[100] This analogy should not be pushed so far as to assert the absence of the Savior in the present, for the Savior is present in the Spirit.

The Savior and the Spirit are so intimately related that the Spirit is sometimes called "our Savior's Spirit." He did not become present until Christ completed his work. He pours out of Jesus' side wound like a pent-up stream to cover the whole earth. He preaches and convinces persons to believe in the Savior and his merits. He becomes the instrumental cause of our salvation, while the Savior and his sufferings are the principal cause.[101]

> All that the Holy Spirit speaks with you, are his [Jesus'] words, it is as much as if he himself spoke to you; all that he takes up with you, is the same as if Jesus took it up with you; he has left him in his stead with you; he is a human, and accordingly in a certain way has gone into his *Hoekje* [closet], he has set himself down and rests, and has left behind for you his busy, omnipresent Spirit, that Spirit who is sufficient for all spiritual and human creatures, who should keep you within his school, and should have at the same time full authority to provide you, in his name and for his sake, all that you need and must have from him in this life: he is to be the dispenser of the degrees of grace, of blessings, of sensations, experiences, and official gifts, which you are to have; he shall take it out of that which is mine, says our Savior.[102]

For the reality of the Spirit in the life of the Christian Zinzendorf argues "not only from revelation [i.e., Scripture], but also from experience."[103] In fact, one might judge that experience was the primary factor. Yet Scripture is crucial to his presentation of the Spirit. The sayings about the Spirit in John 14-16 are important. Here Luther's Bible rendered the word παράκλητος (paraclete, comforter, advocate) by the German *Tröster* (consoler) which has a much more limited meaning than the Greek. Zinzendorf recognized this and included "exhortation and encouragement" among the implications of the term. Through the Spirit God says to the person, "I will encourage you, take you on my lap, speak in a kindly way, and do good to you just as a Mother

[100] Ibid., p. 155 (6 Jan. 1748).
[101] Ibid., pp. 165-66 (6 Jan. 1748). It should be noted that several times in the NT the Spirit is spoken of as the Spirit of Christ. In Gal. 4:6 the Spirit is called "the Spirit of his Son" and in 1 Pet. 1:11 it is indicated that the "Spirit of Christ" worked within the prophets.
[102] Ibid., p. 166 (6 Jan. 1748).
[103] Ibid., p. 156 (6 Jan. 1748).

soothes her little child and speaks kindly to it."[104] Also important was Isaiah 66:13, where God comforts as a mother comforts her child.[105] When preaching on the Lukan Infancy Narrative, Zinzendorf saw the Spirit exercising motherly care of Jesus and understood the words of old Simeon as really addressed to the Spirit.[106] For his understanding that the Spirit proceeds out of Christ's side wound he probably relied on 1 John 5:6-12, besides John 19:34 and John 20:26-29. The latter Zinzendorf used to indicate that Thomas' receiving of the Spirit was from Jesus' side wound, for he was not present when Jesus breathed on the disciples earlier. Scriptural description of the role of the Spirit and the centrality of the incarnate Christ did provide the boundaries for his understanding, and therefore his *religion* did not degenerate into any undefined mysticism, spiritualism, or docetism.[107]

Zinzendorf's Late Broadening of His Christocentrism: The Chief Eldership of Christ and the Mother Office of the Spirit

Zinzendorf's theology seemed to have been in process all of his life, and interesting developments took place in the last decade of his life with regard to Christ and the Spirit.

The Chief Eldership of Christ was determined on September 16, 1741, and proclaimed to the Moravian Church on November 13, a festival still celebrated to memorialize the significance of this realization. On December 19, 1756, a special celebration was held to memorialize the Mother Office of the Holy Spirit. Both of these celebrations were the expression of theological insights from praxis which had matured in both the thought and the experience of the church.

The understanding of Christ as Chief Elder was no claim to a special relationship of Christ with the Moravian Church. Rather was it an expression of the realization of the relationship which Christ bears to all churches — and an attempt to put it into practice. The decision to recognize Christ as Chief Elder was precipitated by an historical crisis. In 1727 twelve persons were elected to the office of elder to administer the matters of the Herrnhut congregation, and from 1735 these persons

---

[104] Zinzendorf, *Öffentlichen Gemein-Reden, 1747*, pt. 1, app. [Anhang], p. 4 (19 Oct. 1746).

[105] Ibid., p. 2.

[106] Ibid., p. 368.

[107] Both Paul and the Johannine literature struggled with the proper role of the Spirit and Christian experience in relationship to the historical Jesus. The Johannine treatment of this is to be found in 1 John 4 and John 14-16. The primary Pauline discussion of it is in 1 Corinthians 12-14. Both biblical traditions relate the experience of the Spirit to the confession of Jesus as Lord or Christ, to the expression of a quality of life (love), to the mission of the church, and to responsibility to the church.

functioned as general elders, headed by a chief elder. Johann Leonhard
Dober, the third chief elder, decided that the responsibilities of this
office were more than he could manage and so resigned. The church
then attempted to elect another chief elder, including the use of to
signify approval,[108] but was not able to do so successfully. The question
was then posed as to whether Christ wanted this position, and for the
first time was affirmative. Though this action was precipitated by an
incident, this was also an expression of the relationship of the living
Savior to the decision-making processes as well as the general life of the
church. The significance of this office for the decision-making processes of the church is indicated in a comment after the Sifting Period,
where Zinzendorf stated that the Elder office of Christ was made public
too soon and should have been limited to the circle of the elders,
implying its special relevance for them.[109]

Because of the Sifting Period, 1743-50, Zinzendorf had to make
correction in the language used to express the relationship of Christ to
the church. This had been a time of excessive use of the imagery of the
wounds, spiritual marriage, and the erotic to express the relationship
with Christ, particularly within the congregations in Wetteravia. For a
while he suspended the Elder office of Christ to spare Christ the shame
for what had happened. In 1751, at the ten-year jubilee of the declaration of the elder office of Christ, Zinzendorf spoke of a new beginning.[110]
This new direction gave birth to a preference of the term "Lord" for
Christ, rather than "Elder," in the late 1750s. He even suggested the
celebration of a "Lord-Festival" on the first Sunday of Advent.

> The idea of Elder, outside of the assembly of the workers, is an
> abstract idea. I have long thought, why do we not introduce the
> name *our Lord. Our Savior* is a term originating with the Pietists,
> which is not to be deserted. We will say it a thousand times when
> we speak of his wounds. But in the communal life it is not
> convenient, and there the Apostles' *our Lord* pleases me much
> more.[111]

By "Lord" Zinzendorf meant Christ as "Housefather," not *Pantocrator*
(almighty ruler of all). As "Elder" was an expression of the relationship
of Christ to the decision-making process of the church, so "Lord"

---

[108] See chapter 5, Christian Life and Ethics, for the Moravian use of .

[109] Dieter Meyer, *Der Christozentrismus des späten Zinzendorf: Eine Studie zu dem Begriff
"täglicher Umgang mit dem Heiland,"* Europäische Hochschulschriften, ser. 23, Theology
vol. 25 (Bern: Herbert Lang; Frankfurt: Peter Lang, 1973), p. 58. (Abbreviated in
subsequent notes as Dieter Meyer, *Christozentrismus des späten Zinzendorf.*)

[110] Ibid., pp. 55-56.

[111] Ibid., p. 63.

(interpreted as "Housefather") is the expression of the relationship of Christ to the life process of the whole church. In 1759, at the last Festival of Christ as Elder that he was to experience, he said:

> If one wants to indicate most completely what the Savior is to the whole church, the "brotherhood," to the smallest as well as greatest, to the brothers and sisters of the Lord's Supper and the bees on the corpse; if one views the workers as members, and nothing more, as if they all stood in one place so that no apple could fall to earth, if they all fell at the feet of their Savior and paid him homage: how would the congregation of souls, the members of the whole church, pay him homage? Then one comes to the point that I have previously often called to your attention, and the object of the 13th of November should be: He is our Lord. I do not understand Lord in monarchical or royal terms, but in terms of the character of a housefather. The whole people, if they as thirty thousand or more stand on one spot, are his family. One calls Lord the one to who one subjects oneself as his property, the one who orders and forbids and troubles himself about everything.[112]

In his last years Zinzendorf thought that the dangers of the Sifting Period were over and that he could feel much more positive about the church's following of its Lord. In 1756 he collected biblical texts about the nearness of the Lord which he bound as a Daily Text Book, covering from June 1, 1756, to December 31, 1757. His last effort consisted of designing a great "Thankfest" which he wanted celebrated in 1760 but did not live to experience.

Parallel to the celebration of Jesus as "Elder" and "Lord" was the celebration of the "Mother Office" of the Holy Spirit on December 19, 1756.[113] Whereas the description of Jesus as "Elder" had to do with church governance and "Lord" had to do with the obedience of Christians to the one who determines their lives as "Father," the Mother Office of the Spirit expressed the way the Spirit cared for the members of the church. This realization of the fellowship with the Spirit is not to be separated from the fellowship with Christ, but is a broadening of the relationship with Christ. The Spirit keeps us in fellowship with Christ, the one who is the Father of our household.

---

[112] Diarium des Jüngerhauses, 16 Sept. 1759, quoted in Dieter Meyer, *Christozentrismus des späten Zinzendorf,* pp. 64-65.

[113] Dieter Meyer, *Christozentrismus des späten Zinzendorf,* p. 60.

The Mother Office of the Holy Spirit even came to overshadow the festival of November 13 commemorating Jesus as Chief Elder of the church:

> Since we have paid homage to the "Mother," according to my understanding this festival (Nov. 13) should cease. It was a festival, a day, which had to be introduced as long as we did not have sufficient acquaintance with the heavenly Mother, and we had not yet devoted ourselves to her as long as we still needed to have a human mother.[114]

The author is not presently aware of what happened to this Festival of the Holy Spirit after the death of Zinzendorf.[115] It seems clear that it never really overshadowed the Festival of Christ as Elder, November 13. Perhaps its emphasis only lived on in the celebration of the Festival of August 13, which commemorated the spiritual awakening of the Herrnhut congregation in 1727, often regarded as the Moravian Pentecost. However, the place of this festival within the vision of Zinzendorf does stress the role of the third Person of the Trinity within the life and practice of the church, an emphasis often neglected by Moravians in favor of the relationship with the second Person. Atwood, in his doctoral dissertation, calls the highly developed worship of the Holy Spirit as Mother under Zinzendorf "one of the best-kept secrets in the historiography of the Moravian Church."[116] Though this is not true of European Moravians who have access to German sources, it is very true of English-speaking Moravians. But it is true that even European Moravians make little of the role of the Spirit, except for those involved in the charismatic movement in the Czech Republic and Herrnhut. And even this movement has not sought roots in the insights of the eighteenth century.

Reflections

It would seem important here to engage in some reflection on Zinzendorf's Christocentric approach to the knowledge of God, something which earned him the title "the noble Jesus freak."[117]

[114] Zinzendorf, source not cited, quoted in Dieter Meyer, *Christozentrismus des späten Zinzendorf*, p. 62.

[115] Atwood, "Blood, Sex, and Death," p. 162. Atwood mentions that in 1759 the Mother Festival was changed to January 1 and that it continued to be celebrated on this date. The last mention of this festival in the material he researched was in the 1774 *Losungen* (Daily Texts) calendar.

[116] Ibid., p. 158.

[117] George W. Forell, introduction to, and trans., *Nine Public Lectures on Important Subjects in Religion Preached in Fetter Lane Chapel in London in the Year 1746*, by Nikolaus Ludwig von Zinzendorf (Iowa City: University of Iowa Press, 1973), p. xxx.

Zinzendorf's approach was Johannine through and through. He understood the Gospel of John to be the culmination of the revelatory process in the New Testament. In his second edition of his translation of the New Testament he rearranged the books in what he understood was their order of historical origin and placed the Gospel of John first as key to the New Testament development which culminated in it. He said that in the New Testament Acts was written in the old ideas held at the time of the Ascension. The Gospel of John was written after all the epistles and is their continuation and conclusion. It presents the whole theology with a clarity which even the letters of the apostles don't have. Though it may appear that sometimes the epistles contradict or say less than John, the truth is that John explains all the epistles.[118] Though Paul's is the standard theology, the final truth is in John, for in the Gospel John again brought to the fore the already set-aside teaching of Paul regarding justification and the divinity of Christ; otherwise Paul would have been forgotten.[119]

It is important to recognize that Christology in the New Testament church (or churches) was in the process of development. The Synoptic Gospels present a Jesus who confronts persons with the Kingdom of God and teaches his disciples about his heavenly Father. The Gospel of John presents a Jesus who is conscious of his own preexistence, speaks openly about his coming from heaven (e.g., 6:38, 16:28), has the power to lay down and take up again his own life (10:17ff), and returns to heaven to prepare there a place for his disciples (14:1-3). He is "the way and the truth and the life; no one comes to the Father, but by me" (14:7). Thus while the Synoptics are theocentric, understanding the relationship with God and God's kingdom as the purpose of Jesus' ministry, John is Christocentric, even including a Prologue which speaks of the Word, become flesh in Jesus, mediating God in creation and Old Testament history. This is similar to the role of Wisdom in Jewish Wisdom literature and is often thought patterned after Sirach 24. In John Jesus draws persons to himself, though he and the Father are one and he was sent by the Father.

While John presents Jesus as from heaven, oddly enough the Johannine materials struggle to maintain the real humanity of Jesus. In John 1:14 the Word of God who was with God from the beginning

---

[118] Minutes of the 1750 Synod, quoted in *Spangenbergs Apologetische Schluß-Schrift*, pp. 475ff.

[119] *Diarium des Jüngerhauses*, 23 Aug. 1754, quoted in Uttendörfer, *Zinzendorf und die Mystik*, p. 352.

becomes flesh. In the resurrection appearances Jesus appears to his disciples with his wounds. And in 1 John the differences of the community with the group which breaks away involve the community's refusal to surrender Jesus' real humanity. Thus it must be remembered that to make Jesus central and divine did not necessarily diminish his humanity. In John's Gospel, which Zinzendorf understood as the fulfillment of New Testament theological development, the centrality of Jesus, the divinity of Jesus, and the humanity of Jesus were all affirmed.

Paul at first glance is quite Christocentric, with a very high Christology. However, when one reads closely, one finds something else. In the opening addresses of Paul's authentic letters one finds the church described as "the church of God." When Paul speaks of divisions of the Corinthians, he also criticizes those who say, "I belong to Christ" (1 Corinthians 1:12). This strange remark, which has puzzled exegetes, seems to find its explanation in 1 Corinthians 1:26ff., where Paul indicates that "he [God] is the source of your life in Christ Jesus, . . . therefore, as it is written, 'Let him who boasts, boast of the Lord.'" In 1 Corinthians 15:20-28 Paul indicates that Christ is now in the process of extending his reign over every rule and authority and power. "When all things are subjected to him, then the Son himself will also be subjected to him, that God may be everything to everyone." In Judaism there was the idea of a preliminary messianic kingdom before the final establishment of God's rule, and this seems to be the way Paul understands the time after Christ's historical ministry. Once Christ has completed the extension of his rule, he steps back and delivers all to the Father, for this is the purpose for which he came: to bring all to the Father. Thus for Paul Christocentrism, if one may speak of his views this way, is a necessity of this age because of what God has chosen to do in Christ, but the final goal and end of Christology is Theology. It is interesting to explore the role of Christology for Paul in the light of the understanding of the role of Christology in the sixteenth-century Spanish mystic, Teresa of Avila. In her *Interior Castle* (VII.5) she reflected on the continuing need for Christ and the sacraments after we have been brought to God. She decided that in our human condition we cannot do without these concrete symbols even when we are in relationship with the One they mediate to us.

Zinzendorf was affected not only by the implications of Johannine Christology, but by the epistemological questions of his time. He believed that God (the Father) in himself cannot be known. The Son is the only Mediator between God and the world and the only person, besides the Spirit, that can be experienced and known in a direct way.

Thus in his *Catechism for the Heathen,* he dealt with the whole of the Christian faith in terms of the Son. He identified Christ as the one they know as "Creator." It is only when the questions turn to Baptism that the Father and Spirit are also mentioned. A question then asks, "Who is that all?" The answers are that the Father is the Father of Jesus and that he is too high to be described. Jesus will tell the person about him when Jesus' Father is her/his Father. The Holy Spirit is Jesus' Father's Helper, and the baptized have him for a Mother.[120]

In the second discourse on the *Augsburg Confession* Zinzendorf felt that it was necessary to explain why the Confession begins with the Father and not the Son. He went on to say:

> Otherwise nothing is more certain than that the whole matter concerning the *mysterio trinitatis* [mystery of the Trinity], does not at all belong to a *systemate catholico* [catholic system] for the whole world and committed to writing; and that if one wants to write a catechism, which shall be in written form for the whole world, for all persons, it ought to treat only of Jesus Christ, who is the God of the whole world, who is the *objectum liturgiae universitatis* [object of the liturgy of the universe], *privative* [solely and exclusively]. Him the Apostles call the *Enchiridion,* the κεφάλαιον, the primary content of all doctrine, in whom the πλήρωμα [fullness] of the whole Godhead dwells σωματικῶς [bodily]; so that we joyously worship the Father on his fatherly throne, the Holy Spirit the Comforter, as well as the only-begotten Son himself, *qua DEUM* [as God], *nec factus, nec creatus, sed aeterne genitus* [neither made nor created, but eternally begotten], with good reason reverenced in the person *Agni Dei,* of the Lamb of God, the sacrifice for sin which is eternally valid.[121]

Zinzendorf explicitly disagreed with Paul's statement that Jesus would hand over the Kingdom to the Father in the end. He said Paul was merely giving his opinion and should have said so. Zinzendorf rather preferred the presentation of Hebrews 10:12: Jesus, after his death and resurrection, ascended to heaven, taking a rest from his labors. The Holy Spirit had been poured out on the world through his atonement, and now the Father was working through the Spirit, subjecting all to the Savior. Jesus was still being experienced through the Spirit, and the mark of conversion is the gaining of a glimpse of the Savior, Christian life to be guided by the glance of the Savior. When ultimately the Spirit

[120] *Büdingische Sammlung,* 3:402ff.
[121] Zinzendorf, *Ein und zwanzig Discurse* [Title page: *Discurse . . . Auctoris*], p. 64 (16 Dec. 1747).

brings all to the Savior in manners and times right for them, then the Kingdom will be handed over by the Father *to the Son*, and the Son will reign for ever. Thus Zinzendorf reversed Paul's description.[122]

The church today is confronted with the Christological issue in very significant ways. For one thing, modern biblical criticism has pointed out that there is a great variety in the Christology of the New Testament. The early church borrowed the religious language available from its contemporary world, Jewish and Greco-Roman, to describe what it experienced in Christ. This language was not carefully thought out as to its coherence and relationship to the experienced reality. It was merely what was available to reflect the reality. The issues related to the variety of Christological expressions were at first worked out only as concerns arose. Paul's Christological expressions (e.g., Colossians 1:15-20 and Philippians 2:5-11) embrace a variety of ideas. This is also true of the traditions embodied in the Gospel of John. Yet when the variety in the tradition produced widely varying Christologies, such as the two Christologically divergent groups portrayed in 1 John, the issues had to be engaged.

As Raymond Brown pointed out in his history of the Johannine community, that which characterized the position of the orthodox group in the Johannine community was adopted by the greater church in the second century which traced its origin to the Twelve. Johannine Christology thus became that Christology which led to Nicea and Chalcedon, and the distinctive elements of Synoptic Christology and Pauline Christology were diminished.[123]

Because of the discoveries of biblical studies we need to be able to take a fresh look at the variety of Christology which clustered around the Christ experience. But this is not the only reason. The church today faces the need to carry on its mission in a world in which other world religions have gained a new sense of their dignity and identity and in which broadening experience of the world makes Christian exclusivism less acceptable. Christian mission theory now takes seriously dialogue, where there is mutual sharing and enrichment without the attempt to convert. The common elements that the great religious traditions share

---

[122] Ibid., pp. 96-97 (23 Dec. 1747).

[123] Raymond Brown, *The Community of the Beloved Disciple* (New York: Paulist Press, 1979), pp. 145ff. The Johannine community consisted of an orthodox element, which took seriously the humanity of Jesus and the atonement, and a Gnostic element, which denied Jesus' relationship with the material world and refused to accept his suffering and death as real. Both accepted a high Christology, but the Gnostic group denied Jesus' real humanity. The high Christology of the Johannine community was adopted in its more orthodox form by the greater church.

can better be seen in terms of a common experience of the Father, rather than the common experience of Christ who constitutes the Christian particularity (as advocated by Zinzendorf and the Johannine tradition). Here the Christology of the Synoptics and Paul comes more to the point. Christ came to call persons to the Father. His post-resurrection activity moves towards the completion of his historic ministry and the subjection of the cosmos to God. When this is done, he will hand over all to the Father so that the God of all may be the God of all. It is important to note this continuity between Paul and the Synoptics, because this represents a major segment of early Christianity. Paul also claims a continuity with Jerusalem Christianity (Galatians 1-2), contrary to what a lot of Pauline scholarship has said.

Having said this, I must affirm the centrality of Christ to our understanding of God and the significance of Christ as a place of entry into the reality of God. I also affirm that there is no other God than the one who is met in the incarnation and sufferings of Christ. I do think that the affirmation of this is what Zinzendorf intended by preserving the eternal mediatorial role of Christ according to the presentation of Christ in Hebrews. Human experience cannot find in history the disincarnate God of triumphalism, the glorious imperial ruler in control of all. Especially in the light of the experience of our century, only *theologia crucis*, the theology of the cross, makes sense. Some have tried to resolve this by understanding God in God's self as a being of great power and relating to the world by accommodations which step down this power.[124] There is truth to this, but there is also the danger that we will understand the God we meet in history as a lesser, different, or modified God. Zinzendorf's approach affirms that the incarnation and sufferings of Christ are not just a temporary or modified way of God's being God, or that this occurred with God only in a particular context. While the early creeds affirmed the divinity of Christ and the union of his natures, they did not reflect on the meaning of his humanity and sufferings for the nature of God. The implications of Jesus taking his humanity and wounds back to heaven and thus into the very nature of God are profound.

A friend who has experienced a great deal of suffering recently sent me a quotation from William Temple's *Readings in St. John's Gospel* in which Temple quoted a poem by an Edward Shillito written just after World War I. Temple remarks, "The wounds of Christ are His creden-

---

[124] For example, Jewish Kabbalistic Mysticism. Christian Gnosticism completely separated the good and supreme God from the God of this world.

tials to the suffering race of men." "Only a God in whose perfect Being pain has its place can win and hold our worship; for otherwise the creature would in fortitude surpass the Creator." The poem expresses the same awareness of the implications of Jesus' wounds that one finds in Zinzendorf:

> If we have never sought, we seek Thee now;
>   Thine eyes burn through the dark, our only stars;
> We must have sight of thorn-pricks on Thy brow,
>   We must have Thee, O Jesus of the Scars.
> The heavens frighten us; they are too calm;
>   In all the universe we have no place,
> Our wounds are hurting us; where is the balm?
>   Lord Jesus, by Thy Scars, we claim Thy grace.
> If, when the doors are shut, Thou drawest near,
>   Only reveal those hands, that side of Thine;
> We know today what wounds are, have no fear,
>   Show us Thy Scars, we know the countersign.
> The other gods were strong; but Thou wast weak;
>   They rode, but Thou didst stumble to a throne;
> But to our wounds only God's wounds can speak,
>   And not a god has wounds, but Thou alone.[125]

In Zinzendorf's approach there is also the beautiful simplicity of coming to Christ and knowing that one has entered the sacristy of all that is, and that in the wisdom of God this will unfold in meaning all of one's life. Yet the very variety of Christology and religious expression to be found in the New Testament should make us more appreciative of variety as expressing the nature of religious experience and reflection. For some, Christ was a teacher, sometimes (Matthew) patterned after Moses and sometimes (John) presented in protognostic fashion as the heavenly revealer of life and light and teacher of truth. Mark, with his emphasis on narrative, presents Jesus as the proclaimer and bringer of the Kingdom of God, exorcist of Satan's dominion, giving his life as a ransom in the pattern of the Isaianic Servant. For some, the meaning of Christ's death is central (Paul and 1 John both stress its atoning significance), but for Luke in Acts the resurrection and Spirit are central, with Jesus' death merely a historic tragedy.

The variety in religious terminology and experience expresses a richness in God. What developed in the Christian Trinitarian formula-

[125] Edward Shillito, poem, quoted in William Temple, *Readings in St. John's Gospel* (New York: St. Martin's Press, 1959), p. 366.

tions is expressive of this. There are Christians today who focus on the Father, others who stress the Spirit, some who would rediscover the feminine in God, some who find their experience with Jesus central. There are those whom the Son introduces to the Father and those whom the Father introduces to the Son. In each person the whole of the Godhead is fully present.

> My God,
> how rich you are.
>
> Our Father who art
> in heaven, and on earth,
> you call me son
> or daughter
>
> as case may be.
>
> You Son who
> shared our flesh
> and history,
> bore our pain.
>
> You fought
> the powers of evil
> gathered there,
> which nailed you fast,
>
> but not so fast
> you could not
> rise
> into our hearts.
>
> And you Spirit,
> maker of holiness,
> transformer of
> the human,
> with some limits,

be everywhere
that God would be
that all you touch
is drawn by
tenderest force

and
with life and justice
express
your new creation,
called to its destiny.

O breath of God,
breathe o'er world
and me, and all;
my heart would be
your sanctuary.

These are your names,
though you are One.
Your many names
do free
to name you more:

Servant, Lover, Mother,
Wisdom, Word,
Adam from Heaven,
eternally Wounded,
Friend,

Fullness, eternal No-thing
beyond all names.
Grant that your names
never become walls
of my making

to keep me
distant
from
your love.[126]

[126] By the author.

Chapter 3

Scripture

Zinzendorf stood within the stream of Protestantism which utilized the authority of Scripture as a means of re-forming the church and thus of finding true and faithful expressions of faith and Christian life. It was the Protestant hope that a return to Scripture would provide a return to true Christianity. The frustrations with the state Protestant churches of Zinzendorf's day led many to search the Scriptures to find new answers. Frequently the image of the ideal church was the Philadelphian Church (Revelation 3:7ff.), the faithful church of Revelation against which no criticism was leveled and before whom God set an open door. Scriptural studies had a rebirth within Pietism, both in scholarship and in popular piety, with a view to renewing the life of the church. Just how Scripture is to do this, to renew the life of the church, is an important question. Though there are those whose personal process is deeply affected by the gathering of information and the intellectual process of arriving at understanding, it is usually true that if renewal, personal growth, and community formation are to occur, the encounter with what is in Scripture must be more than intellectual. The reader must on some level meet that to which, the One to which, the biblical writers bear witness.

Zinzendorf frequently talked of Scripture in a way that at first glance seemed to express an understanding that it was literally inspired, such as in his "Declaration of the Ordinarius to Several Separatists" in Spangenberg's *Antworten:*

> The written Word of God is the oral witness of holy men of God, which flowed from the eternal and living Spirit of God, brought to paper, which then constituted a whole, a closed canon. Thus the collection of the divine truths is the only rule of all knowledge and

faith, doing and being, public and secret matters; and whoever preaches another Gospel, he is accursed, be he pious or evil.[1]

In one of his Berlin Sermons he criticized those who twist and distort Scripture, thinking to improve on it:

> I believe simply what the nature of the words brings and hope that the eternal Wisdom would have known what it was saying and caused to be written, better than all men, better than we know, we who must first learn it there (in Scripture).[2]

He also preferred frequently to speak with a "biblical mouth," using Scripture as it was, without critical questions, using biblical language to communicate Christian truth. And yet, as we will see, such comments in no way portray adequately the profundity of his treatment of Scripture. One has only to become aware of the *Collegium Biblicum* which met in Herrnhut under his sponsorship in 1734, his attempts to create a new German translation of the New Testament, his correspondence with Wettstein in Amsterdam, and his detailed notes about the issues and procedures in translation,[3] to be aware that there is much more here to be explored. His understanding of inspiration allowed for the full participation of God within the full humanity and historical contexts of the writers; therefore to speak of the inspiration of Scripture in no way excluded its bearing the human character of its writers.

Zinzendorf's understanding of Scripture was formed amidst the issues of the Enlightenment, the development of historical criticism, and renewed interest in the original languages of Scripture. The discovery of new Greek manuscripts in the seventeenth century and the

---

[1] *M. Aug. Gottl. Spangenbergs Darlegung richtiger Antworten auf mehr als dreyhundert Beschuldigungen gegen den Ordinarivm Fratrvm nebst verschiedenen wichtigen Beylagen* (Leipzig and Görlitz: In der Marcheschen Buchhandlung, 1751), p. 256 (app. 10).

[2] *Des Grafens von Zinzendorff Inhalt dererjenigen Reden, Welche zu Berlin vom 1ten Januar. 1738. bis 27ten Aprilis in denen Abend-Stunden sonderlich für die Manns-Personen gehalten worden. Dritte Auflage* [3rd ed.] (Flensburg and Altona: Gebrüder Korte, 1743), p. 98 (16 Mar. 1738).

[3] Zinzendorf's first major New Testament translation works were *Eines Abermahligen Versuchs Zur Übersetzung Der Lehr- und Prophetischen Bücher Neuen Testaments Unsers Herrn Jesu Christi aus dem Original Erste Probe* (Büdingen: Joh. Christoph Stöhr, 1739), and *Eines abermahligen Versuchs zur Übersetzung der Historischen Bücher Neuen Testaments Unsers Herrn Jesu Christi aus dem Original Erste Probe* (Büdingen: Joh. Christoph Stöhr, 1739). These two volumes, one on the "historical books" and the other on the "teaching and prophetic books," were later published in second editions, in 1744 and 1746 respectively. To the first edition there is an extended *Erinnerungen Des Hrn. Gr. v. Z. Wegen seiner Ersten Probe Der Übersetzung Des Neuen Testaments An seine Herren Gegener* (Reflections for his opponents by C[ount] v[on] Z[inzendorf] regarding his first attempt at translating the New Testament) (Büdingen: Johann Christoph Stöhr, 1741; also, with a minor change in title, Leipzig: D. Korte, 1741) besides many notes in the text of the translation.

development of critical Greek editions of the New Testament in the eighteenth century made a decided contribution to discontent with the Greek "received text" and the search for a more valid text. Historical criticism portrayed the Bible as originating within historical contexts which determined its nature. It is important to note that Zinzendorf adventuresomely sought to come to terms with the issues of his day and to seek meaningful answers which adequately reflected what was being discovered.

The nature and authority of Scripture are also questions for our day. We live in a world where the sciences are rapidly expanding the frontiers of human knowledge and both the world and the church are well aware of the historically conditioned nature of Scripture. We are more and more confronted with other great religious traditions, not only abroad but within the United States. We have become aware of the value of our theological reflection and our religious experience for the forms of our faith and even for the understanding of Scripture itself. In this milieu it is difficult to maintain Scripture as the only source of insight and truth.[4]

The very variety within Scripture makes the authority of Scripture difficult to formulate, for different movements and traditions find the foundation for their faith in various traditions embodied in the New Testament itself. The variety within Christianity is encouraged by variety within Scripture. It is no accident that the Roman Church before Vatican II preferred the Gospel of Matthew, Lutherans prefer Pauline material, the Orthodox Church prefers Johannine material, and a group such as the Jehovah's Witnesses prefers the apocalyptic materials, such as Revelation. The Ancient Moravian Church, before the second Reformation's discovery of the Pauline materials, was drawn to the Sermon on the Mount while the Renewed Moravian Church under Zinzendorf was particularly influenced by the Gospel of John and Hebrews.

In our day the struggle to define the nature of Scripture's authority has often been focused not so much on doctrinal or sacramental issues as on certain moral issues, participants in the debate seeking some authority for their views. A case in point is the debate which took place

---

[4] The Methodist Quadrilateral indicates that the basis of faith is "revealed in Scripture, illumined by tradition, vivified in personal experience, and confirmed by reason" (*The Book of Discipline of the United Methodist Church* [Nashville: United Methodist Publishing House, 1988], p. 80. See also Donald A. D. Thorsen, *The Wesleyan Quadrilateral: Scripture, Tradition, Reason, and Experience as a Model of Evangelical Theology* [Grand Rapids: Zondervan Publishing House, 1990]). The Anglican Church has a Trilateral, leaving out experience.

within the North American Moravian Church from 1993 to 1995. This focused on the definition of the authority of Scripture in a Moravian doctrinal statement, *The Ground of the Unity,* which originated in reaction to the European Moravian experience of World War II and was accepted by the international Moravian Church at the General Synod of 1957. The statement said that "The Holy Scriptures of both the Old and New Testament are and abide the only source and rule of faith, doctrine, and life of the Unitas Fratrum," and some understood "source" as "source of information," thus ruling out tradition, experience, and reason/science. The debate of 1993-95 in the Moravian Church in North America took place against the background of the Interprovincial Faith and Order Commission's consideration of the issue of homosexuality and ordination for homosexuals.[5]

I will briefly return to this debate at the end of this chapter, indicating it as a model, since it both provides a significant formulation of the Moravian understanding of Scripture and serves as a paradigm for the handling of tradition in a way responsible to both God and present context. Now let us explore Zinzendorf's insights.

The Historical Nature of Scripture

Plitt in his *Theology of Zinzendorf* quoted a statement of Zinzendorf from the Herrnhut Diary which quite well summarizes his understanding of Scripture, using the image of the fruit and the shell used previously by August H. Francke:

In the book which one calls the Bible the whole fruit is together with the shell, as it originated in various times, and as men wrote it, of whom several would never have dreamed that it would sometime be called God's Word.[6]

Zinzendorf was well aware of the differences among the various biblical books. Regarding a question concerning the lack of blood theology (emphasis on the atonement and Jesus' wounds) in parts of the New Testament, he replied:

[5] I have written a full history of this debate in an unpublished manuscript: "The Understanding of Scripture in the Moravian Church (Unitas Fratrum)." This paper was used in various forms during the history of the debate, with the final form dated May 17, 1996. The paper in its final form can be found in the Archives of the Moravian Church in both Northern and Southern Provinces (in Bethlehem, Pa. and Winston-Salem, N.C., respectively) and in the Moravian Theological Seminary Library (Bethlehem, Pa.). The Interprovincial Faith and Order Commission serves both Southern and Northern Provinces.

[6] Diarium des Jüngerhauses, 2 Jan. 1759, quoted in Hermann Plitt, *Zinzendorfs Theologie,* 3 vols. (Gotha: F. A. Perthes, 1869-74), pp. 7-8. (Abbreviated in subsequent notes as Plitt, *Zinzendorfs Theologie.*)

Paul, John, and Christ are in this matter not the same. For Christ
is introduced as speaking briefly and mostly prophetically in the
first three Gospels. Paul speaks of it dogmatically and to be sure
amazingly clear (considering his difficult and argumentative circumstances). Because we have nothing else from him than letters,
which are commonly hypothetical, i.e., relative to other people and
conditions, whom we do not know, therefore the liveliest theology,
most suitable to our times, is to be found in the letter to the
Hebrews, Colossians, Philippians, the Gospel and the Revelation of
John (that biblical theses are more honored in one time than
another is witnessed to in church history).[7]

When speaking of Paul and "the writer of the letter who is known
under the name of James," he observes that they are not of one type.[8]

Zinzendorf expanded on the individual differences of the scriptural
writers in the third of his *Pennsylvania Sermons*, noted as a rich source of
his biblical views. In response to the questions as to why historical
conditions in Scripture are diversely narrated and why there are things
in Scripture which natural scientists prove are different in nature, he
said that Scripture was composed by diverse *geniis* [persons with various
talents] who treated their materials with the greatest honesty and
simplicity. Paul, the most educated amongst them, was the least
understood since he had more *Kunst* [art, skill] to avoid than the others.
The simpler one wrote, the more understandable. Paul, since he was
more educated, became more troubled by qualms and doubts. When he
wrote a truth, he became concerned about how it could be twisted in the
future and so inserted words and lines to protect the meaning. Others
simply wrote their matters and were not concerned with the problem of
future understanding; each simply acted as a servant of Christ according
to his own fashion.

The avoidance of *Kunst* or *Künsteley* [artistry or creativity] was part
of Zinzendorf's understanding of the nature of God's revelation and its
characteristic difference from truth as understood by rationalism. God,
so that God's Word would not be accused of a *Künsteley* and of hidden
meaning, treated Scripture simply, letting authors write as they were
able. Only in doctrinal matters did God enter the process in such a way
as to cause to be written what is true and would serve for the needs of that

[7] *M. Avgvst. Gottl. Spangenbergs Apologetische Schluß-Schrift, Worinn über tausend
Beschuldigungen gegen die Brüder-Gemeinen und Ihren zeitherigen Ordinarium nach der
Wahrheit beantwortet werden, Nebst einigen wichtigen Beylagen* (Leipzig and Görlitz: In der
Marcheschen Buchhandlung, 1752), pp. 145-46. (Abbreviated in subsequent notes as
Spangenbergs Apologetische Schluß-Schrift.)
[8] Ibid., p. 147.

particular period of time. Other things he left to the ordinary notions and information available to persons.

In order then to cause persons to preach the main points of Christian teaching with a simple heart, and not distort it by artistry and creativity, God caused that natural and physical things were not written other than the writers knew them, and if one of them knew these facts differently, they were written differently. Each had the honesty not to make his word agree with that of the other. God thus, both then and now, has protected the Bible from change and emendation, from the attempt to reconcile its problems and so destroy its simplicity and truthfulness.[9]

God then, while protecting the truth of essential doctrines, let the authors speak according to their abilities and understanding. In the fifteenth sermon on the Litany of the Wounds Zinzendorf commented:

[The Holy Spirit] let the people speak as well as they could, he did not give them more understanding and memory than they had, he changed nothing in their natural qualities, but as the person was constructed in body and mind, so he remained, even when he was converted, even when he became a servant of God in the highest degree. There can be another servant of God with the same degree of blessing and estimation in the heart of God, where the one has a poor and the other a great understanding. If the two persons write, the one writes with his great understanding, the other with his poor understanding; if they argue, the one argues according to the school from which he came and the other, according to his. The Holy Spirit does not change this, does not overcome the person's nature, but lets each go his own way.

But the truths, the harmony of the ideas, especially the basic ideas, that which God laid as the basis from the beginning, that must always be the same, whatever variety of styles, whatever difference in the weakness or strength of argument, whatever the differences in reasoning, so that a servant of the Lord, who calls upon the Bible, must be able to say: Of this Jesus witness all the

[9] Nikolaus Ludwig von Zinzendorf, *Eine Sammlung Offentlicher Reden, Von Dem Herrn der unsere Seligkeit ist, und über die Materie von seiner Marter. In dem Jahr 1742. Mehrentheils In den Nordlichen Theil von America der das Englische Canada ausmachet vor allerley Christlichen Religions-Meetings gehalten, von Dem damaligen Evangelischen Lutherischen Inspectore und Past. zu Philadelphia. Erster Theil. [Zweyter Theil.] Zweyte Edition* [2nd ed.] (Büdingen: Johann Christoph Stöhr, 1746), 1:134ff. (7 Mar. 1742). (Abbreviated in subsequent notes as Zinzendorf, *Offentlicher Reden 1742* [Pennsylvanische Reden], 2nd ed.)

prophets so that in his name all who believe in him should receive forgiveness of sin.[10]

In the minutes of the Synod of 1750 there are recorded some of Zinzendorf's comments on the effects of the various types of writers on the language of their books. There are shepherd phrases in the prophets which no one easily uses who is not a shepherd, e.g., Amos. There are also fisherman phrases and tax collector phrases, for Peter was a fisherman and Matthew was a tax collector. In the Epistle to the Hebrews there is a classical dryness and the argument is in many places so "rabbinical, rhetorical, and scholastic" that he doubted this was a Pauline letter.[11]

He was also aware that portions of some of the books are collections without context: for example, some of the prophets. Here the material does not have a logical order, and one should not look for the context of a verse in the surrounding material.[12]

The differences within Scripture are just that, "differences" rather than "mistakes" or "untruths," such differences arising naturally from God's preservation of the human dimensions of the process of revelation.

> If a historian among the canonical writers writes that which is quite opposite to that which another has written (the fact cannot be met with denial but with a transformed view of the places where it is plain), so I call that not untruths, but differences. Because it is not always possible to decide which reading explains the other, so uncertainty remains. Praise God that we never lose or gain much from these places.[13]

Scripture's Reality Is a Reflected Image

For Zinzendorf, Scripture was a *Catoptrisches Bild,*[14] an image which is reflected. Since the Greek verb *katoptrizomai* (κατοπτρίζομαι) appears in the New Testament only in 2 Corinthians 3:18, this would seem to be a clue to understanding his meaning. This passage deals with how Moses

---

[10] Nikolaus Ludwig von Zinzendorf, *Vier und Dreyßig Homiliae über die Wunden-Litaney der Brüder, Gehalten auf dem Herrnhaag in den Sommer-Monathen 1747. von dem Ordinario Fratrum* (n.p.: Zu finden in den Brüder-Gemeinen, n.d.), pp. 145-46 (18 June 1747). (Abbreviated in subsequent notes as Zinzendorf, *Vier und Dreyßig Homiliae.*)

[11] Minutes of the 1750 Synod, quoted in *Spangenbergs Apologetische Schluß-Schrift*, pp. 479-80.

[12] *Collegium Biblicum*, 11 June 1755, quoted in Plitt, *Zinzendorfs Theologie*, 3:12.

[13] Minutes of the 1750 Synod, quoted in *Spangenbergs Apologetische Schluß-Schrift*, p. 643.

[14] Ibid.

reflected the glory of God, but a fading glory, and so veiled his face. Paul then indicates that Christ removed the veil from Moses (i.e., the Law). He then contrasts the Christian with Moses by saying, "And we all, with unveiled face, beholding (or better "reflecting" - *katoptrizomenoi* - κατοπτριζόμενοι) the glory of the Lord, are being changed into his likeness from one degree of glory to another: for this comes from the Lord who is the Spirit." Evidently Zinzendorf saw a parallel between what happens in the Christian life and what happened in the origin of Scripture, namely, that both reflect the glory of Christ.

He explained this term (here *catoptrischen Gesichte*)[15] in one of the sermons on the Litany of the Wounds as something seen by reflection. Because of the illustration he used here (and because of the reference to reflection in the face in 2 Corinthians 3) *Gesichte* here could mean a "face which reflects or is reflected."[16] The reflected image is a picture of a face which is in pieces: an ear is where the forehead should be and the chin is where the eye should be; it is not together and it is not whole.[17] Thus the reflection is not clear and organized. A Christian's knowledge will remain limited in this fashion until the new heavens and earth.

It would seem that Zinzendorf was also affected by Paul's treatment of knowledge in 1 Corinthians 13:8ff., though the verb *katoptrizomai* (κατοπτρίζομαι) does not appear here. Vs. 12 reads, "For now we see in a mirror dimly, but then face to face. Now I know in part; then I shall understand fully, even as I have been fully understood." The first clause in Greek is *blepomen gar arti di esoptrou en ainigmati* (βλέπομεν γὰρ ἄρτι δι' ἐσόπτρου ἐν αἰνίγματι). *Ainigma* gives us *enigma* in English and means a "dark saying" or "riddle." Thus the Greek literally means that we now see in a mirror enigmatically or confusedly. This is what Zinzendorf described.

No System but Christ

Contrary to the attempts of Lutheran scholastic theology, or those of the rationalists in his day, it is not possible to construct a theological or philosophical system, much less to find one in Scripture. Scripture has no system but Christ, and he is its system because he is the person and revealer who is behind all religious truth.

The Holy Spirit will not have that there should be another system than in Christ. The Bible is an image seen in reflection (*catoptrisches*

---

[15] *Gesichte* means sight, vision, face, countenance.

[16] Note that the Greek verb, *katoptrizomai*, can be seen as middle or passive.

[17] Zinzendorf, *Vier und Dreyßig Homiliae*, p. 336 (13 Aug. 1747).

Bild). As soon as the Savior and his person is set upon it, so is everything together. And where the Savior and his person is lacking, there the head and all members are scattered. And whoever would bring out of the Bible a system beyond and besides that of the person of the Savior, I'll let him pass for a master of all masters, if he does not at the same time become a fool to all people with understanding. Therefore there are so many apparent contradictions and mistakes. For if the Savior is not set upon it, so everything sounds different and one does not know what it should mean. But as soon as one views the Bible from the perspective of the Savior, everything fits together.[18]

In commenting upon 1 Corinthians 15, a chapter that frequently troubled him, he noted that there is yet contained there a very precious verse (vs. 55) and he observed how much would have been lost if this chapter were not in the Bible.

I am quite pleased today to become a sinner. I had all sorts of *desiderata* [concerns] in mind about the subtlety of the fifteenth chapter of the first letter to the Corinthians;* but little more than a quarter hour after that I got to thinking a little about the matter of sin and of the protection into which our Savior takes us. Then a verse fell into my mind which I have always considered to be a chief text in the matter and which is from 1 Corinthians 15. Then I thought, it would not be good if this chapter did not stand in the Bible. And so it often happens, and that is the proof as to why the Holy Spirit has let everything be mixed together, even *in Biblicis* [in biblical matters] as it was there said of wheat *in hoc tertio* [in this comparison] "Let both grow together" because very many valuable grains lie among the less esteemed straw, so that if persons who don't understand come and want to make things pure, they would sweep away the good with the bad. So both must remain together; afterwards those with understanding come and seek out of them their concern (thing); for it lies there, it lies there for the seeker who seeks with the longing of his heart: meanwhile others stop with the shell and spring upon it. . . . Now that this may become quite clear, I will once more repeat this fine text, the carbuncle in the writings of Paul, which stands in the fifteenth chapter of the first epistle to the Corinthians, which is otherwise to me mysterious and quite dark.
     * I am sometimes affected by Paul's epistles as St. Peter was, they are difficult for me to understand. I am well protected from this

[18] Minutes of the 1750 Synod, quoted in *Spangenbergs Apologetische Schluß-Schrift*, p. 643. Zinzendorf used the phrase *catoptrisches Bild* in this passage.

danger of the characteristic which this holy Apostle has ascribed to the writings of Paul, because I am intimately acquainted with the *Fontibus* (sources) from which Paul wrote. But I still sometimes remain at a loss about the most immediate meaning of a passage.[19]

Zinzendorf once commented that he was not sure why Scripture was this way, but perhaps it is, as Paul indicates in 1 Corinthians 1, that God chose foolishness to confound the wise of the world. The only thing that really matters is that through it people be able to enter into the sacristy of God's truths.

Why Holy Scripture is composed in this way, as far as externals are concerned, so that one no longer finds a book of this type in the world, that I don't know. The Savior and the Holy Spirit must have had a very important and secret reason for that which he does not feel compelled to explain. We can make a few remarks about that. The Apostle Paul said: Because the world has not known him in its wisdom, so it pleased God to save through foolish preaching, to dress the dear divine truths in purely ridiculous matters, so that it should appear laughable to the world. Therefore one can draw some further conclusions and think: the dear God must not have been very much concerned about the sort of external form and culture in which the book appeared. If only it is revealed to the hearts of his people who are declared worthy to enter into the *penetralia*, into the sacristy of his truths, those who have a right to the *Schechina* if only they also believe: it is certainly true, it is his Word. Therefore I don't get exercised over needing to explain to the brothers and sisters why the Bible is written as it is written.[20]

His approach to Scripture is then different from that of the theologians who look for a coherent system:

There arose the difference which we have with theologians over our judgment on Scripture, that we hold its mistakes and lack for pure beauties, but they think if a book does not systematically hang

[19] Nikolaus Ludwig von Zinzendorf, *Ein und zwanzig Discurse über die Augspurgische Confession gehalten vom 15. Dec. 1747. bis zum 3. Mart. 1748. denen Seminariis Theologicis Fratrum zum Besten auf gefaßt und bis zur nochmaligen Revision des Auctoris einstweilen mitgetheilet* (n.p., n.d.), pp. 168-69 (7 Jan. 1748). (Abbreviated in subsequent notes as Zinzendorf, *Ein und zwanzig Discurse* [Title page: *Discurse . . . Auctoris*].) For information about the two different printings of this work, see chapter 1, note 82.

[20] MS 11, 5 Jan. 1748, quoted in Samuel Eberhard, *Kreuzes-Theologie: Das reformatorische Anliegen in Zinzendorfs Verkündigung* (Munich: Kaiser, 1937), pp. 12f. (Abbreviated in subsequent notes as Eberhard, *Kreuzes-Theologie.*)

together it is a great mistake. One must not say of the Bible that one should find in its chapters and verses and ideas (openly contrary to the nature of a letter) a coherency and get out of them a system, cost what it will. That comes from the point of view that they have established, that it belongs to the nature of a beautiful, real and solid writing that it has a material nexus which one can philosophically demonstrate. The connection in the heart, the connection of central thoughts, is something else. There the Bible most exquisitely hangs together. Indeed, there one can prove the superiority of this divine book above all which we poor humans are able to create.[21]

The Economies of God

Understanding Scripture to be historically conditioned, Zinzendorf divided the history with which Scripture deals into "Economies." He used the German noun *Ökonomie* and the adjective *ökonomisch*, derived from the Greek ὀικονομία (transliterated *oikonomia*), meaning "administration" or "dispensation." The term for Zinzendorf indicated a period in history when God relates to humanity in a particular way. It might well be translated "dispensation," but this is avoided here so that his views are not misread as Dispensationalism. Each period then has its own *sensus numinis* (sense of the numinous) and its own *systema theologicum* (theological system). What matters is not the completeness of one's knowledge, but rather one's obedience to what in one's time is presented to the eyes of the mind and heart.[22]

As to the source of Zinzendorf's derivation of the term *Ökonomie*, Samuel Eberhard suggested that this may have come from Zinzendorf's acquaintance with the Federal Theologians (*foedus* = covenant), such as Cocceius, Vitringa, and Lampe. However, the division of history into periods was not unique with the Federal Theologians. Bengel did the same. Eberhard indicated that there is, however, a basic difference between Cocceius' and Zinzendorf's use of the idea of Economies.[23] Cocceius stressed more of the idea of the growth and broadening of the

---

[21] Records of the 1748 Synod at Krausche, quoted in Eberhard, *Kreuzes-Theologie*, p. 7.

[22] Nikolaus Ludwig von Zinzendorf, *Der Predigten die der Ordinarius Fratrum von Anno 1751. bis 1755. zu London gehalten hat, Zweyter Band, Nebst Einem Anhange einiger an Englische Brüder-Gemeinen gehaltenen Homilien* (London and Barby: Zu finden bey dem Seminario Theologico, 1757), sec. 4, pp. 35f. (24 May 1752). (Abbreviated in subsequent notes as Zinzendorf, *Der Predigten zu London gehalten* [Londoner Predigten, vol. 2].)

[23] Eberhard, *Kreuzes-Theologie*, pp. 32f.

knowledge of God in the stages of revelation. For Zinzendorf this was not so. The essence or substance of revelation, the Savior and his atonement, is always the same because it is bound up with the Person behind revelation, who is always the same. But the person of the Savior addresses each Economy in particular, in ways that are right for it. Though there is growth from one period to another, that which primarily characterizes each period is the entrance of the Savior into that particular time in history with methods pertinent to that time, offering in that time an experience of the truth of which humanity is capable at that moment. Thus each Economy remains an entity unto itself, besides pointing to what is to come. Each period has the theology which is right for its time. The limitations of each Economy are not due to the Savior's inability to reveal truth more fully, nor are they due merely to the human inability to experience truth more fully, although the Savior has taken this last item into consideration. It is rather due to the fact that the Savior chooses to reveal within the terms of the moment of time in which people live. Thus, in contradistinction to Rationalism, truth as it is known is always intensely personal and historical. It is never abstract, truth in itself. It is always truth "for us."

Bengel, as previously mentioned, also divided history into periods, but contrary to Zinzendorf he saw the contribution of each period as cumulative (each time adding to the next) rather than uniquely addressed to inhabitants of each period. His discussion of the revelatory action of God in the succeeding stages of biblical history helped lay the foundation for the *Heilsgeschichte* (Salvation-History) view of biblical history. In the *Ordo Temporum* he said:

> What God teaches we must by all means learn, one thing after another. Step by step God advances in revealing the secrets of his kingdom. What is given to each age by God must be appropriated by the saints. Nothing more must they take to themselves, they must receive nothing less.[24]

Zinzendorf divided history into three to five basic Economies, depending upon whether he considered the period of the Law and that of the Patriarchs as separate Economies. In a sermon quoted by Eberhard from a manuscript, Zinzendorf gave three divisions:

> The first Economy has to do with the invisible God. The Jews were excellent in that they were the teachers of the nations which had to

[24] Johann Albrecht Bengel, *Ordo Temporum*, quoted in Charles T. Fritsch, "Bengel, the Student of Scripture," *Interpretation* 5 (April, 1951): p. 212.

do with the invisible God whom they knew in creation and from whom they received daily blessings. The new Economy has to do with the same God, but in the form of a suffering man, and this knowledge of his divinity which the holy Apostles had received from his wounds (for they knew no word previously that he was God) they had not discovered . . . in the thirty years of his life; but as soon as Thomas looked into the nail marks . . . he had found in the wounds his Lord and his God. And in language they afterwards expressed: God has redeemed the church with his own blood. Therefore, if we want to describe God, our God, the God with us, if we want to describe the creator of all things, so we describe him in his bodily, visible person, with his holy wounds, until he comes. Then a third Economy may arrive.[25]

In the minutes of the Synod of 1750 a discussion is recorded wherein Zinzendorf divided the Old Testament Economy into the Economies of the Law and the Patriarchs. However, it should be noted that, like Paul in Galatians 3, he regarded the Mosaic period as inferior to the period of the Patriarchs and also regarded the period of the Patriarchs as closer to the New Testament than the Economy of the Law.

Ord. [Zinzendorf]. The economy of the Law is poorer than the previous. For with that the appearance of God ceased. From then on everything happened through visions and through the *Schechina*.

L. Therefore the followers of Cocceius say: The time before the Law is closer to the New Testament than the time of the Law. Ord. Excellent. The Jewish people had for 400 years no longer believed in the right God, and had almost forgotten him. Then a quite new way of doing things began. The Patriarchal Economy was forgotten over 400 years, and the new one was much weaker. Then Moses was the only one who still had what was similar to the old style.[26]

Zinzendorf also spoke of times which were distinguished from Economies. In the following quotation Economies are distinguished by covenants:

There are three covenants, that is, that of the Patriarchs, the Law, and the Marriage of Souls. There are more times (than this): for

---

[25] Zinzendorf, sermon, 1750, quoted in Eberhard, *Kreuzes-Theologie*, p. 30.

[26] Minutes of the 1750 Synod, session 8, question 98, quoted in *Spangenbergs Apologetische Schluß-Schrift*, pp. 591-92.

example, 1. the condition of innocence, 2. the status at the time of the Flood, 3. that up to the covenant with Abraham . . . , 4. the Economy of the Law introduced by Moses with wonders and signs . . . , 5. the royal Economy . . . , 6. the epoch of the prophets. . . . The Savior had found everything in the greatest confusion, brought the Law to an end, and began the Soul Economy.[27]

Even though Zinzendorf stated that he was making a distinction between times and the major Economies, one can readily see by his terminology that he was not following a carefully thought-out system of describing religious history. To be so systematic would be somewhat contrary to his whole approach to things. He was not delineating a system, but rather portraying an understanding of the nature of revelation. If it were necessary to enumerate the major Economies, one might outline them as:

1. The Economy of the invisible God, divided into
   a. The Economy of the Patriarchs, characterized by appearances of God (Christ)
   b. The Economy of the Law, when God (Christ) was not so personally known
2. The Economy of the New Covenant, when knowledge of God comes in the form of his suffering Son and which is followed with the giving of the Spirit
3. The final Economy, when Christ will return

Of this last Economy Zinzendorf characteristically said little, feeling that eschatology is one of the mysteries about which one cannot publicly speak.

Zinzendorf also noted successive stages in revelation within the New Testament, as well as within the Old, and lamented the fact that the truths in the Bible are not arranged systematically or *ökonomisch* (according to their historical order). The Bible is more an archives than a chronicle. Many times one finds a truth in the clearest light, then turns over twenty pages, and finds the same truth in darkness as it was expressed some twenty years before its revelation. Therefore the two passages seem to be in opposition. In the Old Testament this did not happen quite so much. There all stands in shadow. In the New Testament the Acts was written in the old ideas held at the time of the ascension. The Gospel of John was written after all the epistles and is their continuation and conclusion. It presents the whole theology with a clarity which even the letters of the apostles do not have. Though it may appear that sometimes the epistles contradict or say less than John, the

[27] Eberhard, *Kreuzes-Theologie*, pp. 31f. (1747).

truth is that John explains all the epistles.[28]   Though Paul's is the
standard theology, the final truth is in the Gospel of John, for in it John
again brought to the fore the already set-aside teaching of Paul regarding justification and the divinity of Christ, otherwise Paul would have
been forgotten.[29] Acts, Paul, and John seem to represent three levels of
revelation in the New Testament.

In his *Nine Public Lectures* Zinzendorf commented:

> It is one of the greatest pleasures to read the Bible according to the
> epochs, according to the periods, according to the stages by which
> the preaching of the Gospel has from time to time been growing
> and ascending. If one starts with the thirties, after the Savior's
> birth, down to the nineties, and keeps this development in sight
> and meditates upon it in a simple and childlike way, then one sees
> what Paul means by saying, "That your love may abound more and
> more, with knowledge and all discernment (Phil. 1:9), that there-
> after you may make such progress that you will measure the length,
> the breadth, depth and height of things" (Ephesians 3:18, alt.).
> You will also be able to speak as plainly of the profoundest mysteries
> of God your Lord as if they were catechism questions. Then you will
> have to stand and say at last, "It is good that Jesus is my Creator and
> my God, that He is the God over everything." But what an observa-
> tion this is, that my Creator has laid down His life for me! All your
> theology, all your theosophy, insight and knowledge will be caught
> up in this as the central point; all of this will run together into the
> wounded heart of Jesus, it will disappear and be lost in love.
> Nothing greater, nothing higher can be thought of. John, full of
> the eternal power and majesty of his God, full of the *causa causarum*,
> full of the *logos* of the Godhead who was in the beginning and was
> with God and was Himself God; "all things were made through
> Him, and without Him was not anything made that was made"
> (John 1:3); full of these stupendous ideas, says, "Jesus Christ has
> loved us and washed us of our sins with His blood" (Rev. 1:5) And
> when he portrays the majestic hours in heaven, the great disclo-
> sures of the heavenly revelations; when he describes the temple of
> God open in heaven and the ark of the covenant; when thunder
> and lightening and trumpets of angels are heard, and hosts which

[28] Minutes of the 1750 Synod, quoted in *Spangenbergs Apologetische Schluß-Schrift*, pp.
475f.

[29] Diarium des Jüngerhauses, 23 Aug. 1754, quoted in Otto Uttendörfer, *Zinzendorf
und die Mystik* (Berlin: Christlicher Zeitschriften Verlag, [1952]), p. 352. (Citation of
the Uttendörfer work will be abbreviated in subsequent notes as Uttendörfer, *Zinzendorf
und die Mystik*.)

no one can number are seen: then their song is, "You have bought us with Your blood!" (Rev. 5:9, alt.)[30]

Zinzendorf made various attempts in his biblical translations to help persons grasp the way Scripture reflected the historical periods of its origins. The most striking was his rearrangement of the order of the books in the second edition of his translation of the New Testament. The Gospel of John was placed first, since it was the culmination of the faith expressions of the early church and therefore served as the key to understanding the whole New Testament and the process which produced its literature. The rest of the books were arranged according to the order of their historical origin, while James, Jude, 2 John, and 3 John were omitted.[31] His *Enchiridion* should also be noted, a work of his late years. Though by his death he only was as far as Exodus 31, it was his intention to produce a handbook from the whole Bible for daily use, leaving out repetitions and genealogies and abbreviating those things which are already past or concern the Jews only. It was entitled, *Enchiridion, i.e., The Main-Sum of the Whole Holy Scripture Brought Together into a Handbook, with the Greatest Possible Retention of the Words of the Book.*[32]

Distinctions in the Content of Scripture

The nature of Scripture indicated that there were inspired and uninspired portions and that each writer wrote according to his style,

[30] Nikolaus Ludwig von Zinzendorf, *Nine Public Lectures On Important Subjects in Religion Preached in Fetter Lane Chapel in London in the Year 1746*, trans. and ed. George W. Forell (Iowa City: University of Iowa Press, 1973), pp. 39-40 (6 Sept. 1746).

[31] Nikolaus Ludwig von Zinzendorf, *Eines Abermaligen Versuchs zur Übersetzung Der Historischen Bücher Neuen Testaments Unsers Herrn Jesu Christi aus dem Original Erste Probe Zweyte Edition Von den vorigen Schreib- Druck- und andern Fehlern gebessert* (Büdingen: Joh. Christoph Stöhr, 1744). *Eines Abermahligen Versuchs zur Übersetzung Der Lehr- und Prophetischen Bücher Neuen Testaments unsers Herrn Jesu Christi aus dem Original Erste Probe zweyte Edition Worinnen die meisten besagter Lehr-Bücher befindlich sind, Von den vorigen Schreib- Druck- und andern Fehlern gebessert* (Büdingen: Joh. Christoph Stöhr, 1746). These two were later bound together into one and published together. The same arrangement that is to be found in this second edition of the New Testament is to be found in a rebound copy of Bengel's Greek text, used by Zinzendorf, and now residing in the Herrnhut Archives. In the afterword [*Nachrede*] to the 1746 edition of the *Lehr- und Prophetischen Bücher* Zinzendorf comments (pages in the afterword are not numbered) that he omitted James, Jude, 2 John, and 3 John because he was not inclined to revise Luther's translation. However, his attitude to James was much the same as Luther's, and these books had difficulty finding their way into the canon of the early church. Thus one might guess that his motivation might have been other than stated.

[32] Zinzendorf's work is entitled *Enchiridion das ist, die Haupt-Summa Der ganzen Heil. Schrift, in ein Hand-Büchlein gebracht, mit möglichster Beybehaltung der Worte des Buchs* ([London]: n.p., 1752). This was only on Genesis. The *Des Seligen Ordinarii Fratrum letzte Bibel-Arbeit im Alten Testamente* (n.p., [1760]) expanded this into the thirty-first chapter of Exodus and was published after his death.

expressive of the issues of his context. This rendered very complex the whole matter of biblical interpretation, something that will be discussed later. It was this very complexity that encouraged the scholarly study of Scripture in which Zinzendorf engaged. Yet he believed that Christianity at its heart was simple and that it was for everyone, not only the educated and the scholars, though the congregation would need a great deal of help in how to handle it. God must have provided for some things to be clear and simple, though this was not true of everything.

Zinzendorf formulated the idea that the truths of Scripture could be seen according to three categories.

In the *Pennsylvania Sermons* he said:

The Apostle said in 1 Corinthians 12:8, "To one it is given to speak from wisdom." That is the one gift. "To another it is given to speak from knowledge." That is the second gift. Now no more gifts appear. For to know the Basic Truths (*Grund-Wahrheiten*) is no special gift: no one has it alone, but all must have it, otherwise they could not be saved.

Therefore the Apostle said: I busy myself to present complete each person, in Christ and knowledge. Colossians 1:28. Each person of God must be gifted for every good work through Scripture. 2 Timothy 3:17. The knowledge of the glory of God in the face of Jesus Christ is for all humanity. This same knowledge is called Basic Truths.

But that which is only for the wise and skillful, and for the educated (although only those that are of God), one calls Knowledge (*Erkenntnis*).

And for the sort of people that God has gifted not only with understanding but especially with the deep insight into his divine Mysteries (*Geheimnisse*), that is called the gift of wisdom which is not for all people because not all could bear it. And therefore out of great faithfulness it is not given to all persons, but it is often held back. And that is the nature of divine Mysteries.[33]

Zinzendorf believed that one needs the gift of God, i.e., the Spirit and the relationship with the Savior, to understand Scripture at all, but to understand the *Basic Truths* one needs no *special* gift. Every Christian has what they need in this regard since Basic Truths have to do with one's salvation and they are essentially factual and historical in nature —

---

[33] Zinzendorf, *Offentlicher Reden 1742* [Pennsylvanische Reden], 2nd ed., 1:138-49 (7 Mar. 1742). (Full citation earlier in this chapter, at note 9.) Zinzendorf's reference to no more gifts appearing than wisdom and knowledge must mean no more in relationship to his concern, for more are mentioned in 1 Cor. 12.

having to do with Christ and the Atonement — and embody the experience of the Savior which is the core of the church's existence. The very act of God which saves one and the very presence of the person of God (the Savior) in the heart also grant the ability to understand the truth about salvation.

However, not everyone in the congregation is able to go beyond Basic Truths in interpretation. To go beyond this, the Spirit must bestow special gifts. To understand *Knowledge*, the second level of truth within Scripture, one must have certain skills, and thus there is a special place for the skilled interpreter in the life of the church. However, Zinzendorf did not understand the person able to deal with Knowledge as one who has merely acquired information and skills, but this was also a gift.

> Matters of Knowledge are divine truths which do not belong among deep matters, but exist in clear fashion in Scripture. Each person who reads Scripture industriously and basically thinks about it, can know well these matters of Knowledge. And it is a great blessing for a type of teaching, it is a gift of God to have all matters of Knowledge.[34]

The element of gift played a role because Zinzendorf saw understanding as a matter of knowing not merely the words and their historical meaning, but the realities to which they refer. Thus, having information is only a first step to knowing what a text is about.

Matters of Knowledge are materials in Scripture which are basically clear, but need explanation and are the affair of the teacher. Among them are such scriptural questions as the election of the Jews in Romans 9 and the problem of the relationship of the Law and Gospel.[35] It is within this area of passages needing explanation that the interpreter, teacher, and theologian do their work.

Although matters of Knowledge are clear in Scripture, they are not at first readily apparent, and differences of interpretation will result. One interpreter will stress one passage. Another will stress a different verse. One interpreter, therefore, must not force his interpretation on another, but should bear these religious differences in love and give the other as much time to understand as the Savior gave him.[36]

Mysteries are indeed difficult to understand and take a special gift above that needed for matters of Knowledge. Since this special insight is not granted to all, and since Mysteries are concerned with matters in Scripture the explanation of which is not possible from Scripture itself, several considerations should be observed:

[34] Ibid., p. 73.
[35] Ibid., pp. 73ff.
[36] Ibid., p. 77.

First, they are not necessary for all people. Second, one should not dispute about them, neither with Satan nor with the world nor with the children of God. Third, have patience with people who can't follow you. Fourth, no one should speak about understanding Mysteries which he does not understood, for he might misjudge the counsel of God and thereby deceive.

If one lets oneself be satisfied with Holy Scripture and presents the teachings about the Mysteries with the style of speaking and expressions that stand there, then it is all right. But if one wants to make clear the true form of the Mysteries, that is going too far. People to whom it is disclosed are astonished over it, but they know that it is not disclosed to everyone, and to each one just as much is given to know as one can bear.[37]

Mysteries included such matters as the nature of the presence of Christ in the Lord's Supper, the Trinity (insofar as its essential nature is concerned), and eternal election. If one sought to explain these, one would be venturing into the area of the metaphysical. In the last analysis, it "is no one's duty to explain such Mysteries, except the Holy Spirit's."[38]

The Clarity of Scripture

It has long been a Protestant principle that Scripture was basically clear and that clear understanding could be derived from it. Richard Simon, a Catholic who is considered the father of historical biblical criticism, in his *Histoire critique du vieux Testament* (1678), argued against the Protestant position. The Bible could not really be understood without the Christian tradition which supported it and helped interpret it. The Catholic Church has frequently reserved the Scriptures for those who are equipped to understand and urged interpretation which was responsible to the teaching authority of the church. The development of the complexities of modern criticism, as well as the recognized complexity of Scripture itself, have called attention to the lack of clarity within the Bible and the special training which is needed to understand. Even then, the scholars do not agree.

Zinzendorf showed sympathy with those who in the history of the church have taken the Bible out of the hands of the people because their respect for the Bible was such that they did not wish to see the Bible misused. In the *Sermons on the Litany of the Wounds* he made an extended statement on this:

[37] Ibid., p. 72.
[38] Ibid.

Thus there is a definite incorrectness in the esteem of Holy Scripture which is widespread. This is because some persons who want to be better and more intellectual than others have found many things to find fault with in Scripture (its expressions, stories, chronology) and in certain of its facts and sentences which contradict one another. Others have believed if they cannot assert and prove such matters as true, that black is white and no is yes, then the authority of the Holy Spirit has been destroyed. These have dealt with the *loca vexata* [problematic locations] (as they are called) in whole folios and have saved Scripture according to their understanding. However, because of this, all intelligent persons have become suspicious. Finally there are those persons who being responsible to the church have become impatient over all this and because they have seen that Holy Scripture is so violently and at the same time so inadequately defended, and they have not known how to defend it better, and partly because they have seen with their own eyes the misuse of Holy Scripture by dry minds (e.g., the books of Moses, the Song of Songs, several stories of David and the Patriarchs) as a secret scorn by people who treat these matters without Spirit—so they have finally forbidden that the Book be allowed in all human hands, have made it a holy thing and have closed it. The accusation has been brought against them that they did not want to let people know the truth, but I don't believe that was their purpose. They did it with good intent because they didn't know a remedy against the many misuses of the all too dull and pretentious reader and therefore rather made it into a holy thing, set apart, and wanted it to be higher than the people so that they could not tread it under foot. That is their true reason.

On the other hand, in our Protestant Church, especially in a certain part of it, some have sought to make the Holy Scripture so common and from time to time have published news of how many thousand copies have been distributed. They have made people feel that it was a duty to read it and have made it a duty for the general populace not only to have it at home but also to bring it into many hands.[39]

Finally, in recent times a type of Bible reading has arisen where people believe that if they don't read so and so many chapters a day, they would not be Christian. I cannot deny that I do not consider the reason why the Bible was taken out of the hands of the people the

[39] Evidently a criticism of Halle, where there was a large enterprise to print Bibles and religious books.

reason for which those who hold this opinion are accused. I also have not been able to consent in my heart to the manner and way the Bible is treated and read. The cause if this: Holy Scripture is in my and the Brethren's eyes the true Word of God. . . .

We are invited to the Spirit of Scripture, and he who does not have the Spirit, about this person the Apostle says: It is impossible that he can understand it, for understanding must occur under the direction of the Spirit; the spiritual person discerns everything and no one can lay any charge upon him, no one can dispute him on anything.[40]

In one of his apologetic writings Spangenberg put to Zinzendorf a question on the darkness of Scripture, and the answer which Zinzendorf gave seemed to be a bit too much for Spangenberg, so that he felt the need of qualifying it by another quotation from Zinzendorf which asserted the essential clarity of Scripture. Zinzendorf's reply was, in effect, that he who has read Scripture cannot help being aware of the problems of understanding it.

Who finds no dark places in Scripture, he must not read it very well. And who then believes that all points over which theologians reason hang so systematically together, as the eighty different schools believe, each according to their understanding, he must be able to believe eighty contrary things. And who does not want to be content with the insufficiency even of the knowledge of the Ortho-dox, to this person must the approach of Paul in 1 Corinthians 13 be dark, for he places our whole knowledge in darkness. Indeed, he must, contrary to Peter, who calls Paul's manner of speaking δυσκόλους [*duskolous* - difficult], still admit the experience: the theologians not only from Christ to Luther, but even the Lutherans since Luther, every year produce something new for the clearing up of Scripture.[41]

This problem of the historical nature of Scripture and its lack of clarity, except in Basic Truths, caused Zinzendorf to engage extensively in biblical translation. His attempts at a new translation of the New Testament and his work on an *Enchiridion* of the whole Bible have already been mentioned.

His advice to people seeking to understand was to begin with the Gospel of John, which really offered the key to the whole process of biblical revelation. Of course, understanding John meant understanding the Savior

---

[40] Zinzendorf, *Vier und Dreyßig Homiliae*, pp. 141-44 (18 June 1747).

[41] *Spangenbergs Apologetische Schluß-Schrift*, p. 146. The text that Zinzendorf refers to, 2 Pet. 3:15-16, contains the word δυσνόητα (difficult to understand) in all Greek editions I reviewed instead of δυσκόλους (difficult).

who is also our Creator, and so what one brings to Scripture is not so much the theology of John as the Person of the Savior as portrayed in John. "The Holy Spirit will not allow that there be another system other than that in Christ. The Bible is a 'Catoptrisches Bild' (an image that is reflected). As soon as the Savior and his Person is set upon it, so all is together."[42]

If one wants to make a decision about which of Jesus' words in the Gospels are actually Jesus' words, Zinzendorf advised making the decision according to the Gospel of Matthew, for Matthew was the only one of the Synoptists who personally heard Jesus' words.[43] Zinzendorf may have felt comfortable with this because Matthew has a high Christology, and such a passage as Matthew 11:25-30, often called a Johannine thunderbolt in the Synoptic sky, presents Jesus in a Johannine fashion.

Another approach to gain clarity is what he called his "Wounds Hermeneutic":

If only the words which one reads, which the prophets and apostles have spoken, are sprinkled with the wounds, if one reads them in the wounds-light, then one reads quite another Bible, another New Testament, other sayings than one read before this. And a person who during his life has learned no Greek or Hebrew, can see into the true, pure meaning and can observe and become such an exegete through his wounds-hermeneutic. If he had sweated twenty years over the original text, so would he have gained a lot of wind, a lot of probabilities, a lot of scruples in his head, and would have become half a rabbi; but he would have gained darkness from that, he would have more error than before, more uncertainty than before, he would have learned that he knew nothing, that would have been the whole effect. But as soon as he began to get the wound-vision (i.e., seeing from the perspective of the wounds) and understand the mystery that a Lamb was slain, and that the Lamb is his Creator; then is everything clear before his eyes according to which he can know the natural language of Holy Scripture, that which belongs to the heart. Then he knows that can be so, that can not be so, that can have the meaning, that cannot have the meaning: that he knows with certainty, so that he does not have to fear being misled and cannot be deceived by any commentary, however skillful it is. He has the text, he knows how one must test the Word, in what sort of light the truth must appear, if it is truth. And if to him a little saying, a text, an old word, a biblical word comes to attention, which he holds with the wounds, so he says: you

[42] Minutes of the 1750 Synod, quoted in *Spangenbergs Apologetische Schluß-Schrift*, p. 643.

[43] *Spangenbergs Apologetische Schluß-Schrift*, p. 493.

are God's Word, you are the word of my Lord, I hear my dear Lord
speaking, yes, that is the truth, it is as if I heard him speak; I feel that
that is the meaning, it harmonizes with his ideas, for I have his mind
(*Sinn*), I have seen him, I have seen his royal law which he has in my
heart, I have studied it, I have studied the law that he had made: to
die for my sins. And he has fulfilled that to the last iota, through
which he freed me from all bonds and established me and created
me to be a little cross-bird.[44]

Besides his New Testament translation and the *Enchiridion*, he
engaged in many other attempts at Bible translation, one of the most
significant being his "Story of the Days of the Son of Man upon Earth
Extracted from the Four Gospels." Two editions were published during
his later years (1757 and 1759). This provided Moravians with a
harmony of the Gospels without the problems inherent in viewing four
Gospels. From this a Passion Story was derived (earliest version in 1769)
which could be read privately and in church services. In its presently
revised North American form it is now called *Readings for Holy Week*
(formerly the *Passion Week Manual*) and is used in Moravian churches
from Palm Sunday to Easter.[45]

Another approach was to limit extensive Bible reading only to those
who were equipped to do so. This withdrawing of the Bible as a whole
from the majority of the church was to be continued only until they were
strong enough in the kernel of Scripture, and then he would again
restore the whole of Scripture to them.[46] This is one of the reasons why
the Daily Texts or Watchwords became so important in the church.
These Daily Texts were selected verses of Scripture, accompanied by
interpretive hymn verses, which would not be misleading or confusing
to the congregation because they were removed from context. Such
verses, apart from contextual issues, then could become daily watchwords through which the Savior might work in a direct way.

Simplicity and Scripture

For Zinzendorf Scripture had about it a simplicity, in spite of its
complexity. This is because the process which produced it is so simple
that it reflects the reality with which it deals, rather than hiding it.

[44] Zinzendorf, *Vier und Dreyßig Homiliae*, p. 362f. (13 Aug. 1747).
[45] Nikolaus Ludwig von Zinzendorf, *Die Geschichte der Tage des Menschen-Sohns auf
erden aus den vier Evangelisten zusammen gezogen. Zweyte Edition.* [2nd ed.] (Barby: n.p.,
1759).
[46] Diarium des Jüngerhauses, 17 Feb. 1756, quoted in Uttendörfer, *Zinzendorf und
die Mystik*, p. 351.

Zinzendorf's description of scriptural language was much like what in linguistic analysis is called primary language. It is not language carefully thought out, but borrowed from the culture to reflect the reality experienced. Thus its purpose is not to provide language for careful and critical analysis, but to reflect the original reality.

Zinzendorf saw God working simply with the writers of Scripture, letting them write as they were able, and the writers of Scripture responding from the heart rather than the head, i.e., responding from their intuitive perception of the reality about which they spoke, avoiding the interjection of their own artistry and creativity. So Zinzendorf said:

> The reader then has there [in the Bible] what the listener had, and that distinguishes Holy Scripture from all that is called scripture and book. Whoever heard this talk, will scarcely recognize it on paper, and it is still quite well written down. But what one should read that would have the ability to stir one, must be written out of the heart; and what one should hear with effect, must be spoken out of the heart.[47]

In the minutes of the Synod of 1750 Zinzendorf had been discussing his views on spiritual books. He pointed out that the Herrnhut Diary is of a different nature from other books, and then went on to indicate that Scripture is of the same type, for it brings a *viva vox* [living voice].

> For the Herrnhut Diary is also a book, but therein distinguished from others, because it contains a *vivam vocem* [living voice], which condition also distinguishes Holy Scripture from other books. For it is by and large constituted by spoken material which was written down: and minutes of spoken material are very different from that which one ordinarily calls a book: not *sensu volumnis* [in the sense of a volume], but *scripti* [of something written]. If one wants to quibble about the word "book," then everything is a book which is bound. But as one opposes *vivam vocem* to a book, one truly opposes minutes to τὸ γραμμά [to *gramma* - what is written]. This former contains words which have come out of the fullness of the heart at the moment and out of the ideas presented and keeps them for those who have not heard what was said.
> But if one writes a book, so one thinks and reflects on what one will write. There is something dangerous in writing. For one may be so ambitious that he does not want to write what other people can

---

[47] Nikolaus Ludwig von Zinzendorf, *Eine Predigt Vom Geheimniß der Religion, Über die Worte Es geschah, daß er mit dem Tode rang, und betete hefftiger. Es war sein Schweiß wie Bluts-Tropffen die fielen auf die Erde. Luc 22,44. Aus erheblichen Ursachen dem Druck überlassen* (Frankfurt and Basel: Johann Brandmüller, Jünger, 1740). From the foreword [Vorrede] (pages not numbered).

harm. Thus he twists his whole book, only to avoid being criticized and still have the honor that one has written something, but not with the intention that people really learn something.[48]

The purpose of Scripture is to put us in touch with the living voice behind it and the person of the Savior. It is important to keep from being caught up in its complexities. In fact, if improperly used, Scripture may get in the way of the Savior, and that must be avoided.

> Only the Word itself must not get in the way of the true and close connection with him. That this can happen the Savior says: "You seek, he says, in Scripture, and you think to find therein eternal life, and it is that which witnesses of me; but you don't want to come to me," John 5:39-40. He presupposes then that the use of the Word, and industrious studying in Scripture, can certainly get in the way of and interrupt fellowship with him, and of that he warns. For he always remains the main matter: the speaker is above his word and never against his own word. . . . The reading and studying in the Bible, the consideration of Scripture must never be made by us equal to the fellowship which we should and can have with our God and Savior in person.[49]

Anointing

It is interesting that Zinzendorf provided for a personal interaction with the Savior which results in individual and differing theological expression, most but not all of which is scriptural:

> There [in matters of the soul] each soul addresses itself immediately to the Savior and allows their theological slip of paper which is prepared for them to be filled out by him and no one else. The greatest part of this slip of paper or memorial is pure Bible. That all people have equally who hold to the Savior. There Christianity is, in a sense, the same. But what constitutes the especially distinguishing mark between the Savior and the soul, that the Savior now speaks with me and not with you, and then another time acts with you and not with me; there no one must be consulted but him.[50]

---

[48] Minutes of the 1750 Synod, quoted in *Spangenbergs Apologetische Schluß-Schrift*, p. 456.

[49] Zinzendorf, *Der Predigten zu London gehalten* [Londoner Predigten, vol. 2], sec. [Abtheilung]4, pp. 85f. (18 Oct. 1752).

[50] Ibid., p. 341 (22 Sept. 1754).

The Savior thus does not merely relate to us in terms of the Bible, though our "theological slip of paper" is for the most part pure Bible. The relationship is personal and so not only goes beyond the Bible, but also differs from person to person. Since Zinzendorf interpreted the ascension of Jesus in the light of Hebrews 10:12, where Jesus takes his rest in heaven, this conversation with the Savior is usually mediated through the Spirit, who functions like a Mother, to keep the family aware of the Husband and "Father" who is away. Zinzendorf spoke of this in terms of "anointing," as in 1 John.

> When the Gospel is set forth, then begins the anointing which gives each one his light, his portion of insight which is holy to him, which exercises itself upon this holy ground. And upon this ground (for no other foundation can anyone lay, 1 Corinthians 3:11) each one builds his own system; for each one must have his own practical system, each one must be able to speak for himself. That he learned out of the Savior's heart. . . . In John we have an example, that one leaned on his breast, and if one asks he can get the answer to his question.[51]

In the Herrnhut Diary *anointing* is defined as "partaking in his Spirit, which makes us sensitive to what is true and that harmonizes with Holy Scripture."[52] The last comment is important. Zinzendorf always affirmed Scripture as the final arbiter as to the legitimacy of what was perceived to be the leading of the Spirit.

> But we can be certain whether each matter is truth or whether it only seems so and is a leading of our nature; for this we have the Word in the sayings of the Savior and the apostles and their conduct. There we see their whole plan and become acquainted with it.
> If the devil now wishes to deceive us or to trip us up through reason; then it offends the general plan, it does not conform to Scripture, and then we extricate ourselves and see always the way before us.
> There is a continual *rapport* with the Word of God, and through that things go well.[53]

[51] Ibid., p. 342.
[52] Diarium des Jüngerhauses, 18 Sept. 1750, quoted in Uttendörfer, *Zinzendorf und die Mystik*, p. 87.
[53] *Des Herrn Grafen Ludwig von Zinzendorff Sieben Letzte Reden So Er In der Gemeine, Vor seiner am 7. Aug. erfolgten abermahligen Abreise nach America, gehalten. Denen noch beygefügt sind zwey in Gelnhausen von demselben gehaltene und ehemals einzeln gedruckte Predigten* (Büdingen: Johann Christoph Stöhr, 1743), p. 22 (18 June 1741).

In the Synod of 1750 he further defined the relationship of anointing and Scripture. Anointing and feeling (the perceived effect of anointing) can be the norm of faith and life where *in thesi* nothing is determined or decreed; or it can be the norm in the application of that which is already biblically decreed. If something is in the Bible, no one can call on feeling against that. However, the definition of the Bible is difficult. Is Habakkuk the Bible, or only a piece of it? And must not all the pieces be together, standing in their right place, if the Bible is to be used? Because of the problems caused by the makeup of the Bible, feeling may come to one's help in determining the interpretation of a passage which is not clear or may be merely suited to a particular historical period.[54]

The School of the Holy Spirit

The function of the Holy Spirit in the church is to care for the Savior's family and to help them in their growth in truth and life. The church becomes a school of the Spirit.

For Zinzendorf, faith started simply with the Savior. The Savior then

will tell you what family he is of, what Father he has; then will he explain to you what his Holy Spirit is. . . .

And when you have spiritually grasped it in general, he will send you afterwards into the *Repetition*-school with the Holy Spirit, who will then remind you of everything in *specie* [particular] which you heard from him [Jesus]. He will, as far as is necessary for you to know, pray the heavenly Father and keep the liturgy to the heavenly Father in your hearts, even if you yourself cannot find the words for it.

This is the consolation which we can give persons, our hearers from the world, who with their whole heart want to be blessed; although we do not *directe* [directly] preach the holy Trinity to them. Our little children, who are baptized in the name of the Father, of the Son, and of the Holy Spirit, who grow up where they were hatched (born from his side), who know to go nowhere else than to him, to whom a thousand *notiones* [ideas] of the world remain hidden, but who day and night live with the dear Lamb and are accustomed to live with him, adhering to him even in their third and fourth year with heart and mind, closer than to their own life (in a way

[54] Minutes of the 1750 Synod, quoted in *Spangenbergs Apologetische Schluß-Schrift*, pp. 471f.

in which it could not be brought about with great effort and *studio* [study] in fifty years if it happened by continual presentation or if one insisted upon bringing the matter into his mind mechanically), these little students of the Holy Spirit, I say, doubtless learn to become acquainted with their *Abba* and divine Mother too at the same Time, as soon as they are able to think — which is quite natural.[55]

Without the Spirit the inner life with God is not sustained and our attempts to express our faith do not come out right.

We know not only through revelation but through experience that the Holy Spirit is indescribably near us and stands in such a near *connexion* with our hearts that if we speak with the Savior and with the Father, if we pray and want to bring certain divine matters together which are over our *captum* [head], and yet occur, so he prays them for us: and if he does not pray them for us as we are accustomed to pray before our little children morning and evening prayers, nothing pertinent comes out of it for we ourselves do not know what we want: and if he does not put together for us the matters which we think and the words which we want to speak, it does not come out right.

It is not of significance that we have learned something, that we read it in a book, that we deduce it mathematically or have an admirable eloquence to bring matters to light: for as long as the Holy Spirit has not been present in it, as long as he has not formed the thoughts and words, as long as we do not owe the foundation and *stimulum* [impulse] to him; then an experienced child of God can immediately hear that what is there spoken, said, and asserted is not the language of the Holy Spirit, and consequently also no certain truth. And here may a person labor and toil as much as he will, and may he have the most incomparable *ingenium* [genius] and memory of the world, and have the best intention; yet, if he has not learnt it from the Holy Spirit, so there will always be a *sibilus*, and the time will never come for a *Shiboleth*.[56]

Theology starts simply with an experienced reality which can be described on a single page. One's theological manual must be filled out by God alone, and one does not have to know everything — only what God

[55] Zinzendorf, *Ein und zwanzig Discurse* [Title page: *Discurse . . . Auctoris*], pp. 66-67 (16 Dec. 1747).
[56] Ibid., pp. 156-57 (6 Jan. 1748). In Judges 12 the Gileadites tested the Ephraimites by their ability to pronounce this word.

provides. Not to know some things is permissible and does not matter greatly if one is in relationship with the source, the original.

> We have a principle that is different from the theologians: we believe that the whole theology, with which we can stand before all holy angels without shame, can be written upon an octave page with large letters. Who neglects this theology is without salvation in this time.
> That was the first point. The disciples allowed an ignorance. Today this is no longer allowed: one no longer ignores anything. One can not experience a matter other than at the source, at the original. Other guides, if they have honest intentions, cannot give one much of an answer which, by the distribution of ideas which happen by the inexpressible wisdom of God, should fill out the page so that my book is my manual. That no one can fill out oneself for one's use; each one must get it filled out by God alone. They will all be taught by God. John 6:45.[57]

He commented that the Holy Spirit always interprets the Bible as one does to a catechetical student, proceeding step by step. If the Savior gives one to understand something, it is as sweet as honey and the student rejoices greatly over it. But one must be patient. Theologians make the mistake of trying to understand everything at once.

Reflections

When Zinzendorf's understanding of Scripture is reviewed, it is difficult to avoid some sense of excitement about the breadth of his concerns, his appropriation of the thought and questions of his time, and the very personal way in which he integrated ideas and formulated answers. If we feel that he did not go far enough, it is important to recognize that most in his own time, even such scholars as Bengel, thought him far too radical. We cannot expect him to approach issues in the light of modern insights, but it is always amazing how modern he is.

With regard to Scripture he maintained the Protestant principle of *sola Scriptura* (Scripture alone), but his practice and understanding of this was different from many who claimed this principle. In an intriguing way he provided for the role of the Spirit, the contemporary experience of God, as a way of personalizing truth and growing in its meaning. There was provision for new revelation, but this was always very carefully held in

[57] Zinzendorf, *Der Predigten zu London gehalten* [Londoner Predigten, vol. 2], sec. [Abtheilung] 6, pp. 337f. (22 Sept. 1754).

tension with Scripture. This was the pattern of his developing understanding of the Spirit as Mother.

He affirmed the historical nature of Scripture, saw clearly the difficulties that this posed for understanding, and struggled with various ways by which the Bible could be more understandable and serve its purpose within the church. He became aware of the categories of truth within Scripture and the natural slowness with which the understanding of truth comes. Above all, he did not make salvation dependent upon the extent of biblical or theological knowledge. All that was needed was the relationship with the Savior. All else grew from that.

To reflect on the issues which arise out of this chapter means that the relationship of Scripture to other sources of truth needs exploration.

God and variety

The Christian faith has the gift of being a historical *religion* with rootage in historical events and a long tradition, but is also beset by the problems inherent in being a historical *religion*. It claims eternal truths and values while it confesses a special history which became embodied in Holy Scriptures (salvation history from Abraham to Christ, the life of Christ, and the history of the Spirit in the early church). The church's confession of history was complicated by the variety of responses and traditions embodied in its special tradition (Scripture) and the variety of responses and traditions which arose out of this in the history of the church.[58] Thus the experience of the church with variety, and even its inclusion within Scripture, ultimately made it difficult to identify eternal truth and values with any singular expression of it. The development of historical criticism has reconfronted the church with the variety it experienced in its origins and embraced in the development of the biblical canon.

The church in its ongoing proclamation and application of its truth and values has to contend not only with variety in its present context, but with the variety of its tradition. It needs to find some way of sorting out and affirming that which is eternal, formulating faith statements in a variety of contemporary contexts, and working on ethical issues complicated by ambiguous guidance from its tradition.

One solution to the sorting out of the eternal from the contingent is to listen seriously to what the Bible says about God as "person," which is a central

[58] This variety was encouraged by the church's move from Palestinian culture into the Greco-Roman world while its literature that was to become sacred was being produced. Accompanying this cultural change was the need to translate all of the information from Jesus from Aramaic into Greek, thus encouraging an interpretive handling of the tradition.

Zinzendorfian emphasis. The Person of God transcends all actions and expressions and remains a constant entity behind one's experience of God's action or reflection on God. Consistency is to be found in the Person experienced and in the fact that several covenants and commitments are made with the same Person even though the specific covenants may be contextually conditioned. Changing historical contexts do not change the Person of God, even though God acts contextually and calls humans into relationship in a context. Thus God entered into relationship within the framework of covenants with Abraham and Moses, redefined and clarified the nature of relationship/covenant in Christ, and through the Spirit continues to enter into relationship.

The name YHWH, revealed to Moses in the Exodus experience (Exodus 3:14) may emphasize God's consistent presence or creative activity ("I am who I am," "I will be who I will be," or "I will cause to be what I will cause to be"). However, I suggest that in response to Moses' request to be given God's name, God answers "I am who I am" only as a way of indicating that God is beyond naming and even refuses to be named. Attention is directed to Godself as the core reality, rather than a name or description. The First and Second Commandments also affirm the uniqueness of God and that God must be recognized to transcend all images and all attempts to explain and describe. Only God is God, and God cannot be limited or fully defined by naming.

The name revealed in the New Testament, "*Abba*, Father" (Galatians 4:6), emphasizes the caring and dependable nature of God's relationship and is really functional rather than descriptive of God's essence. The giving of the Spirit clarifies that the relationship with God is not distant, a relationship of a God up there with humans down here, but a relationship with a God who is present on the level of human existence, down here. Thus to call God Spirit (as Person) does not describe God's being any more than to say Father describes this. In a sense both are affirmations that God is relational.

One may have difficulty arriving at clear, final answers in matters of doctrine and morality. But behind the variety of the tradition, the variety of our experience, and the variety of our formulations, there is the God who engages us in the gift of relationship and who is not only the common denominator in the variety but the one who contains all of the possibilities and potential answers. In the reality of God one has all there is to have, though the answers and issues may not be clear.

In the practical process of formulating faith and ethical decisions, one needs to find a way of proceeding. It seems to me that there are two helpful foci. The first is to analyze the dialogical relationship of Spirit (the active presence of God) and tradition (the deposits from previous experience of God and reflection upon such experience). The second is to examine creation (or "general revelation") as a source of knowledge. Creation has long been felt to disclose information supportive of and supplementary to "special revelation." As tradition is in a dialogical relationship with Spirit, so the religious traditions about creation need to be in dialogue with new scientific studies which also disclose the nature of creation.

Zinzendorf has provided starting points for this in recognizing the historical nature of revelation, the central role of the person of God (Christ) in revelation, the role of the Spirit in theological understanding and ongoing revelation, and the relationship of creation and salvation in the person of Christ who is Savior and Creator.

Spirit and Tradition

The role of the Spirit, affirmed in most of the New Testament traditions, has implications that are often neglected. Usually the Spirit is relegated to the role of inspirer and interpreter of tradition already established — or the creative impulse of early Christianity which is not active in the same way since the days of the apostles or the early councils. In this way all authority is placed in the tradition. Taken seriously, the Spirit means that things are never settled and the church is continuously engaged in rethinking in the light of God's engagement with the present age. One must respect the tradition, but cannot idolize it in any form. Only God is God, and God keeps on being God by not abdicating to the tradition.

The biblical tradition may be seen as follows: The divergent traditions of Judaism which bear witness to God and God's relationship to life are converged, clarified, and evaluated in terms of a unique action of God in history in Christ. However, this self-disclosure of God is itself rendered ambiguous and multiform by the humanity and culturally conditioned perceptions of those who witnessed it, bore witness, and transmitted this witness. Though God in Christ is an unambiguous reality, the perception of this reality is not. It was then left to the church, under the guidance of the ongoing activity of God (the Spirit), to do two things:

    1. To affirm valid understandings and clarify misconceptions by distinguishing, in the light of ongoing history, where the God-in-Christ event had or had not been adequately understood — or had been actually misunderstood in the light of cultural and religious presuppositions

2. To be open to the speaking of God to newly developing issues and circumstances not adequately anticipated or treated in the tradition

In their approaches and results the first-century Christians were varied while seeking to remain faithful to God's intention. As a result, there was diversity both within and between Christian communities.

The diversity produced called for some standards by which to discern whether the Spirit of God was active in experiences, understandings, and what was claimed to be divine guidance. This is treated extensively in the Reflections in chapter 6. Both the Johannine literature and Paul reflect some common principles:

1. The role of the Spirit must be recognized.
2. One must stand within the available tradition of the Christ event, recognizing Jesus as Lord and listening to what he taught.
3. A quality of life, congruous with God, should be manifested if one claimed one was expressing knowledge of God. This might be expressed in gifts, but should be particularly expressed in love.
4. The involvement of community in the discernment of perceptions of God's will and truth were important.
5. Especially in the authentic Pauline materials, there is a recognition of the limited nature of all human perception and the ego-centered use of knowledge (note particularly 1 Corinthians 8:1-3 and 1 Corinthians 13).

It is true that, from the later first century on, the developing church in various ways became sociologically and theologically less tolerant. But this must be understood as related to its internal and external struggles. One must listen to its solutions without surrender of the freedom to be faithful to both tradition and Spirit.

If the Christian of today opts to stand within tradition and yet be responsible to God's contemporary action (the Spirit), one is in the uncertain situation of driving a road with many markers, but with the destination unclear. (The analogy of a road takes seriously the long span of history through which the church has lived. The biblical analogy of the church as the temple inhabited by the Spirit was appropriate when the church was seen not so much in terms of extended history.) There is no other foundation than Christ, but one does not stand still on this foundation. Life flows out as a ribbon or highway through varied landscapes, and one must follow. One may protest that if the future is open to the Spirit there are no absolutes, but that is not true. There is the absolute of God, expressed in the Christ event and active in ongoing history. In this way God remains God, and all witness and interpretation remain just that.

The first two Commandments have been taken seriously. The answers formulated by the church(es) over the centuries must be heeded, but not taken ultimately. In the best sense, the traditions always lead us beyond themselves to the God who is beyond them.

Creation and science

In the history of Christianity the doctrine of creation has played a significant role. This has been used to explore creation's intent, predicament, and restoration by God's saving action. Up to the development of modern science, creation has been interpreted primarily mythologically, expressing experienced phenomena and the projections of the human psyche. Views on creation were varied, witness the diverse Old Testament creation accounts — especially the two in Genesis 1-3. There are also several New Testament creation accounts (e.g., John 1:1-18, Colossians 1:15-20, and Hebrews 1-2) which are reinterpretations of Old Testament traditions. It would seem that as God and traditions regarding God are continuously interpreted by the Spirit, so creation should be by the discoveries of science and God's continuing revelations about creation. Thus our stories about and descriptions of creation should continuously be changing so as to contribute to our understanding of God's intention for creation and creation's evolution and devolution. Our perception of what is so by nature cannot be determined only by the ancient myths, which in themselves bear no uniform witness.

There is no desire either to depreciate the insights of ancient myth or to lay claim to false objectivity on the part of modern science. It is merely to affirm that our understanding of creation, from which we might formulate positions on issues, is constantly in process and that it is legitimate that this be so.

Zinzendorf's affirmation of Christ as Creator should be heard here. The New Testament creation stories understand Christ as God's agent in creation. Creation and salvation are united in the person who is agent of both. The consequence of this is that the meaning and purpose of creation, the direction of creation in its process and evolution, is to be found in Christ. Christ is the second great act of creation, which completes God's vision for the world and impels creation towards the realization of its future. For the Christian to understand creation is not merely to set in creative tension the creation narratives of Genesis with the discoveries of modern science. Christ is in some way the meaning of all that we can know mythologically and scientifically about creation. Thus the tradition about

Christ and our attempts to understand it become very important here. What has been said about God as Person is also important, for if we are undecided on the meaning of Christ for creation, we are still in relationship with the Person who is Creator and with whom our puzzlement over creation may be lived out.

Viewed this way, the dialectic of Spirit and tradition, and that of modern science and the creation myths, provide two foci from which to approach the church's concerns in ways responsible to the past, yet open and committed to God's continual unfolding and application of love and purpose. In all of this the person of Christ who is Creator (and thus embodies the meaning of creation) and Savior (and thus embodies the meaning of the original Christian tradition) is crucial.

This dialectic occurs always within a context which shapes its concerns and becomes the situation to which God would address a word. Zinzendorf was well aware of this. Today this has been significantly explored on a technical level in Robert Schreiter's *Constructing Local Theologies* and in a more popular vein in such books as Robert McAfee Brown's *Unexpected News: Reading the Bible with Third World Eyes* and Letty Russell's *Changing Contexts of Our Faith.*[59]

A Moravian model for the understanding of Scripture

I now return to the debate on the nature of Scripture's authority which took place in 1993-95 in the North American Moravian Church, mentioned at the beginning of this chapter. The resolution of this debate provides not only a significant formulation of the Moravian Church's understanding of its tradition, but a model for the way the tradition of the past may live into the present in a way responsible to God's concern for the present.

The debate focused on the nature of Scripture's authority against the background of the Interprovincial Faith and Order Commission's consideration of the issue of homosexuality. The Commission itself determined to deal first with the nature of Scripture's authority so that it might have an approach to dealing with Scripture's statements on homosexuality. As the church itself became aware of this, a debate developed in which persons of varying perspectives argued their understanding of Scripture in letters to the editor and articles in the *Moravian* magazine. In this debate historic Moravian positions on Scripture were explored. The Ancient Moravian Church understood Scripture as a *minis-*

---

[59] Robert J. Schreiter, *Constructing Local Theologies* (Maryknoll, N.Y.: Orbis, 1985). Robert McAfee Brown, *Unexpected News: Reading the Bible with Third World Eyes* (Philadelphia: Westminster Press, 1985). Letty Russell, ed., *Changing Contexts of Our Faith* (Philadelphia: Fortress Press, 1985).

terial which serves the one *essential* of relationship with God. Zinzendorf understood Scripture as mediating the relationship with the Savior and reflecting a process by which God worked in each historical context to bring persons to what was needed for that time.

The focus of the debate was the statement about Scripture which was part of the *Ground of the Unity*, a doctrinal statement accepted by the Moravian General (international) Synod of 1957. This statement had its origins in the European Continental Province of the Moravian Church as a reaction to the experience of the Second World War and was firmly rooted in a concern for God's authority over against human authority. Part of its statement about Scripture was: "The Holy Scriptures of both the Old and New Testament are and abide the only source and rule of faith, doctrine, and life of the Unitas Fratrum." As some were reading this in the debate in North America, there was no room for tradition, experience, or reason. Only Scripture is our source, understood as source of information for understanding God and God's will. The 1994 Northern Provincial Synod revised this statement to read: "The Triune God as attested to in the Holy Scripture of the Old and New Testaments is the only source of our life and salvation; and this Scripture is the sole standard of our doctrine and faith and therefore shapes our life."

In arriving at this new statement, the Synod Committee on Faith and Order that prepared the revision at Synod first discovered that there was common agreement among all perspectives present that Scripture was to be our *only rule for doctrine.* Then it was discovered that there was common agreement that the ultimate *source* of Christian faith and life was God God's self, and that Scripture itself was not this source, but attested to God as source. It was also concluded that though the Moravian Church has a valued Christocentric heritage, the church must affirm all of *the Trinity* as the source of the church's life. For Scripture's function in relationship to *doctrine and personal faith*, there was prefer- ence for "*sole standard,*" rather than using the word "rule" because it was felt that Scripture's relationship to this was profound and "rule" might be misunderstood as implying merely "rules," thus oversimplifying this relationship. Then, with regard to the role of Scripture in defining the *Christian life,* there was recognition that it was not possible to arrive at moral rules from Scripture that all could accept, and that living the Christian life was more than rules: it is a living out of the life of Christ with the empowerment and guidance of the Spirit. It was also remembered that historically the church recognized a relationship between doctrine and life: what is believed defines and shapes life. Attention was called to Romans 12:1 and the word "therefore" which Paul used to connect the doctrinal chapters 1-11 with the ethical concerns in the remaining chapters. The term "*Scripture*" was used instead of "Scriptures," because there was a desire to connote the canon of the Bible as our authority, and not just the individual books or the Old and New Testaments seen separately, which might be indicated by the term "Scriptures." The process was one in which God seemed to be participating, and this issue, the debate over which was expected to last the duration of Synod, was settled in one day. Many noted that this took place just a few days before the celebration of August 13, which commemorates the spiritual renewal of the Moravian Church in 1727.

The Southern Province Provincial Synod of 1995 accepted the Northern Province revision and added to this a statement about tradition: "In interpreting Scripture and in the communication of doctrine by teachers and preachers in the Church, we look to two millennia of ecumenical Christian tradition and the wisdom of our Moravian forebears in the faith to guide us as we pray for fuller understanding and ever clearer proclamation of the Gospel of Jesus Christ."

Some additional changes were made at the international Synod of 1995 in Tanzania, with the resultant final form being:

God's Word and Doctrine

The Triune God as revealed in the Holy Scripture of the Old and New Testaments is the only source of our life and salvation; and this Scripture is the sole standard of the doctrine and faith of the Unitas Fratrum and therefore shapes our life.

The Unitas Fratrum recognizes the Word of the Cross as the center of Holy Scripture and of all preaching of the Gospel and it sees its primary mission, and its reason for being, to consist in bearing witness to this joyful message. We ask our Lord for power never to stray from this.

The Unitas Fratrum takes part in the continual search for sound doctrine. In interpreting Scripture and in the communication of doctrine in the Church, we look to two millennia of ecumenical Christian tradition and the wisdom of our Moravian forebears in the faith to guide us as we pray for fuller understanding and ever clearer proclamation of the Gospel of Jesus Christ. But just as the Holy Scripture does not contain any doctrinal system, so the Unitas Fratrum also has not developed any of its own because it knows that the mystery of Jesus Christ, which is attested to in the Bible, cannot be comprehended completely by any human mind or expressed completely in any human statement. Also it is true that through the Holy Spirit the recognition of God's will for salvation in the Bible is revealed completely and clearly.[60]

It should be indicated that neither in the North American Synods that first formulated the revision nor in the international Synod that revised and finally accepted the above expression of faith was there a single person who voted against the revision. Sufficient dialogue had previously taken place to enable persons of different perspectives to understand each other and arrive at a common solution which could preserve the integrity of the Church's variety.

> Triune God,
> Source of life and salvation,
> Mystery of Christ,
> Word of the Cross,
> from pages wonderfully
> filled with the humanity
> of those who
> bore You witness,
> and filled with You:
> arise into my heart
> through them
> that I may truly live
> and discern You
> among the pages
> of my daily life.[61]

---

[60] See Appendix B, which includes the whole of the *Ground of the Unity*, as revised in 1995.

[61] By the author.

Chapter 4

The Significance of Christ and the Spirit for the Human Predicament

The Christ event, extending from the Incarnation to the Ascension, is the central and definitive act of God in history. Though it is central and unique, its treatment within the New Testament is contextual, and in reality it was also contextually experienced by those who bore it witness. This is evidenced not only in the variety of perspectives and language by which it is approached, but in the selectivity which is exercised upon the tradition about Jesus. The Spirit, the post-Ascension ongoing presence and action of God, is also experienced contextually and variously described.[1] The language about the Spirit affirms not only the ongoing presence of God after the life period of Jesus, but the participation of God in human formation. Both Christ and Spirit were described according to the needs of the audience for which the description was intended and the religious language available to both the author and audience, while seeking to be faithful to the reality being described.

That the church's witness is contextual keeps us from finalizing it in a particular form. God always transcends God's actions, and the full meaning of the actions transcend the particular witness borne to them. There is a richness or a fullness in all of this, explicit and implicit, that is not exhausted by the way we draw from the well of its meaning, for "from his fullness have we all received, grace upon grace,"[2] endlessly.

---

[1] Not all of the description of the post-Ascension experience of God in the New Testament used the language of the Spirit to describe such phenomena. In describing the origin of spiritual gifts, Paul in 1 Cor. 12 uses the language of the Spirit (though also speaking of God's working in all), in Eph. 4 the author speaks of the ascended Christ, while in 1 Pet. 4 they come from God.

[2] John 1:16.

This richness is enough for our needs, whatever they are in the context of our culture and life-experience. This richness also reminds us that the One from whom we draw what we need is the One who ultimately fulfills our needs, not merely as a composite of answers and resources, but as Person. This is very much the perspective of Zinzendorf.

The contextual character of the way the church draws from this fullness is most simply illustrated by Paul's statement in 1 Corinthians 9:19-22 about differing contexts for the proclamation of the Gospel. He indicates that sensitivity to context is not a compromise which diminishes the Gospel, but it is "all for the sake of the Gospel." "To the Jews I became as a Jew.... To those outside the Law I became as one outside the Law.... To the weak I became weak.... I do it all for the sake of the Gospel." How this worked in different cultural contexts can be seen when one compares his treatment of the symbol of the cross in his letters to the Galatians and Colossians. In Galatians 3 Paul feels it necessary to treat the cross as signifying that Christ bore the curse pronounced upon those who disobey the Law, thus freeing from the Law those for whom the Law is central. In the Judeo-Christian context, in which the Law was taken seriously as the binding expression of the covenant between God and Israel, it could not merely be set aside. It must be satisfied. But in Colossians 2 there is no discussion of Christ's satisfaction of the Law because for the Gentiles this is not an issue. Rather the crucifixion is presented as a freeing from the condition of the flesh and the cancellation of "the bond which stood against us with its legal demands." This bond God "set aside, nailing it to the cross. He disarmed the principalities and powers and made a public example of them, triumphing over them in it [the cross]."[3] This is a description of the manumission of those who have been enslaved by the conditions of fleshly existence and the domination of the cosmic powers. To be freed from the flesh and the cosmic powers was as major a concern for the Greco-Roman world as were obedience to the Law and freedom from sin for Jews. The change in language in Colossians is one of the reasons why Colossians is often said not to have been by Paul. However, Paul has indicated that in different contexts he must draw upon the Christ event differently, focusing on issues as perceived within the culture he addressed and borrowing language from this culture to describe what he wishes to communicate.

Paul's comment about "to the weak I became weak" is especially worthy of attention. *Weak* was a term used in Stoicism for those who did not adequately understand. In the treatment of the weak, in 1 Corinthians

[3] Col. 2:13-15.

8-10 and Romans 14, the concern is not cultural context but rather a modification in application of what the Gospel means in life: thinking that idols have a reality and power which they do not; believing that there are aspects of creation that are unclean, not belonging to the Lord; and feeling the need to follow certain religious observances which were a part of one's background but are not really called for by the Gospel. At issue are the lack of knowledge and varying opinions which are part of each human context. Paul's comment in 1 Corinthians 8:1-3 places in perspective a one-sided emphasis on correct knowledge and practice: Knowledge puffs up, but love builds up. If anyone imagines that he knows something, he does not yet know as he ought to know. But if one loves God, one is known by him.

Thus contextual variety should be allowed. One should not pass judgment on the servant of another (for each Christian is a servant of Christ); only the master, has this right of judgment. Each stands before his own master, and the master will uphold the servant (Romans 14:4). This allowance of variety should not, however, compromise the heart of the Gospel itself. In Galatians 1 Paul clearly indicates that no other Gospel should be tolerated, even if it comes from him.

With this legitimization of contextuality in mind, a brief analysis of the human predicament is in order, for this predicament, in its many aspects, is what God addresses as God comes to us in the Christ event and in the Spirit.

The beauty/order and disorder of existence present a paradox. There seems to be purpose and meaning in creation, and yet existence seems also to be distorted and problematic. The primary species of living being, homo sapiens, where existence comes to consciousness and is the subject for reflection, would seem to hold such promise but also suffers greatly and inflicts terrible suffering upon itself and other forms of life, even the cosmos itself. Nature cannot seem to adequately nourish and protect its own creatures and may inflict indiscriminate destruction. Perhaps it would not be so hard to understand and bear if there were a reason for all the pain and suffering. One of the major issues in dealing with the human predicament has been to grapple with existence and the strange and unfathomable powers which affect it. While modern science has to some extent demystified the cosmos and turned gods and elemental spirits into the forces of nature and history, the development of depth psychology has made humanity aware of the strange world of forces within persons that populate the unconscious. There are two issues here: how can persons relate to, gain power over, or be freed from these powers that are without and within one; and what is the problem with humanity that we cannot do this more successfully.

There are other existentials that are central to human experience: for example, the need for development and transformation, the need for meaning and a future which can shape the present, the need to face death, and the reality of the Transcendent or spiritual as a significant component of existence.

Cultures come to have traditional perceptions or presuppositions about human existence. Hellenistic religions had as primary concerns the freeing of persons from the *cosmic powers* and *death*. Judaism was less individualistic and focused on the realization of God's sovereignty over humanity and creation, believing in the promises of God inherent in the call of Abraham and the Exodus experience. But it was apparent that the promises of God were not being realized as one nation after another conquered the Jews and life remained tragic. Judaism came to feel that the failure to realize what was promised was due to the *failures of humanity*. Humans had not been faithful enough or pure enough or righteous enough for the promises of God to be realized. They had not sufficiently obeyed the covenant with God and God's Law. For life and world to be different, *sin and impurity* needed to be dealt with. And there were problems with human nature, for to enable persons to live in this world God had given them an evil impulse which came to be problematic and ill-suited for obedience to God. Fleshly existence was governed by *two impulses*, one good and the other evil. The evil impulse functioned much like Freud's *libido*, expressive of self-interest and the basic life-drives, necessary for such human tasks as getting ahead, taking a wife, and raising a family. Yet not all of the problems were with the human being. There was also *Satan*, the ruler of this world who sought to deceive and influence persons and had demonic forces at his disposal.

This *dualistic perception of flesh and world* has been transmitted within Christianity.[4] It expressed the presuppositions of the context in which Christianity arose and was then transmitted in Christianity's formative

---

[4] Dualism in Judaism and Christianity was not an absolute dualism, with good and evil representing equal powers and separate worlds, the material completely separated from the spiritual. God created all and the problems of the world were due to a fall from the goodness of original creation. This limited dualistic perspective on flesh, world, and the spiritual powers was part of early Christianity's heritage from intertestamental Judaism and was supported by some of Hellenistic culture. This limited dualism, as a worldview, became imbedded in the literature of the New Testament. A more extreme dualism came to exist in Jewish and Christian Gnosticism, where the worlds of spirit and matter, good and evil, became completely separated. The good God had nothing to do with the creation of this world. For Christian Gnostics this world was the work of a lesser creator God described in Jewish tradition, not the work of the ultimate God of light and true knowledge revealed in Christ.

tradition, the New Testament. Many Christians today would still express the central need for the Christ event to *free them from their sins and flesh in a world ruled by Satan.* This is not to deny that there is meaningful insight in seeing that sin and flesh and Satan describe important aspects of human experience, but the consequent negativity towards world and flesh has not seemed to produce any resolution to the problems of human existence. One might argue that they have not been taken seriously enough. But one might also argue that this negativity has undermined the very resources we need to deal with our existence. Jungian psychology, for example, in dealing with the problematic side of human nature sees the shadow side of humanity not as something to be rejected and repressed. We cannot not be what it is to be human, and it is when we reject a part of our humanity that it is most destructive, operating autonomously within the psyche, without control. It is more productive to become conscious of the shadow and to integrate it into conscious life. Then the power of what could be destructive may be creative and in the service of the person. In this integration a strong ego is not a sin against God but a way of structuring the psyche so that some control and responsibility to God can be managed. Alice Miller, a Swiss psychiatrist concerned with what happens to the child when raised in ways destructive to the child's unique identity, traces the rise of Nazism to European child-rearing practices. She discusses the way in which Christian theology and pedagogy were often companions in the destruction of the self.[5] We must ask not only about the correctness of our theology but about its consequences.

The Jewish perception of existence was expressed in the story of the *Fall*, a Jewish Pandora's box which unleashed the troubles of the world. There was a *human Fall.* By this the human predicament was located in an historical or mythical event, though in Jewish Wisdom literature lack of understanding and wisdom was often a way of explaining the world's condition. Generally within Judaism Genesis 1 was understood to portray the ideal world, a world created good and humans made in the *image of God.* Genesis 2-3, besides providing a different description of creation, portrays the *temptation* of woman by the serpent and the involvement of the man in eating from the tree of knowledge of good

---

[5] Alice Miller, *Prisoners of Childhood: The Drama of the Gifted Child and the Search for the True Self*, trans. Ruth Ward (New York: Basic Books, 1981); *Thou Shalt Not Be Aware: Society's Betrayal of the Child*, trans. Hildegarde Hannum and Hunter Hannum (New York: Meridian, 1986); and *For Your Own Good: Hidden Cruelty in Child-Rearing and the Roots of Violence*, trans. Hildegarde Hannum and Hunter Hannum (New York: Farrar, Straus, Giroux, 1983). (Citation of the last mentioned work will be abbreviated in subsequent notes as Miller, *For Your Own Good.*)

and evil. This had been forbidden by God and so was an act of *disobedience*. All are *punished* and *excluded from the ideal world* of the "garden." The symbolism of excluding humans from access to the tree of life located in the garden means that *death* is a consequence of this Fall. The exclusion of man and woman from the ideal world, together with the new experience of pain in childbirth for woman and a new resistance of the ground to man's labor, portrays the way *existence and nature had changed, now resisting* rather than supporting human existence.[6] Rabbinic interpretation pointed out the ways that both human nature and the world had changed.

Besides the human Fall there was an *angelic Fall* described in Genesis 6.[7] In the same chapter there is the flood during Noah's time and, because of its proximity to the story of angelic Fall, it was interpreted as the consequence of this Fall.

Humans were then presented with a situation not only due to their contemporary behavior, but created by the acts of their ancestors and of the angels. Both were extensively explored by intertestamental Judaism. Influenced by this, early Christianity, and subsequently Christianity down through the centuries, has described the human situation in terms of the Fall of Adam, from which we inherit both predicament and guilt, and the Fall of Satan, who still opposes God and seeks the conquest of our souls.[8]

Though the above constituted the existentials of the human situation, there was still much that needed definition in the developing

[6] It is interesting to note that Philo, a contemporary of Jesus and Paul influenced by Plato's philosophy, understood Genesis 1 to describe the creation of the ideal heavenly human after the pattern of which the earthly human of Genesis 2 was made. This heavenly Man (Son of Man) then developed into a Savior figure, one who could restore God's original intent for humanity. Some modern interpretations would like to portray Genesis 2-3 as a story of human maturation, not of fall, but that does not suit the way this story has been handled historically.

[7] In the OT materials the serpent of Genesis 2, the fallen angels of Genesis 6, and Satan as presented in Job are indicated as oppositional forces, though not evil in themselves. Satan in Job is presented much as a district attorney in the Court of God to make accusations against Job. In the literature of the intertestamental period the angels of Genesis 6 are imprisoned by God in the underworld for their role in the condition of the world that led to the flood. Satan has become prince of this world, head of all the forces of evil, opposing not only humans but also God. The change in the presentation of Satan, from oppositional to evil, is understood as due to his fall, similar to the fall of the angels of Genesis 6.

[8] It should be noted that in Judaism and in the NT the Fall produces a *predicament*, a distortion of existence, that humanity must now live with, but not *inherited guilt* to be removed by baptism as Christians often later came to believe. Rom. 5:12 and following provides a Christian description of the impact of the Fall on humans, bringing death into the world and also bringing sin as a power from which humans could not extricate themselves.

theology of the church. The effects of the Fall and the remaining human capabilities were discussed, including the nature and possibilities of the human will. The sovereignty of God over history and human salvation (or damnation) and the definition of grace (the help humans would need) were discussed. Augustine's (354-430 CE) formulation was a watershed in Christian theology and was still part of the theological discussions in Zinzendorf's day. Augustine distinguished between the graces necessary for meritorious acts unrelated to salvation and the grace necessary for salvation. The latter was absolutely gratuitous and efficacious (irresistible). Human will was still free to choose, but was determined by inner motives and the objects presented for choice. God must provide both the motives and the objects which will enable a choice for salvation. Thus the human is free to choose but cannot unless God provides the right circumstances. Saving grace is an act of pure mercy on God's part, without consideration of individual merit. God in absolute power and knowledge, from all eternity, has predestined some for salvation and others for damnation.[9]

This is background for considering Zinzendorf's approach to the human predicament and the meaning of Christ and the Spirit for the resolution of this predicament. All of the above came to him in his churchly tradition and formed his understanding of world and life. His historical context, e.g., the issues of the Enlightenment and the perceptions of Pietism, sharpened the questions for him, while his own experience of life and the significance of relationship with the Savior caused him to see the predicament and its resolution in particular ways. Especially important is his understanding of the human predicament in terms of loss of relationship with the Creator who is Savior and the resolution of the predicament in terms of the restoration of this relationship. The Creator-Savior is also the archetype of the human, and human destiny is defined in him.

The Human Predicament

Creation - Image of God

Humanity as originally created was made in the image of God, which for Zinzendorf was defined in terms of Jesus Christ. When God said, "Let us make man in our image" (Genesis 1:26), God was speaking of making humans in a likeness which would eventually be revealed in Christ and

[9] For a discussion of the development of Augustine's theology and the debate over its issues to the time of Zinzendorf, see Jan Miel, *Pascal and Theology* (Baltimore : Johns Hopkins Press, 1969), pp. 1-63.

was constituted by all that Christ is, not some aspect of Christ such as spirituality, rationality, or moral perfection. Christ is the original of what it is to be a human and therefore should be imitated as a model for life.

> Here is the archetype, the original image and the first thought of the original, as God wanted to reveal himself in Christ, as he wanted to present himself with eyes, ears, and all human members. Therefore human members were already ascribed to him in the Old Testament. He is the original model according to which the human being was created. The human is a copy, an imitator of God. Thus it is a shame for a human creature to imitate someone else who is not the true image and original. Thus it is said, "Be imitators of God" (Ephesians 5:1).[10]

Zinzendorf's description of this image in terms of Christ's having human members was only a way of saying that all that humanity is intended to be is found in Christ, and this includes the human body. The body is neither foreign to God's intention for human existence nor foreign to God's self. That the Savior is both Creator and human archetype intimately links the Savior with creation. Creation and humanity must be understood in the light of the Savior who embodies creation's intent: not out of what they are or have come to be, but out of what they have not yet come to be but were intended to be. The Savior's creative/saving acts form both humans and creation in the direction of their destiny.

The Fall

Zinzendorf did not see Adam's fall as due to disobedience to God. Disobedience is only the effect of an estranged and deceived mind, not of the natural state of mind. Thus something must have happened with humanity before it would have disobeyed. Unbelief made Adam prey to the persuasion of Satan.

> Through what then did the first human fall? Answer. Only through unbelief. His Creator had said to him: Do not eat of this fruit, otherwise you will die. The Devil came and said: Eat from it; then when you eat of it you will become another god. The woman believed his word, Eve believed what the Devil said (you will be as

---

[10] Nikolaus Ludwig von Zinzendorf, *Auszüge aus des Seligen Ordinarii der Evangelischen Brüder-Kirche sowol ungedruckten als gedruckten Reden über biblische Texte, nach Ordnung der Bücher heiliger Schrift gefertiget und herausgegeben von Gottfried Clemens* [Drei Bände über die Bücher Mose] (Barby: n.p., 1763-65), 1:29 (2 Aug. 1748). (Abbreviated in subsequent notes as Zinzendorf, *Auszüge aus Reden über biblische Texte* [OT].)

god) and was, on the other hand, unbelieving, doubtful and distrustful towards her Creator, and so she allowed herself at least to be persuaded that she would not die and on the other hand persuaded that there would be advantages. That was her fall. So long now as man is unbelieving, so he is subject to all deceptions, games, foolish matters which the Devil makes him believe. As long as he is in unbelief, so is he the fool of Satan, who does with him what he will. He preaches his fables to him and the man believes them. He plays before him his comedies, and the man gazes at them. He does for him his tricks of magic, one after the other; the man is amazed at them and can not get away. The Devil puts him to sleep, lets him dream this and that, and the man cannot awaken from this sleep. He gives him this and that to try and taste; the man becomes accustomed to it and can not again break away. . . . Such is the economy which Satan and humans conduct with each other in the time of unbelief.[11]

The Fall had little to do with sex, as some were wont to say. The shame felt after the Fall was not sexual, but due to an awareness of the animal nature that was part of human existence — and fear of what it could do.

The Fall does not then really consist of that which spiritually fantastic persons think, fleshly desires and earthly circumstances, but that shame which the nakedness of human members excited in fallen man was already the first fever-fit for the cure of man, that was the beginning of a vehement regimen and at the same time the proof that man was certainly animal, but at the same time was gifted with a soul which could not think as a sow, as a horse, and as another fleshly creature which was less highly developed and had no spirit from God. For man was ashamed of his similarity to the animals, his animal nature which showed forth all too strongly. And because he still knew no help against it, because the consolation for it was still a secret to him, he thus could not endure himself.[12]

If unbelief is the cause of the Fall, the Fall consists in one's rejection of the proper role of the Savior as one's sovereign. Through the

[11] Nikolaus Ludwig von Zinzendorf, *Ein und zwanzig Discurse über die Augspurgische Confession gehalten vom 15. Dec. 1747. bis zum 3. Mart. 1748. denen Seminariis Theologicis Fratrum zum Besten aufgefaßt und bis zur nochmaligen Revision des Auctoris einstweilen mitgetheilet* (n.p., n.d.), pp. 216-17 (14 Jan. 1748). For information about the two different printings of this work, see chapter 1, note 82. Citation of the printing used in this book will be abbreviated in subsequent notes as Zinzendorf, *Ein und zwanzig Discurse* [Title page: *Discurse . . . Auctoris*].
[12] Ibid., p. 173 (7 Jan. 1748).

rejection of the proper sovereign, one becomes subject to the wrong sovereign, Satan. For "nobody can own himself. There is something in the whole situation of man, in the nature of such a creature, which makes it impossible for him to own himself. He must have a lord."[13]

Certain things have happened to humanity in the Fall to change it from its nature as created. The change does not cause humans so much to sin actively, but their nature is impelled by a being not a part of them. Fallen human nature, though not pious, is not evil in itself.

> Nature is not pious, my brothers and sisters, but it is thoroughly infected with the common corruption and with *peccato originis* [original sin], but human nature does not sin *primario* [primarily], it is not active in sinning, it has no inclination a priori to sin, to do evil. But nature is driven by a foreign being, it is ridden by someone else who has his holiday with the children of unbelief.[14]

Zinzendorf's view of original sin and its consequences should be seen along these lines. The guilt humanity bears is not a guiltiness for something that the first humans did, but a guilt which is humanity's own by virtue of becoming subject to Satan resultant upon the conditions created by the Fall.

> Now also a *reatus* (accusation) stands against us which is no mere *imputation*, as the righteousness of Jesus Christ, but such a one as is mixed with its own guilt. Because we by nature stand not only as servants under sin but we so easily marry our tyrant and consent to his government because we are indeed bound to him, because sin is pleasant to us, *naturell*, and suitable to our taste; on the other hand the intercourse with God and divine matters are foreign, unreal, *fatal* and unpleasant, and the more precious a truth is, the closer it is to the heart, the more offensive it is to the heart by nature.[15]

When one sees that bad children come from good parents and good children come from bad parents, one finds

> repeated proof, that the son does not bear the iniquity of the father, and that not in the least is there any spiritual inheritance, neither among the good or bad; but in the case of the Gospel it

[13] Nikolaus Ludwig von Zinzendorf, *Nine Public Lectures On Important Subjects in Religion Preached in Fetter Lane Chapel in London in the Year 1746*, trans. and ed. George W. Forell (Iowa City: University of Iowa Press, 1973), p. 89 (2 Oct. 1746). (Abbreviated in subsequent notes as Zinzendorf, *Nine Public Lectures* [1973].)

[14] Zinzendorf, *Ein und zwanzig Discurse* [Title page: *Discurse . . . Auctoris*], p. 262 (18 Feb. 1748).

[15] Ibid., p. 81 (17 Dec. 1747).

depends upon each person obtaining his allotted little Spirit for himself, and that the Holy seven Spirits go out to kindle a fire from the hole in Jesus side, that out of the element of soul, out of the *parente communi animarum* [universal parent of souls] (so the eternal fire is called - Isaiah 33:14, Hebrews 12:20) sparks enter the heart, living sparks, as the Protestant confessions say, which ignite in persons and enthrone the spirit of Christ in such a body and soul.[16]

Moreover, since the coming of Christ another factor affects the impact of Adam's Fall upon the world. By the death of the Savior/ Creator the effects of the Fall were erased. The atonement is not merely an event the application of which deals with our needs.

Even the remembrance of sin is blotted out in the tribunal of God; for no longer will a single human soul be damned because Adam has fallen; not a single human creature needs to look pained because Adam has fallen. For all at once all sin is atoned for on the Cross, the entire Fall is erased, and the whole obligation to Satan and the entire sentence passed upon the fall of Adam is torn up, canceled, and annulled by the nails of Jesus, so that on our side there is not the least question regarding this: "As in Adam, all die, so in Christ are all made alive" (I Cor. 15:22), all who nevertheless go to the devil, all who nevertheless go to hell, not excepted. On the wood of the Cross the world was saved all at once, and whoever is lost loses himself, because he will not receive the Saviour, because he falls again and repeats the fall of Adam, because from a certain opposition and hostility toward his Reconciler he takes the side of his enemy, who is still alive, who is still active, who is still unbound, and who is still trying the very same thing on each soul that he tried on the first man.[17]

The universal presence of the Spirit since Pentecost also means that the power of God is now available to assume sovereignty over those whose freedom from Satan has been won. Sin, after the atonement and the pouring out of the Spirit, then happens by a relapse of humans into the circumstances of the Fall.[18]

---

[16] Ibid., p. 83 (17 Dec. 1747). Zinzendorf describes the Spirit, which issues from Jesus' side wound, as bringing with it the little spirits allotted for each person, thus restoring the spiritual dimension to human nature lost in the Fall.

[17] Zinzendorf, *Nine Public Lectures* [1973], p. 68 (18 Sept. 1746).

[18] See Zinzendorf, *Ein und zwanzig Discurse* [Title page: *Discurse . . . Auctoris*], pp. 160-62 (6 Jan. 1748) and pp. 124-25 (26 Dec. 1747).

Effects of the Fall on human nature

Besides the way in which the Fall brought humanity under the power of Satan, it also affected human nature, robbing it of its natural faculty for fellowship with God and knowledge of God.[19] Even a decided bodily change has taken place, though Zinzendorf does not speculate over its nature. Humans are now only the first among living creatures, having lost their heavenly body and now needing to live in an earthly body:

> What sort of fads speculation about this matter has produced is not our matter. What sort of alterations the structure of our body has undergone is not a suitable question. But we positively know that we have lost the heavenly body and have a merely natural earthly body which was not natural to our first earthly parents . . . but now is our nature through reproduction. . . . The human being after the Fall is nothing more than first among the living creatures who have flesh and bone, veins, and such a structure which distinguishes them from the vegetables.[20]

The Fall has created in humans a loss of awareness of why they are in the world.

> The human being is more noble than the cow which is still as its Creator made it for the purpose that it might be of use to humanity.
> But humans are quite perverted and twisted in their hearts and heads; they do not know why they are in the world. They live without purpose and want what happened to them a long time ago (the Fall).[21]

The Spirit which God breathed into humanity at creation has been lost, leaving humans cold and dead in spiritual matters.

> What does it mean to be dead and cold? A person can be spiritually dead, even if he speaks so much of God and of Christ and weeps over them. All members are moved over these matters, the emotions become incited, the reason agrees with this, and still the heart is dead. There is no life, no feeling in the heart, i.e., no truth.

[19] *Des Grafens von Zinzendorff Inhalt dererjenigen Reden, Welche zu Berlin vom 1ten Januar. 1738. bis 27ten Aprilis in denen Abend-Stunden sonderlich für die Manns-Personen gehalten worden. Dritte Auflage* (Flensburg and Altona: Gebrüder Korte, 1743), pp. 195-96 (9 Apr. 1748). (Abbreviated in subsequent notes as Zinzendorf, *Reden zu Berlin für die Manns-Personen* [3rd. ed., 1743].)

[20] Zinzendorf, *Auszüge aus Reden über biblische Texte* [OT], 1:63f. (11 Mar. 1754).

[21] *Des Herrn Grafen von Zinzendorff Inhalt einiger öffentlichen Reden, welche im Jahr 1738. vom Januario bis zu Ende des Aprils in Berlin an die Frauens-Personen daselbst gehalten worden. Vierte Auflage* (Leipzig and Altona: Gebrüder Korte, 1749), p. 151 (24 Feb. 1738).

That means: God's Spirit is lacking. As Adam fell, he lost the spirit which he had when he was like God. His body and soul, to be sure, did not die that day. Still God's prophecy has been fulfilled that he has died. And so it is that his spirit has departed. All humans are Adam's natural children, without spirit and life. Therefore David prayed not only for a pure heart, but a new spirit. Indeed, it is said of the new covenant (Jeremiah 31, Ezekiel 36) that God wants to write his law in our heart and give us a new spirit. Since we by nature have a stone, rock-hard, despiritualized heart, quite as unreceptive as the heart of Nabal, even so is the human heart naturally hard against the Savior and his message, against the word of the cross, against his wooing, against his promise to redeem it from curse and ban, from the power of the devil, and to lead it into holiness. The heart remains as it is, if the Spirit of God does not come upon it.[22]

This is crucial, because for Zinzendorf the heart that God created in persons through the Spirit is the organ of religious perception, intellectual capacity not sufficing and often misleading.

Zinzendorf's analysis of the capacities of "natural man" is intriguing. Here one sees his "psychological" interests as he seeks to analyze the way persons function.

A person either becomes brutish, as is quite ordinarily the case amongst the common people, among people who because of their manual labor, scraping in the earth, and other such like corporeal things, have no time to cultivate their spirit; or else the person applies himself to the cultivation of his mind. When a person becomes brutish, his body gets the upper hand, and he desperately lives on in this way; he knows he must yet die; so the *stimulus* of death which in time helps him to his grave, which harasses his body until it is laid there, must in the meanwhile serve him as an *amusement*: death must obtain a pungent gout [taste]. It is a thing which happens *toto die* [every day]; one knows, for example, that if he drinks wine, beer, brandy, it will kill him; and yet he cannot leave it alone. Thus what actually kills a person is his amusement: the fire in the blood, the fury in the members. And then he becomes so accustomed to it that the Apostle *Paul* compares it to a marriage: sin and the members have become so accustomed to one another as if they belonged together, they now want to be and remain together and they decay in the midst of their *ebats* [frolic]. People who think either think very *subtil* [subtly] so their reason, i.e., their overdriven reflection and speculation, consumes their *materiam corpoream* [fleshly matter] resulting in a *espece* [kind] of statue; or where the mind is not so highly developed that it can attain any thing of this sort, the persons perish comfortably and quickly in their desires. Others live for a long time if they are not crushed by the burden of their mental work. A *philosophus* [philosopher] grows to old age if the attention to abstract matters and his daily and nightly work on this does not sublimate him too soon. On the other hand, when anyone is half studious and half animal, half philosophical and half human, that occasions a continual contrast of pleasure and displeasure. When at any time the animal impulse is too strong, it brings him into subjection to it; but then the person afterwards would take his life, would shoot or drown himself. Sin, when it is finished, brings forth death; one cannot bear to look at oneself, until by and by another fit carries one away again.

Hence there is not a more unhappy person than an unconverted scholar; he is such a miserable creature, that one can scarcely find anyone under the sun like him; no post-horse's fatigue is comparable to that of such a person. Such a person lives in a continual confusion and restlessness of his mind, under an incessant alternation of the dominion of the body and of the soul; and there is no remedy. But there are people who are either totally or half fleshly, which is true of every person whose inward sensibility (feeling) is not entirely stifled, whose conscience is not yet seared, whose spiritual *remors* [remorse] has not yet died, with whom in any case, if it does not go farther, it can come to a silly whining. But who becomes spiritual in that part; who in the likeness of the evil enemy has actually grown in pride and conceit and in a false θείῳ (divinity), in the daemon-character, and is become a *genius*, a person who goes and flies on in his impudence, flying until his wings melt, until the body returns to the earth and the soul to its own place: such a one is in the condition which Paul so lamentably describes in Romans 7.[23]

However, the predicament of natural man is not only a matter of observation, it is so *ea lege* [by this principle/law] from the perspective of the Christ event. The Christ event, by its inherent nature and its remedy of our predicament, defines our predicament without the need for introspective analysis. The solution has defined the problem. We needed a Savior because we have a Savior.

[23] Zinzendorf, *Ein und zwanzig Discurse* [Title page: *Discurse . . . Auctoris*], pp. 175-76 (7 Jan. 1748).

Free will

Zinzendorf's discourse on free will in the *Discourses on the Augsburg Confession* is one of his shortest. This gives a clue as to his view. He believed that Luther from the perspective of his *De servo arbitrio* would not object to what he wrote, though Luther later changed his mind allowing a greater role for free will.[24] Zinzendorf advocated taking a practical approach rather than theoretical. He described free will as not a benefit, but an ἀνάγκη, a necessity to human existence. For "free-will is an inherent property of a thinking creature."[25] Without free will real faith in and love for God is not possible, which is why it is necessary. "But so much as one can become free and give up free will, so much as we can let the Father, the Savior, and the Holy Spirit think for us, so much have we gained, so much more have we added to our blessedness beyond our previous condition."[26]

In his *Nine Public Lectures* Zinzendorf engaged in an extended discussion of free will, treating also the differences between Lutherans and Calvinists. Here his affirmation of free will was bound up with his view of Christ as Creator and that "all human souls, actually and universally considered, are designed for salvation."[27] Thus each needs the freedom to choose, though all souls are not actually saved unless they receive the Savior who appears before their hearts. The Savior will no longer exercise his power to force choice as he did in the Old Testament. As Zinzendorf expressed the Savior's words:

> If they will not be acquainted with me in this way, and if they are not inclined to love me in this manner, they may leave it alone; I shall force them no more — I do not want forced people. I do not want a seraglio [harem] of souls: I want free souls. I want to have bride-hearts; I will voluntarily be their bridegroom, and they will voluntarily be my bride.[28]

Though the Savior/Creator provides an appropriate time for the exercise of one's free will in the life of each person, this is complicated by Satan, who may possess the soul. Then the soul must say: "Ah, for God's sake! I should really be saved, but I cannot perceive any right will. Satan must have possessed me; he must have captivated my heart." Then the Savior will say, "Oh, you poor people, you will never manage; come

[24] Ibid., pp. 285-86 (21 Feb. 1748); Zinzendorf, *Nine Public Lectures* [1973], p. 61 (18 Sept. 1746).

[25] Zinzendorf, *Ein und zwanzig Discurse* [Title page: *Discurse . . . Auctoris*], pp. 287-88 (21 Feb. 1748).

[26] Ibid., p. 287 (21 Feb. 1748).

[27] Zinzendorf, *Nine Public Lectures* [1973], p. 62 (18 Sept. 1746).

[28] Ibid., p. 64 (18 Sept. 1746).

to me." The Savior then explains: "I will stretch out my invisible hand of blessing over them, and as soon as Satan sees my wounded hand, he retreats, and the soul does not know how it comes to freedom."[29]

Humanity in Christ and the Spirit

Zinzendorf described the human predicament in traditional language reshaped in the light of his own theological perspective. He also did this with the language used for describing the impact upon humanity of the Christ event and the gift of the Spirit. This will be discussed in terms of the categories of grace, faith, salvation, sanctification, new birth and mystical marriage.

Centrality of Grace

For Zinzendorf all was of grace as all was of God. Humanity cannot know God without the mediation of Christ. One cannot be freed from the power of Satan without the sacrifice of Christ, nor become a new creature without Christ and the Spirit. All of humanity's real possibilities stem from God's free grace, and not from the possibilities one brings into being by one's own efforts. Zinzendorf tells of an interesting struggle he had with various Lutheran censors when he tried to get one of his hymns printed. The hymn was:

> When one in the splendor of the light
> Looks at himself and sees he's of no worth,
> And goes and takes control,
> And no more does what he once did,*
> And labors much in many ways,
> He never learns what a Savior is.
>   * He really improves himself.[30]

Zinzendorf received the book back twice from the first printer, who tried to insert the word "not" in the third line, making it "And does not go and take control," meaning that the right way to the Savior is to correct one's ways. After Zinzendorf sent it back the second time, the

---

[29] Ibid., pp. 72-73 (18 Sept. 1746).

[30] The full stanza is to be found in *Graf Ludwigs von Zinzendorff Teutscher Gedichte Erster Theil* (Herrnhut: Zu finden im Waisenhause, 1735), p. 309, and in the 1766 edition of the same work, *Graf Ludwigs von Zinzendorf Teutscher Gedichte Neue Auflage* (Barby: Heinrich Detlef Ebers, 1766), p. 366. In this latter edition, the explanatory footnote keyed to line 4 is added, "He really improves himself." The first four lines of the verse are given in Zinzendorf, *Ein und zwanzig Discurse* [Title page: *Discurse . . . Auctoris*], pp. 208-9 (14 Jan. 1748). Here he discussed the problem he had with censors over this hymn.

printer refused to print it. The Count eventually printed it himself. It is as above in the 1735 edition of his *German Poetry*. Some time later, when it was included in the hymnal which was printed by another printer, a Wittenberg divine who was the corrector tried to change the same line and Zinzendorf believed that it remained in the first edition of the hymnal as "Lutheranly corrected." In the second edition the problem line was changed to "And does more than he should and can."[31] It is interesting to observe that in the *German Poetry* of 1766 there is a footnote (included in parentheses above) which tries to explain the line.

Even Zinzendorf's blood and wounds theology was an emphasis on grace. The grace of God is given concrete imagery in the vivid description of Jesus' suffering, and the believer enters into the experience of what God has done, not as an emotional experience within but as an objectification of God's grace which comes from without. The side wound becomes the place of security, as in Toplady's hymn "Rock of ages, cleft for me," and the Savior's sacrifice is the garment which the Christian wears as she or he comes to final judgment (as Zinzendorf expressed in "The Savior's blood and righteousness my beauty is, my glorious dress"[32]).

Since all depends on grace, there is nothing that can be done in preparation or study. What is needed is the preaching of the Gospel (which can occur in many varied and simple ways) and the activity of the Spirit in the heart (for the Spirit is the Savior's chief preacher and restores the spiritual dimension to a person's life, the "little spirit," which enables the heart to know the Savior).

> It really depends then upon the general plan of this Article which consists in this: we speak against our own preparation, work, and action. This is opposed in the Article: the studying and meditating as to how we may find out a way to blessedness, or to God, besides the Savior himself, and may make ourselves *habil* [qualified] for that through certain *preparationes* [preparations] according to academic taste. To this is a person naturally inclined according to pride and high thoughts about himself and the higher he has climbed, the more he is apt to devise such *preparationes* [preparations] and what he himself can cook up.

[31] Zinzendorf, *Ein und zwanzig Discurse* [Title page: *Discurse . . . Auctoris*], pp. 155-56 (14 Jan. 1748).
[32] Nikolaus Ludwig von Zinzendorf, "The Savior's blood and righteousness," in Moravian Church in America, *Moravian Book of Worship* (Bethlehem, Pa., and Winston-Salem, N.C.: Moravian Church in America, 1995), p. 201 (1739).

Now because the whole *Augustan Confession* was written in this spirit, to take away everything from the human being, and to vindicate grace, . . . therefore we are to reflect upon nothing in this whole fifth Article, but only this, that the Holy Spirit, and not the person, must make the beginning of human blessing (or salvation), even the plan for it, and that the news of all that which God has already bestowed upon us must convert persons. . . . What matters therefore is the message to the heart of the person which an apostle, or an angel of God, or a printed book, or a letter, or a student who sings before the window, or whoever brings it to the human heart — so is it always *evangelium* [Gospel]. If someone sends for a *paquet* [bundle] of herbs from the shop, a natural human being who never thought much about God all his life, or if someone sends to the apothecary for a bag of cloves and finds a paper wrapped around it upon which, among other things, there is something about Christ's merit and sufferings and which paper perhaps got there because the book from which it came did not do well, and this strikes him and he comes to be aware of his heart — who then will doubt that the bag is *evangelium* [Gospel] to him? And when this person one day comes before the throne of the Lamb of God and is blessed (or saved), then will this torn-off piece of paper have been as good to him as to another his book bound in velvet and covered with silver. . . . Therefore nothing is more inconclusive, than to rest the conversion of souls upon the *illumination* of the teacher, and this whole controversy is *de lana caprina* [of no import — of goat's wool]. For what is required for the conversion of one person through another? There is no qualification demanded of the instrument, but it is merely necessary that the *materia medendi* [material for healing] be rightly conveyed to the patient and be apprehended by faith. Thus then the merit of Christ is the treasure, the means for alluring forth and igniting faith, upon which the blessing (or salvation) of the person and the whole of temporal and eternal well-being are present all at once. That can come into being from a small opportunity, for that the Savior can make use of the meanest circumstances out of his great care for poor souls. But if a person would denigrate this, thinking, "What then will he teach us? How shall that thing help us? I will grasp it another way," and then set himself down like the Jewish Scribes and Cabbalists and prepare himself for the worthy contemplation of divine things, ten, twenty, thirty years, reducing himself to a skeleton over it, and the close *attention* and longing for speculations of this kind make him externally so pious and all other ideas and natural powers so dissipate him that one scarcely anymore knows whether he is a spirit or an ordinary person; yet he would be so unblessed after twenty years as he had previously been, and even a bit more unblessed. And during the time when he was thus preparing himself, perhaps the Savior may have conveyed the Word of his sufferings and atonement to many thousand uneducated hearts. . . .

If we are therefore to teach suitable to this Article, we must oppose all self-preparations and precursors of grace and say: "If the Holy Spirit awakens a longing in the heart, only the creaturely, human longing for one's creator, for one's origin, for one's joy, for one's flesh and bone (though yet unknown), and the heart is not stiff-necked, and does not forget it immediately but waits and reflects, not dissipating the inner stirrings brought about by the Holy Spirit but much more preserving them within and, as it is said about Mary, the *Evangelium* [Gospel] stirred; then the little creature becomes a student, a hearer of the *Evangelii* [Gospel], a church-child of the Holy Spirit, may the circumstances be as they will.[33]

Faith

For Zinzendorf then "faith is not everyone's thing," for it is God's "gift and act of compassion."[34] "This is a sovereign *remedium* [remedy] against all inappropriate passion and all vain undertakings which are not for the benefit of souls but more often turn out to their harm."[35] There is an aspect of faith which is the human response, and to this Zinzendorf assigns the infinitive *to believe* (τὸ πιστεύειν). The noun *faith* (ἡ πίστις) describes what God creates.[36]

[33] Zinzendorf, *Ein und zwanzig Discurse* [Title page: *Discurse . . . Auctoris*], pp. 223-27 (12 Feb. 1748). The reference to Mary probably has behind it Luther's translation of Luke 2:19, which reads: "wie es von Maria steht, bewegt das Evangelium." *Bewegen* means to move or stir. The English-language translation does mention 2:19, though the German-language text does not give biblical references. The story of Mary and Elizabeth in Luke 1:39-45 may also have been in mind. As John the Baptist leapt for joy in Elizabeth's womb, so the Gospel, Christ, stirred in Mary's womb, something not specifically referenced, but presupposed by, Zinzendorf's use of this story as a primary paradigm of the communication of the Gospel.

[34] Zinzendorf, *Reden zu Berlin für die Manns-Personen* [3rd. ed., 1743], p. 192 (9 Apr. 1738).

[35] Zinzendorf, *Ein und zwanzig Discurse* [Title page: *Discurse . . . Auctoris*], p. 239 (18 Feb. 1748). The eighteenth-century English-language translation uses the wonderful phrase, "the itch of making many converts."

[36] Zinzendorf, *Reden zu Berlin für die Manns-Personen* [3rd. ed., 1743], p. 192 (9 Apr. 1738). (A typesetting error numbers this page 170.)

Since faith as verb, as response, does not create faith as noun, which is God's gift, then faith can never be seen as a work which saves.

There (in some universities with a spiritual concern) I have observed that the very toiling and praying to obtain faith is made into a work, and this puts on the robe of faith in which faith stands before God when it enters heaven. Faith makes one blessed (or saves one), but why? Because faith costs so much until one attains it, with this one is rewarded by God and from this comes the way of speaking about this: the noble struggle of faith, from Paul's "fight the good fight of faith, lay hold of eternal life"; a matter concerning which we can speak another time.

It is too complicated for now, but I will only say this much now: that if we do not carefully pay attention, we can turn faith itself into doing, we can be caught in a certain net which is set out for self-righteous people and turn forgiveness of sins into a reward for the struggle of faith.

The *Augsburg Confession* says something quite different. What then do these people do who so teach and inform their hearers? Answer. They seek a way to God contrary to the Gospel and despise Christ. As it is expressed in the Augsburg Confession: Only through faith, and even that not of yourselves. Moreover, to faith you must bring nothing, there you must do nothing through art, science or other effort; but God must give faith and, as the *libri symbolici* [creeds] say, kindle it in the heart.[37]

There are also various types of faith. There is the faith of the devils which James speaks about. This is a recognition of the existence of God, but with no love for him. This cannot save. Then there is the faith of the ungodly, of humanity in general. What is needed is the heart, disposed and made fit, and this is a creation of God.

What then is the faith of the godless and of all ordinary persons who have not seen and yet say they believe? Answer: That is a light-minded faith, a faith in fables, a vulgar faith, a *credulitas* [credulity], which is not the same as *fides diabolica* [diabolic or devil's faith]. One comes and tells an old fairy tale: there was once a man, etc. Afterwards there comes another and says that there are ghosts in a house. Then one tells about Rübezahl in Silesia, and finally one comes and tells a story from the Bible, and the child believes the three, one as well as the other; that is truly no faith that makes one blessed (or saves) and that, I think, really needs no proof. . . .

[37] Zinzendorf, *Ein und zwanzig Discurse* [Title page: *Discurse . . . Auctoris*], pp. 257-58 (18 Feb. 1748).

That is a true Christian whose heart is so constituted that he (he, not this or that person, not in this or that country, not this or that *religion*, but he for his own person) finds forgiveness of his sin with *Christo* [Christ] and who to the glory of Christ knows so much about the dear God and believes in the dear God, because we have heard it from Jesus, and he has done such things which no one can do unless God were with him, God in whom the church believes because of *Jesu* [Jesus].

Neither Satan nor atheists believe in this Article, says the Augsburg Confession. This is our position and therefore they do not at all believe in *sensu theologico* [a theological sense].

The heart is compliant when faith is present, and that is an important matter, for nothing else is required except the heart.[38]

Faith then cannot be mere intellectual assent or an ignorant credulity, but must be an encounter of the whole person in his/her particularity and inmost being (heart) with the Savior. Without this response faith as content cannot even be understood, for only when God's gift is received does it begin to unfold its meaning. Thus, as Augustine said, "I believe in order that I may understand."

Zinzendorf also discussed faith according to the traditional distinctions of *fides implicita* (implicit faith) and *fides explicita* (explicit faith). The distinction concerns the difference between the faith response necessary to salvation and the intellectual formulations about and reflections upon what one believes in (faith seeking understanding). It is good if both can be together, but if not, "then it is sufficient if only the first is there, the *fiducia implicita*, the undisclosed but affective believing within the heart."[39]

Fides implicita is viewed according to two aspects: faith-in-distress (*der Glaube in der Noth*) and faith-in-love (*der verliebte Glaube*, which might best be defined as faith which in its nature is love). Faith-in-distress, which comes out of the natural human state and one's longing for help, has the infallible promise of God's grace.[40] It is in this condition that one receives the Savior. In this sense salvation is passive. Our job is not to oppose it. We have to come as a spiritual beggar.[41]

Faith-in-love is the response of the heart which in need has been open to the Savior. Zinzendorf's favorite term for faith is love. He believed that Paul calls saving faith love in 1 Corinthians 13,[42] and that

[38] Ibid., pp. 260-62 (18 Feb. 1748).
[39] Zinzendorf, *Nine Public Lectures* [1973], p. 35 (6 Sept. 1746).
[40] Ibid., p. 36 (6 Sept. 1746).
[41] Ibid., p. 71 (18 Sept. 1746).
[42] Ibid., p. 47 (11 Sept. 1746).

this is also to be found in John 21 in the conversation between Peter and Jesus.[43] Commenting on Peter's response to Jesus:

> And at that time he really did love Him more than all the others. Before he had loved Him in his imagination; he had honored Him and out of esteem for Him had rashly claimed to be ready to suffer death for Him rather than forsake Him. He did make a bold beginning, but he got stuck, because his love was dry and intellectual. But when the Savior forgave him everything, when He acquitted him of his sins, when He declared a renegade to be His apostle, then Peter could hold back no longer. If anyone said anything about his Lord to him, tears filled his eyes, and his body and soul were humbled. . . .
>
> All this is still *fides implicita*, the faith which is God's work in the heart in the middle of our stillness, where we and He have to do with each other alone, where nothing comes between us and Him — no man, no book, no knowledge, no learning, not even the most necessary truths — but only the distress, the sinner's shame, and the faithfulness of the Shepherd.[44]

Fides explicita may be described in two ways. It is the faith which we speak about and know while we are still learning of the Savior. "Not seeing and yet loving makes one ask afterwards, 'Who is that? What is that which I love this way?' And then one soon enough gets information for one's heart."[45] *Fides explicita* is also the faith about the Savior which we teach to others.

The whole life of the Christian consists

> in the increasing and growing in this knowledge, so that we know Him better today than yesterday and in a year know Him a year better, in twenty years twenty years better, and in eternity an eternity better than now. This is the great science; this is the great knowledge, without limit and end, the inexhaustible knowledge. In Him and His person lies hidden a treasure of wisdom and knowledge which cannot be fathomed or exhausted.[46]

Zinzendorf found this unfolding of faith's understanding in the biblical material itself.

---

[43] Ibid., p. 38 (6 Sept. 1746). Zinzendorf does not mention this, but it should be noted that belief and love are in a synonymous parallelism in 1 Pet. 1:8: "Without having seen him you love him; though you do not now see him you believe in him."

[44] Ibid.

[45] Ibid.

[46] Ibid., p. 49 (11 Sept. 1746).

One has only to compare the first sermons of the apostles with the subsequent ones, one has only to read Paul's epistles which he wrote at the beginning and to contrast them with the others which came out later. One has only to read John's letters and after that his Gospel, with which he concludes. Then one will see how the apostles' faith itself evolved, how the solid ideas of God the Creator as a human being successively develop. They obtained one important grace and power of demonstration after the other in their addresses. They had grace not only for confessing in the face of all the world, but also for learning to prove what they preached and for finding words to make themselves clear on these subjects.

It is one of the greatest pleasures to read the Bible according to the epochs, according to the periods, according to the stages by which the preaching of the Gospel has from time to time been growing and ascending. If one starts with the thirties, after the Saviour's birth, down to the nineties, and keeps this development in sight and meditates upon it in a simple and childlike way, then one sees what Paul means by saying, "That your love may abound more and more, with knowledge and all discernment (Philippians 1:9), that thereafter you may make such progress that you will measure the length, the breadth, depth and height of things" (Eph. 3:18, alt.).[47]

The Councils erred, not in the content of the Council's truth, but in making salvation a matter of conceptions and correct understanding.

We, according to our understanding in our communion, know how to manage this issue. We can help the councils out, because we hold that one has ordinarily no knowledge in the matter of salvation without being at the same time saved. We differ only on this point, that we do not believe that when someone does not know this or that, that he is therefore damned. For knowledge has degrees, and knowledge of important things does not come all at once. But since there are, nevertheless, still certain people who have insights into truths and yet are not saved, it cannot be made a universal principle that knowledge saves. But it is an exception to the rule if at some time knowledge does not save a person. I mean that which can be called true knowledge, the central knowledge that really matters, the point into which everything runs together: the *cardo*, the hinge of knowledge, does save; that is certain.[48]

[47] Ibid., p. 39 (6 Sept. 1746).
[48] Ibid., p. 45 (11 Sept. 1746). *Cardo* in Latin means "hinge" or "the point around which everything else turns."

That which saves is the knowledge called love, which is interpersonal knowledge between the soul and the Savior, expressed in the language of mystical marriage where one declares of Christ: "this is indeed bone of my bone and flesh of my flesh!"[49] Zinzendorf commented:

> I would like this love to be the only pleasant and blessed reality, the pearl toward which all souls extend their desires, so that they might win it and forget everything else, so that each soul would ask itself honestly and candidly, "Do you have this love?" Can you feel it? . . . Do you feel a condition which you have not had before? Has something happened to you which you need explained, if you cannot explain it yourself?[50]

The nature of salvation

Salvation has become a comprehensive term for what God brings about through Christ. It means to be kept from or rescued from danger or destructive forces, and in the passive has the connotation of prospering and well-being. There are many things that one is saved from: sin, enemies, death, the Devil, sickness, and particularly the final judgment and the wrath of God. One is also saved for life, heaven, God. Here I use the term *salvation* as a general and comprehensive term by which to describe Zinzendorf's understanding of the process involved and not so much as a term he utilized. His equivalent to our word *salvation* involves the use of the words *selig* (blessed - an adjective) and *Seligkeit* (blessing - a noun) which have broad connotations. To be or be made *selig* is to be saved because it is to be blessed with God's gift(s).

Salvation for Zinzendorf involved a process in which the Savior, as Creator, is engaged with each person. It is a process in which we may have confidence, because as Creator of all souls the Savior has designed all souls for salvation, though this may not actually come to pass. The sixth Lecture of his *Nine Public Lectures* is a good presentation of his views. This Lecture, taking John 1:11-12 as its text, is on the theme "That it is Blessedness and Happiness to be a Human Soul." This is so because to be human is to be one who is created to have eternal life.

Though the Savior forced people in Old Testament times, he does so no longer.

> I will appear before the heart with my truth which they shall have within. They shall not give themselves the least trouble about it; they shall not take a single step for it; they shall have no occasion

[49] Ibid., p. 49 (11 Sept. 1746).
[50] Ibid., p. 53 (11 Sept. 1746).

to expend the merest trifle upon it. Before they are aware of it, they shall have it in their hearts, as the wind turns into a corner and cannot find its way out again. It shall come close to them in their hearts, and thus shall they know me: without having to be taught, they shall acquire a love and affection for me, small and great, children and old people; and I will draw no distinctions. . . . If they will not be acquainted with me in this way, and if they are not inclined to love me in this manner, they may leave it alone; I shall force them no more.[51]

The matter is simply that the Savior comes, and then he is or is not received. This is the proper interpretation of the Second Advent of the Savior. The coming of Jesus into the heart consists simply in nothing else than that the Restorer of our nature, who is at the same time the Creator of its being, begins to become important in one's heart, be it from necessity or through a special dispensation, so that one is really concerned to become acquainted with Him.[52]

Thus if you have serious thoughts about the Savior, conclude that the bleeding Savior stands before your hearts, that he is there in person. He longs to have you glance at his wounds. He would like you to "look to him" (Hebrews 12:2) and your hearts to be so affected as if the bleeding Prince stood there with his opened side, ready to embrace your souls or, as Augustine states it, as if he were crucified before your very eyes.[53] Awareness of one's sins or spiritual poverty may create sadness, but the main point is whether you and the Savior want each other. It is not complicated, but simple.[54]

The major obstacle to salvation is the power of Satan, who also seeks his sovereignty over souls. As previously indicated, the similarity of Adam's sin and ours is in the submission to Satan's sovereignty. The death of the Savior atones for all sin on the cross so that "the entire Fall is erased" and humanity is freed from Satan's sovereignty. But this enemy is still alive, active and "trying the very same thing on each soul that he tried on the first man."[55] The process that the Savior undertakes with each person leads at some time to the response of one's free will to the coming of the Savior, if Satan has not complicated things.

No human soul, as such, need be lost in the entire world; a pure, simple man would certainly be saved. But he who has allowed Satan

[51] Ibid., p. 64 (18 Sept. 1746).
[52] Ibid., p. 66 (18 Sept. 1746).
[53] Ibid.
[54] Ibid., p. 67 (18 Sept. 1746).
[55] Ibid., p. 68 (18 Sept. 1746).

to put the notion in his head of being a fool, of one who wants to be like God, who has allowed Satan to flatter him into a kind of deification, an idolatry of himself, and to make him a self-idolator, a person who is in love with himself, who admires himself, who wants to balance accounts with God Almighty, who wants to measure himself by Him, who would gladly conclude an agreement with Him for salvation — whoever has allowed Satan time to build such castles in the air is not a simple man, no plain human soul; rather he is pregnant with demonic ideas; he participates in the spirit of Satan; he is spiritually possessed.[56]

Such a soul must be exorcised. "Therefore the Saviour says, 'The unclean spirit must depart from every man' (Luke 8:29, alt.); there is no other remedy."[57]

Yet one must not be too quick to judge the possibilities of salvation in terms of lack of response within this life. The basic principle is that "all souls are his." The Devil makes exception to this rule in our world. But

this says nothing about the place where everything is brought together, where all threads, all guideropes, all rays of the entire universe and all courses of time converge at one point. There the almighty grace of the atonement, the incontestable council of the atonement, is triumphant, and as long as a soul has not attained to thinking, to reflecting, to bidding and bargaining, it goes straight into the Saviour's arms.[58]

Although Zinzendorf used all of the traditional theological terminology to describe God's saving action in Christ, there were two central elements to his thought. The first was that Christ is Creator, all souls belong to him, and he is the initiator of salvation. This places salvation at the heart of creation and explains the passion of the Savior for salvation. Secondly, salvation is not primarily salvation from sins, human predicament, final judgment, etc., but was viewed in ways that make persons central to a drama involving personal cosmic powers. One is saved from the power of Satan, who deceives us about the nature of human existence, to the Savior, who comes to us in gentleness and love. In turn we respond in love, and in our embrace we find the destiny for which we were created, becoming "bone of his bone and flesh of his flesh." One might add a third element. It is all exceedingly simple and available to all, even a child.

[56] Ibid., p. 71 (18 Sept. 1746).
[57] Ibid., p. 72 (18 Sept. 1746).
[58] Ibid., p. 68 (18 Sept. 1746).

Sanctification

The term *sanctification* is traditionally used to describe what happens to the person in the forming of his or her life after salvation. Christianity has had various opinions about how far this formative process was able to go, some arguing for the ultimate perfection of a person, thus affirming that complete transformation was possible. The significance of sanctification for salvation has also been debated, seeing it as contributing to or a necessary prerequisite of salvation. Others have understood it as a divine gift, as is salvation, not as a human process.

As one might expect, Zinzendorf came to view sanctification not as a process towards Christian perfection, but as a gift of God's grace and an aspect of salvation. The best way that this can be dealt with is to share here the conversation, which I have translated from the Latin, in which Zinzendorf and John Wesley engaged over this very issue. Zinzendorf's point was that humans are sanctified at the same moment as they are justified, and that from the point of view of the Gospel one is holy only in Christ, not in oneself.

Z. I do not recognize any inherent perfection in this life. This is the error of errors. I prosecute this with fire and sword throughout the whole earth, I despise it, I annihilate it. Christ is our only perfection. He who seeks inherent perfection, denies Christ.

W. I truly believe that the Spirit of Christ produces perfection in those who are truly Christian.

Z. Not at all. All of our perfection is in Christ. All Christian perfection is faith in the blood of Christ. The whole of Christian perfection is imputed, not inherent. We are perfect in Christ, in ourselves we are never perfect.

W. We argue, I think, over words. Is not everyone who truly believes holy?

Z. Excellent. But only in Christ, not in himself.

W. But does he not live in a holy fashion?

Z. Indeed, he lives in every respect in a holy fashion.

W. And does he not also have a holy heart?

Z. Certainly.

W. And does it not follow that he is holy in himself?

Z. No. No. Only in Christ. Not holy in himself. No one has holiness at all in himself.

W. Does he not have in his heart love for God and neighbor, even if not the whole image of God?

Z. He does. But this is the holiness of law, not the Gospel. The holiness of the Gospel is faith.

W. All our strife is about words. Do you concede that the whole heart of the believer is holy and totally alive, that he loves God with all his heart and serves him with all his strength. I ask nothing more. I desire nothing else in my idea of perfection or Christian holiness.

Z. But this is not his holiness. He is not more holy if he loves more, nor is he less holy if he loves less.

W. What? Don't you believe that when he grows in love he also grows in holiness?

Z. Never. At the same moment as he is justified he is also sanctified. From that point on he is never more holy or less holy, even up to his death.[59]

Though the differences between these two great men are to be regretted, the difference is not a personal matter but involves a significant theological issue.[60] For Zinzendorf the focus was only on what the

---

[59] *The Journal of the Rev. John Wesley, A.M., Enlarged from Original MSS, with Notes from Unpublished Diaries, Annotations, Maps, and Illustrations,* Standard Edition, ed. Nehemiah Curnock (London: The Epworth Press, 1938), 2:487ff. (3 Sept. 1741); translated from the Latin by Arthur J. Freeman. (Abbreviated in subsequent notes as Wesley, *Journal.*) This encounter was also retained for Moravians in the *Büdingische Sammlung Einiger In die Kirchen-Historie Einschlagender Sonderlich neuerer Schrifften. Erster Band. Nebst darzu gehörigen Registern. Sind wir doch sein ererbtes gut.* (Büdingen: Joh. Chr. Stöhr [vol. 1], Korte [vols. 2, 3], 1742-44), 3:1026f. (Abbreviated in subsequent notes as *Büdingische Sammlung.*) The conversation was held in Latin and recorded in Latin. In a note later added to his *Journal* Wesley indicated that "to spare the dead, I do not translate." Zinzendorf was dead at the time the note was added (see Wesley, *Journal,* 2:488). The good memories of the Methodist-Moravian relationships were hard to eradicate even in the presence of their theological differences.

[60] Wesley writes in his *Journal,* 15 June 1741: "Mond. 15. I set out for London; and read over in the way, that celebrated book, *Martin Luther's Comment on the Epistle to the Galatians.* I was utterly ashamed. How have I esteemed this book, only because I had heard it so commended by others; or, at best, because I had read some excellent sentences, occasionally quoted from it! But what shall I say, now I judge for myself, now I see with my own eyes? Why, not only, that the author makes nothing out, clears up not one considerable difficulty; that he is quite shallow in his remarks on many passages, and muddy and confused almost, on all: but that he is deeply tinctured with mysticism throughout, and hence often dangerously (1st ed., fundamentally) wrong. To instance only in one or two points. How does he (almost in the words of Tauler) decry reason, right or wrong, as an irreconcilable enemy to the Gospel of Christ? Whereas, what is reason (the faculty so called) but the power of apprehending, judging and discoursing? Which power is no more to be condemned in the gross, than seeing, hearing or feeling. Again, how blasphemously does he speak of good works and of the law of God. Constantly coupling the law with sin, death, hell or the devil; and teaching, that Christ delivers us from them all alike. Whereas it can be no more proved by Scripture, that Christ delivers us from the law of God, than that he delivers us from holiness or from heaven. **Here (I apprehend) is the real spring of the grand error of the Moravians. They follow Luther, for better, for worse.** Hence their, "No works, no law, no commandments" (Wesley, *Journal,* 2:467. Also recorded in English, with German translation, in *Büdingische Sammlung,* 3:1023ff.). A note is added to Wesley's *Journal* indicating that while Charles Wesley and William Holland had found Luther's preface to *Galatians* most precious on May 17, 1738, John Wesley seems not to have known the book until now, that is, June 1741.

Christian is because of God's gift. Holiness, defined as the quality of belonging to God, is ours in Christ and has nothing to do with personal growth and development. This is the way the term is used biblically (e.g., note 1 Peter 1:2 and 1 Corinthians 1:2). There is also the truth that as humans we remain sinners so that we are *simul justus et peccator* [at the same time just and sinner], never believing that in this life we attain any state of perfection.

> We are not people who from the first moment of our spiritual life until into eternity itself remain unassaulted and unattacked. From a distance something comes at us; there is something in our own selves which we cannot name, to which we have as yet been unable to give the right name, until the proper position of the soul has been determined. . . . No reading, no hearing, no moral doctrine guards against it. For the only remedy against all such alluring demands, gross or subtle, is the doubtful glance of the Savior, when the form of Jesus does not seem so pleasing, so joyful to our hearts, when He seems to us to be no longer so sweetly before our hearts as usual.[61]

It is important to remember that even in eternity our holiness will be a "sinner-holiness," dependent on God:

> In short, the Savior has so constituted my heart, that I am a sinner and must remain so even into eternity, and when eternity arrives, I know with certainty that I will not be able to change: but I will remain in my sinner-form, in my sinner-poverty, in my sinner-shame in eternity and certainly will never encounter the persons nor attain the stage of perfection in the blessed eternity of which I have read and heard a great deal and which transforms one into a person that exists on one's own, who knows oneself as divinized. On this understanding I stand fast, by this I live and die: that in time and eternity our concern is nothing else than grace. Everything which is not God, which is not Creator, in a word which is not the Savior himself, is as the other poor creatures are which exist by grace. On that is built our whole system, our approach, our Church, our preaching of the Gospel, and matters of our *religion* and community.[62]

---

[61] Zinzendorf, *Nine Public Lectures* [1973], p. 85 (25 Sept. 1746).
[62] *Büdingische Sammlung*, 3:197.

New birth

New birth is the terminology often used to describe a certain type of conversion experience where the quality and character of life change. But more importantly new birth expresses a new beginning in life characterized by new dimensions, just as physical birth was the beginning of one's biological existence. The way the term *life* is used in the Gospel of John makes it clear that new birth brings with it a life with new characteristics and resources. In John 3:7 "You must be born anew" also may be translated "You must be born *from above*" (italics mine) indicating the introduction into life of transcendent dimensions. The Greek word ἄνωθεν actually has these two meanings.

Since Zinzendorf saw Christianity primarily as real relationship with Christ and the coming into being of a new reality within persons in the relationship with the Savior, not merely having a new status or new understanding, the imagery of new birth is important. It is focused on experienced realities.

Out of the pierced side of the Savior flowed the Spirit who is the agent of Christian life. The Spirit brings with himself all of the little spirits which are to be the basis for restoring the spiritual dimensions to human existence.

And as for the Holy Spirit who constructed himself as it were out of the *matrix* of his holy Side's Wound, he was not *en vogue* before, he did not before exist in the thoughts and knowledge of humankind. He then first, when the spear penetrated the dear Lamb, gushed out along with the incorruptible blood and life of the Lamb and with the Source of all, during this time, into human *individua* [individuals] to restore their little spirit (John 7) and has taken along the whole host of souls in his πληρώματι [fullness]. Now as all souls come from God, all human souls in general; so, *ut ita dicam* [if I may speak thus], these little spirits, these imperceptible, invisible, incomprehensible, gracious and Jesus-like spirits, which came forth out of our Savior's Side (preserved, sealed, and locked up in the Holy Spirit) by and by are distributed amongst the human *individua* [individuals], so that if one will describe himself, he says: "I know him. I know that I belong to him." Why? I have received one of the little spirits which have proceeded out of his Side, αὐτὸς ἐγω, I myself, my *individuum* [particular self] has that belonging to it which was destined for it, namely the little spirit sealed up until now in the Holy Spirit, which did not exist in me before, which I did not have since I was still fleshly, since I was still a natural person. I am now possessed by this so that I am now spiritual; so that now in me, that is, in my body and soul, something sits as it were upon the throne, so that it rules over soul and members and whose eminence the others (body and soul) do not desire to dispute but gladly recognize its divine origin and know that it is a little daughter of the Father and Mother in heaven.[63]

Zinzendorf compared new creation through the Spirit to the creation of woman.

The creation of woman, and the new creation, new birth of persons, is as if they were one act. "He took a rib out of his body and made a woman out of it. They stuck him in his side, and immediately blood and water flowed out. That was now the Spirit whom those who believe in him should receive, as the prophet has said: Out of his body will streams of living water flow." John. 7:38-39. Who believes should experience placing his hand in his side in faith, and saying: My Lord and my God![64]

The spirit, breathed into humanity at creation and lost in the Fall, is restored, becoming once again the basis for human spiritual existence and perception, representing God in the inner life of the person. The possibilities for the human to be what God intended and the Savior patterned are now available.

The mystical marriage

For Zinzendorf the mystical marriage is the primary expression of the relationship with the Savior/Creator. In this Erich Beyreuther calls him a straggler in the eighteenth century, for the high point of this was in the seventeenth century.[65] Yet in Zinzendorf's struggle with the Enlightenment, and in the light of his own experience, this was a natural expression. *Religion* consisted of a personal relationship with the Savior through the recreated heart and was constituted by the reality of the Savior ("You are bone of his bone and flesh of his flesh"). This, said

[63] Zinzendorf, *Ein und zwanzig Discurse* [Title page: *Discurse . . . Auctoris*], pp. 76-77 (16 Dec. 1747). The footnote to this passage indicates: "John says, 1 John 4:13, that God has given us something of his Spirit which is called our spirit, and so far contradistinguished from God the Holy Spirit. Αὐτὸ τὸ πνεῦμα [the Spirit itself], the Holy Spirit bears witness with our spirit. Rom. 8:16."

[64] Zinzendorf, *Auszüge aus Reden über biblische Texte* [OT], 1:77. The last reference is, of course, to the story of Thomas in John 20, which was a favorite of Zinzendorf.

[65] Erich Beyreuther, *Studien zur Theologie Zinzendorfs: Gesammelte Aufsätze* (Neukirchen-Vluyn: Kreis Moers, 1962), p. 72. (Abbreviated in subsequent notes as Beyreuther, *Studien zur Theologie Zinzendorfs.*)

Zinzendorf, is implied by the German term for a Christian. *Ein Christ* indicates that we bear the name of Christ and "we are Christians in the same way that, in our European countries, a wife takes the name of her husband and afterwards is called not by her maiden name but by her husband's name."[66]

> With pride the Christian says: "My Maker is my husband" (Isa. 54:5, alt.); He has not only created me, and He is not only the potter of my clay, but "He is the husband of my soul, who has betrothed Himself to me for ever and has betrothed Himself to me in grace and mercy, yet, has betrothed Himself to me in Faith" (Hos. 2:19f., LT, alt.). I am certain who my Husband is; I know Him.[67]

In his lecture on "That which, Properly Speaking, can Secure Us from all Fear, Danger, and Harm," he insisted that he who is "our true and eternal Husband" must have the most intimate claim on our lives.

> Therefore by faith and love we must so enter into the Saviour, that we can no longer see or hear anything else above or beyond Him, that we and He remain inseparably together. "I will know Him, as I am known by Him" (I Cor. 13:12, alt.). He knows me so well; He knows my hours and days; He knows my motions and emotions; He knows my abilities and inabilities; He knows my inclinations and my fears; He knows my danger and my security; in short, I can be nowhere better than in His arms.[68]

Sometimes his marriage imagery sounds strange to our modern ears, such as when he says that the Christian is to be perceived as "a consort, as a playmate for the marriage-bed of the blessed Creator and eternal Husband of the human soul."[69]

Erich Beyreuther's essay "Marriage —*Religion* and Eschaton" is a very helpful treatment of the use of this imagery by Zinzendorf.[70] He began with a brief discussion of Oskar Pfister's attempt at a psychoanalytical treatment and continued with a more extended examination of Leiv Aalen's attempt to understand this as an un-Lutheran foreign element in Zinzendorf's theology, derived from Augustine's teaching on grace

---

[66] Zinzendorf, *Nine Public Lectures* ([973], p. 77 (25 Sept. 1746).

[67] Ibid., pp. 77-78 (25 Sept. 1746).

[68] Ibid., p. 102 (16 Oct. 1746).

[69] Ibid., p. 86 (25 Sept. 1746).

[70] Beyreuther, "Ehe-*Religion* und Eschaton," *Studien zur Theologie Zinzendorfs*, pp. 35ff., 57ff.

and nature and transmitted through Jacob Böhme.[71]   Beyreuther was convinced that it is better to understand this in terms of Zinzendorf's search for pictorial language which would communicate the experience of the Savior, the use of the erotic language of baroque poetry, and as an outgrowth of the orthodox Lutheran teaching of the *unio mystica*.[72]

This is a central image for Zinzendorf. As Beyreuther commented: "The image of the marriage-*religion* stands unambiguously and prominently at the summit of all of his images."[73] Yet this image is "wedded" to his theology of the cross. The beauty of the Bridegroom, even when speaking of the Song of Songs, is the beauty of his wounds. Zinzendorf mentioned the story of a bishop named Martin, to whom Satan appeared in the likeness of the Savior, but in the form of a king surrounded with heavenly glory. Martin said to him: "If you are Christ, where are your wounds? . . . a Saviour who is without wounds, who does not have the mark of his sufferings, I do not acknowledge." To this Zinzendorf added:

> For the Saviour is never in all eternity without His sign, without His wounds: the public showing has His holy wounds as its ground. . . . If we, therefore, want to invite people to the marriage, if we want to describe the Bridegroom, it must be said like this: "I decided to know nothing among you except Jesus as He hung upon the cross (I Cor. 2:2, alt.), as He was wounded. I point you to His nail prints, to the side, to the hole which the spear pierced open in His side. . . . As soon as this look strikes your heart, you run to the marriage feast.[74]

The marriage imagery was widely used. It described the preaching of the Gospel as the invitation to the wedding with the Savior.[75] It was the basis for ethics, describing the Christian *praxis pietatis*, shaping life

---

[71] Oskar Pfister, *Die Frömmigkeit des Grafen Ludwig von Zinzendorf: Ein psychoanalytischer Beitrag zur Kenntnis der religiösen Sublimierungsprozesse und zur Erklärung des Pietismus*, Schriften zur angewandten Seelenkunde, vol. 8 (Leipzig: Franz Deuticke, 1910). Leiv Aalen, *Den unge Zinzendorfs Teologi* (Oslo: Lutherstiftelsens Forlag, 1952). Aalen believed that in dependence on Jacob Böhme's theosophy Zinzendorf developed a view about a continuity in creation, sin and redemption in which grace developed and completed what was in nature (p. 59). Beyreuther argues that Zinzendorf never viewed humanity as leaving behind the "sinner-holiness" and attaining some sort of completeness — even in eternity (p. 61). Aalen's work was translated into German as *Die Theologie des jungen Zinzendorf*, Arbeiten zur Geschichte und Theologie des Luthertums, vol. 16 (Berlin and Hamburg, 1966).

[72] Beyreuther, "Ehe-*Religion* und Eschaton," *Studien zur Theologie Zinzendorfs*, pp. 36ff., 43, 67.

[73] Ibid., p. 42.

[74] Zinzendorf, *Nine Public Lectures* [1973], p. 28 (4 Sept. 1746).

[75] Ibid., pp. 24ff.

and behavior.[76] It was also central to the Christian expectation and anticipation of the future, keeping in mind the biblical image of the marriage banquet. However, it never degenerated into individualism, for individuals are seen as part of the church which is the bride.

As Creator/Savior Christ embodied the male principle of existence, while all souls were female:

He has made all souls, which souls are his wife. He has formed no *animos*, no male souls among human souls, but only *animas*, female souls. These are his bride, candidates to rest in his arms and for his eternal bedroom: . . . In the kingdom of spirits there is only one husband who regards us as Esther and we regard ourselves as sisters.[77]

Human marriage then was provisional, since Christ is the only true male and in the end-time all males, as all females, will be married to Christ. In the interim before the end, man in the marriage is the representative of Christ and the woman is the image of the receptive and blessed church:

Amongst the married it is determined that the husband should be the image of the Atoner, of the Husband of all souls, and the woman is the image of the church, of that little community which has been won by the precious blood of Jesus.[78]

Though provisional, marriage is then not merely a means of handling sexual desire or for having children, but is a mystery which expresses the relationship between Christ and the church, as Paul describes it in Ephesians 5. This explains Zinzendorf's attention to sexual counseling for those newly married, though for the unmarried there was strict separation of sexes within the church. Marriage, even in its physical and sexual aspects, was sacramental:

It is a churchly grace (*Gemein-Gnade*) to sanctify marriage, to recognize the One who establishes it, to experience God in the

[76] Ibid., pp. 74-87 (25 Sept. 1746). This lecture on John 21:16, "Do you love me," speaks of how the husband of our soul directs us in life with his eyes, calling for our love and the realization that we are "a consort," "a playmate for the marriage-bed of the blessed Creator and eternal Husband of the human soul."

[77] Nikolaus Ludwig von Zinzendorf, *Die an den Synodum der Brüder, in Zeyst vom 11. May bis den 21. Junii 1746. gehaltene Reden, Nebst noch einigen andern zu gleicher Zeit in Holland geschehenen Vorträgen* (n.p.: Zu finden in den Brüder-Gemeinen, n.d.), p. 208.

[78] *Ehechor-Reden*, p. 210, also pp. 103, 105, 119, 294; quoted in Beyreuther, *Studien zur Theologie Zinzendorfs*, p. 59. These sermons to the Married Choir, 1747ff., exist in the Herrnhut Archives as a printed manuscript with Zinzendorf's corrections written in, but evidently were never published. Beyreuther notes that they are in the style of the Sifting Period (p. 44).

marriage, to find in heart and mind even the Holy Trinity active in the marriage at certain times.[79]

Reflections

The issues raised in this chapter are central to the Christian faith. What is our human predicament which keeps us and our world from realization of our destiny, and how is this to be resolved? Our world and our human nature are problematic, but they are not evil. It is important to know this; otherwise we reject the very vehicles of our life which are necessary, but incomplete.

As was stated at the beginning of this chapter, the problems of the human predicament are often culturally and contextually perceived. The Christ event is sufficiently comprehensive to provide resources to deal with the issues of each culture and person. And yet the solution is not just something we discover and implement when the problems are adequately understood and defined. It is really the solution which indicates the nature of the problems. The Creator/Savior God, in whom the meaning of creation and the paradigm of human existence are to be found, has offered himself as the Husband of the soul, and it is this relationship which is the solution beyond all solutions and which indicates that the foundational problem of human existence is relational. The foundational human need is not for solutions, but for the One who transcends us but is for us and with us. Here one has not just some helpful resolutions of some problems, but one has the Giver of all gifts, the Creator of each soul and all life, the One who is the true pattern and nature of human existence, the One who will work in a personal way towards the solving of all issues. It is in this relationship that true life is possible and the forces which would use and destroy us are overcome.

This relationship is gift. Not only can we not qualify ourselves for this relationship, but any relationship is always gift. It is not possible unless it is given — and received. It is given because it was always intended by the One who created us; it is given because this One has always loved us and would not let us go; it is given because the Lover of our soul would follow us into eternity with this gift; it is given because we cannot live without relationship with the Transcendent. How wonderful to know that it is given in a world where life seems to depend upon qualification and accomplishment! Who would have guessed it is given if the secret had not been told us?

And into eternity we will remain human and limited, so that we always need the relationship. Would we really want to qualify for eternity

[79] *Ehechor-Reden*, p. 210, quoted in Beyreuther, *Studien zur Theologie Zinzendorfs*, p. 53.

on our own, to become divinized and so autonomous? How lonely this would be: to be in ourselves what we can now be in relationship! Why would we want to be autonomous when even God in God's self is community, relationship, Trinity? Even married to the Husband of our souls we remain in relationship, never absorbed, never disappearing into the One who loves us and was wounded for us. This One preserves us in our identity and is gentle with us, never forcing us.

The relationship of the soul and her husband

In some ways Zinzendorf's view of the relationship with the Savior/ Creator was affected by hierarchical patterns of life in both the ancient world and his own time. His understanding of the term *Lord* for Jesus in the 1750s was also related to this: Jesus was the Father who ruled the house. It is amazing that Zinzendorf, both in speaking of the relationship with the Savior and in his approach to pedagogy, was able to transcend his own experience of authority, though still speaking of the need for a Lord. The dominance of his life by an absent mother, tutors, and educational discipline at Halle, all affected him. Alice Miller, writing of child-rearing practices in Europe up to the twentieth century, speaks of "poisonous pedagogy" bent on breaking the will of the child,[80] exactly the advice of Zinzendorf's mother to Francke at Halle. Yet Zinzendorf came to believe in the goodness of the child and the loving nature of the "house-father."

Zinzendorf's understanding of Christ as Husband and Lord needs more than the "humanization" he provided. Is it possible to preserve the truth of one's need for a "Lord" while allowing for a different style of relationship between humanity and God? Paul in Galatians 3-5 seems to imply this. In Christ and through the Spirit one was freed from Law and the "elementals" to function in freedom and maturity. What are the functional implications of this maturity?

The new role of women in Jesus' ministry and the early church would also seem to have implications for this, both as an expression of their special value and dignity within the life and mission of the church and as an expression of a new styling of relationship within the social institution of marriage. This latter is especially important because marriage is at times used as a metaphor of the relationship of Christ and the church (e.g., Ephesians 5:21ff.), and thus one might expect to learn about the relationship of the person with Christ from the style of relationship in Christian marriage. Unfortunately the new freedom of women in the life of the church is often misunderstood from the

[80] Miller, *For Your Own Good* (full bibliographic information in n. 5, above).

ambiguity in the New Testament material. The favorite Gospel of Matthew provides little role for women (in contrast to Luke and John). Paul has often been seen as calling for limitations on the public role of women, but this is primarily based on later additions to Paul's letters by those who tried to borrow his authority for a more conservative and restrictive position on women.[81] When Paul's authentic literature is analyzed, it is clear that women were engaged with him in mission (see Romans 16), and he indicates that in Christ there is "neither male nor female" (Galatians 3:28). In 1 Peter 3, although women are to be submissive to their husbands, the husbands should recognize that women are "joint heirs of the grace of life." Thus there are various advocacies of traditional social roles, but much recognition of women's equal status and sufficient evidence of their engagement in significant roles.

Besides the liberalization of the role of women, there is the new stylization of the human relationship with God. This is reflected in both Romans 8 and Galatians 4, where Paul uses Jesus' term "Abba, Father" as central to his description of the human relationship with God.[82] *Abba* is a term of intimacy, not subservience, and in Paul's world is almost a feminization of God in a world where "father" is usually the authority and head of the house.

However this relationship might be styled in the present, of course God remains God and humans remain human. But perhaps the soul is called into maturity and responsibility in relationship with her Husband, rather than dependence, and is offered a measure of autonomy. Thus in relationship with our Husband we are called upon to gain ourselves as well as lose ourselves. Christ wants persons who can think and act, while always remembering who leads them into both their and his future, and remembering who is the Source of their life. This allowing of maturity and intimacy should also allow the struggle with God so characteristic of many Old Testament stories about relationship with God, out of which we, like Jacob, may come both lamed and blessed.[83]

[81] Materials in 1 Corinthians and 1 Timothy assigning a very restricted role to women seem to be later additions to Pauline materials. Paul mentions a number of women in Romans 16 who were his associates and in Gal. 3:28 indicates the equality of men and women in Christ.

[82] *Abba* was the word for "Father" with which Jesus began the original form of the Lord's Prayer in Aramaic. It was a familiar form of address, made polite with the addition of a pronominal suffix, such as in the beginning of the Lord's Prayer in Matthew: "*Our* Father who art in heaven." This was part of Jesus' teaching about the familiar and loving nature of the relationship with God.

[83] Gen. 32:24ff.

While Zinzendorf spoke of the gift of the marriage of the soul with Christ at the beginning of the relationship, there is also a process in which the partners in the marriage grow into a oneness where distinctions become very difficult if the marriage is fulfilling its purpose. Teresa of Avila, who saw the marriage with God as the end of a process rather than a gift at the beginning of the Christian life, described her experience, distinguishing between betrothal, which allows some autonomy to the soul, and spiritual marriage, when distinctions can no longer be made. While I agree with Zinzendorf that the marriage of God and the soul is a gift at the onset of the Christian life, what Teresa says is worth considering:

2. "You must understand that there is the greatest difference between all the previous visions and those of this dwelling place. Between the spiritual betrothal and the spiritual marriage the difference is as great as that which exists between two who are betrothed and between two who can no longer be separated."
4. In spiritual betrothal the two may still separate; the union is different because even though a joining takes place, in the end the two can be separate and remain by themselves. In spiritual marriage, "the soul always remains with its God in that center." "In the spiritual marriage the union is like what we have when rain falls from the sky into a river or fount; all is water, for the rain that fell from heaven cannot be divided or separated from the water of the river."[84]

The soul between the powers

Living between the powers pretty well describes what most of us experience in life. This can be described in terms of the *powers of world and society* which affect our lives from *outside* us, but it can also be described as an experience which occurs *within* us, expressing the varied *dynamics of the psyche*. If we do not choose a dominant and creative power which would lead our lives to their appropriate destiny and form our lives in creative and good ways, we are either driven in other directions or torn between the powers.

For Zinzendorf the soul lived primarily between the power of the Creator/Savior and the power of the Devil, understood in the New Testament sense as the head of the powers of evil. If one did not take the opportunity of choosing the Creator, the Devil took over by default. These two powers vied for influence over human life.

[84] Teresa of Avila, *The Interior Castle*, trans. Kieran Kavanaugh and Otilio Rodriguez, Classics of Western Spirituality (New York: Paulist Press, 1979), pp. 177-79.

I have come to take seriously the reality of radical Evil, or the Evil One: a purposive, intentional, and personal presence of evil in the world. To recognize this should not make life more frightening, but less, for one then has a chance to deal with what impacts and influences life. Without our awareness, Evil may use us, to others' and our own destruction, with little understanding of the real dynamics with which we must cope. It is interesting that we have been living in an "enlightened" age since the eighteenth century, with new confidence in human reason, self-understanding, and historical and scientific methodology. And yet look at what has happened within this history, the terrible, terrible tragedies of this history. I have lived through the Second World War, the Holocaust, the Communist Empire, the Korean War, the Viet Nam War, countless tragedies in Africa and presently in Yugoslavia, hatred against minorities in my own country, besides the many local incidents which appear in the newspapers each day. Can one explain this only in terms of the problems of human beings? However, in no way does this mean to see Evil around every corner and to excuse our actions with, "The devil made me do it."

The *religion* of the Old Testament, by and large, interpreted the significant spiritual dynamics of the world and human existence as being only God. There were no other forces of any consequence. There were human and historical forces, but God was always in control of these. This made life seem simple: do good and get good and get God's blessing. By the time of the intertestamental period Judaism came to interpret its world dualistically, as indicated at the beginning of this chapter. This was, I believe, not just because Jews became acquainted with the thought systems of Greeks and Persians, who were dualistic. This different interpretation of human existence came because the old interpretation no longer adequately explained what was experienced in life. The hoped-for realization of God's promises did not occur. The righteous did not receive what they deserved. And moreover, there seemed to be other powers operating within the world which indicated that the world was more complex than they had previously thought. One system of powers was what we might call the neutral powers which they understood were behind nature, political and economic systems, and the stars. They were neutral, as humans were neutral, and could do good and evil. Another system of powers involved Satan and demons, the inherently evil powers. Whereas in the book of Job Satan is God's district attorney, bringing accusations against Job, in the intertestamental period Satan is a fallen angel who has taken over this world and is its ruler. Satan is described as a real power in the world, and so is attractive to those who find the world and its powers difficult to manage.[85] Satan also opposes God and God's values and wishes for the world. In the Gospel of Mark the proclamation of the Kingdom of God is accompanied by the attack on Satan's kingdom and authority.

Growing spirituality necessitates one's dealing with all of the spiritual dimensions of existence, for it calls those who do so to the attention of Evil. Increasing one's spirituality is an invitation to Satan, and a most dangerous invitation for those who think Satan does not exist. Satan would seem to bother primarily with those who are potentially good and God's. Paul's linking of the "messenger of Satan" with his "abundance of revelations" in 2 Corinthians 12 is a theme repeated in Christian mysticism. It is also important to recognize that the issues, problems, and struggles of the inner life can also be used by Evil for the destruction of the person and his or her relationship with God. Thus involvement in the spiritual world calls for growing wisdom and discernment and particularly staying close to the relationship with God by which we are sustained. We might ask, if relationship with God opens up to us the whole of the spiritual world, including elements which are dangerous, why get involved in the first place? But this is our destiny. We are made for relationship with God, and we are spiritual beings. The nature of life does not go away if we refuse to see it.

Related to the spiritual dimensions of being human is the sacred task humans have as an essential dimension of creation. The human being, as the primary place where the world comes to consciousness and develops the possibility of implementing intentions, is the primary location for the operation of the spiritual powers. As asserted in Lukan theology of Jesus, we become the place of God's Spirit and Kingdom for the transformation of life and society (Luke 4:17-19). This is implied in the role assigned to humans in the creation stories of Genesis 1-3.

While I do not want to buy into the negative appraisal of world and human existence which is a part of dualism, I have come to believe that one ignores the reality of Evil to one's own detriment. Nothing is helped by ignoring what is real on the personal or cosmic level. If one cannot accept the existence of a personal force of evil, the phenomena of recent history call upon one to recognize the reality of evil beyond the merely individual level — if one only calls it corporate and systemic.

[85] Today many who are attracted to Satanist cults are seeking to gain control over the powers and forces in life.

Between the powers of the psyche

Ordinarily we have thought of the powers as being outside of us. Jungian psychology has given us some interesting insights as to the powers which operate within us, but which also may be the media through which the powers outside us operate. If Jung is right in his description of interior powers, and most persons experience this, then the resolution of the dynamics of the psyche becomes as important (and as much a religious issue) as the resolution of the dynamics of the outside world. The world to which Christ comes is also our inner world.

Jung understood that there was an archetype, a structure within the psyche inherited as a part of human nature, that functioned as God. He called this the self, "a term on the one hand definite enough to convey the essence of human wholeness and on the other hand indefinite enough to express the indescribable and indeterminable nature of this wholeness."[86] Christ, as the image of God, psychologically refers to the self. Jung says, "He is in us and we in him. His kingdom is the pearl of great price, the treasure buried in the field, the grain of mustard seed which will become a great tree, and the heavenly city. As Christ is in us, so also is his heavenly kingdom. These few, familiar references should be sufficient to make the psychological position of the Christ symbol quite clear. *Christ exemplifies the archetype of the self.*"[87] Thus the Christ story addresses the self within persons and enables the integrating and healing action of the self within the psyche. If this is true, then it is absolutely necessary that Christ be taken into the inner life of the person or that the Christ story inform the self-structure that is already there.

However, Jung sees the Christian symbol of Christ as incomplete, because it seems to call upon persons to be completely good, to the exclusion of the dark side of the psyche represented by the archetype of the *shadow*. The shadow is the opposite of our conscious values and understandings, unintegrated with consciousness and usually autonomous. While being a part of the psyche it may function against us. Jung's *Answer to Job* is an interesting presentation of how when challenged by Job, a righteous man, even God comes to consciousness of his shadow. God realizes the way he has harmed Job, and grows through this.[88] Thus

[86] C. G. Jung, *Collected Works*, trans. R. F. C. Hull, ed. Sir Herbert Read et al., Bollingen Series 20 (Princeton: Princeton University Press, 1953-79), XII, 20, quoted in John Welch, *Spiritual Pilgrims* (New York: Paulist Press, 1982), p. 192. (Citation of the Welch work will be abbreviated in subsequent notes as Welch, *Spiritual Pilgrims*.)

[87] C. G. Jung, *Collected Works*, trans. R. F. C. Hull, ed. Sir Herbert Read et al., Bollingen Series 20 (Princeton: Princeton University Press, 1953-1979), IXii, 60, 70, quoted in John Welch, *Spiritual Pilgrims*, p. 192.

[88] Carl G. Jung, *Answer to Job*, trans. R. F. C. Hull, Bollingen Series (Princeton: Princeton University Press, 1969). The God Jung describes here as discovering his dark side is really the archetypal God of the psyche, and not the God outside the person.

Christ and the shadow (or evil) are foundational or archetypal aspects of the psyche, not merely external to the psyche.

Wholeness in Christian perspective is often thought to be freedom from evil and an overcoming of the opposites that we find within us. Jung believed wholeness came by integration of the shadow into consciousness and "self" so that it might creatively contribute. John Welch, who follows Jung's psychological paradigm in his approach to spirituality, suggests that there is an approach to the Christ story which includes both self and shadow. This can be found in the image of the crucifixion, where Christ enters into the mystery of all that is human and thus embraces the shadow.[89]

One must question whether Christianity, in its dualism inherited both from Judaism and Hellenism, adequately has come to terms with the fullness of what it is to be human. Christian ethics often presumes the elimination of evil within humanity, rather than the integration of darkness and light. We pretend that if we are faithful and righteous we have no shadow. When this is done the shadow functions autonomously below consciousness, emerging to the harm of ourselves and others where it finds excuse.

Zinzendorf's, and Luther's, view of the Christian as *simul justus et peccator*, at the same time just and sinner, comes closer to Jung's perspective. Zinzendorf's emphasis that one is *both sinner and just into eternity* is even more so, though he does not see the creative possibilities of the human shadow. Zinzendorf's emphasis on Christ's humanity and his remaining the crucified one to all eternity also has interesting possibilities. Thus one might find Zinzendorf on the way to a more modern understanding of what it means to live between the powers.

Jung noted the difficulty in distinguishing between what is within and outside the psyche when dealing with the Transcendent.[90] This points up the possibility of some relationship between these two dimensions of reality.

[89] Welch, *Spiritual Pilgrims*, pp. 199ff.

[90] "I have, therefore, even hazarded the postulate that the phenomenon of archetypal configurations — which are psychic events *par excellence* — may be founded upon a *psychoid* base, that is, upon an only partially psychic and possibly altogether different form of being. For lack of empirical data I have neither knowledge nor understanding of such forms of being, which are commonly called spiritual" (Carl G. Jung, *Memories, Dreams, Reflections*, recorded and ed. by Aniela Jaffe, trans. R. Winston and C. Winston, rev. ed. [New York: Vintage Books, Random House, 1965], p. 351). This is a statement about the difficulty, according to his scientific methodology, in knowing what is beyond the psyche. Yet this statement also affirms his attraction towards what is beyond. To a young clergyman in 1952 he wrote, "I find that all my thoughts circle around God like the planets around the sun, and are as irresistibly attracted by Him. I would feel it to be the grossest sin if I were to oppose any resistance to this force" (Ibid., p. xi).

One needs to ask how the Transcendent that is outside the psyche can affect human and historical processes. It is not that God as energy could not affect matter, but when one observes how one experiences the Transcendent (good or evil), it seems that the primary agency is the human being. The reality of the unconscious and the complexity within the psyche offers opportunity for the transcendent powers. God may act through us both through the archetypal materials within the psyche and what has been learned or introjected through our religious traditions. God may also use whatever the psyche has experienced and become developmentally. Evil may use the parts of the psyche that are susceptible, either the archetypal structures we have not made conscious and integrated or the anger, hurts, and fears which originate within our life experience. God and Evil may not only use individuals, but groups who share common dynamics. *It is, however, important that what is within us not be seen as evil in itself, thus disassociating ourselves from it with consequent great danger.* We cannot reject that which we are and with which we must learn to live. We cannot deal creatively with what we reject. We need freedom from the evil outside us and union with the Savior outside us so that we can explore and integrate what is within, calling upon the "image of God" within, the "self," empowered by the external reality of Christ. I view this as part of the creative process to which Christ, as both Savior and Creator, leads us.

If the above is so, then attention to the psyche is not merely a developmental task, contributing to human well-being, maturity, and functioning. Nor is it merely spiritual in the sense of encouraging human evolution in a spiritual direction.[91] It is spiritual because it contributes to what the Savior/Creator intends us to be. It is through what we are that the spiritual powers impinge upon human experience, history, and economic and political systems. What tragedies of recent history might have been averted if we had only realized that what we are and to whom we submit ourselves is the root of all that happens in life!

Does this sound complicated, to seek to deal with life between the powers, without and within? Then simply accept the Savior/Creator

[91] Ira Progoff, in *Depth Psychology and Modern Man* (New York: McGraw-Hill, 1959), presents his psychological model for his journaling process. He sees the development of the human psyche in the history of evolution as the creation of an instrument by which the biologic process of life could one day transcend itself. Thus the persons who reach a high level of spiritual achievement are carrying "the evolutionary process of life further within their individual existence than nature herself had taken it." Such persons "have also become channels through which the purposes of God's creation could be drawn closer to fulfillment, as they have worked toward the perfectibility of man within their own existence" (pp. 260-61). Thus they move human existence in a spiritual direction.

into your life, and he will care for what needs to be done if you are willing to follow his leading. Life does not all have to be understood or lived now, but one does have to surrender to the Savior/Creator for the process to begin. What should come then will come when it should.

There is a throne
deep in my heart
I pray
you'd take
to center
me in you.

and by your love
and power
help me to live
'midst all
the powers
within, without.

But I do pray
that I would grow
mature with you,
with others,
to take my
place in life.

Whate'er
you'd make of me
I'd not forget
you are my life.
I can't create
your gift,

nor would
I
ever
wish
to be
alone.[92]

[92] By the author.

Chapter 5

Christian Life and Ethics

We often think of the primary concerns of Christianity as having to do with solving the God-human relationship, formulating statements of truth, and establishing correct institutions. And yet one has only to read the Bible to see the centrality of life and ethics. This is central not only because of a concern for patterns of behavior responsible to God and others, but for the resourcing of the life of the person. How does a person live suitable to human possibility and destiny when confronted by interior and exterior, or environmental, forces and limitations?

Romans 12:1-15:18 constitutes the primarily ethical portion of Paul's great letter which explained his theology to Roman Christians. This ethical section is connected by the "therefore" of 12:1 to the theological argumentation of the first eleven chapters. But one only has to glance at the first eleven chapters to see there also the ethical interwoven with the theological. This is true of every New Testament treatment of the Household Codes,[1] each being supported by prior theological argumentation and introduction about the basis and nature of the Christian life. It might even be argued that the primary concerns of the early church were ethics and life, and often theological assertions were focused on the life which they facilitated. Thus the treatment of Christian life and ethics calls for a profound investment.

For the beginnings of both the Ancient and Renewed Moravian Church, Christian life was an essential focus. They were part of movements for the reform of the life of the church. The Ancient Church in its beginnings was called "Brethren of the Law of Christ," following a

[1] The Household Codes are discussed in the Reflections at the end of the chapter. They are to be found primarily in 1 Peter, Colossians and Ephesians and deal with conduct within the Christian household.

semimonastic life expressed in the Sermon on the Mount. Gradually the church became more open to society, included the nobility, embraced education, and listened to the insights of the "Second Reformation." Though it always remembered that the essential of Christian faith and life was the gift of relationship given by God, which all else served, the rootage of life in the soil of grace was not always fully appreciated or trusted. Zinzendorf, on the other hand, asserted that *all was dependent on grace and the Savior.* Life is the outcome of the graced realities in one's life. While the human responsibility for ethical behavior was taken seriously, there was no thought of attempting to attain a *human* perfection. This was impossible because one was always, at one and the same time, *justus/sanctus et peccator,* "justified/holy and sinner." For Zinzendorf not only justification but holiness would always depend on the Savior's grace, even in eternity. One could never outgrow the need for grace. The ethical imperative then was the appreciative and loving response to God's gift lived out from the resources of this gift. In the earlier stages of both the Ancient and the Renewed Moravian Church, community also played a central role in guiding and resourcing behavior.

Law and Grace

In some sense the relationship of Law and Grace was an issue faced by earliest Christianity as it explored the place for the Jewish Law and tradition in Christian life. But it soon became also a question of the role of moral law and ethical principle when God in grace had already provided justification and even holiness. Paul's contemporaries raised the question of whether sin really mattered anymore. Why not continue in sin that grace might abound? (Romans 6:1) Over the years the argument for retaining a place for the Law has represented both a desire to preserve the Law as a part of God's revelation and the need for moral structure, along with grace, rooted in the history of God's provision for life.

Zinzendorf distinguished the laws of the state from the laws and principles of morality. Public law and the authority of the state are related to the institutions of the community in which one lives and are matters of policy. They concern the patterns of community life. But they do not concern the inner person, the heart, or what is spoken of in Scripture.[2]

---

[2] Minutes of the 1750 Synod, as recorded in *M. Avgvst. Gottl. Spangenbergs Apologetische Schluß-Schrift, Worinn über tausend Beschuldigungen gegen die Brüder-Gemeinen und Ihren zeitherigen Ordinarium nach der Wahrheit beantwortet werden, Nebst einigen wichtigen Beylagen* (Leipzig and Görlitz: In der Marcheschen Buchhandlung, 1752), p. 487. (Abbreviated in subsequent notes as *Spangenbergs Apologetische Schluß-Schrift.)*

Morality, viewed as the ultimate principles by which one lives, and not seen as the institutions which a community may establish for its life, can be based only upon God and not upon observation of any natural law (as advocated by many in the Enlightenment).

> What is moral can not be determined outside of the revealed will of God, but what God makes moral, that is moral.
> Since the Lord Jesus became a man, so are all things moral which the Savior, according to his heart, has indicated to be thought and done; and what his heart rejects . . . that is immoral. . . . now what is suitable to Jesus decides morality.[3]

Morality must begin with faith, and particularly the graced reality of the Christian life, for otherwise it is attempted without its proper foundation and is condemned to failure.

> The beginning is not to be made with doing what our Savior has commanded. For, as has already often been said: who begins with doing, when he is still without power in the Spirit, when he is still dead, when he is still blind, when he still has no grace, when he still has not experienced the power of God but still stands in his own strength, he is in no way prepared. And if he does something he weaves a cloth which is of no use.
> He has a false ground the shallowness of which he does not see and take note of, which draws him still deeper because he thinks that he stands upon a ground.
> We can give nothing before we have something.[4] We must have grace, forgiveness in the blood of Jesus.
> We must first know why he is Lord of the whole world and us, so that each soul must experience in himself why he is its Lord. Each soul must be able to say with joy, he is my Lord.[5]

The statement "We can give nothing, before we have something" should be written in bold letters, framed, and hung upon the wall of

---

[3] Nikolaus Ludwig von Zinzendorf, as recorded in *Spangenbergs Apologetische Schluß-Schrift*, p. 484.

[4] In the eighteenth-century translation this sentence is rendered "We can do nothing before we have something." The verb in German is *geben* (give), and this is important. Ethical action does not just do something but when based on a spiritual reality it also gives something of the reality on which it is based.

[5] Nikolaus Ludwig von Zinzendorf, *Inhalt dererjenigen Reden, Welche zu Berlin vom 1ten Januario 1738. bis 27ten Aprilis in denen Abend-Stunden sonderlich für die Manns-Personen gehalten worden* (Berlin: Christian Ludewig Kunst, n.d.), pp. 162ff. (1738), reprinted in vol. 14 of Nikolaus Ludwig von Zinzendorf, *Ergänzungsbände zu den Hauptschriften*, ed. Erich Beyreuther and Gerhard Meyer (Hildesheim: Georg Olms, 1964-85), 14:66-67 (12 Mar. 1738). (Abbreviated in subsequent notes as Zinzendorf, *Reden zu Berlin für die Manns-Personen* [1st ed., n.d.].)

every church and Christian home. It is so easy to be practical and focused on the needs at hand without looking to the life resources which enable both life and action. In fact, knowing what to do is not a second step beyond the spiritual realities which constitute us; rather it is from these spiritual realities that we learn what to do. For this Zinzendorf quoted the Augsburg Confession and Luther.

When it finally and really happens that a heart believes on the wounds and the atonement which occurred through Christ, and receives this Atoner in the heart, then ought we surely to take such a one to school and tell him: "Look! Now you have become a believer, now will I tell you what to do and what to let alone?[6] No, not at all; the Augsburg Confession says whoever believes will by faith itself be led to good works and fruits, and that for the sake of God. A believer can make mistakes, can not reach the goal, can err; for such is a poor sinner and remains so until death. But a believer either does not know that there is something good to be done, or he does it if he has an opportunity and understands that there is nothing bad about it; or he leaves it alone. That is the character of a believer; at least it is certain that when he reads it in a book or someone tells him you must do good, that tells him nothing more than his faith itself. You have an anointing from the one who is holy and knows all. Item. This I do not say to you as one who does not know it, for you have the anointing which teaches you everything.

The "anointing" is nothing else than another name, another designation which expresses that which faith signifies, the oil in the vessel. Why does the little lamp burn so well? I continually pour into it. Where does that come from? From what then does the heart live? From what does it then so burn? O, it lives in faith in the Son of God who loved me; its nourishment is faith in the Son of God who gave himself for me, who became a spring which never in all eternity will dry up. John 4:14. Why then does that other lamp burn so poorly? It is wanting in faith; when that is true so would even works be judged as of no value according to God's mind, as it says in an ancient verse. What should be is to proceed on the foundation of our Savior's mind and will: one would make no detour, one would not think back and forth, one would not so long twist and turn; but what one would think would well please one's Lord, that

[6] The eighteenth-century English-language translation omits the question mark in this sentence even though the following sentence is preserved with its strong "No." One might guess that the translator had a problem with this as a question. What follows is difficult to translate and almost might be taken two ways. The German is "Nein, eben so wenig, die Augspurgische Confession sagt, wer gläubt." It cannot mean "No, just as little as . . ." because that would deny what the Augsburg Confession says.

one would do with joy. One would love much because one has been forgiven much. An old Halle hymn reads: "Command as Lord your child, redeemed at great cost." That is true, but they should also diligently sing what they previously so orthodoxly sang:

What should I yet desire,
o'erwhelmed by grace's flood,
now that I have entered
the Holy through your blood;
there eternal redemption I've found,
now freed from hell's dominion,
salvation's garment I've obtained,
wherein my faith in eternity's displayed.

This is a main point in the Article (of the Augsburg Confession): for God's sake, for the Savior's sake, for our Redeemer's sake, because we forget how much it cost him to redeem us. From awareness of this I will study how I should adorn my heart, my whole spiritual garment, inasmuch as that depends on me — for very little depends upon me. The Holy Spirit always cares for this. I seldom get so much as a pin to stick; he does it, he adorns me for the wedding-day. But what I can do with regard to this is a trifle, and that I will learn from Jesus' suffering, faith in his wounds, the glance into his wounds which endures for all time, which should make me holy and educated for the Kingdom of Heaven, which should make such a God-human out of me that all persons should recognize whence I come, that my origin is from heaven on high, that I come from Jesus' side, in which I found again through grace what I had lost.[7]

---

[7] Nikolaus Ludwig von Zinzendorf, *Ein und zwanzig Discurse über die Augspurgische Confession gehalten vom 15. Dec. 1747. bis zum 3. Mart. 1748. denen Seminariis Theologicis Fratrum zum Besten aufgefaßt und bis zur nochmaligen Revision des Auctoris einstweilen mitgetheilet* (n.p., n.d.), pp. 239-41 (18 Feb. 1748). For information about the two different printings of this work, see chapter 1, note 82. Citation of the printing used in book will be abbreviated in subsequent notes as Zinzendorf, *Ein und zwanzig Discurse* [Title page: *Discurse . . . Auctoris*].
There are several rather long quotations from Zinzendorf in this chapter. It is important to let him speak for himself. The first line of the hymn quoted in German is *Was soll ich noch mehr verlangen.* For Zinzendorf the side-wound of Jesus functioned much as indicated in Augustus Toplady's familiar hymn (1776):
Rock of ages, cleft for me,
Let me hide myself in Thee;
Let the water and the blood
From Thy riven side which flowed
Be of sin the double cure;
Cleanse me from its guilt and power. (Moravian Church in America, *Hymnal and Liturgies of the Moravian Church* [Bethlehem, Pa. and Winston-Salem, N.C.: Moravian Church in America, 1969], hymn 334.)

In regards to God's Law in the Old Testament, Zinzendorf held it in high respect. However, what he respected is the *materia legis*, the content of the Law. What he rejected is "the legal method" and the attempt to see one's own righteousness through the Law.

> The Law is still valued by us even to the present, and so it must remain. For although the legal method and way is at an end, yet the *materia legis* is always something fine and desirable.[8]

Thus morality and behavior become not a *Muss* [must] and a *Last* [burden] but a *Lust* [pleasure—note the play on words in the original German]. It is no burden, but a joy, grace and privilege.[9]

The problem with the Law is that it doesn't answer to the use to which humans try to put it. Law does not put an end to sin, but rather stimulates sin, as Paul experienced it (Romans 7).

> Indeed, says Paul, there is even a certain power, a *cordiacum* [cordial], which again and again brings sin to life, which nourishes and cares for sin, which is to sin what the cushion is to the *podagra* [gout], upon which it can rest softly, where it can suitably sustain itself and continually gain fresh *courage*. O, for God's sake! what can we call that *cordial?* Answer: It is called the Law which is to sin its foster-mother, its nurse which feeds it, which patches it up again.[10]

This is because the Law stands in opposition to what the natural human is within, the natural aptitude and propensity to sin. It appears to be an infringement of freedom and not only opposes what a person by nature might do but in its challenge to one's freedom (pretended freedom) one reacts against that which is forbidden.

> From this rebellious *genio* [spirit] arises a certain *inclination* to things, to which one should otherwise have had no *inclination* one's whole life time; one tries the things. No sooner does one see lust described, as soon as one hears, that thing should not be, so one experiences desire, one tries it as something extraordinary,

[8] [Minutes of the] 1750 Synod, as recorded in *Spangenbergs Apologetische Schluß-Schrift*, p. 487.
[9] *Spangenbergs Apologetische Schluß-Schrift*, pp. 480, 482.
[10] Zinzendorf, *Ein und zwanzig Discurse* [Title page: *Discurse . . . Auctoris*] p. 170 (7 Jan. 1748). The central role of grace for Zinzendorf, and his opposition to Law as an approach to ethics, becomes quite clear in the differences which develop between Zinzendorf and John Wesley. See discussion of this in chapter 4 (including note 60) and in George W. Forell, ed. and introduction to *Nine Public Lectures on Important Subjects in Religion Preached in Fetter Lane Chapel in London in the Year 1746*, by Nikolaus Ludwig von Zinzendorf (Iowa City: University of Iowa Press, 1973), pp. xvii-xix. (Abbreviated in subsequent notes as Zinzendorf, *Nine Public Lectures* [1973].)

one becomes curious about it, gets an *appetit* for it and is drawn into that which indeed is afterwards troublesome; but in *illo momento* [that moment] one could not help oneself, lust was excited by the prohibition; *nitimur in vetitum* [we strive for what is forbidden], that is an old and true proverb.[11]

The Law, which is spiritual and given to humanity to maintain order within God's world, does not solve the human problem because it does not change human nature, and Zinzendorf as well as Paul sees this as the real problem. The human is still fleshly; the inward self, heart, has not been changed so that obedience to the Law would be a possibility. The human must have a changed heart and a new nature — must be born again.[12]

The Law was originally given in God's world, where order was fast disintegrating, to maintain order. *It was not intended as a final solution to the human problem.* The proper definition of Law is to be τάξις (order), not νόμος (law); τάγμα (that which provides order) not ἀνάγκη (necessity). *Its intent is not to pass judgment but to enable life and create order.*[13]

He illustrated this from contemporary law.

There are two forms of government in our ordered civil world; they exist together, and I wish just to mention them. Represent to yourselves a town, and in the same an official or the hereditary judge on the one side, and the mayor or community *Syndicum* (Syndic) on the other. The judge does not issue as many commands as the mayor, who to all appearance commands without ceasing. On those few occasions when people come to the judge of their own accord they regard him as a good man; but when he sends out after any one who does not come on his own, then bitterness presently shows itself; whereas when the mayor comes or gives his commands, there is nothing but willingness.

Why is that so? Answer The former is the guardian of law, and the latter of order. Law is a death-pang to people while order makes things easier; the latter is a yoke[14] while the former is a burden. This goes so far that the most absurd orders, burdensome orders, such as some handicraft association customs are, find however quite willing persons who venture their lives for the sake of their miser-

---

[11] The proverb is from Ovid and reads, *Nitimur in vetitum semper capimusque negata* (We strive for what is forbidden and always desire what is denied us). Zinzendorf, *Ein und zwanzig Discurse* [Title page: *Discurse . . . Auctoris*], p. 184 (7 Jan. 1748).

[12] Ibid., pp. 183ff. Reference is made here to Paul's treatment of the Law in Rom. 7 and Gal. 3.

[13] This is the purpose of the Law as discussed by Paul in Gal. 3.

[14] Probably in the sense of sharing the load.

able guilds which function through compulsion and are full of misery: On the other hand, who in the world ever dies for his lord's law? Who is concerned whether there be more or less law? Who does not welcome the daily reduction of the laws of his lord?[15]

And so it is with church discipline:

As long as church discipline consists of nothing but orders which already lie in the minds of informed brothers and sisters; with which they must necessarily be at one, because they are orders *stantis & cadentis ecclesiae* [by which the church stands or falls],[16] since it is impossible that congregations could exist one day, if things did not go in this order, according to this *ressors* [jurisdiction]; that is good.[17]

What must happen then is that the First Table of the Law become our nature and that we become one heart and soul with the Savior.[18]

On what does this whole matter depend? It depends upon our belonging to the Savior and becoming one heart and one soul with him. His death and suffering, till soul and body part, must continually rest in the heart, fill up all our thoughts, captivate all our powers, possess our entire mind, and tinge even our body. Then are we a people out of danger, and the First Table then becomes our nature: I no longer live, but Christ lives in me. The few matters, the few *casus* [cases] specified in the Second Table which we accept with a few thousand others which already exist in our hearts, which arise out of the nature of the matter and have developed, one after another, in our church regulations for 1700 years and which remain the business of the Holy Spirit who makes those matters into inner rules for his good hearts which other people consider to be despotic law; and that which creates bitterness in their hearts is that within which our hearts live, and we stand by this with body and soul.

This is called establishing the Law, to bring it about that people, who have all their lifetime looked upon the Law as an unfortunate thing and perhaps would have spit upon it, do now kiss it, lay it

[15] Zinzendorf, *Ein und zwanzig Discurse* [Title page: *Discurse . . . Auctoris*], pp. 177-78.

[16] *Stantis et cadentis ecclesiae* within the Lutheran tradition indicated what was essential to the church's existence, much as the *essentialia* (*essentials*) did for the Moravian Church. In Lutheran theology this was primarily applied to justification by faith.

[17] Zinzendorf, *Ein und zwanzig Discurse* [Title page: *Discurse . . . Auctoris*], p. 179.

[18] According to tradition the First Table of the Law contains the commandments about God on which those on the Second Table concerning morality are based.

upon their heart, and say it was a fine thing that it formerly came into being; things have advanced farther with us indeed and we no longer raise questions at all about a hundred matters; for instance, the seventh commandment, You should not steal: I only want that the little I have suffice for my fellow humans. You should not commit adultery: I want to be able to 'inscribe the marriage of the Savior to persons in their hearts and make it possible that all men function as deputies of Christ,[19] which is their ministry (belongs to them) — and thus through all the commandments. It would be *ridicul* [ridiculous], one must have lost his healthy understanding, must be crazy in his head before it can be made conceivable to one that the mind of a Jesus-like person could be turned against such good order and matters, that it might be able to act counter to such ideas: this we cannot comprehend, we cannot imagine it. One can have no *suspicion* that it would be possible with the *disposition* wherein the heart stands, wherein one lives, and which has become our second nature. Therefore because the First Table has its rightful place, because we are with body and soul in the heart of Jesus, because we are at home with him, because we may not out of curiosity climb up to heaven (for from heaven high we have our origin) but in dependence we wish to enter again his mother-like body [i.e., his side wound].[20] Whether now I say to our Savior, You shall not steal, You shall not bear false witness! or whether I say to a soul who lives in our Savior, who rests in his arms, who thinks in agreement with him, You shall not steal, You shall not bear false witness, that is, *a posteriori*, the same, though indeed *a priori*, the Savior has not the capacity of sinning which we have. Therefore we thank our Lord: whenever we can do good, we do it gladly. But when there comes an evil desire (for death is at hand, it lies in the members even of the children of God), then we thank God, that there is no obligation to obey it. We reflect upon our *privilegium* [privilege], to be as holy as Jesus' wounds. We reflect upon our

[19] The reference to husbands acting as Christ's deputies has to do with Zinzendorf's understanding of marriage where the husband's relationship to the wife is to be as the relationship of Christ to the soul, and marriage is paradigmatic of the relationship of Christ, the only true bridegroom, to all souls, which are feminine (whether of women or men).

[20] This sentence seems to be missing an independent clause in German. If the "but" (*sondern*) could be omitted from the last clause, it could read: "Therefore because the First Table had its rightful place, because we are with body and soul in the heart of Jesus, because we are at home with him, because we may not out of curiosity climb up to heaven (for from heaven high we have our origin), in dependence we wish to enter again his mother-like body [i.e., his side wound]."

charter, our right for which our Lord hung upon the cross. Ask Jesus, we say, whether I must serve you? We do, as is sometimes done when by chance tax collectors or *exactores* [another term for tax collectors] come into a free house and demand something which one is not responsible to give; we protect ourselves and say, I have a *privilegium* [privilege], prove first that I am obliged, otherwise I am free. I thank God, that I have carried our suit, through Jesus Christ my Lord.

When this is once settled and certain; and when afterwards that blessed point is added, that our mind is become like the Lamb's mind; when we so keep the community-creating, churchly, constitutional Supper where sin in the members is given the stunning blow through the corpse of Jesus which beats it down so that it can scarcely recover itself during the interval until we again receive his corpse's powers, until we apply the *antidotum* [antidote] anew; that it cannot rally from one time to the other, nor find its way out of its *etourderie* [stun], but lies there as something which one has hurled with a sling and must reflect for a long time before it can again come to itself out of its stupor. So I still cannot say that I have no sin; indeed it is there: but I can say it is as dead, it is dazed, it lies there as dead, it is hurled down, it has scarcely tried to get up again when I have again received the corpse's power, so have I anticipated it afresh. And then that blood of the Lamb of God, not like the poor, miserable blood in other human bodies (for it all looks the same), is instilled into our little tabernacle; so that no longer does our blood have the upper hand but his, so that the flame of his blood precipitates, quenches, sweetens the flame of our animal blood, to the end that our walk and our actions in this mortal body may from one time to another be carried on moderately, spiritually, Christ-like, suitable to the human body of our Husband and Head.

Yet this is not our, but his, matter; we cannot do it for ourselves, it does not come from our nature, as if we were perhaps a sort of angel; but it comes from the constant, indispensable genuine *connexion* with the dear Lamb, with our Husband. Therefore what is in the Questions and Answers in Luther's Catechism sounds so right when it is asked, Why does a person go to the Lord's Supper? and the Answer is, Because he has flesh and blood about him, and has the devil and sin around him he will go to the Lord's Supper. This is a right conclusion, and I only wish it may be taken in this following sense. Who does not desire and pant after the Savior's corpse, to whom the time does not seem long from one meal (Lord's Supper) to the other, to be as the child, and let the wounds of the Savior embrace him like *Elisha*, such a one is really a poor person who has but a shallow connection with our Savior and does not know what it means; he does not know how he needs it; for it is not only a *plaisir* (something to be desired), it is not only a great blessedness, that a person is covered, embraced, and moistened by the corpse of Jesus, that his blood flows and circulates in our blood and veins; this is not only something pleasurable, a festival; but necessity demands it. We need that the mind of the Lamb be like our mind and our body may become like his corpse. Our body must actually have been long dead before it goes into the grave, our members must have long decayed before they decay in the grave, so that really nothing new happens to them there: It must be only a completion of that *mortification*, of that νεκρώσεως [mortification, dying], which has already here begun in our living body where the death of the Lamb rules and stirs already in our soul, hands and feet, and all our members; inasmuch as the natural powers would not have been sufficient to perform those natural functions which are entrusted to us if we were not living in the power of and faith in the Son of God.[21]

Hence the Christian life is characterized by a spontaneity and a naturalness because the change effected in human nature makes one's nature more congenial to right action. Even though the old aspects of one's humanity remain, one can trust one's nature in a new way.

This is the nature, the disposition, that new human whom he created for us, which is formed and fashioned according to God; there we have a holiness and righteousness that is as natural to us as swimming is to the duck, water to the fish, and flying in the free air to the bird.

There is nothing premeditated, nothing artificially effected, nothing forced; but it all comes of itself, because we are his children, his servants, his members, his playmates, his little sheep — in short, because we participate in his divine nature.[22]

[21] Zinzendorf, *Ein und zwanzig Discurse* [Title page: *Discurse . . . Auctoris*], pp. 186-91. Some sentences are long and complex, but that is the nature of the original. If one imagines this being preached, it would seem to have a homiletical style where in climactic fashion one phrase builds on another.

[22] *Des Herrn Grafen Ludwig von Zinzendorff Sieben Letzte Reden So Er In der Gemeine, Vor seiner am 7. Aug. erfolgten abermahligen Abreise nach America, gehalten. Denen noch beygefügt sind zwey in Gelnhausen von demselben gehaltene und ehmals einzeln gedruckte Predigten* (Büdingen: Johann Christoph Stöhr, 1743), pp. 47-48 (16 July 1741).

It becomes clear why "we can give nothing before we have something." This style of ethic cannot be lived out unless one has something: the reality out of which the ethic comes to expression. Since this is a reality, not an understanding, age is not a primary consideration. In fact, this becomes easier for an adult when the adult becomes like a child and lives in simplicity and spontaneity.

The Christian as a Living Expression of Christ

When one allows oneself to act under the guidance of Christ, then the reality of Christ in the heart becomes expressed outwardly so that others may indeed see that there has been a Savior in the world. It is not only that ethics do not work well without the resources Christ brings to the heart, but ethics without consideration of these resources fails as a witness and points to no new reality which enables life. Ethics must point to more than noble principles.

> It [the Moravian community] is a school for those gaining wisdom, a present opportunity to get that from the Savior which we need; it is the blessedness of so walking in the world as he walked.
>
> We get such a nature given us that without reflection, without long excursions or scrupulosity, without seeking advice or approval in books, we can behave as if we had thoughtfully studied it.
>
> It flows of itself.
>
> Therefore Scripture speaks so much of the divine nature, of the mind of Christ; Let this mind be in you, which was also in Christ Jesus.
>
> For things are now so as the Apostle says, Be followers of God, as dear children. Not such followers as students, not as *academici* [those who belong to the academy] and *sectarii* [sectarians]; but if you will be followers of God, of that God manifested in the flesh, be it then as a child is a follower or *successor* of his father; so that one says he is the father's likeness. The memory is perpetuated that there was once such a man in the world, who was created thus, who now lives in his children and posterity by the likeness and family-face in his children.
>
> So likewise Jesus, who was the Son of God in the world, openly lives in all those in whom he has taken form, until he comes again; so that we can see that there has been a Savior in the world; a man who was the true essential living Law of God and had it in his heart and did not need first to study and meditate much upon it.[23]

[23] Ibid., pp. 57-58 (23 July 1741).

This belief in the effect of one's faith and relationship with Christ upon one's outer appearance (so that the reality of Christ becomes evident in one's life) interested Zinzendorf in physiognomy. Uttendörfer comments that Zinzendorf had read a book on this in 1717.[24]   One of the sermons on the Litany of the Wounds is devoted almost entirely to this subject.[25]

The Look of the Savior

In ethics Scripture would undoubtedly be that which it is in the realm of doctrine, partially a *source* of ethical knowledge, but also a *rule* which provides standards for issues not scripturally defined. It also helps to discern the inner reality of the heart which expresses itself in ethical action. But even as a source and a rule it must be remembered that, though some of its advice transcends historical conditions, much is contextually determined and limited by the perceptions of the writer. Thus one must also look to the contemporary God and Christ for ethical direction. In the New Testament this is often expressed in the church seeking the guidance of God's Spirit to resolve various issues (e.g., 1 Corinthians 14). God remains intimately involved in ethical issues.[26] This means that finding answers to ethical issues may be complex.

But not all are equipped, by education or natural gifts, for intellectual and analytical treatment of ethical issues. Not only must the realities of the relationship with God be available to all beyond the ability to treat doctrinal issues, but ethical life must be available to all beyond the ability to analyze the ethical issues. As the relationship of the Savior with the heart transcends intellectual development and is available to all, so the presence of the Savior to the heart makes at least the attempt of ethical response a possibility for most.

Ethics can be simple. If one has the crucified Savior continually before one's eyes, one can watch the Savior's eyes as he looks upon us. Morality is "what the Savior would have us do." While life may be complex and one may not know what to do, the Savior can direct us so that ethics, as well as *religion*, can be a matter of the heart.

[24] Otto Uttendörfer, *Zinzendorf und die Mystik* (Berlin: Christlicher Zeitschriften Verlag, [1952]), p. 6.

[25] Nikolaus Ludwig von Zinzendorf, *Vier und Dreyßig Homiliae über die Wunden-Litaney der Brüder, Gehalten auf dem Herrnhaag in den Sommer-Monathen 1747. von dem Ordinario Fratrum* (n.p., Zu finden in den Brüder-Gemeinen, n.d.), pp. 89ff. (28 May 1747).

[26] Here Paul describes the Christian community gathered to seek God's will. Prophecy and speaking in tongues are spiritual gifts that provide guidance.

I suppose that we remain men; it is a part of the state of sin not to think more highly of ourselves. But we shall succeed, if our Head but look now and then upon us.

We are not people who from the first moment of our spiritual life until eternity itself remain unassaulted and unattacked. From a distance something comes at us; there is something in our own selves which we cannot name, to which we have as yet been unable to give the right name, until the proper position of the soul has been determined. This must be handled with great caution and watched over carefully; and even if it should stick in the deepest recesses of the mind, even if it is also lying imprisoned, so that it is actually not able to block our course in following Christ, yet it is still there, and no reading, no hearing, no moral doctrine guards against it. For the only remedy against all such alluring demands, gross or subtle, is the doubtful glance of the Savior, when the form of Jesus does not seem so joyful to our hearts, when He seems to us to be no longer so sweetly before our hearts as usual.

People who have murdered someone have said that the person and image of the murdered one always hovered before their eyes; they have neither been able to bear it nor escape from the sight of it. We also say of people who are very important to us, I see him as clearly as if he were here; I could paint him right now. This David applies to his Savior, "I have placed Him so directly before my eyes that I will never lose Him from my thoughts, from my point of view; I need only look up, and I have Him immediately there." (Ps. 139) Suppose, then, that one might fall into all sorts of questionable situations, if possible to go astray in something, to allow oneself to be implicated in something by one's thoughts, to wander from the Savior with one's senses. The Savior need only look at me, even though one does not look toward Him, and the glance of His eyes goes through one like a flame of fire: one is transparent, known throughout by Him; He knows the moment when He is to look at us, and He also knows how He is to look at us, for He has read our thoughts before they have formed themselves. When Judas came and betrayed Him, He preached him a sermon: "My friend, you give me a kiss and betray me." When Peter denied Him, He spoke no words but rather looked upon him. In the case of Judas the sermon availed nothing; the look had this effect on Peter: "He went out and wept bitterly" (Matt. 26:75); he bathed himself in tears. What kind of tears? Tears of love. He wept for love, for he had not owned, confessed, or affirmed his Master, for he had not risked his life for Him. And when the Savior said a few days later, "Do you love me?" the answer was, O dear Lord! I appeal to you; you have looked upon me: you have also seen me, an unfaithful heart. You do know what your look has effected; you know indeed how your look operated upon my heart; my eyes were wet with tears; it went through body and soul. Yes, the Savior was obliged to say, it is true; you already have the right doctrine, and you are a good theologian; you know what you shall set forth to the church; you shall be a bishop. Point your diocese only toward my merits; point them only toward this method of coming to me, toward this method which I have used, the method which you have experienced, which immediately brings a person out of all labyrinths into the right way. "Strengthen your brethren" (Luke 22:32) with the example of your conversion by the glance of my eyes.

It is this also, beloved in the Lord, which we have to wish each other at the end of this discourse, that we may be looked upon by the Savior so graciously, so powerfully, so essentially; and that at the same time we may be so blessed, so happy that we turn away our view and our eyes from everything which otherwise seemed to us proper or improper and turn them toward Him with no desire to look at or into anything else; that our eye may not be able to throw a glance anywhere else but to this point.

And when you have once caught sight of the beauty of His suffering, so that in all your life you will not be able to get rid of that sight, then He conducts you with His eyes wherever He will have you; then with His eyes He teaches you what good and evil is. Your knowledge of good and evil lies in His eyes, not in the tree from which Adam poisoned himself, from which Adam ate his curse, but rather in the eyes of the tortured Lamb, there lies your blessed, happy knowledge of good and evil. As far as the same image looks upon you, into the midst of your mortal bodies, so far shall you be changed, pervaded, captivated by the person of Jesus, so that your other brethren perceive you no longer as a man in your denomination, as a brother of the same persuasion only, but rather as a consort, as a playmate for the marriage-bed of the blessed Creator and eternal Husband of the human soul.[27]

[27] Zinzendorf, *Nine Public Lectures* [1973], pp. 84-87 (25 Sept. 1746). Note how in the last paragraph of the quote it is asserted that the perspective upon life should not be determined by Adam's fall, but Christ's eyes. Life should be viewed from the perspective of grace.

Living with the Savior and His Family

Ethical life is based upon the daily living with the Savior. Zinzendorf's favorite phrase for this was *Umgang mit dem Heiland.* This is somewhat difficult to translate. Literally *Umgang* means "going around," but it implies relationship with, living with, going with, conversing with. *Umgang* is the German equivalent of the Latin *conversatio* (intercourse, conversation, turning oneself towards, devoting oneself to), which was used to describe the monastic life. Dietrich Meyer also points to Bernard of Clairvaux's use of the Latin phrase *commercium cum deo* (commerce, communion with God) as a technical term for mystical union, equivalent to *Umgang mit dem Heiland,* known by Luther and entering Lutheran orthodoxy through John Arndt and Philipp Nicolai. This was regarded as a high point in the order of salvation.[28] Of course, as indicated in the discussion of mysticism in chapter 1, Zinzendorf saw *Umgang* as the Saviour/Creator's gift of relationship at the beginning of the Christian life, not its climax at the end of an extended process.

The discipline of *Umgang* can be understood as rules which enable one in the end to attain a perfection of life and relationship with God, or it can be undestood as itself "a whole new mode of being."[29] Within mysticism and monasticism there has been a debate as to whether discipline leads to new life and being or whether it *is the practice of* new life and being. Within the perspective of the latter *Umgang mit dem Heiland* is not a means of getting something or becoming something, or even of attaining some goal. *In itself living with the Savior is the practice of that which is the goal and nature of faith, rather than a way of going beyond itself.* Moreover, *Umgang* is living with the one who is both the source of life and guidance and who is the very incarnation of Christian life. As Peter Zimmerling points out:

> Because Jesus Christ, as well as the Trinity as a whole, is that which he does, action and being come together in him, "he has become virtue for us." Only presupposing this can virtue become visible in him: "Whoever considers virtue in the abstract will not get much out of this. But when we seek and find virtue in the person of the Savior and acknowledge that he has become our wisdom and righteousness: and with regard to virtue, that one sees the finest

[28] Dietrich Meyer, "'Christus mein ander Ich': Zu Zinzendorfs Verhältnis zur Mystik," *Zeitwende* 54 (1983): p. 97. (Abbreviated in subsequent notes as Dietrich Meyer, "'Christus mein ander Ich.'")
[29] Thomas Merton, *Mystics and Zen Masters* (New York: Farrar, Straus and Giroux, 1967). Merton comments: "One might say that the monk is not so much one who denies himself and practices virtue in order to find God, but one who is more or less fervent in his monastic *conversatio* in proportion as he realizes that he has found God in it" (p. 155).

virtue in his eyes, that his word and action are pure virtue, then for us virtue becomes incarnate."[30]

Ethics has often been seen as the imitation of Jesus, but in Zinzendorf this is transcended in three ways.

First, this is not to be understood in a legalistic or narrow way. What is called for is not to repeat *what* he did, but to do something *the way he did it.*

> The concern is not that in everything one has to consider what the Savior would have done, but rather how the Savior would have done it if he had done it. . . . As he is, so also are we in the world.[31]

Second, in *Umgang* Jesus becomes the companion of life, resourcing and directing it. He also becomes an alternative center of awareness (besides myself), so that it is appropriate to use of him the term "my other I."[32]

Third, the Savior mediates the Godhead to those in this relationship. The Spirit which enters the world from the side of the wounded Savior also preaches him and draws persons into the living relationship with him, caring for them with her Mother-heart. Living with the Savior then becomes living with the Trinity, the family of God, or within the community of the inner life of God. Thus Zimmerling, in a section "Concerning the Trinitarian Foundation of Ethics," quotes Zinzendorf:[33]

> There's nothing better, dear brothers and sisters, than as a little fish swims in the water, contented and undisturbed into eternity, we live in the family of our Husband, his Father and our dear Mother. As little as a child thinks, reasons, and speculates who for his whole life knows nothing else than he was born in the family constituted by his father and mother, so must we think in no other way than to forget all previous matters and do not concern ourselves that we have lived before this point: we know nothing other than we are in the family of our Father and our Mother who have begotten and borne us and have given us so much which is true, eternal, and capable of bringing us blessing.[34]

[30] Diarium des Jüngerhauses, 29 Oct. 1756, quoted in Peter Zimmerling, *Gott in Gemeinschaft: Zinzendorfs Trinitätslehre* (Giessen and Basel: Brunnen, 1991), pp. 212-13. (Abbreviated in subsequent notes as Zimmerling, *Gott in Gemeinschaft*.)

[31] Manuscript collection of Zinzendorf's sermons, 11 Dec. 1746, quoted in Zimmerling, *Gott in Gemeinschaft*, p. 214.

[32] Dietrich Meyer, "'Christus mein ander Ich.'"

[33] Nikolaus Ludwig von Zinzendorf, *Der Öffentlichen Gemein-Reden im Jahr 1747. Zweyter Theil* [pt. 2] (n.p.: Zu finden in den Brüder-Gemeinen, 1749), p. 262 (19 Oct. 1747), quoted in Zimmerling, *Gott in Gemeinschaft*, pp. 216ff.

[34] Zimmerling, *Gott in Gemeinschaft*, p, 217.

The Use of the Lot

To shape ethics by the living relationship with Christ still leaves many individual and practical decisions within life's complexities unclear. Some way of seeking guidance from Christ was needed when decisions needed to be made. The use of the lot enabled the church to do this.

The use of the lot in the Moravian Church determined much of the life and decisions of the church in the eighteenth and nineteenth centuries ; so it is important to look its role in decision making. Here I am primarily indebted to Erich Beyreuther's "Lot-theory and Lot-Praxis."[35]

The lot's widespread use was primarily due to the influence of Zinzendorf. Whereas the first Moravian generation used it naïvely, the second generation asked the question as to its origin. The Synod of 1769, which collected the ideas of Zinzendorf on the use of the lot and gave guidance to the church for the next hundred years, explained the origin in the following words:

The blessed Disciple (Count von Zinzendorf) had already in his early years used a similar method in his conversations with the Savior to speak with him, and he later more and more did this, since he, as well for his person as in the early time of the community, found himself in very difficult circumstances and therefore, against all human understanding, was wonderfully and rightly led. In the community it occurred as early as 1727 and 1728. When it came to the founding of the community in Herrnhut, the primary offices and those who filled them were determined through the lot. And in the very difficult circumstances which followed and were related to its founding, in which no human understanding was sufficient to find the right way, they used the lot with such effect and such consequences that one must be astonished. The congregational workers made a convenant with one another neither to follow their heads nor to give way to the advice of others, who otherwise meant well, but to ask the Savior himself and to trust in him as a child, so that he might guide them on the right way. However, the lot was used very little in the early times and only in matters of the greatest importance, for which previously all had been determined and ventured upon according to Holy Scripture.[36]

[35] Erich Beyreuther, "Lostheorie und Lospraxis," *Studien zur Theologie Zinzendorfs: Gesammelte Aufsätze* (Neukirchen-Vluyn: Kries Moers, 1962). (Abbreviated in subsequent notes as Beyreuther, *Studien zur Theologie Zinzendorfs*.)

[36] Supplement to the [minutes of the] 1769 Synod, Herrnhut Archives, R2B45,2, quoted in Beyreuther, *Studien zur Theologie Zinzendorfs*, p. 112.

This historical account in the Supplements to the Synod of 1769 gives little actual information other than that it was an expression of the relationship with the Savior which Zinzendorf introduced into the church in 1727-28. Zinzendorf himself, both at the Synod of 1749 and in his *Kreuzreich* (1745), pointed out that the use of the lot already had great currency in both sacred and secular areas,

> that the lot had general use in the Protestant Church in more "dangerous" matters, as it is with us, and that it was more decisively used in matters of government and ministry in many places, as is true with us.[37]

Besides encountering this in the court and church life, Zinzendorf later in increasing measure called upon Luther for support. Luther, in connection with his interpretation of Jonah, said:

> And what else is the casting of the lot than a covenant that we find agreement with one another regarding a matter. . . . Here there is nothing bad. . . . God is so pious and just that he does not let the lot go wrong.[38]

Pietism also probably had its influence. Zinzendorf at Halle ate daily at the table of A. H. Francke, whose book *Blessed Footsteps of the Still Living and Guiding Loving and True God*[39] expressed his faith in God's providential guidance. His method was to understand all his plans, to prepare carefully, to reflect on things, and to pray about them. Then, having done his part, he would wait passively for God to give some indication.[40] Though Francke's belief in God's guidance would have influenced Zinzendorf, for Zinzendorf it would have to take another form, for his ever-active life could not wait passively for God's guidance to show up in his circumstances.

[37] Nikolaus Ludwig von Zinzendorf, *Die gegenwärtige Gestalt Des Creutz-Reichs Jesu in seiner Unschuld d. i. Verschiedene deutliche Wahrheiten denen unzehligen Unwahrheiten gegen eine bekante Evangelische Gemeine In Dreyen Abtheilungen entgegen, Und allen unpartheyischen Gemüthern vor Augen gestellet, Dem aber der die Hertzen kennet und lencket, und nicht nach dem Ansehen richtet, sondern ein recht Gerichte. Zu selbst eigener Symmartyria einfältig überlassen.* (Frankfurt and Leipzig: Zu finden bey Johann Christoph Stöhr, 1745), p. 47, quoted in Beyreuther, *Studien zur Theologie Zinzendorfs*, p. 113.
[38] *Büdingische Sammlung Einiger In die Kirchen-Historie Einschlagender Sonderlich neuerer Schrifften. Erster Band. Nebst darzu gehörigen Registern. Sind wir doch sein ererbtes gut* (Büdingen: Joh. Chr. Stöhr, 1742), 3:760, quoted in Beyreuther, *Studien zur Theologie Zinzendorfs*, p. 114.
[39] The title in German of Francke's book is *Segenvollen Fußstapfen des noch lebenden und waltenden liebreichen und getreuen Gottes.*
[40] Beyreuther, *Studien zur Theologie Zinzendorfs*, p. 115.

That Zinzendorf found the lot especially agreeable to his needs did not mean that he saw it as necessary for expressing the guidance of God for all Christians.

The Savior has various ways of leading a person. One he leads through understanding. To another the Savior gives many feelings in his mind. To the third he gives a systematic connection to the word of God. . . . We do not direct our own way, but the Savior does according to our characteristics. . . . He reveals himself to humans according to their understanding through a distinctive way, so that, if they only have that which the Savior gives them, they are blessed in the world.[41]

Zinzendorf considered himself of the second type which knew himself directed through "feelings of the heart, daily watchwords, and prophecies."[42]   His use of the lot must also be understood in relation to the idea of *Salbung*, "anointing," the guiding activity of the Spirit who is "Mother" to all Christians.[43]

Though the lot is God's gift to the Christian, it is not infallible. This is not because God is unfaithful and fallible, but rather because the human to whom the lot is given is fallible. Nor was it understood as a guarantee of success and glory. Zinzendorf was too much influenced by the theology of the cross to believe that. The lot would lead one into the difficulties which were a part of following Christ. By following it one could know that one was not merely following one's own inclination:

The lot and the will of the Savior has been one for me for a long time, until I become wiser. I am not yet so wise that I can discern the Lord's will out of my ideas. An innocent little piece of paper is for me more certain than my feeling.[44]

In fact, in order to avoid forcing God to express his will Zinzendorf used three lots, one of which was affirmative, another negative, and the third blank.[45]

[41] Zinzendorf, *Reden zu Berlin für die Manns-Personen* [1st ed., n.d.), pp. 161-62 (4 April 1738).

[42] Beyreuther, *Studien zur Theologie Zinzendorfs*, p. 116.

[43] See chapter 4, which includes a treatment of anointing.

[44] Gerhard Reichel, *August Gottlieb Spangenberg: Bischof der Brüderkirche* (Tübingen, 1906 [1905]), p. 89, quoted in Beyreuther, *Studien zur Theologie Zinzendorfs*, p. 119.

[45] Beyreuther in the second volume of *Die große Zinzendorf Trilogie* mentions that there still exist in the Herrnhut Archives three round mother-of-pearl disks in a silver case. On one there is "Ja" (yes), on another there is "Nein" (no), and on the third there is nothing (Erich Beyreuther, *Die große Zinzendorf Trilogie* [Marburg: Francke, 1988], 2:95 [Abbreviated in subsequent notes as Beyreuther, *Trilogie*]).

History of the use of the lot

The first knowledge which we have of the use of the lot in Zinzendorf's life is in connection with the "Four-Brother-Covenant" for the spreading of the Kingdom of Christ in Oberlausitz, formed in 1724. Friedrich von Wattewille, Pastor Scheffer of Görlitz, and Pastor Johann Andreas Rothe in Berthelsdorf, together with Zinzendorf, were the participants. Institutions were planned much after the pattern of Halle, and various responsibilities were assigned among the four. Here the offices of each were selected by the lot. This laid a background for the use of the lot in 1727-28 when, as mentioned in the supplement to the Synod of 1769, the lot was used in selecting people to fill various offices in the newly founded congregation at Herrnhut.[46]

The next decisive use of the lot of which we have information was in 1731. Zinzendorf had hoped for a position in the court of the king of Denmark, who was his cousin. Meanwhile the awakening at Herrnhut (1727) had already occurred and the Diaspora workers were at work expanding the influence of Herrnhut. He lacked not only money but a real determination as to whether he should make the trip to the coronation of his cousin. He submitted to the lot whether he should go *"doucement, rigoreusement, indifferement oder prudement"* [quietly, rigorously, indifferently, or cautiously]. He decided on the last. The consequences of his decision for the Moravian Church were extensive, not only in terms of the initiation of the foreign mission work of the church, but also in providing the church with his continuing leadership.[47]

Though the lot was at first used sparingly, it came to have more and more frequent use. It became important not only for selecting officers of the congregations, but for the selection of mission fields and the missionaries to be sent and in the arrangement of marriages. The application of the lot to many aspects of church life became important because the Moravians were not part of a long established tradition with traditional ways of doing things, but a part of a new enterprise which was seeking the will of the Lord to lead it into areas without precedence. The exile of Zinzendorf from Saxony and the formation of the Pilgrim Congregation heightened the need of the church to seek the will of the Savior for the unanticipated moment. As Zinzendorf described the Pilgrim Congregation,

> I wanted that it would be so in a congregation [or church] that we
> would not know in the evening what we should do early in the

---

[46] Beyreuther, *Studien zur Theologie Zinzendorfs*, p. 120.
[47] Ibid., p. 121.

morning. To do that in a congregation, inspiration is necessary. Where that does not exist, there is no congregation. If in a congregation we want to venture everything for the sake of salvation, so he [Jesus] must reveal himself to it, through his Spirit and eyes must direct it, otherwise, like Moses, it cannot take a step. And the lot serves for that purpose in the congregation.[48]

It is not to be denied that the use of the lot was open to abuse. Zinzendorf had said, "The matter of the lot is a charisma of the community and belongs among the miraculous powers in his church. It is however true that when one is near the fire, one can be burned."[49] One notes this happening at the synods at the end of the 1730s, when the first order of business was the acceptance of the order of business and the second matter was the selection of the person who should cast the lot. After the Sifting Period the use of the lot also finds a greater measure of maturity.

It was presupposed that the person who used the lot brought to its use a willingness to obey the results. At the Marienborn Synod of 1744 Zinzendorf said :

In casting the lot it is a basic plan that it only binds the one who does it. . . . The lot is, for just this reason, a difficult thing, because it is binding in an astonishing way to the person who casts it. The person who commits himself to the lot is certainly the greatest mystic, for he must be quite without a will.[50]

However, later one finds statements which seem to modify the binding nature of the lot. When one does not know what to do in a situation and uses the lot,

in the most part the lot is only a counsel and does not bind one to follow it. If one therefore gets a better counsel on another day, since the mind is clearer than on the previous, so perhaps the advice has been only given on the first day so that the mind might be informed *pro iterim* [literally: for the way; temporarily], and one is no longer bound to the lot which one drew in anxiety and confusion.[51]

---

[48] [Minutes of the] 1739 Synod at Ebersdorf, 15 June 1739, quoted in Beyreuther, *Studien zur Theologie Zinzendorfs*, p. 127.

[49] Herrnhut Archives, R2A43bI, quoted in Beyreuther, *Studien zur Theologie Zinzendorfs*, p. 127.

[50] [Minutes of the] 1744 Synod at Marienborn, 21 May 1744, quoted in Beyreuther, *Studien zur Theologie Zinzendorfs*, p. 134.

[51] Diarium des Jüngerhauses, 9 Sept. 1750, Herrnhut Archives, R2A43bI, quoted in Beyreuther, *Studien zur Theologie Zinzendorfs*, p. 135.

In its best usage the lot was used to determine the will of the Savior where it could not be otherwise understood and expressed the belief that the Savior led the church in its daily activity.

As previously mentioned, the Synod of 1769 codified Zinzendorf's use of the lot. However, opposition was already rising to its use. In 1782 the Berthelsdorf Synod agreed to reject the use of the lot in connection with questions of property. By 1818 the use of the lot for marriages was abolished for all except ministers and missionaries residing outside Europe, and in 1825 made no longer obligatory for ministers. In appointments, the Synod of 1869 made it obligatory only in appointments of bishops and acceptance of candidates for missionary service. By the Synod of 1889 the lot was no longer mentioned in connection with the decision-making processes of the church.[52]

The State and Citizenship

Zinzendorf's treatment of the state is an interesting example of his awareness of contextuality, both in the biblical materials and in his own time. He notes the variety of perspectives on the state in the biblical materials and explains it according to the different historical situations in which the material arose. But he also makes the point that God's people have always been subject to legitimate authority[53] and are not really much interested in meddling in public affairs, something that sounds strange to Christians today, who have become accustomed to social and political concerns.

Zinzendorf indicated that during the time of the prophets the secular government was not instituted by God, but permitted by God and chosen by the people; so the prophets corrected the magistrates, whose reign was sometimes an infringement upon the theocracy. In the time of Jesus Israel was a republic, though a dependency of Rome under conditions which allowed it great freedom. The Jewish kings had no authority unless they usurped it as tyrants. Jesus was a public-spirited man, educated in republican principles. Though he rejected Jewish kings, he directed people to the head of the republic, the emperor.

> The Savior established nothing new, but left everything in *statu quo* [as he found it]. He directed his disciples to be respectful and obedient towards the *Sunedrium* [Sanhedrin], towards the high council of the Jews. He commanded to give to Caesar his tribute,

[52] Gillian Lindt Gollin, *Moravians in Two Worlds: A Study of Changing Communities* (New York: Columbia University Press, 1967), pp. 62-63.

[53] Zinzendorf, *Ein und zwanzig Discurse* [Title page: *Discurse . . . Auctoris*], pp. 338-39 (3 Mar. 1748).

and decided the matter of taxes and *accis* [excise] in *favorem magistratus* [favor of the magistrate]. That is the *casus* which we have from our Savior, that he absolutely forbade his disciples to involve themselves in matters foreign to them; and the example of his disciples proves that they left everything lie and stand when they followed him.[54]

The next historical period is that of the disciples and Apostles. Here the Jewish Republic was hastening towards its dissolution. Paul spoke of this and John lived to see it. The remaining powers were monarchical, so Paul taught his people to be subject to the higher powers (Romans 13, 1 Timothy 2) and described the magistrate as a minister of God for good.

> Consequently, it is not only a matter of conscience, not even only a policy that Christians are subject; but there is added to that an *inclination,* their heart is inclined to it, they are partisans for the magisterial rights; and among the several forms of magistracy despotism is the most agreeable in temporal matters.
>
> Whoever in Germany and in monarchical countries attacks us on this topic of authority is a bad person who only wants to pick a quarrel with us: but who attacks us in republics must be given a more careful reply, and it should be done with more Christian dexterity than we often like. For the children of God are often among the most suspect persons in republics, *quia sunt oves* [because they are sheep].[55]

Zinzendorf recognized that a republic calls for a different type of citizenship, though Christian character also minimizes possible participation. He did say that the magistrate should be refused when what he asks would lead to sin or is against the Savior.[56] Christians may be magistrates according to the Augsburg Confession, but they do this "with a great deal of encumbrance."[57] It is also no sin for Christians to partake of the ordinary business of life: buying and selling, taking an imposed oath, having possessions, marrying and having children.[58]

His emphasis on loyalty to the ruler, rather than the state, was before the days of the rebirth of Germany in the nineteenth century, when German nationalism might have claimed loyalty beyond the ruler. In his day loyalty to the state was expressed primarily in terms of loyalty to the

[54] Ibid., pp. 336-37 (3 Mar. 1748).
[55] Ibid., pp. 338-39.
[56] Ibid., p. 356.
[57] Ibid., p. 339.
[58] Ibid., pp. 346-47.

ruler.[59] Yet Zinzendorf, as one who studied law in preparation for court responsibilities, was also readily aware of the importance of law and argued for living by the law and not making the law at or after the case. "As soon as the citizens know what is law and justice, they may then regulate themselves accordingly; and the administrators of the laws are obliged to keep to that rule."[60]

The ruler is head of all "Religions" in the country, whatever they are; but he cannot say, "I am in charge of truth or *religion* insofar as it makes one holy: that belongs to the office of the Savior."[61]

It is all right to ask God for victory in a righteous war — i.e., when one's country is invaded. However, war in itself is a mystery. It is hard to understand why some sovereigns are overthrown. War is a work of providence where, though it may be a plague, still it may have its purposes and values. It has become a school and academy affair, which may even become a school for souls. A Christian can neither sanction war, nor forbid it. One must choose *pro tempore*, "how a Person is to behave in his special and personal circumstances, this the Savior must teach him."[62]

The major concern of Zinzendorf was that Christians be involved in their primary area of responsibility.

> Scaliger once said, *tacebam, quia eram ovis* [I am silent because I am a sheep]: and this is the favorite fault of Christians who live in proximity to the Gospel, and seems to be instilled into them with the mother's milk of the Holy Spirit. They do not like to meddle in foreign matters, they do not like, under the *pretext* of being a patriot, to engage in discussions of others' right or wrong. Now if such a simple brother should drop in amongst a company of Tories, and hear them reasoning about *obedientia passiva* [passive obedience], about inactive, simple obedience, he might easily slip and say, "Yes! that is all right, that is my mind too"; and a patriot could take this very ill of him. The Augustan Confession does not determine these circumstances on either side. It teaches us no *jus publicum* [law for the state], my brothers and sisters! But all it says is that Christians are such persons who will never put anything in

---

[59] Hermann Plitt, *Zinzendorfs Theologie* (Gotha: F. A. Perthes, 1869-74), 2:538. (Abbreviated in subsequent notes as Plitt, *Zinzendorfs Theologie*.)

[60] Zinzendorf, *Ein und zwanzig Discurse* [Title page: *Discurse . . . Auctoris*], p. 340.

[61] Plitt, *Zinzendorfs Theologie*, 2:531. By stating that the ruler is head of all religions, he is stating the principle which came out of the Treaty of Westphalia, which settled the Thirty Years War, *Cuius regio, eius religio* (Whose rule, his *religion*).

[62] Zinzendorf, *Ein und zwanzig Discurse* [Title page: *Discurse . . . Auctoris*], p. 346.

the way of the magistrate; it only establishes the position that all may live in peace from the Christian perspective.[63]

This implies that most Christians are out of their element in politics, for this is not their basic concern or interest. It is interesting that the nobleman Zinzendorf did not hesitate to intervene with governors and kings as it concerned the mission of the church and the benefit of those carrying out the mission. However, he was first a servant of Christ, and his understanding of the role of government was affected by his historical context. Government was cared for from the top down, by the appointees of princes and kings and governors. There was no thought to changing governmental structures and accepted practices of society. However, one must remember Pietism's, and Zinzendorf's, concern for the poor and the orphan and provision for human needs, especially education, characteristic of the Pietistic enterprises. Here one is reminded of some of the approaches of early Christianity where, though powerless to effect any change in social and political structures, Christians did seek to transform society within the Christian communities.

Reflections

Resources

Zinzendorf knew that resources are needed for living, because life is difficult. His statement, cited at the beginning of the chapter, that "we can give nothing, before we have something," is crucial. *Christian life is the product of having something — or Someone.* With his Christocentrism he saw what one has as growing out of the relationship with the Savior who, in the marriage with the soul, becomes bone of our bone and flesh of our flesh. Living as a Christian is not merely a matter of having sufficient resources or living out of inner transformation. It is of ultimate concern that life bear witness to the One who is in us, but beyond us. It is not our life with Christ's help that counts, but it is *Christ's life through us.* Therefore what is of grace in life bears witness to grace and God. This is similar to Paul's statement in 2 Corinthians 4:7: "But we have this treasure in earthen vessels, to show that the transcendent power belongs to God and not to us." The New Testament language which identified a person of the Godhead with the resources was varied. Both the Son and the Spirit could be seen as agents of God's action in the present. While for the Johannine community, with all of its language about the Spirit, the center of the Christian experience is really Christ, for Paul the Spirit is God's gift of Godself, the fulfillment of the promise made to Abraham (Galatians 3:14), out of which relationship one may say,

[63] Ibid., p. 339.

"Abba, Father," with the help of the "Spirit of his Son" (Galatians 4:6).[64] It is the presence of this relationship which makes possible Christian life (Galatians 5:16-25).

Thus the New Testament literature seems to recognize in various ways Zinzendorf's concern to call attention to the need for the resources of Christian life. "We can give nothing before we have something."

Simplicity

Besides concern for the resources of the Christian life, Zinzendorf was also concerned for simplicity. In Zinzendorf's understanding of *religion* as "the heart-relationship with the Savior," *religion* becomes available to all, even the embryo in the womb. It does not depend upon intellectual ability to understand, conceptualize, and systematize. The same problems exist in formulating ethical behavior as in formulating theology. Some people will not be able to handle complex issues. How then can all persons be ethical and live a Christian life? Zinzendorf is clear that when one has Christ, one has all one needs. It is within this relationship that the ethical issues are to be dealt with. As Jesus in a personal way will fill out one's "theological page," helping one to know what one needs to know, so Jesus in a personal way will direct behavior. One has only to look at the eyes of the Savior to find out what to do.

Simul justus (and *sanctus*) *et peccator* is also important here.[65] Holiness is God's gift, as is justification, while in ourselves we are still sinners. We do not need to produce holiness, in fact we cannot; we can only try to live responsibly. We will be human, as Zinzendorf indicates, all through eternity. Existence will always depend upon grace. Thus we may joyfully, from the perspective of grace, live out life with its failures and complexities.

That there are to be failures and complexities must be noted. Whatever our approach to ethics, whether we have a rule for every

[64] In Gal. 4:6 Paul indicates that Christians have received "the Spirit of his Son" who helps them to say "Abba, Father." This means that the resurrected Christ continues to do what he did historically, i.e., teach persons to pray to the Father. In Rom. 8:15, in the passage comparable to Gal. 4:6, the wording is that Christians have received "the spirit of sonship" (RSV), rather than "of his Son," which has quite a different meaning.

[65] *Simul justus et peccator* is the Latin phrase which represents the heart of Lutheran theology. At one and the same time (*simul*) the human being in Christ is justified (*justus*) and sinner (*peccator*). One is justified in Christ, not in oneself. Thus one may be at the same time sinner and justified, for what one is in God's eyes depends on God and not on our limits. For Luther and Zinzendorf one is also *simul sanctus et peccator* : one is holy in God but still sinner in oneself. Holiness is God's gift, not our accomplishment. Holiness is here understood as a status, as is justification. God as a gift declares us to be just and holy while in ourselves we are sinners. Thus what God does for us frees us to deal with our predicament and to attempt what God declares and calls us to be.

occasion or watch the eyes of the Savior, there will always be failures and complexities. That is our nature, and it is in the nature of life. Therefore one cannot say that to trust our perception of the eyes of the Savior is to take an *unusual* risk because we may misunderstand. All ethic involves the risk of doing something wrong.

As Zinzendorf's understanding of simplicity does not deny the intellectual task in theology, though recognizing its limits and its varied expression, so simplicity in ethics cannot deny the responsibility of the church to work at the complex ethical issues of today which may produce varied answers. Important in doing this is not only the intellectual acumen specialists may bring to the issues, but the way the issues are *lived through with God.* The living through at times will be the most significant witness which arises out of the struggle with difficult issues, for it indicates the acceptance of ethical responsibility and points to the Transcendent Reality which (Who) resources life, makes it graced (gracious), and calls to life and responsibility.

Discipline

Zinzendorf's understanding of discipline is that it helps and supports the life God has given — and it is the practice of the life God has given. It is not a means of proving or attaining righteousness or holiness or gaining God's acceptance. Neither is it the orders of a religious community about matters which are peripheral. And it does not consist of orders forced upon one which one does not really desire. Rather does it provide an order which supports life already desired, chosen, and being lived.

The need for discipline becomes clear when it is realized that what God gives and would realize in us is not yet, but is coming to be in a process analogous to the biological, psychological, and moral developmental processes. To be given the resources for life does not mean that the realization of the gift is present, but persons are engaged in a process of living upon and towards the gift. The incompleteness and ambiguities of undeveloped human nature, and even of developed human nature, make discipline a necessary, but friendly and supportive, structure. Both gift and discipline are necessary.

In the New Testament there are two basic approaches to life and discipline. One is behaviorist. Tell persons what to do, and they will become what they should become by doing what they should do. This is the approach of the Gospel of Matthew, with its large collections of Jesus' sayings understood as commandments. Chapters 5-7, the Sermon on the Mount, are often described as the discipline of the Matthaean community, a topical arrangement of Jesus' sayings with Jesus presented as a new Moses giving a new Law from a new mountain. The other approach is that of Luke, Paul, 1 Peter, and John. They stress the importance of being open to transformative realities (Christ, the Spirit, the Gospel), and then discipline is provided to furnish structure and facilitate the life which these realities are bringing into being. Neither of the approaches neglects discipline, but each understands it quite differently.

Scholars have noted that there is a body of ethical teaching in the New Testament which, though differing in content in the places where it is expressed, treats common topics and expresses a common style of social relationship This is given the descriptive name "Household Code," for it describes relationships within the ancient household. This included relationships of children and parents, husbands and wives, servants and masters, and, at times, relationships with the state. The primary locations for this are Colossians 3:1-4:6, Ephesians 4:1-6:20, and 1 Peter 2:1-4:11.

This material was part of the catechetical instruction of the early church, providing new members with a summation of Christian discipline. Each citation of the code is introduced by a discussion of the spiritual realities which empower the Christian life, particularly the death and resurrection of Christ, through whom the believer dies to the old life and rises to the new, a reality made concrete in baptism. Thus In Colossians 3:1-4 it is said:

> If then you have been raised with Christ, seek the things that are above, where Christ is, seated at the right hand of God. Set your minds on things that are above, not on things that are on earth. For you have died, and your life is hid with Christ in God. When Christ who is our life appears, then you also will appear with him in glory.

The Ancient Moravian Church stressed the importance of discipline, as did the Renewed Moravian Church in what was originally called the *Brotherly Agreement.* As part of the process of resolving the divisions which existed in Herrnhut in 1726-27, on May 12, 1727, Zinzendorf brought together the members of the community to express allegiance to *Manorial Prohibitions and Injunctions,* to which was added the *Brotherly Agreement*[66] expressing the spiritual life of the community. The Agree-

---

[66] In German the two documents were called *Herrschaftlichen Gebote und Verbote* and *Brüderliche Verein und Willkür.* An English translation of the original *Brotherly Agreement* can be found under the title "Brotherly Union and Agreement at Herrnhut, 1727," in *Pietists: Selected Writings,* ed. Peter C. Erb, The Classics of Western Spirituality (New York: Paulist Press, 1983), pp. 325ff.

ment was understood as a voluntary commitment of the community to a discipline which would foster what all held to be important. This has been revised a number of times over the years, and in recent times in North America has been renamed *The Moravian Covenant for Christian Living*. The *Agreement* expresses the relationship between what one has and what one does, which Zinzendorf believed was crucial to ethics and life. In the void of values characteristic of our world and in the modern hunger for spirituality, persons ask how and with what shall we live? This is not merely a search for morality, but also a search for meaning, as expressed in the poem which concludes this chapter.

Community

Zinzendorf was clear that it is very difficult to be ethical without community, whether it is on the congregational level or that of smaller groups: bands and choirs. Community makes possible the practice of a Christian life that would be difficult without it. Community consists of all those who join around the crucified Savior or who share the heart relationship with the Savior, but community is also with the "family" of God: Father, Son, and Mother. Though many of the Moravians were involved in extended journeys and in continuous contacts with society all over the world, behind their endeavors there was always the community to which they could return, and the mystical community in which they shared wherever they were.

In the New Testament one finds Christian community of various sorts. In the Pauline churches, modeled after the Jewish synagogue, ongoing contacts with society were maximal and relationship with Christian community was occasional. However, in the communal life of the Jerusalem and Matthaean churches, contact with Christian community was maximal. The Matthaean community seems to have been similar to Qumran, a semimonastic community with discipline expressed in the sayings of Jesus now preserved in large collections. Yet, however much time was spent in community, whatever the model of community, there was nevertheless always some community. This makes sense not only from the perspective of the resources of and responsibility to community which were part of the Christian experience, but because the religious life was social in nature, participating in God's inner community and exploring the meaning of this for human relationship.

World

Zinzendorf's understanding of the state and Christian civic responsibility was so much tied to the governmental structures of his time and the division of life into the two realms of the church and state, characteristic of Lutheran teaching, that it provides little guidance for those living in democratic societies. Moreover, the horrors of the Holocaust in Europe and the Vietnam involvement of the U.S. have made it imperative that religious groups exercise a prophetic role within society. Christians cannot assume that they should be involved only in the affairs of the Lord and that the matters of the state would be properly cared for. We have learned from our history, as Zinzendorf was constantly learning from his. I would guess that his advice to us today would be quite different.

It has usually been clear for Christians that the world and its systems function according to their own value systems, and so the Christian brings to his/her society some counter-cultural values. For many then decision making within society becomes complex, needing not only clarification of one's values, but prioritizing and honing of the fine art of compromise, knowing when it is possible and when it is not. It is also true that on many contemporary matters the Christian tradition does not offer clear guidance, and on some the guidance which it does offer seems in question. The church must struggle with the issues for the sake of its members, providing direction and guidance while recognizing that approaches to issues will be differently conceived by those loyal to Christian values. Thus ethical decisions are not fully possible without grace and forgiveness and the recognition of the legitimacy of variety.

There were various approaches to the relationship of Christians with the world in early Christianity. Christians did not think they could do much about the world (which God would soon bring to an end), and they divinized its power structures (as in Romans 13) or demonized them (as in Revelation 13). Often the world was seen as ruled by either Satan or neutral powers who opposed or did not understand God's purpose.[67] Because of the resistance of the world to God and life, and the tragedies of history, Judaism had moved in a dualistic direction, which it passed on to early Christianity's worldview. This dualism involved more than rejection of the world's power structures (with a

---

[67] In 1 Cor. 2:8 Paul speaks of the "rulers of this age" who crucified Christ because they did not understand what God was doing in him. In 1 Cor. 5:5 the power of Satan in the world is mentioned. Paul's treatment in Rom. 13 of the state, as ordained by God, would thus seem to reflect sensitivities to the Roman reader. In Gal. 4 the "elementals" (equivalent to political structures) were given by God along with the Law to control human impulses until the time arrived for human maturity, but now one was freed from them in Christ.

hope for God's intervention and establishment of theocracy). World, matter, and flesh were often seen as hostile to the spiritual. The Johannine tradition barely tolerates the world, except for the Prologue to the Gospel.[68] Now there is a sense in which negative assessment of the role of world and flesh in life frees one to recognize the spiritual and the tenuousness of the world. But we are here, and we are in the world, and we are flesh. Too strong a dualism denies the meaning of the life we now have and calls us to long for what is not yet ours. Incarnation is not an accident. Even God does it. Then there must be meaning here. There must be something we are to become and learn in this world besides patience and tolerance.

The tasks of life

The clarification of the nature and purpose of life and its tasks is an important part of an ethics concerned with being and becoming, not just doing. There are *several tasks* that are part of the Christian perspective on life in this world, besides the usual developmental tasks. Though the treatment of these is not phrased in Zinzendorfian terminology, all but number 5, Christian responsibility for creation, find themselves at home in his theology. And even this fifth is consistent with Zinzendoef, if his emphasis is on Christ as Creator, a major theme in his theology, is kept in mind. That the contemporary concern for creation is not addressed is a consequence of the nature of the religious questions within his context. The central concern of Zinzendorf's time was the fate of persons, not of creation as a whole. Consequently he understood the significance of Christ as Creator as related to the salvation of the person whose Savior was also her or his Creator and thus passionately concerned with his or her destiny. Understanding Christ as Creator in the modern context calls us to explore how this might be applied to the Savior/Creator's relationship to world and cosmos, as well as persons.

1. There is the *moral aspect* of the person's formation, engaging us in becoming persons with values and commitments, though not without mistakes and failures. Holiness is a gift, not an accomplishment, while formation is a process in which we can participate. What we become morally not only constitutes us in certain ways, but it equips us for whatever God would call us to in the future — even beyond this life.

[68] I believe that the prologue is added by the final editor of the Gospel (John 21:24-25) as a way of diminishing its dualism. That it is an addition becomes clear because it stands over against the dualism supported in much of the Gospel. That this addition occurs at the beginning of the Gospel indicates that the prologue provides the perspective by which the Gospel is to be read.

2. *Our formation, our becoming, witnesses to the Transcendent,* to what is more than us, to God, to Christ. We are an experiment in becoming, in whose process the nature and possibilities of life with God are realized and shown.

3. There is a *spiritual aspect* to formation. It involves the process of discovering our own spirituality and the reality of God and God's world, concerns which are easily neglected as one engages in the tasks of life in this world. It is as if, when we are born and move into the experiences of this life, we begin forgetting whence we came and to whom we go. Discovering our spirituality and God is part of our developmental process. In our discovery we bear witness to the world in which we live.

4. There is an *interpersonal aspect* to formation. In the New Testament this is characterized as *love.* Our ability to love affects the possibility of interpersonal relationship, for love has to do with relating to others beyond our own needs, the ability to care for others and to be patient and persistent in relationship. In a way it manifests the redemptive process of God.

5. With our learning to care for others we *need to learn how to care for creation,* a proper love of the world. The creation narratives speak of the responsibilities humans have been given for the world. An interesting aspect of living in this world is that we have learned about creation from within creation, not as something apart from it and us. Thus both it and we are engaged in a process of formation together. The world here prepares us for the world beyond, whose nature we cannot yet imagine but whose God we trust.

6. All of this is part of *being for God in the world.* There was a time before modern science when it was felt that the forces of nature and history were the primary ways of God's being in the world. Within the last three centuries we have been developing an understanding of both nature and history which sees them as operating largely by their own dynamics. Thus we have come to realize that the primary way of God's being present is where the world comes to consciousness and can be influenced: in humanity. We need to learn to be willing and open to God, allowing our lives to be formed by God. Therefore we become those who can be used in God's purposes and who can re-present God, like living sacraments. Thus the Kingdom of God is within us and among us (two possible meanings of Luke 17:21).

Living into Zinzendorf's language

One of the reasons for the long quotations from Zinzendorf in this chapter is to expose the reader to his imagery. Some of the language about Jesus' wounds and the mystical marriage with Jesus may be offensive to those unaccustomed to it and unacquainted with similar language in mysticism. Yet over the years I have constantly found myself strangely moved by it. It leaves me with images in my head and heart which somehow make Jesus and what he did a part of me, or me a part of him. I find myself changing under its impact. This language was the language Zinzendorf used to paint the Savior before the mind and heart of believers so that they could experience the objective, not subjective, reality of the Savior and thus be equipped for life. In some sense the first Tablet of the Law enters my heart. I see him in his suffering which more than his resurrection makes him God to me. His side-wound becomes the womb of my birth and life. His blood flows in mine. In his dying I not only live but die. And I feel his eyes upon me and hear him ask, "Do you love me?" And as the Mother Spirit comes upon me I surrender to her care and find myself in the family of Father, Mother, and Son. If this language at all works for the reader, what does this say about our overintellectualization of the Christian message, though the raising of this question should not be seen as anti-intellectual?

The neurologist Oliver Sacks, well known for his sensitive appreciation of persons with various disabilities, argues that the glory and identity of being human is to be found not in the abstract and conceptual (of which not all are capable), but in concrete thinking.

> But of much greater interest, much more human, much more 'real' — yet scarcely even recognised in scientific studies of the simple (though immediately seen by sympathetic parents and teachers) — is the *proper* use and development of the concrete.
>
> The concrete, equally, may become a vehicle of mystery, beauty and depth, a path into the emotions, the imagination, the spirit — fully as much as any abstract conception [perhaps indeed more, as Gershom Sholem (1965) has argued in his contrasts of the conceptual and the symbolic, or Jerome Bruner (1984) in his contrast of the 'paradigmatic' and the 'narrative']. The concrete is readily imbued with feeling and meaning — more readily, perhaps, than any abstract conception. It readily moves into the aesthetic, the dramatic, the comic, the symbolic, the whole wide deep world of art and spirit. Conceptually, then, mental defectives may be cripples — but in their powers of concrete and symbolic apprehension they may be fully the equal of any 'normal' individual. (This is science, this is romance too. . . .) No one has expressed this more beautifully

than Kierkegaard, in the words he wrote on his deathbed. "*Thou plain man!*" (he writes, and I paraphrase slightly). "The symbolism of the Scriptures is something infinitely high . . . but it is not 'high' in a sense that has anything to do with intellectual elevation, or with the intellectual differences between man and man. . . . No, it is for all . . . for all is this infinite height attainable."[69]

World
within, without,
strange,
I struggle
to be somehow
and to relate and act.

Who
am I
midst all I am
and what does life
and God
expect of me?

I need
some place
to stand,
someone to say
"you are"
and who I am.

I need
some cosmic arms
me to embrace,
unfailing love
to set me free
from all that binds.

[69] Oliver Sacks, *The Man Who Mistook His Wife for a Hat and Other Clinical Tales* (New York: Summit Books, Simon and Schuster, 1985), pp. 166-67.

Down
from the cross
arms reach towards me
and gather me into
his pain and wounds
and lasting love.

I know he knows
how hard life is
and how I need
one who will
join his pain
and hope with mine.

And I need
others to call me
home, be my people,
my freeing
paradigm of life
to be — with me.

And
to remind of stories,
sprinkle life's waters,
hold forth life's food,
and direct my eyes
above and yet below.[70]

---

[70] By the author.

Chapter 6

The Church, Ministry, and the Sacraments

The Renewed Moravian Church in the first thirty years of its existence engaged in extensive experimentation on the forms of church appropriate for its mission. Even in the beginning of the Christian community one can discover various forms of church. The community of disciples that Jesus attracted around himself was one form, out of which Jesus selected twelve for mission but also as a symbolic reconstitution of the twelve tribes. While the Pauline churches developed after the pattern of the Jewish synagogue, the Jerusalem and Matthaean churches seem to have adopted the pattern of a religious society similar to the Essenes at Qumran. In Matthew, Peter was seen as having been given special authority, while at Jerusalem, James, the brother of Jesus, assumed leadership. The life of the Christian community flowed into forms available within the culture, which were in turn affected by the dynamics of Christian life and mission.

The apostles, and the tradition they could transmit, seemed to play a central role. Paul made several trips to Jerusalem to confer with apostles, one after his conversion when he spent two weeks with Peter, and a later visit during which he shared his understanding of the Gospel (Galatians 1:18-2:10). But in spite of a common loyalty to apostles and Jerusalem different forms of Christianity developed, each with particular traditions which they preserved. One way to explain the several Gospels is by taking seriously the uniqueness of each Gospel tradition as part of the formative memory of a Christian community. Differences gradually caused complementary and oppositional dynamics between and within communities. Distances also affected the ability of one segment of Christianity to link with another. Some intentional efforts were made to link developing communities, such as the first church council in Acts 15 and the offering collected by Paul as gift to the mother

Jerusalem church from the younger churches.

Paul was deeply concerned with the divisions developing within and between churches with which he was involved. He found that what we as humans bring to the development of Christianity leaves upon it the stamp of our gifts and characteristics. Since human differences create differences, the way to unity and reconciliation was not to be some formula for conceptual and institutional reconciliation. Rather the churches must be called back into relationship with the common realities which brought them all into being. Paul did this by speaking of the relationship of God, Christ, and the Spirit to the origins and on-going life of the church. For example, while the Corinthian church seemed to be constituted around loyalty to certain leaders or teachers, Paul points out that it is not the leaders whose eloquence or style constitutes the community. Rather it is God who constitutes the church, in Christ, and God is the only one of whom we should boast (1 Corinthians 1:26-31). He also indicates that the church is the church *of God* in a particular place (1 Corinthians 1:2), but is not to be identified by the place in which it exists. In 1:30 he points out that the church exists "in" Christ, who is our Wisdom from God, and also our righteousness, holiness, and redemption. The image of the body of Christ in 1 Corinthians 12 indicates both the origin of the church in Christ and its re-presentation of him in the world. It is an active image and reminds the church that its mission remains connected with him, for it functions as his body. The events of Christ's life, especially his death and resurrection, constitute the events through which God brings the church into being and are symbolized in the initiatory rite of baptism. Through the Spirit God gifts the church for its well-being and its mission. The language of 1 Corinthians 12 speaks in Trinitarian terms of the spiritual gifts as given by the same Spirit, serving the same Lord, energized by the same God (vs. 4-6). The action of the Spirit is important, for it prevents the church from understanding itself as once and for all historically constituted in some form only in the lifetime of Jesus. Whatever the importance of historic events such as Jesus' commission of the church, whatever the importance of apostolic tradition and apostolic succession, church is not church unless it also lives out of God's ongoing presence in the Spirit. And even Pentecost as historic event does not have the last word about the church. The realities which constitute the church are also contemporary and must be related to as *present* sources of its life. The church has its traditions, and these traditions and the society provide institutional forms, but the church cannot exist without drawing from the contemporary realities which initially gave it existence.

There is one Gospel which would seem to say otherwise, and unfortunately this Gospel is placed first. In Matthew Jesus is presented as a new Moses giving a new Law on a new mountain (chapters 5-7). Jesus' sayings are organized into a Pentateuchal pattern with five narrative and five sayings sections, thus with five divisions like the Old Testament Law. Though Jesus will be with them to the end of the age (28:20), he has primarily left with them his commandments, and their mission is to go and make disciples of all nations, baptizing them and teaching them his commandments (28:19-20), functions which have to do with inclusion and instruction in the established community. There is little *active* role for the resurrected Jesus, now that he has given his commandments and disciples are being instructed in the tradition. There is also little role for the Spirit in Matthew, unlike John and Luke. The church already has what it needs. And there is a system of authority. Jesus has been given all authority (28:18) and he has given authority to Peter (16:13-20). This happens to Peter only in Matthew. Since Peter was dead by the time of the writing of Matthew, it is quite likely that the question of Peter's authority was important because this also gave authority to Peter's successors, who likely remained the leaders in the Matthaean church. This church then lived from a tradition and established authorities with minimal sense of needing to find its existence in the living realities which initially brought it into being. Of course all institutions need structure, and one finds the Pauline churches also developing this, so that in 1 Timothy there are bishops (overseers), deacons, and an order of widows. Yet in the Pauline tradition one generally finds a better balance of the need for both institutional structure and contemporary response to spiritual realities without which the church becomes only institution.

Zinzendorf's understanding of church respected the ecumenical creeds and confessed special loyalty to the Augsburg Confession and the Synod of Bern (Reformed),[1] the traditions which came to him in the

---

[1] Vernon H. Nelson, archivist of the Moravian Church Archives, Northern Province, Bethlehem, Pa., has a printed lecture, "Synod of Bern, Switzerland, 1532," delivered on 1 March 1987 and preserved in the Archives. (On the same occasion Lane A. Sapp also presented a lecture, "The Doctrinal Themes of the Bern Synod: Why They Were Important for Zinzendorf and the Renewed Brethren.") Nelson concluded: "The Synod of Bern, particularly the first 18 articles, is of great importance to the Renewed Moravian Church, even though the name of the Synod has almost disappeared. The Synod of Bern is in fact more important to the Moravian Church than to the Swiss Reformed Church. In the Moravian Church, under Zinzendorf, the first 18 articles of the Bern Synod permeated the life, the hymns, the liturgies, and particularly the message of the Church." See also Ernst Saxer, "Zinzendorf und der Berner Synodus," *Unitas Fratrum* (Hamburg: Friedrich Wittig), nos. 29/30 (1990): pp. 157ff.

Moravian settlers on his estate, and the Anglican tradition. In fact, for one hundred years after its renewal in Herrnhut the Moravian Church preserved the identity of the Reformed, Lutheran, and Moravian traditions in its own membership. The reestablishment of the Moravian episcopacy indicates not only a concern for recognized church order but a desire to be in continuity with apostolic traditions.[2] The concerns of those hoping for the renewal of the church, such as the Pietists, meant returning to the original sources of the church's life. The institutional churches may live primarily by their traditions; but the "real" church, which transcends but lives within all traditional churchly expressions, must live from the heart relationship with God, from the reality which gives it birth. As Zinzendorf expressed his vision for Herrnhut in a hymn:

Herrnhut should no longer stand
than the works of your hand
unhindered there are done,
and love be the bond,
until we (are) ready and expectant
as good salt of the earth
to be usefully poured out.[3]

Zinzendorf grounded the church primarily in its relationship to the contemporary Christ and the Spirit who is the Mother of the church, not in the institutional forms with their differences and distinctives. But he was well aware that the church cannot live a disincarnate life, for incarnate life was the pattern established by Christ himself.

The church is necessary not only because there is the tradition of a community behind it in Christianity's Jewish heritage, not only because God in Trinitarian existence has modeled it, not only because Christ has called it into being, not only because the experience of Pentecost constituted it, but because community is needed for human existence and plays a role in creation itself. Community is needed as the place where the wisdom of the centuries may be shared, where the individual

[2] This intent was recognized recently in Church of England–Moravian Church in Great Britain and Ireland conversations, which issued in the following document: Church of England and Moravian Church in Great Britain and Ireland, *Anglican-Moravian Conversations: The Fetter Lane Common Statement with Essays in Moravian and Anglican History*, Occasional Paper No. 5 (London: Council for Christian Unity of the General Synod of the Church of England, 1996). See paragraphs 45-48, pp. 26-27.

[3] Nikolaus Ludwig von Zinzendorf, as quoted in Erich Beyreuther, *Die große Zinzendorf Trilogie* (Marburg: Francke, 1988), 2:179. The verse, and the hymn of Zinzendorf form which it is taken, can be found as hymn 349 in *Gesangbuch der Evangelischen Brüdergemeine*, 2nd ed. (Hamburg: Friedrich Wittig, 1982).

human struggle may be shared and supported, where interpersonal possibilities may be explored, where the presence of God may be experienced out of the shared gifts and resources of many, and from which the reality of God may be reflected back into the world. This last is very important. The metaphor of the mirror is present in the language of experience in many religious traditions. It appears in the New Testament in 1 Corinthians 13:12 and in the language about reflection from the face of persons in 2 Corinthians 3. The Genesis 1 story of the creation of humans in the image of God indicates that humans were placed here to reflect God into the world. God is present in the whole world, but humans are the place where creation comes to consciousness and the possibility of response-ability, and so may reflect God's purposes. This is a most holy aspect of human existence.

To properly understand Zinzendorf's views regarding the nature of the church, we need to consider his use of the German terms *Kirche, Religion, Sekte,* and *Gemeine.* In order to maintain clarity regarding his use of these terms, the German terms will be retained. The plural of *Religion* is *Religionen* and of *Gemeine* is *Gemeinen.* Various compounds of *Gemeine* are used.

Kirche

The *Kirche* (German for church) itself is invisible and not to be equated with the visible and historical Christian traditions and institutions which Zinzendorf calls *Religionen* (Religions, Denominations). To the *Kirche*

> belong all souls who through the Word, through the voice of Jesus, wherever they are, let themselves be woken to life, who are desirous of salvation, who love him, who belong to him in time; and who someday come from the east and west, north and south, and will sit at table with Abraham, Isaac, and Jacob in heaven.[4]

It is this invisible church which cuts across all confessional lines:

> Therefore we want to place minimal limitations on the true right-believing church of Jesus Christ, but believe that in the various religions of the Lutherans, Reformed, Mennonites, even in the

---

[4] *Eine Sammlung Offentlicher Reden, Von Dem Herrn der unsere Seligkeit ist, und über die Materie von seiner Marter. In dem Jahr 1742. Mehrentheils In den Nordlichen Theil von America der das Englische Canada ausmachet vor allerley Christlichen Religions-Meetings gehalten, von Dem damaligen Evangelischen Lutherischen Inspectore und Past. zu Philadelphia. Erster Theil [Zweiter Theil] Zweyte Edition,* [2nd ed.] (Büdingen: Johann Christoph Stöhr, 1746), 1:94 (7 and 18 Feb. 1742).

Roman Catholic there are persons who are blessed. However, with this proviso, that they gained salvation not through their confession but merely through the true faith in Jesus Christ and his merit.[5]

Religion

The term *Religionen* is used for the great historical churches,[6] the confessional bodies such as Lutheran and Reformed which we often call denominations. To these, people give external allegiance as *Christianern* (Christians) rather than *Christen* (those defined by Christ and bearing his name).[7] In Zinzendorf's *Nine Public Lectures* he comments:

In all languages one says, a Christian, and in our German alone one says, *ein Christ*, and that is the right word. . . . In no way are we called by the name of Jesus or Christ in the sense of a religious denomination, as if Christ were our teacher, as if Christ were our prophet, our lawgiver, as if He were the founder, the author of our *religion*, as it is sometimes expressed by a pagan historian, as for example in Lucian. "The founder of this *religion* was crucified." In this sense we are not Christians. Rather, we are Christians in the same way that, in our European countries, a wife takes the name of her husband and afterwards is called not by her maiden name but by her husband's name. Thus every soul who has the right to call herself by this name, "because she was taken out of Man"(Gen. 2:23), belongs to Christ, is Christian.[8]

[5] Nikolaus Ludwig von Zinzendorf, *Der Freywilligen Nachlese, Bey den bißherigen Gelehrten und erbaulichen Monaths-Schrifften, 1. Sammlung. Etiam inter manipulos colligat, et pudore non afficiatis eam. Ruth. C. II. v. 15.* collection 13,(Frankfurt and Leipzig: M. Christ. Gottfried Marche, n.d.), p. 1544, quoted in Hermann Plitt, *Zinzendorfs Theologie,* (Gotha: F. A. Perthes, 1869-74), 1:458. (Citation of the Zinzendorf work will be abbreviated in subsequent notes as Zinzendorf, *Freywilligen Nachlese.* Citation of the Plitt work will be abbreviated in subsequent notes as Plitt, *Zinzendorfs Theologie.*)

[6] Nikolaus Ludwig von Zinzendorf, *Jeremias, ein Prediger der Gerechtigkeit, allen redlichen Predigern in der evangelischen Kirche einfältig und als ein Exempel vorgestellt, wie man in seinem Amte mit Gott, mit der Obrigkeit, mit den Lehrern, mit seinen Zuhörern überhaupt, und mit seinen Brüdern insonderheit wandeln könne. Von Nicolaus Ludwig, Grafen von Zinzendorff. Nach der zweiten verbesserten Auflage wieder abgedruckt* (Berlin: Franklin und Comp., 1830), p. 15 (1740). (Reprint of the 2nd rev. ed.) (Abbreviated in subsequent notes as Zinzendorf, *Jeremias.*)

[7] *Des Grafens von Zinzendorff Inhalt dererjenigen Reden, Welche zu Berlin vom 1ten Januar. 1738. bis 27ten Aprilis in denen Abend-Stunden sonderlich für die Manns-Personen gehalten worden. Dritte Auflage* [3rd ed.] (Flensburg and Altona: Gebrüder Korte, 1743), p. 29 (3 Feb. 1738).

[8] Nikolaus Ludwig von Zinzendorf, *Nine Public Lectures On Important Subjects in Religion Preached in Fetter Lane Chapel in London in the Year 1746,* trans. George W. Forell (Iowa City: University of Iowa Press, 1973), p. 77 (25 Sept. 1746).

Zinzendorf always affirmed that valuable teachings exist within the historical *Religionen* and that their confessions are right for them. Also, there are true Christians in every Christian *Religion*, along with the nominal members. The Savior sees to this.[9] Zinzendorf saw something of special value in every *Religion*. Each had its treasure. Hence he did not encourage separatism, nor was he among those Pietists who did not see the value of the church.[10] In fact, he said to those within the *Religionen*, "Whoever wishes to help his *Religion* must not consider it a 'Babel,' but a broken Zion, and do that from the heart."[11] Anyone acquainted with the history of the Moravians in this period will remember the extreme reticence they had concerning receiving a member from one of the *Religionen*. They usually insisted that each person remain a loyal member of their own confessional body and carried out the *Ecclesiola in Ecclesia* (little church within a church) concept of Spener and Francke wherever they went. Moreover, Zinzendorf affirmed the unique value of each *Religion* through the *Tropus*[12] concept. The *Tropi Paidiae* were "ways of teaching" which characterized each historical tradition. Within the Moravian Church for about the first 100 years separate membership lists for the Lutheran, Reformed, and Moravians were retained. The *Tropus* concept was partially fostered by Zinzendorf's ecumenical perspective and partially urged upon him by the persistence of the settlers from Moravia, who insisted upon reviving their ancient Church. Thus the identity of the Ancient Moravian Church was preserved, as well as that of Lutherans and Reformed.[13] These three *Tropi* then constituted the

[9] Plitt, *Zinzendorfs Theologie*, 1:460. See note 5 for full bibliographic information.

[10] Though Zinzendorf was likely influenced by Philadelphianism, a movement to create ecumenical communities in Europe, he did not have the separatist tendencies of the more radical types of Philadelphianism. Peter Vogt discusses Zinzendorf's contacts with this movement and the existence of a Philadelphian interconfessional *Schloßecclesiola* ("little church at the castle," similar to Pietism's *ecclesiola in ecclesia*) in the court of Reuß-Ebersdorf, from which Zinzendorf's wife came (Peter Vogt, "Zinzendorf and the 'Pennsylvania Synods' of 1742: The First Ecumenical Conferences on the North American Continent" [Honors paper in *religion*, Moravian College, Bethlehem, Pa., May 1992], pp. 98-104 [Abbreviated in subsequent notes as Vogt, "Zinzendorf and the 'Pennsylvania Synods'"]). Zinzendorf did use the term *Philadelphian* in relationship to the Moravian Church. The use of the term *Philadelphian* was ultimately derived from Revelation 3, where Philadelphia is described as the ideal church.

[11] Zinzendorf, *Jeremias*, p. 20 (1740).

[12] *Tropos* is the transliteration of the Greek and *tropus* is the Latin. Both are used. The plural of *tropos* is *tropoi* and of *tropus*, *tropi*. *Paideia* (or *paidia*) is a transliteration of the Greek word for training or discipline, and *paedia* is the Latin. Thus a *tropus paediae* is a way of discipline, and Zinzendorf uses this to describe the approach of each religious traditon.

[13] Hermann Plitt, *Die Gemeine Gottes in ihrem Geist und ihrem Formen* (Gotha: Friedrich Andreas Perthes, 1859), pp. 181-82. (Abbreviated in subsequent notes as Plitt, *Die*

Unitas Fratrum or the *Brüdergemeine* (Unity of the Brethren).[14] This Unity
of the Brethren adopted the church order of the Ancient Moravian
Church, but the understanding was never lost that

> the external form of churches, even if it is the best, is never the
> *Geistes-Gemeine* [*Gemeine* of the Spirit] nor does it create this, but it
> serves it as its bearer and must confer on this a *jus reformandi* [a
> principle to bring about reformation] in Spirit and power which
> is always divine. As long as it does that and lets its external affairs
> always be spiritually directed, both essence and form, inner and
> outer, remain unseparated in reference to persons as well as
> institutions, even if some particulars are wanting.[15]

Zinzendorf strongly spoke out against the pestilence of Christian
criticism of other Christian traditions:

> This critical and sarcastic spirit is a pestilence of our times, and
> ruined to the ground for the Savior more than one *Gemeine* which
> doesn't deserve the name. . . . With this opportunity it very specially
> lies upon my heart, how all my brethren in the *Religionen* . . . are
> quite seriously to seek to purify themselves from that in the blood
> of Jesus (insofar as there remains in their minds, especially from
> the perspective of the academy, one and another *idea secundaria* for
> the despising of form, liturgy, external administration and impart-
> ing of the sacraments, the confessional, ordination, etc.).[16]

Gemeine Gottes.) Plitt quotes the following from Zinzendorf without indicating a source:
"They have accused us of wanting to begin a new sect. But we can easily contradict that
if we are asked in appropriate fashion. The renewal of the Ancient *Brüder-Kirche* (*Unitas
Fratrum* or Ancient Moravian Church), to which we owe our external church order
through the gracious leading of the Savior, happened only out of respect for the
Ancient *Brüder-Kirche* founded 300 years ago, the ancient sister of the Protestant church.
People who do not understand the matter believe they are doing God a service if they
can merge and hide the remaining descendants of the Ancient *Brüder-Kirche* in another
church. In our time they want to put them among the Lutherans as in earlier times in
Poland they were placed among the Reformed. But by doing this they overlook that in
the many and varied Christian church differences there lies the deep intent of God, so
that in place of his spiritual kingdom whose inner unity is not disturbed by differences
in *incidentals* there not emerge again a common political church-realm which is
dependent on the mind and type of thought of each ruler and then calls that 'right
belief' which in each period knows how to gain the upper hand."
  [14] It is interesting that *Brüdergemeine* and *Unitas Fratrum* have essentially the same
meaning. Thus the Latin name of the Ancient Moravian Church was really taken over
as the name for the whole Renewed Moravian Church.
  [15] Plitt, *Die Gemeine Gottes*, p. 185. This is the description of Plitt, not Zinzendorf's
words.
  [16] Zinzendorf, *Jeremias*, p. 227f. (1740).

Sekte

In regards to the word *Sekte,* in an essay titled "Simple (*Unmassgebliche*) thoughts on the name and meaning of the word *sect,*" he showed that from the external and historical point of view a Christian group can be called a *Sekte,* if one means nothing else than "an association of such persons who prefer the party of a person or an idea, although not always exclusive of other teachers and doctrines."[17] So the term may be used if it has no exclusive implications, though on the whole Zinzendorf was wary of the term. The Gospel is no sect, but the only universal *religion.* Christians are not sectaries of certain earthly teachers, but Christians have one Teacher, come from God, who said that his teaching was not his, but that of him who sent him.

Gemeine

The term *Gemeine* was the term which Zinzendorf most frequently employed for the church.[18] This was quite distinct from *Religion. Gemeine* was used for the real church, which lived with and from Christ and expressed the reality from which it lived. This term described a living organism which is universal as well as local.

> And because I always make a great difference between a *Gemeine* and a *Religion in genere* [in kind]; and with respect to a *Gemeine* I am of the opinion that she stands in need of no new system, because she is herself a daily system of God, a system which the angels themselves study: so, on the other hand, in the *Religionen* from whence the *Gemeine* [here not congregation but universal church] is made up, from which it issues, where it has its old knowledge and in which it would also like to remain in order to set forth certain points freely, one must point out people who have spiritual eyes and ears, people with whom μετάνοια [repentance] is going on.[19]

[17] Zinzendorf, *Freywilligen Nachlese,* collection 4, pp. 456ff., quoted in Plitt, *Zinzendorfs Theologie,* 1:470.

[18] Plitt, *Die Gemeine Gottes.* This is an intriguing presentation by the author of the three-volume *Zinzendorfs Theologie.* In it he begins with a doctrinal treatment of *Gemeine* and *Kirche* and then moves to a historical consideration in three sections: The Preformation of Christian *Gemeine* in the Old Testament and the Savior's Disciple-family; the Original Formation of the Christian *Gemeine* or the Apostolic *Gemeine*; and then the Continuation of the Christian *Gemeine* from the Patristic Age to the Moravian Church or *Brüdergemeine.* He argues that the nature of the *Gemeine* is "spiritual, eternal, based on the community of life of its members with God and each other, in Jesus Christ, through faith and love, but its form is necessarily subjected to the changeability of human relationships, local and temporal conditions" (ibid., p. 2).

[19] Nikolaus Ludwig von Zinzendorf, *Ein und zwanzig Discurse über die Augspurgische Confession gehalten vom 15. Dec. 1747. bis zum 3. Mart. 1748. denen Seminariis Theologicis*

Bettermann explained the use of the term *Gemeine* in the German of the eighteenth century. *Gemeine* and *Gemeinde* are two forms of the same word. Where Luther used the term *Gemeine*, the eighteenth century used both forms in a similar way. In the nineteenth century *Gemeinde* emerged as the only form. Whereas the term *Gemeinde* came to designate a local congregation, *Gemeine* amongst the Brethren in the eighteenth century had a broader meaning. *Gemeine* refers not only to the local congregation, but also to the church as a whole, and wherever the local congregation is meant, the orientation of the local to the whole invisible church is always seen. Thus the local *Gemeinen* are joined in a living unity.[20] The *Gemeine* in its universal sense is then made up of all *Gemeinen*, both within and without the established *Religionen*, and also the heavenly *Gemeine*.

"The only true *Gemeine*, the only foundational *Gemeine*, the only genuine original *Kirche* is the Holy Trinity."[21] Any *Gemeinen* formed on earth were made after this pattern. The first earthly model of this *Gottes-Kirche* (church of God) was the creation of humanity. Because of the failure of this, God acted again and said:

> The *Kirche*, which had been formed in my heart from eternity, must still be: and that went so far that the Creator became human in his own person and passed through the stages of human life; and there he hung on the cross . . . : so he hung there in all stillness, and established the model of the *Kirche*, which had been betrayed, which did not wish to come into being, which had not wanted to be created for 4,000 years, doing this nakedly and simply at the cross, and declared his [sic] John and his mother to be the first cross brother and sister.[22]

Thus Christ, his mother, and John became the earthly model of the heavenly *Gemeine*, a relationship brought into being at the cross. The reader will remember Zinzendorf's emphasis on the side-wound of Christ as the birthplace of the church. In this sermon he speaks of the

Fratrum zum Besten aufgefaßt und bis zur nochmaligen Revision des Auctoris einstweilen mitgetheilet (n.p., n.d.), pp. 86-87 (17 Dec. 1747). For information about the two different printings of this work, see chapter 1, note 82. (Abbreviated in subsequent notes as Zinzendorf, *Ein und zwanzig Discurse* [Title page: *Discurse . . . Auctoris*].)

[20] Wilhelm Bettermann, "Warum wir Gemeine und nicht Gemeinde sagen," *Jahrbuch der Brüdergemeine* (Gnadau, Unitätsbuchhandlung) (1935/36): pp. 16-17.
[21] Nikolaus Ludwig von Zinzendorf, *Der Öffentlichen Gemein-Reden im Jahr 1747. Erster Theil. Mit einem Anhang einiger zu Ende des Jahres 1746. gehaltenen Homilien* (n.p.: Zu finden in den Brüder-Gemeinen, 1748), p. 78. (Abbreviated in subsequent notes as Zinzendorf, *Öffentlichen Gemein-Reden, 1747*, pt. 1.)
[22] Ibid., p. 79.

arms and the wounds of Christ as being the only place for all Christians. The possibility of this relationship did not depend upon understanding or ability to consciously respond; thus Zinzendorf reduced it to the relationship of the embryonic Jesus and John the Baptist:

> I reduce it to two persons. John and Jesus, both in their mother's womb, and their mothers, in any case together constituted a Christian *religion*; there began the feeling, the experience, and the inner movement which today in Christianity is regarded as dream and imagination.[23]

The understanding of the church as a counterpart of a heavenly reality anchored the *Gemeine* in this transcendent realm.[24] It was in the world, but it took its life from God's world, and it, in a sense, anticipated the end time when the heavenly reality would become the total reality.[25] Thus the end time was perceived as being near, though Zinzendorf regarded eschatology as one of the biblical mysteries and refused to

---

[23] Nikolaus Ludwig von Zinzendorf, *Einiger seit 1751. von dem Ordinario Fratrum zu London gehaltenen Predigten in Dreyen Haupt-Abtheilungen edirter Erster Band.* Sec. [Abtheilung] 2 (London and Barby: Zu finden bey dem Seminario Theologico, 1756), pp. 154 (17 Jan. 1753).

[24] Hartmut Beck has written on Moravian settlements on three continents, stressing the intentional organization of the settlements with Herrnhaag as a pattern. The Saal was the place "where the members of the congregation, wherever and however they might otherwise live, gather in worship as the congregation 'below' (which is here on earth), which knows itself bound to the congregation 'above' of those members of the congregation who have fallen asleep, completed their course, and so departed" (Hartmut Beck, "Für Zeit und Ewigkeit: Herrnhuter Siedlungen auf drei Kontinenten im 18. Jahrhundert und deren transkulturelle Orientierung," in *Geisteshaltung und Stadtgestaltung, Referate, gehalten auf dem Geographentag in Potsdam, 1995*, ed. Manfred Büttner [n.p.: Peter Lang, 1997], p. 171). Beck emphasizes that the Moravians took to where they went a common community design while respecting and adapting to local cultures. The article includes photos and diagrams of various communities.

[25] Peter Vogt calls attention to Zinzendorf's desire to establish *Gemeinen* as representing a new "Ökonomie Gottes" (Economy of God). Zinzendorf comments: "The holy people have to be brought together from all four winds at the due time. Of that there now are appearing dawnings and examples which are the *Gemeine*" (*Teil 1-4 Theologische und dahin einschlagende Bedencken Welche Ludwig Graf von Zinzendorff, Zeitheriger Bischoff Der Böhmisch- und Mährisch- Evangelischen Brüder, Seit 20. Jahren entworffen. Mit des Autoris Zuschrifft An alle Hohe Obrigkeiten Und einer Vorrede Polycarpi Müllers, Ehemahligen Professoris zu Leipzig und Directoris des Gymnasii zu Zittau, nunmehrigen Episcopi Fratrum* [Büdingen: Johann Christoph Stöhr, 1742], pp. 166-67, quoted in Vogt, "Zinzendorf and the 'Pennsylvania Synods,'" pp. 95-96. [The Zinzendorf work will be abbreviated in subsequent notes as Zinzendorf, *Theologische Bedencken*]). It should also be noted that the conversion of persons in the mission fields was seen as the gathering of the First Fruits (see Rev. 14:4), as represented in John Valentine Haidt's paintings of the first converts of Moravian missions. Haidt was a Moravian minister and one of the first colonial American painters to treat religious subjects. He produced several renditions of the First Fruits.

speculate about it. The experiences of this time are the first fruits of the end time and a new economy of God. One finds this same perspective in Jewish and early Christian apocalyptic thought, which was both mystical (spoke of a transcendent reality in which the believing community participated) and eschatological (concerned with the end time, when God would establish this reality within world and history). Often the mystical tendencies in apocalyptic are neglected in favor of eschatological interests.

As Zinzendorf described it: Jesus has "given us a certain sketch of the primal temple, of the primal *Gemeine*."[26] The extent to which this governed Zinzendorf's thinking on the church is realized by few Moravians in North America. The liturgy of the worship service was viewed as the participation by the congregation in the heavenly worship,[27] the division of the church according to age and station ("choirs" of the married, single, etc.) was considered expressive of the nature of the heavenly *Gemeine*, and the organization of seating in the saal for worship and of burial in the cemetery, or God's Acre, in choirs also had this purpose behind it. The churches were not dark and mysterious gothic buildings, but bright, with a great deal of window space and extensive use of white both on the interior of the place of worship and as the liturgical color.[28] The surplice which was adopted for use at the Lord's Supper was not a white liturgical gown but after the manner of those robed in white in the book of Revelation, and it reminded the congregation that they belonged to a heavenly reality.[29] I believe that this is why Christ remained so near to the experience of Zinzendorf and the Moravians, even though he was understood to have ascended to the right hand of God, with the Spirit commissioned to act on his behalf in

[26] Zinzendorf, *Öffentlichen Gemein-Reden, 1747*, pt.1, p. 84.

[27] The Moravian Hymnal of 1735 has an interesting plate on its title page which shows the relationship of earthly to heavenly worship. It portrays a time of *Anbeten* (prostration) before the Lamb. There is a sanctuary (or *Saal*) with at least two levels. On the ground level there is a congregation prostrating itself before the Lamb. Then there is another group in a balcony in the back of which the Lamb is located, along with the seven lampstands and four beasts. Those in the balcony are prostrated in front of chairs (thrones). Though there are only twenty visible (ten on each side), they must represent the twenty-four elders in heaven (Evangelischen Brüder-Gemeine, *Christliches Gesang-Buch, der Evangelischen Brüder-Gemeinen von 1735 zum drittenmal aufgelegt und durchaus revidirt* [n. p.: Zu finden in obbesagten Gemeinen, 1741]). The imagery is borrowed from Revelation, chapters 1-5.

[28] See Peter Vogt, "The Shakers and the Moravians: A Comparison of the Structure and the Architecture of Their Settlements," *The Shaker Quarterly* (Poland Spring, Maine) 21, no. 3 (fall 1993): pp. 79ff.

[29] Cf. Wilhelm Bettermann, *Theologie und Sprache bei Zinzendorf* (Gotha: Klots, 1935), pp. 122ff.

the world. Although in heaven, he was not far away, and one could still live from him, and he would enter one's daily life (*Umgang mit dem Heiland*). The church, and each one whose soul was his bride, participated in the reality in which he now dwelt.

The primary mark of the *Gemeine* would be the relationship with the Savior, and thus with God.

The second mark would be its relationship with the Spirit, who cared for the church as a Mother. The Spirit called persons to the ascended Jesus and assisted in carrying out his mission. The *Gemeinen* were congregations of God in the Spirit transcending all denominational lines. Such a concept he sought to bring into reality in 1742, when in the Pennsylvania Synods he tried to create a fellowship which would include members of all the German-speaking Protestants in Pennsylvania.

The Spirit had a decisive effect upon the nature and forms of the *Gemeine*. During the Synod of 1750[30] Zinzendorf spoke of the "*Gemein-Geist*," the Holy Spirit in regards to its influence on the *Gemeine*, "*das agens, motor, Spiritus activus*" ("the agent, mover, active Spirit"). This Spirit is the "*je ne sai quoi*" (absolute essential) or the "*Schibboleth*" (see Judges 12:6) of the *Gemeine*. The effect of the *Gemein-Geist* on the hearts of the members of the congregation is the "*Gemein-Sinn*" (common mind), and when this is put into action it is called the "*Gemein-Plan*" (common plan). The "*Gemein-Wille*" (common will) is the common willingness to contribute to the purpose for which the Savior has brought the members of the *Gemeine* together. The "*Gemein-Gefühl*" (common feeling or intuitive perception by the heart) is that "*inne werden*" (inner becoming) which the "*Gemein-Geist*" causes us to experience from time to time. Thus the life of the congregation or church is dependent upon the Spirit, and the Spirit creates a *Sinn, Plan, Wille*, and *Gefühl* which are expressive, not of the individuality of the members of the *Gemeine*, but of their unity. Moreover, as one might understand from previous consideration given to revelation and interpretation as *ökonomisch* (right for a particular economy or time), the Spirit would lead the church to forms and institutions which would be appropriate to the Lord's purpose for the church in every situation. In other words, form shall not determine the *Gemein-Geist* but the *Gemein-Geist* shall determine the form.

[30] Minutes of the 1750 Synod, as reported in *M. Avgvst. Gottl. Spangenbergs Apologetische Schluß-Schrift, Worinn über tausend Beschuldigungen gegen die Brüder-Gemeinen und Ihren zeitherigen Ordinarium nach der Wahrheit beantwortet werden, Nebst einigen wichtigen Beylagen* (Leipzig and Görlitz: In der Marcheschen Buchhandlung, 1752), pp. 542ff. (Abbreviated in subsequent notes as *Spangenbergs Apologetische Schluß-Schrift*.)

A third mark of the *Gemeine* was mission. Christ had given his church a mission. Each one of the Gospels concludes with some equivalent of a commissioning of his disciples. In John, Jesus sends his disciples as his Father had sent him (e.g., John 17:18). Both the life and activity of the *Gemeine* carry out this mission. Its *life* expresses the very relationship which Christ calls the church to facilitate for others and which gives those exploring the Gospel an experiential referent. In 1 John 1:3, others were invited into the fellowship with the Father and the Son which constitutes the life and fellowship of the community.

Hence for Moravians a crucial step in mission was always the planting of a *Gemeine* where the life with Christ was lived out and could be experienced by others. The mission as *action* was going where Christ would have the *Gemeine* go, keeping in mind that mission and evangelism were God's business. One had to discern, follow, and participate in what God was doing. What began as preaching excursions into areas surrounding Herrnhut following the spiritual experience of 1727 in a few years brought Moravians to the West Indies and North America and then to many other parts of the world to "win souls for the Lamb." Within ten years Moravians had gone also to Greenland, Suriname, South Africa, the Gold Coast, Algeria, Arctic Russia, and Ceylon.[31]

The Development of Forms of the Gemeine: A Tale of Two Cities

During the Zinzendorfian period the Moravian Church engaged in amazing experimentation to discover the forms of church structure which were suitable to sustain the spiritual life of its community and its members and to support the mission to which it felt called. Some forms of church were also necessary to relate the church to the social and political structures of the time, and some forms were the ones available within a particular context. An interesting example of this is the initial use of the office of village elder at Herrnhut, an office which eventually evolved in a spiritual direction.

However, the *Gemein-Geist* (the Spirit of God in the congregation), and not merely traditional forms, was to determine what was right for the times. What follows is the story of this experimentation in the first thirty years of the Renewed Moravian Church. This will be described primarily in terms of the developments in Herrnhut, the place of the Moravian

[31] For Zinzendorf's theology of mission see David Allen Schattschneider, "'Souls for the Lamb': A Theology for the Christian Mission according to Count Nicolaus Ludwig von Zinzendorf and Bishop Augustus Gottlieb Spangenberg" (Ph.D. diss., University of Chicago, 1975). For an excellent contemporary discussion of mission as the essence of the church, see Wilbert R. Shenk, *Write the Vision: The Church Renewed,* in the series Christian Mission and Modern Culture (Valley Forge, Pa.: Trinity Press International, 1995).

Church's eighteenth-century rebirth, and Bethlehem, its first sustained development in North America, where the ability to maintain European traditional forms of church life was in question and there seemed to be opportunity for a new ecumenical experiment. It would also be interesting to explore the developments in Herrnhaag, an ideal Moravian community which was begun in 1738 after much of the initial experimentation at Herrnhut, but space does not allow.[32] The story of Herrnhut and Bethlehem, the "tale of two cities," should best represent what was occurring at this time in the Moravian Church. For those interested in the form and mission of church for our time, these thirty years in the eighteenth century are a powerful model.

That the Moravian Church, with serious intent and commitment, entered into this experimentation meant that it did not immediately claim to have the answers. It knew directions it wanted to pursue, but not the details. And it was willing to keep on making the changes needed. It perhaps needed clearer discernment of the ways that the Spirit and Christ as Chief Elder were involved in its life so that the intent of Christ could be more clearly distinguished from the dynamics of persons and community. It also needed a more adequate appraisal of what it meant to be *simul justus/sanctus et peccator* (at the same time justified/holy and sinner). Though this was believed theologically, many did not always recognize what one might call the "persistent humanity" of even those most deeply committed to Christ. This will be dealt with under the Reflections at the end of this chapter in a section on "Following Christ in the Church." But what is of greatest concern is not that they made some mistakes, as do we all, but that the time came when experimentation diminished and forms hardened into institutions. As Erbe comments on the period after Zinzendorf's death, previously cited in the Introduction:

> The Moravians, who previously had spread abroad so much noise, so much excitement and unrest, the Church which had been like a volcano, now became — it is scarcely to be believed — the "Welt der Stillen im Lande" (the world of the quiet in the land), a piece of German Biedermeier, middle class and noble, closed in upon

---

[32] See the writings of Hans-Walter Erbe on Herrnhaag in the journal *Unitas Fratrum*, listed in footnote 69 later in this chapter. Issue 12 of *TMDK*, though focused on contemporary ecumenical relationships, also includes comments on the development of the Moravian Church in various European locations: Denmark, Germany, the Baltic, Switzerland, etc., and an article by Hartmut Beck, "What Are We? How Do We Understand Ourselves?" Particularly, are we a society or a church? (*TMDK: Transatlantic Moravian Dialogue Correspondence*, English[-language] edition [Bethlehem, Pa.], issue 12 [July 1997]). Issues 11 and 12 also deal with ecumenical relations in Great Britain and North America. All of this bears on the Moravian Church's search for forms of Gemeine right for various contexts.

itself in its Settlement Congregations, these quiet and proper villages, simple and distinguished, separate from the greater world, at the same time intimate and worldwide, with its culture in lifestyle and the arts worthy of respect, in constantly new realizations of community (*Gemeine*) shaped by its focus upon itself.[33]

Herrnhut

Pietism in Halle, under the influence of August Hermann Francke, had already begun experimentation with the development of institutions for the benefit of orphans and poor besides schools, a seminary for teachers, a printing office and bookstore, a Bible house, and infirmary. Zinzendorf had originally intended to develop at Herrnhut something similar to Halle. However, circumstances dictated otherwise, and soon communal forms were developed to suit the needs of the developing community at Berthelsdorf and Herrnhut and its mission.

Herrnhut was shaped by the settlement of refugees from Moravia and elsewhere. At first, there was little structure, and Zinzendorf entrusted the care of this developing community to Johann Andreas Rothe, the Lutheran pastor of Berthelsdorf. In 1725 Rothe initiated the first stage in the development of offices for a community of about 60 persons from Berthelsdorf and Herrnhut. Especially influential was a sermon he preached on Romans 12:7-8, urging the use of apostolic offices for the developing community. Christian David reported on this sermon that

he proved how very unfair it would be that everything would be allowed to depend on one or two poor preachers. For (1) no one would have all the gifts which are needed for a whole community (*Gemeinde*); (2) even if he would have all gifts, the time and strength would be lacking to care for this according to the need of each member . . . , but where members are committed to one another and one serves the other with that gift which each received from the Lord for the common good, then can the whole body be built up for its self-improvement.[34]

[33] Hans-Walter Erbe, "Herrnhaag–Tiefpunkt oder Höhepunkt der Brüdergeschichte?" *Unitas Fratrum* (Hamburg: Friedrich Wittig) no. 26 (1989): pp. 45-46.

[34] Johann Andreas Rothe, sermon in Rom. 12:7-8, as reported in *Christian Davids Beschreibung von Herrnhut 1731*, in Herrnhut Archives, R6Aa22,1, pp. 32ff., quoted in Hanns-Joachim Wollstadt, *Geordnetes Dienen in der christlichen Gemeinde: Dargestellt an den Lebensformen der Herrnhuter Brüdergemeine in ihren Anfängen*, Arbeiten zur Pastoraltheologie, vol. 4 (Göttingen: Vandenhoeck und Ruprecht, 1966), p. 139. (Abbreviated in subsequent notes as Wollstadt, *Geordnetes Dienen.*)

On February 2, 1725, a four-hour meeting was held for the assignment of offices. There is a little writing in Zinzendorf's hand which lists seven women and seven men representing both Berthelsdorf and Herrnhut at the top and then lists their assignments as "Helpers in the Work of the Lord." The categories of assignment seem closely related to Romans 12:7-8 as it existed in Luther's translation:

Helpers in the Work of the Lord
1. in prophecy
2. for service (εἰς τό διακονεῖν)
3. in teaching
4. in exhortation
5. in administration and care
6. in advocacy and giving attention
7. in working out all of the works of love,
    especially the difficult and unpleasant[35]

The second stage of development happened in relationship to the differences and resultant quarrels of the settlers, which necessitated pastoral work by Zinzendorf (1726-27) and further organizational development. Zinzendorf prepared the *Manorial Injunctions and Prohibitions,* binding upon every resident of Zinzendorf's estate and signed by them on May 12, 1727. To these were added the *Brotherly Agreement,* which was binding only on those who voluntarily wished to be a part of the religious community. The residents of Herrnhut were free citizens under the protection of the count, who became overseer and represented the community to the outside world. An elected body of elders, patterned after customary Upper Lausitz village government, cared for the life of the community. There were initially twelve elders selected, from which four chief elders were selected by lot. The elders represented and preserved the identity of the several groups within the community, with two elders and one chief elder for each group: (1) the first ones (i.e., the exiles), (2) those from Zauchtenthal, (3) those from Kunwald, (4) the foreigners (*Frembde* i.e., *Nicht Exulanten* [not exiles]).[36] There is a document in the Herrnhut Archives in the hand of Zinzendorf which provides a list of offices under the title "Worldly Direction of the Republic of God at Herrnhut":[37] the elders and other such offices as craftmaster, almsgiver, overseer of streets, carer for the sick, etc. The development of the bands in 1727 are considered to be a third stage in the development of offices, especially concerned with pastoral care.

[35] Zinzendorf, as quoted in Wollstadt, *Geordnetes Dienen,* pp. 130-31.
[36] Ibid., p. 143.
[37] Ibid., p. 140.

These beginnings of the ordering of communal life underwent many changes. For example, the office of elder by 1730 became primarily a spiritual office, and the administrative tasks were taken over by the General Council (*Gemeingericht*). That the forms of community life should be engaged in a process of constant change fitted Zinzendorf's understanding of the nature of institutional forms:

All institutions exist for the sake of their purpose. When the purpose is no longer attained or falls away, one lets go of the thing itself, and so must it be in a *Gemeine* of God; otherwise there is no salt, and it only goes on *ex opere operato*.[38]

There was initially a clear intent by both Rothe and Zinzendorf to establish an apostolic community patterned after the early church. Zinzendorf said:

What we have in our *Gemeine*, to which we hold, is apostolic, and is recognized by others, because it has for its foundation the simplest Scripture. That is our goal by which we measure ourselves.[39]

However, as various developments took place, it became clear that biblical patterns were not the only determinant, and that the needs of the present situation were also important. At the Synod of Gotha in 1740, when he presented the reasons for the beginnings of the choir system, he commented:

Regarding Choirs . . . in the New Testament there is nothing about a similar division. . . . Therefore we want to present this not as a biblical, but a Moravian Brethren's institution . . . , only that ours is more developed (German *ordentlicher*) than the old Brethren had theirs. And if it would even be neither biblical nor Moravian, yet the circumstances in which we stand demand it. It is now a new world.[40]

In the summer of 1727 Zinzendorf began the use of "bands" to deal with the spiritual and interpersonal life of the community. The bands

[38] Herrnhuter Diarium, Rückblick auf das Jahr 1734 beim 31. 12. 1734, von 15 Januar 1735, quoted in Wollstadt, *Geordnetes Dienen*, p. 125, n. 10.
[39] Zinzendorf, *Theologische Bedencken*, p. 75, quoted in Wollstadt, *Geordnetes Dienen*, p. 43.
[40] Herrnhut Archives, R2ANr.3A1, session [Sessio] VII v. 16 June 1740, pp. 143ff., quoted in Wollstadt, *Geordnetes Dienen*, p. 108. Uttendörfer indicates "that Zinzendorf approximately since 1740 gave up the idea of measuring all by the Apostolic Age" (Otto Uttendörfer, *Das Erziehungswesen Zinzendorfs und der Brüdergemeine in seinen Anfängen*, Monumenta Germaniae Paedagogica, vol. 51 [Berlin: Weidmannsche Buchhandlung, 1912], p. 144, n. 2).

were voluntary associations of a small group of persons. Each band was led by a band convenor or director [*Bandhalter*] who assumed primary responsibility for the pastoral care of persons in the band. By 1734 the number of bands in the Herrnhut congregation had grown to 100. The 1745 description by Zinzendorf and a description by Christian David (the second below) make clear the insights into the nature of pastoral care embodied in this development:

> That we meet as bands with each other, that we confess one to the other the state of the heart and diverse imperfections, is not done in order to consult with our brothers and sisters because we could not get along without the counsel of a brother or sister. Rather is it done that one may see the rightness of the heart. By that we learn to trust one another; by that no brother or sister thinks of the other that things are going well with them if they are really going poorly. Then no one can imagine that the brother or sister feels well when they are in pain. That's why you talk to each other, why you unburden your hearts, so that you can constantly rely on each other.[41]

> Initially there were among the brothers and sisters several who had a special trust in each other so that they began especially to form an association with the purpose (1) that they want to say to each other everything that they have on their heart and mind; (2) that they want to remind and encourage each other concerning everything they can see or think of each other and yet always to encourage one another to the good in everything; (3) that they want to come together once every week, in the evening, to hold conference or bands with which they might get to know one another well from within and without; (4) that they wish to give each other the freedom for heart, life, and journey, to test and express everything, and so love one another as their own life, to keep watch, pray, struggle and fight for one another, and to bear,

[41] Nikolaus Ludwig von Zinzendorf, *Zwey und Dreyßig einzele Homiliae Oder Gemein-Reden in denen Jahren 1744. 1745. 1746. Daß ich euch immer einerley sage, verdrüßt mich nicht, und macht euch desto gewißer* (n.p.: Zu finden in den Brüder-Gemeinen, n.d.), p. 17 of homily 20, quoted in Gottfried Schmidt, "Die Bänden oder Gesellschaften in alten Herrnhut," *Zeitschrift für Brüdergeschichte* 3 (1909): p. 154, quoted in Peter Zimmerling, "Seelsorge in der Gemeinschaft: Zinzendorf als Seelsorger," *Theologische Beiträge* (Theologischer Verlag Rolf Brockhaus) 26th year (April 1995): pp. 76ff., translated under the title "Pastoral Care in the Community: Zinzendorf and Pastoral Care," *TMDK: Transatlantic Moravian Dialogue Correspondence*, English[-language] edition (Bethlehem, Pa.), issue 11 (March 1997): pp. 58-59. (The translation will be abbreviated in subsequent notes as Zimmerling, "Pastoral Care.")

spare one another, and help make life easier which is otherwise difficult, and therefore have the community which is proper *Evangelio* [to the Gospel].[42]

By 1731 another form of community division came into being under the influence of the Pietistic attempt to analyze spiritual development and to assign persons to stages in this development. This is what Wollstadt characterizes as the "small classes," to be distinguished from the "great classes," a term used for the division of the community into groups according to age, status, and sex before the application of the term "choir" to these larger divisions. Unfortunately these small classes gradually took the place of the bands. In 1731 at a lovefeast for the married men their bands were dissolved and they were divided into three classes: Young Men, Children, and Beginners. The difference between the Children and the Young Men is:

When a trespass takes place, one pities the Children, but one punishes the Young Men. One asks and charms the Children, but one orders the Young Men and demands of them that they carry out the matter laid on them. When Children do something good, one is amazed and praises it; with the Young Men one takes it for granted.[43]

From the division according to spiritual development there is only a short way to the Warrior (German *Streiter*) ideal which meant much to Pietism and the eighteenth-century Moravian communities. The Warrior was committed to complete obedience and surrender to Christ and to live for the ultimate mission in service of the Lord.[44] For example, Zinzendorf and his wife were committed to this Warrior ideal, and their marriage was regarded as a *Streiterehe*, a "warrior marriage."

The Ancient Moravian Church in a similar way had divided persons into Beginners, Progressing, and Perfect.[45] Zinzendorf came to see the

[42] Christian David, *Beschreibung und Zuverläßige Nachricht von Herrnhut in der Ober-Lausitz, Wie es erbauet worden, und welcher Gestalt Nach Lutheri Sinn und Meinung Eine recht Christliche Gemeine sich daselbst gesammlet und eingerichtet hat. Vormals von einem Mitglied andern Freunden der Wahrheit schriftlich ertheilet, nun aber von einem, der nur Wahrheit suchet, und sehnlich wünschet, daß an mehr Orten in der Freyheit Christliche Gemeinen nach diesem Muster, zur Verherrlichung Gottes in Christo, angeordnet werden möchten, durch den Druck gemein gemacht.* (Leipzig: Samuel Benjamin Walther, 1735), pp. 33ff., quoted in Wollstadt, *Geordnetes Dienen,* pp. 93-94. (Citation of the Christian David work will be abbreviated in subsequent notes as David, *Beschreibung und Zuverläßige Nachricht.*)

[43] Herrnhut Archives, R6Aa18, 1e,XX, quoted in Wollstadt, *Geordnetes Dienen,* p. 102.

[44] Wollstadt has an extended discussion in his *Geordnetes Dienen,* pp. 317ff.

[45] Wollstadt, *Geordnetes Dienen,* p. 100.

division of persons into classes according to spiritual development as a mistake. He realized this as he turned to the centrality of grace in Luther by 1734 and came to reject the Pietistic teaching about the conversion struggle (*Bußkampf*). He later said that it was unfortunate that the class divisions should have been mixed in with the bands.[46]

> Through that [the establishment of classes] the bands were destroyed and the classes were never considered by the Sisters for the purpose that the bands had served. As soon as one distinguishes between souls, the bands stopped. But when it happens that people come together, who regard each other as decent people and good friends, that is a band. . . . But there is no band where one censures another or where one must fear that one or the other is wounded. Then people separate from one another without arriving at anything substantial. . . . As soon as the first hurtful remark is directed at someone, then the band is finished.[47]

Wollstadt comments that the result of this period was not completely negative. With this division of members the idea of spiritual development became a conscious principle, and the Young Men class of the single brothers became the first messengers in foreign lands.

Following the division of the *Gemeine* into four groups in 1727, according to the area from which the settlers came, this was further developed to seven and then ten areas in the years 1728 to 1730, each intended to have its own male and female Teacher and Administrator and its own bands, though the only offices we know of in the records are the Helper and the Almoner. With the development of the classes and developing self-awareness of the community, the division according to place of origin did not really seem to persist.[48]

The choir system had its beginnings in earlier "great classes" of the *Gemeine* according to sex, age, and station in life.[49] It did not at first supplant the bands and small classes, but rather slowly subsumed them.

[46] Ibid., p. 101.
[47] Minutes, 6 Sept. 1753, 8th session [Sitzung], quoted in Gottfried Schmidt, "Die Bänden oder Gesellschaften in alten Herrnhut," *Zeitschrift für Brüdergeschichte* 3 (1909); p. 200, quoted in Wollstadt, *Geordnetes Dienen*, p. 101.
[48] Wollstadt, *Geordnetes Dienen*, pp. 102-4.
[49] Wollstadt indicates that there were up to eleven great classes designated: *Armkinder* (infants or children carried on the arm), *kleinen Knaben* (little boys), *kleinen Mädchen* (little girls), *großen Knaben* (older boys), *großen Mädchen* (older girls), "*jungen Purschen*" (unmarried young men), "*Jungfern*" (virgins or young women), *verheirateten Männer* (married men), *verheirateten Weiber* (married women), *Witwer* (widowers) and *Witwen* (widows) (ibid., p. 106).

The name "choir" (*Chor*)was not employed until 1735.[50] An important part of the choir development was the building of the great choir houses in which each group lived and carried on their life and crafts. The origin of the term *Chor* (choir) is not to be solved.[51] In the bands and then the classes there had been a strict segregation of the sexes, which was to be the foundation for the development of the Single Brothers and Single Sisters choirs. Zinzendorf was here concerned not only with the moral stature of the community but with avoiding the dangers inherent in a religious awakening where emotionalism could develop sensual relationships.

We know from experience that in times of religious agitation, sensual relationships, with their attendant evil consequences, may develop all too easily out of the spiritual influence of the time[52]

The Brotherly Agreement of May 12, 1727, also indicated that

familiar or intimate relations between single men and women are to be positively forbidden; moreover the elders have the power to prohibit social intercourse as soon as they have even the slightest suspicion, no matter how worthy its purported goal.[53]

The division of men and women and according to age and status provided for an interesting approach to spiritual life, for the Savior in his life paralleled the stages of human development and life experience. The life of Jesus and Mary then became a paradigm for the classes and choirs. Each group should, in its circumstances and with its gifts, model a part of the nature of Jesus, particularly in relationship to the stage of his life which related to theirs.

The Single Brothers choir was the first to develop in Herrnhut, followed by the choir for Single Sisters. The Widows choir also developed early because of the economic needs of this particular group, but the choir for Widowers was not formed until 1746. In the 1740s the choir

[50] Ibid., p. 104.

[51] Ibid., pp. 104f., n. 183.

[52] Minutes of the 1740 Synod in Gotha, 16 June 1740, Herrnhut Archives, quoted in Otto Uttendörfer, *Zinzendorf und die Jugend: Die Erziehungsgrundsätze Zinzendorfs und der Brüdergemeine* (Berlin: Furche, 1923), p. 82. (Abbreviated in subsequent notes as Uttendörfer, *Zinzendorf und die Jugend.*)

[53] *Brüderliche Verein und Willkür* (Brotherly Agreement), Herrnhut Archives, 15 June 1727, reproduced in Joseph Theodor Müller, *Zinzendorf als Erneuerer der alten Brüderkirche: Festschrift des theologischen Seminariums der Brüdergemeine in Gnadenfeld zum Gedächtnis der Geburt Zinzendorfs am 26. Mai 1700* (Leipzig: Friedrich Jansa, 1900), pp. 106-10, quoted in Gillian Lindt Gollin, *Moravians in Two Worlds: A Study of Changing Communities* (New York: Columbia University Press, 1967), p. 69. (Abbreviated in subsequent notes as Gollin, *Moravians in Two Worlds.*) See also chapter 1, note 58.

for Married Persons also came into being, along with a choir for Children, where as a matter of necessity children had often to be cared for apart from parents who were engaged in the building up of the settlements or the various mission enterprises of the church.

The institution of the choirs is described by Zinzendorf in his *Eventual Testament* of 1738.[54] Though the choirs and their houses also provided a solution to the problem of living space and a context in which trade and the industrial life of the community could be carried on, their purpose was primarily religious. The rules of the Single Brethren in Herrnhut in 1736 state: "No one is permitted to live here who is not primarily concerned with the welfare of his soul."[55] The Single Sisters of Herrnhut vowed to dedicate their lives completely to the Savior and, to this end, to leave all decisions to Christ and the Elders of the community, and to "retain no will or choice of their own."[56] The choirs did provide experience of a communal life style similar to that of the early church.

The membership of a person in the choirs, when the system was fully developed, began even before birth. Zinzendorf said:

> When the marriage has been consecrated to the Lord and the mother lives in continuous interaction with the Savior, one may expect that already in the mother's womb the children form a choir, that is, a grouping of the community consecrated to the Lord's work.[57]

By the age of about one and a half the child was then given to the care of the nursery, and education and spiritual care under the supervision of the choir began. From age twelve to seventeen the children were in the Older Boys and Older Girls choirs which prepared them to take their place in the community. Here the children were often apprenticed to

---

[54] Zinzendorf, *Eventual Testament* (1738), in *Theologische Bedencken*, p. 181.

[55] The Constitution and Regulations of the Brethren in the Inn, Herrnhut Archives, 29 Feb. 1736, quoted in Otto Uttendörfer, *Alt Herrnhut: Wirtschaftsgeschichte und Religionssoziologie Herrnhuts während seiner ersten zwanzig Jahre (1722-1742)* (Herrnhut: Verlag der Missionsbuchhandlung, 1925), pp. 85-86, quoted in Gollin, *Moravians in Two Worlds*, pp. 70-71.

[56] David, *Beschreibung und zuverlässige Nachricht*, p. 19, quoted in Gollin, *Moravians in Two Worlds*, p. 71.

[57] Diarium des Jüngerhauses, 19 Sept. 1755, quoted in Uttendörfer, *Zinzendorf und die Jugend*, p. 85, quoted in Gollin, *Moravians in Two Worlds*, p. 80. Those responsible for the Embryo Choir provided prenatal care for the mothers, but also care for the embryos. It was taken seriously that the Savior was in relationship with all his souls, even the unborn child. One of Zinzendorf's favorite stories about the nature of *religion* was the instance when the embryonic Jesus in his mother's womb came into the room where Elizabeth was with John in her womb, and John lept for joy in his mother's womb.

specific trades. From the Single Brothers or Single Sisters choirs they would move, upon marriage, into the Married People choir.

There is no indication that the eighteenth-century Moravians consciously made the choir system a substitute for the family except in the Pilgrim Congregations. It was primarily a subordination of family loyalties to the needs and work of the church, and particularly reflected an understanding of the broader loyalties created among all those who were one in Christ. Such would be the relationship of Christians in heaven, and so this was anticipated in the congregational relationships and even in the organization of God's Acre.[58] The choir leaders, or "Helpers," had primary responsibility for the members of the choirs.

An alternative form of the *Gemeine* was expressed in the Diaspora work of the Moravian Church in Europe, beginning in 1727. From Herrnhut members were sent to preach in surrounding areas, a ministry which was ultimately to extend even to Russia and the Baltic. According to the Pietistic idea of forming a "little church within a church," societies were begun within congregations of the state churches for the nourishment of spiritual life, but with the insistence that members remain within their own churches.

In 1735 David Nitschmann was ordained as a Moravian bishop by Daniel Ernst Jablonski, the grandson of Comenius, and regular orders of ministry were reestablished. In 1736 at Marienborn the first Synod of the Moravian Church was held. Communal structures continued to be modified with the departure of Zinzendorf for North America, and a special Elder became overseer of Herrnhut, and a General Conference of a number of prominent Moravians, including two bishops, was established. While Zinzendorf was gone they pursued recognition of the Moravian Church as an independent episcopal church. When Zinzendorf returned in 1743, he protested and took over as *Advocatus et Ordinarius Fratrum,* abrogating the powers of this General Conference and now possessing absolute power.

It is interesting to explore the offices and titles which Zinzendorf used of himself to express his role in the *Gemeine.* Though he used many

---

[58] It would be interesting to investigate Zinzendorf's idea of life after death and its implications for the de-emphasis on the family and the husband-wife relationship. Certainly he, like Paul in 1 Cor. 7, subordinated personal interests and marriage to the Christian mission. Paul, in 1 Cor. 7, argues that this was especially important since the time of tribulation had arrived and the world was passing away. However, there is also the presupposition of Jewish Apocalyptic that there will be no marriage in the afterlife. This understanding was expressed in practices at Corinth where some couples were living together in a spiritual marriage, without sex. The broadening of human relationships, already experienced within the Christian community anticipating the afterlife, would seem to be expressed within the Moravian communities.

titles, his office was usually anchored in the order of the *Gemeine* at that time and thus often changed as the *Gemeine* or circumstances changed. Some of these changes were connected with his need to manage events in the development of the Moravian Church, as described near the beginning of chapter 1. His frequent changing of titles likely meant that he was never completely satisfied with any. From time to time he caused himself to be called Administrator (*Vorsteher*), Helper (*Helfer*), Overseer (*Aufseher*), Bishop (*Bischof*), Disciple (*Jünger*), Papa, Teacher (*Ordinarius*), and, while in Pennsylvania, Brother Lewis, giving up his title of Count (*Reichsgraf*). One intriguing title, which was applied also to others but particularly described his role, was *Charnier* or Hinge:

> The most necessary and unavoidable office in every *Gemeine* is that which I wish to call the *Charnier*, which is as the key to the clock. The Elders, Helpers, Teachers, and Dieners are reminded of their offices through these persons and opportunity to observe such is indicated for them. They are always prepared and ready to depart and to stand before the Lord. . . .
>
> The time, the conditions, the manner of all our holy activities, and how these same must from time to time be conducted, are regulated through this office.[59]

Bethlehem

Moravians first came to Pennsylvania in 1734 to aid the settlement of Schwenkfelder exiles who had temporarily settled on Zinzendorf's estate in Berthelsdorf. However, the first Moravian settlements in Pennsylvania occurred later, following a failed settlement in Georgia. Christopher Wiegner,[60] one of the Schwenkfelders who was later to provide hospitality for Moravian immigrants, participated in the formation of the ecumenical Associated Brethren of Skippack. The Brethren of Skippack also included Henry Antes, a justice of the peace who was of Reformed background. Antes was later to arrange for the purchase of the 500-acre tract that was to become the Moravian settlement of Bethlehem. He eventually moved to Bethlehem, but left in 1750

[59] Zinzendorf, *Eventual Testament* (1738), in *Theologische Bedencken*, p. 174, quoted in Wollstadt, *Geordnetes Dienen*, pp. 169-70. Zinzendorf's image of this office as the key to the clock (probably meaning that it winds up everything and keeps it going) can also be translated as "the key to the hour," meaning the key to what is going on in the present.

[60] For the extended contacts of Wiegner with the Moravians, see *The Spiritual Diary of Christopher Wiegner*, trans. and ed. Peter C. Erb (Pennsburg, Pa.: The Society of the Descendents of the Schwenkfeldian Exiles, 1978).

because he objected to the effects of the Sifting Period on Bethlehem.[61] However, even then he retained his relationship with the Moravians. Joseph Dubbs, a Reformed Pastor, wrote a poem about his significance shortly after the centennial of his death. It included,

> He greeted the mild Moravians,
>   As the servants of the Lord;
> And with Zinzendorf and Boehler
>   He labored in sweet accord;
> For they sought to unite the churches
>   In a brotherhood of love,
> By a "union in the Spirit,"
>   Like that of the Church above.
>
> . . . .
>
> When his heart was almost broken,
>   And he felt that his end was nigh,
> To his farm in Frederick township
>   Henry Antes returned to die;
> And when his spirit departed
>   To dwell in the land of the blest,
> Ten loving Bethlehem Brethren
>   Bore his corpse to its final rest.[62]

When Zinzendorf came to Pennsylvania in late 1741, he brought with him his ecumenical vision and hopes for a Church of God in the Spirit that would be similar to the Moravian *Brüdergemeine* which within itself preserved the heritage of the Moravians, Lutherans, and Reformed. The Brethren of Skippack had a similar vision. How much it was influenced by previous contacts with the Moravians is uncertain.

[61] In his opposition to the excesses of the Sifting Period, Antes had the support of the older community and a number of the leaders, but Bishop John Nitschmann was unyielding, and so Antes quietly moved back to his farm (Joseph Mortimer Levering, *A History of Bethlehem, Pennsylvania, 1741-1892, with Some Account of Its Founders and Their Early Activity in America* [Bethlehem, Pa.: Times Publishing Co., 1903], pp. 250-51 [Abbreviated in subsequent notes as Levering, *History of Bethlehem, Pennsylvania*]). In 1751 Bishop Nitschmann was recalled and by December Bishop Spangenberg had returned from Europe. In his doctoral dissertation, Edwin Sawyer discusses the religious experience of colonial Moravians, with particular attention to the impact of the Sifting Period: Edwin A. Sawyer, *The Religious Experience of the Colonial American Moravians*, in *Transactions of the Moravian Historical Society* (Nazareth, Pa., Moravian Historical Society) 18, pt. 1 (1961).

[62] Joseph Dubbs, *The Moravian* (Bethlehem, Pa.) 27, no. 5 (2 Nov. 1881). The poem and the notes on the stanzas (also quoted in *The Moravian*) were originally published in the *Guardian*, a Reformed Church monthly, in 1872. Dubbs was a pastor in Pottstown and later served on the faculty of Franklin and Marshall College.

With the agreement of Zinzendorf, Henry Antes sent a letter of invitation to a Conference of Religions to be held New Year's Day:

> Inasmuch as frightful evil is wrought in the Church of Christ, among the souls that have been called to the Lamb (to follow Christ) mainly through mistrust and suspicion towards each other — and that often without reason — whereby every purpose of good is continually thwarted — although we have been commanded to love; it has been under consideration for two years or more, whether it would not be possible to appoint a general assembly, not to wrangle about opinions, but to treat with each other in love on the most important articles of faith, in order to ascertain how closely we can approach each other fundamentally, and, as for the rest, bear with one another in love on opinions which do not subvert the ground of salvation; and whether in this way, all judging and criticising might not be diminished and done away with among the aforesaid souls, by which they expose themselves before the world and give occasion to say: those who preach peace and conversion are themselves at variance. Therefore this matter, so important, has now been under advisement again with many brethren and God-seeking souls, and been weighed before the Lord; and it has been decided to meet on the coming New Year's Day at Germantown.[63]

What began as a Conference of Religions after several meetings evolved into a desire to create Zinzendorf's envisioned Church of God in the Spirit and came to be called the "Pennsylvania General Synod," the meetings being called Pennsylvania Synods. They at first included Lutherans, Reformed, Moravians, Quakers, Mennonites, Dunkers, Ephrata monks, Schwenkfelders, Separatists, and the Inspired. Seven Synods or Conferences were held from January to June 1742, but after the fourth only the Lutherans, Reformed, and Moravians remained.[64]

---

[63] Henry Antes, 15 Dec. 1741 (26 Dec. New Style), included in *Avthentische Nachricht Von der Verhandlung und dem Verlass Der am 14den und 15den Januarii Anno 1741/2 Im sogennanten Falckner-Schwamm An Georg Hübners Hause gehaltenen Zweyten Versammlung Sowol Einiger Teutschen Arbeiter Der Evangelischen Religionen Als Verschiedener einzelen treuen Gezeugen und Gottsfürchtiger Nachbarn. Nebst einigen Beylagen.* (Philadelphia: Gedruckt und zu haben bey B. Franklin, n.d.), quoted in Levering, *History of Bethlehem, Pennsylvania*, pp. 97-98.

[64] Levering, *History of Bethlehem, Pennsylvania*, pp. 97-118. Levering includes a discussion of the intent for these meetings and their public statements. See also Vogt, "Zinzendorf and the 'Pennsylvania Synods.'" For a brief treatment of this subject see Peter Vogt, "The Pennsylvania Synods of 1742: Precursors of Modern Ecumenical Dialogue?" *TMDK: Transatlantic Moravian Dialogue Correspondence*, English[-language] edition (Bethlehem, Pa.), issue 11 (March 1997): pp. 24-27. For a treatment of the Pennsylvania Synods in German see Peter Vogt, "Zinzendorf und die Pennsylvanischen

It was only at the seventh Synod in June that the Moravians were officially represented, since before this they were not organized and recognized, and could only participate unofficially. Zinzendorf, however, was fully involved, being chosen as moderator at the second meeting, and some identified as Lutheran or Reformed were also associated with the Moravian fellowship in various ways. Zinzendorf took his position at the Synods strictly as a Lutheran. He became Inspector of the Lutheran department of the Synod and John Bechtel was Inspector of the Reformed department. Several congregations were established under this arrangement. The Synod also was to be involved in the Moravian mission in the West Indies and South America and among the North American Indians.[65] The recognition of the Moravian Church and its joining the Synod occurred at the seventh meeting. This was facilitated by the arrival of the first Sea Congregation of 56 persons, who with the Moravians already in Pennsylvania (including missionaries from the West Indies and Indian converts) made up a group of 120 persons. Henry Antes received them and addressed them in the name of the Synod, as recorded in the minutes:

> Henry Antes testified in the name of all, that the undenominational (*unpartheyische*) Synod of Pennsylvania recognized, in general, the arriving old Moravian Church as a true Church of the Lamb; in particular, its ministers as brethren and fellow-laborers; but, in accordance with the fundamental rules of the Synod, on the other hand, the Church, in itself, as independent, and, within its

Synoden 1742," *Unitas Fratrum* (Hamburg: Friedrich Wittig), no. 36 (1994): pp. 5ff. The minutes of the Synods were published in German by Benjamin Franklin: *Avthentische Relation Von dem Anlass, Fortgang und Schlusse Der am 1sten und 2ten Januarii Anno 1741/2 In Germantown gehaltenen Versammlung Einiger Arbeiter Derer meisten Christlichen Religionen Und Vieler vor sich selbst Gott-dienenden Christen-Menschen in Pennsylvania: Aufgesetzt In Germantown am Abend des 2ten obigen Monats* (Philadelphia: B. Franklin, n.d.). This German-language work has been reprinted in Nikolaus Ludwig von Zinzendorf, *Materialien und Dokumente*, ser. 2, vol. 30 (Hildesheim: Georg Olms, 1997) along with an English-language translation of the same, based on an eighteenth-century manuscript translation held by the Moravian Archives, Bethlehem, Pa., and with an introduction, notes and bibliography by Peter Vogt. See also Ernst Benz, "Zinzendorf in Amerika," *Zinzendorf-Gedenkbuch*, ed. Ernst Benz and Heinz Renkewitz (Stuttgart: Evangelisches Verlagswerk, 1951), pp. 140-61.

[65] Levering, *History of Bethlehem, Pennsylvania*, p. 106. For a discussion of the Moravian work among the Indians see: Georg Heinrich Loskiel, *Geschichte der Mission den evangelischen Brüder unter den Indianern in Nordamerika* (Barby: Zu finden in der Brüdergemeinen, 1789); Karl-Wilhelm Westmeier, *The Evacuation of Shekomeko and the Early Moravian Missions to Native North Americans*, Studies in the History of Missions, vol. 12 (Lewiston, N.Y.: Edwin Mellen, 1944; and David Zeisberger, *Herrnhuter Indianermission in der Amerikanischen Revolution: Die Tagebücher von David Zeisberger 1772-1781*, ed. Hermann Wellenreuther and Carola Wessel, Selbstzeugnisse der Neuzeit: Quellen und Darstellungen zur Social- und Erfahrungsgeschichte (Berlin: Akademie Verlag, 1995).

own limits and regulations, with which the Synod never meddled, as inviolate; and wished that the grace of the Lamb might rule over them.[66]

The Pennsylvania Synod would continue to meet quarterly, but its efforts were to fail. The Lutherans and Reformed were to be lost as Mühlenberg, sent by Halle in 1742, undertook his mission among the Lutherans,[67] as did Michael Schlatter, sent by Reformed Synods in Holland in 1746, among the Reformed. Thus the leadership was provided to order and establish European traditions in North America. In 1747 the Reformed Synod was formed, and the Reformed withdrew from the Church of God in the Spirit. In 1748 the Lutheran Synod was formed. In Europe in 1747 the Moravian Church made plans to withdraw from the Pennsylvania Synod since the Moravians were the only ones left. It was decided to continue the three *Tropi* of Lutheran, Moravian, and Reformed *within* the Moravian Church, as was done in Europe. At this time also it was determined to extend the Chief Eldership of Christ (as a governmental principle) to North America, which meant that Bishop Spangenberg's function as General Elder in Bethlehem was to be abolished. This was formalized in North America on November 13, 1748, and so Spangenberg resigned.

As the possibilities for an ecumenical association declined, the intentional development of Bethlehem received more attention. The initial settlement of Bethlehem had been in 1741 after unsuccessful attempts at a settlement in Georgia and a failed relationship with George Whitefield in Nazareth due to his insistence on predestination. In 1741 500 acres were purchased on the site of what was to become Bethlehem, a log house was built, and work on the Gemeinhaus was begun. In June 1742 the first Sea Congregation of 56 persons arrived, settling in Bethlehem and Nazareth. On June 25 the congregation at Bethlehem was formally organized, and in November the first formal arrangements were made for the government of the Moravian Church in North America. In spring of this year Zinzendorf for a while had served Lutheran and Reformed congregations in Philadelphia, being called in May to serve as a Lutheran pastor. In the latter half of 1742 Zinzendorf made three excursions into Indian country, and before he returned to Europe in January 1743, he organized a Moravian congregation in Philadelphia.

[66] Levering, *History of Bethlehem, Pennsylvania*, p. 115, source not given.
[67] Zinzendorf's November 1742 quarrel with Henry Mühlenberg especially concerned his vision for an ecumenical German-speaking Protestant association of churches, whereas Mühlenberg came to order and establish Lutheran congregations.

Peter Böhler was the first administrator of Bethlehem (1742-44), but for the next eighteen years Bishop Augustus Spangenberg was administrator and helped to define the character of this new community (except for the period of three years, 1748-51, when he was recalled to Europe).[68] He and the Moravian Church had viewed Bethlehem as a *Pilgergemeine*, a Pilgrim Congregation, primarily committed to mission and thus practicing a more extensive communal life than characteristic of other Moravian congregations. For example, families did not live as units; husbands and wives lived separately, and children after infancy were raised in community nurseries. Those not engaged in outreach worked for the congregation in various ways and had their needs cared for by the congregation. This freed both men and women for the mission outreach of the congregation. Only a few of the Moravian congregations were ever called Pilgrim Congregations. This term came into use during Zinzendorf's first exile from Herrnhut, when in 1732 he leased several properties in Wetteravia, 30 miles east of Frankfurt, and began the building of Herrnhaag as an ideal Moravian community.[69] The executive conference of the church located there, and this congregation functioned also as a training place for those who had a vocation to proclaim Christ to the world. The members of this Pilgrim Congregation, later to be called *Jüngerhaus* (House of Disciples), often traveled as a mobile community with Zinzendorf to such places as England, Holland, Berlin, Livonia, and Switzerland, maintaining the Moravian communal discipline wherever they went.

In the descriptive terminology applied to congregations, there were several types. *Brüdergemeine* (Church of the Brethren, Unity of the Brethren) was the name applied to the whole Moravian Church. Where the Moravian Church established closed communities or settlements, the term *Ortsgemeine* (Place or Settlement Congregation) was used,

---

[68] He was recalled because he would not support the changes being implemented in Bethlehem during the Sifting Period. In 1749 in Europe Zinzendorf called to an end the experimentation of the Sifting Period and the role of Christ as Chief Elder was approached more soberly. See Zinzendorf's comments on the tenth anniversary of the declaration of Christ as Chief Elder in 1751, contained in chapter 1, and the discussion of his late broadening of his Christocentrism in chapter 2. The end of the Sifting Period paved the way for Spangenberg's return.

[69] Whereas some buildings in Herrnhut were constructed in the early stages of communal development and then later buildings were added which expressed the growing Moravian vision of the community, Herrnhaag was designed to express the Moravian ideal before it was built. For information on Herrnhaag see Hans-Walter Erbe, "Herrnhaag: Eine religiöse Kommunität im 18. Jahrhundert," *Unitas Fratrum* (Hamburg: Friedrich Wittig), nos. 23/24 (1988): pp. 8ff.; Hans-Walter Erbe, "Herrnhaag – Tiefpunkt oder Höhepunkt der Brüdergeschichte?" *Unitas Fratrum* (Hamburg: Friedrich Wittig), no.26 (1989): pp. 37ff.

except where the whole community was geared for mission and organized a community life which would free adults for their mission responsibilities. This latter was the *Pilgergemeine*. In the Pilgrim Congregation there were those who were sent by the congregation into mission and these also bore the name *Pilgergemeine*, while those who stayed at home to support the mission enterprise were called *Hausgemeine* (House or Home Congregation). Then there were congregations which were not part of a closed community but existed as congregations in the general communities where they were located, taking their name from their environment. These were of two kinds: *Stadtgemeine* (City Congregation) and *Landgemeine* (Country Congregation).[70]

The amazing accomplishments of the Bethlehem Pilgrim Congregation are expressed in its construction programs. Within twenty years of its beginning they constructed 50 buildings, started 50 industries, and cleared 2500 acres of land. Besides this, in satellite congregations they constructed another 50 buildings and developed another 5000 acres of land.[71] Following Zinzendorf's death in 1760, Spangenberg was asked, partially because of the financial pressures on the Moravian Church, to develop a plan to transform Bethlehem from a Pilgrim Congregation into a Settlement Congregation, something which he at first strongly resisted and with which he then complied. This was the second time in his leadership of Bethlehem life that he was called upon to follow directions with which he did not agree. In 1762 the unique communal life of Bethlehem as a Pilgrim Congregation entered a process which within three years brought it to an end, though its life as a closed community and Settlement Congregation was to continue into the next century. One difficult aspect of this change was the task of reconstituting families and returning children to the care of their parents.

In the Settlement and Pilgrim Congregations there was a process of inclusion into the community which began with permission to stay, then acceptance into membership, then candidacy for admission into Communion with permission to observe celebrations of Communion, and finally permission to receive Communion. The experience of first Communion was often described as a very special experience in the memoirs of persons. If misbehavior occurred, discipline involved the subtracting of privileges, as appropriate. Transition would occur within the choir system with appropriate rites as one's age or marriage status changed.

[70] Beverly Prior Smaby, *The Transformation of Moravian Bethlehem: From Communal Mission to Family Economy* (Philadelphia: University of Pennsylvania Press, 1988), p. 25. (Abbreviated in subsequent notes as Smaby, *Moravian Bethlehem.*)
[71] Ibid., p. 86.

The concern of the life of the congregation was to acquaint a person with the Savior, to keep him or her close to the Savior to experience all his benefits, and to give religious significance to all of the matters of life. For this there was a full routine of daily worship and weekly, monthly, and annual devotions and events. Some of the events took place within the choirs, and some were for the whole congregation.[72]

Preaching

The Office of Preaching was central for Zinzendorf, as expressed in the Lutheran confessions. He began his Discourse XII on the *Augsburg Confession* with a discussion of the definition of the Gospel in the *Augsburg Confession* and in the *Smalcaldic Articles*. In the *Augsburg Confession* the Gospel is the name given to the Office of Preaching. In the *Smalcaldic Articles* the Gospel includes preaching, Baptism, the Holy Sacrament of the Altar, and the office of the keys or brotherly exhortation. Zinzendorf argues for the broader perspective on the Gospel contained in the *Smalcaldic Articles* and suggests that since the *Augsburg Confession* calls it an office, this office might also be understood to dispense all the other graces. Even the Law should be included as part of the Gospel, which signifies the whole counsel of God, the whole of revelation.[73] It is wrong to understand as the Gospel only what is said in the pulpit. The Gospel is the message of God addressed to the human heart, by whatever means it comes,[74] and it is the characteristic of the true church that the Gospel is preached purely and the sacraments are administered according to all which the Gospel indicates.[75] Zinzendorf's hymn on the Augsburg Confession affirms:

> I believe even for all time,
> (there is) a holy Christianity, a gathering
> which believes,
> a church which is and remains.
>
> Where the Gospel is purely preached
> and according to all
> which the Gospel indicates
> the sacraments are administered.

[72] Ibid., pp. 13ff. There are a number of books helpful for exploring the communal life of Moravian congregations which are listed in the bibliography under the category "Moravian Communal Life and Sociological Studies."

[73] Zinzendorf, *Ein und zwanzig Discurse* [Title page: *Discurse . . . Auctoris*], pp. 221-22 (12 Feb. 1748).

[74] Ibid., p. 224.

[75] Ibid., p. 311 (2 Mar. 1748).

For that is enough at this time
for a true unity of the Christian church
that we hold profitably
to this:

that one confesses the Gospel
according to the purest understanding
and according to the Word
gives the sacraments true meaning.

And beloved Christianity
has not yet come to true unity,
so that ceremonies human-made
look alike.

St. Paul wants that one Spirit
and body, one hope of your calling remain,
to which you were called,
one Lord, one faith, one baptism.[76]

Two additional comments should be made about preaching. First, besides the preaching to communicate the Gospel there was *Gemeinreden* (congregation sermons or, literally, congregation-speaking). This was a talking with the congregation about realities which members already assumed and which lived within their hearts. Thus one might describe it as giving expression to the realities which inspired the life of the congregation so that all might better understand what was already experienced and that these realities might become more alive for them.[77] This is in contrast to preaching to communicate the Gospel to persons who did not understand and had not accepted it and to preaching or theological reflection within a particular theological tradition where one has obligation to use a particular language. In

---

[76] Ibid., pp. 301-2 (2 Mar. 1748). Zinzendorf wrote lengthy hymns on both the Augsburg Confession and the Synod of Bern, two confessions central to him and to the Renewed Moravian Church.

[77] The Moravians of the eighteenth century also had *Gemeinmusik* about which Zinzendorf made the following statement: "It is the beauty of *Gemeinmusik* to make the natural beauties, namely the divine simplicity and the gravity of the scriptural text, pleasurable to the ear. The art of worldly music and of the so-called church music is totally opposed to the purpose of the *Gemeinmusik*" (Nikolaus Ludwig von Zinzendorf, quoted in *Zinzendorf und die Herrnhuter Brüder: Quellen zur Geschichte der Brüder-Unität von 1722 bis 1760*, ed. Hans-Christoph Hahn and Hellmut Reichel [Hamburg: Friedrich Wittig, 1977], p. 232 (25 Nov. 1759), quoted in Peter Vogt, "Gemeinmusik: Moravian Music in the Context of Moravian Spirituality in the Eighteenth Century," paper prepared for the Second Bethlehem Conference on Moravian Music, 24-27 Oct. 1996).

Gemeinreden there is great freedom as to language, and theological language from different traditions may be used together in the system of the Savior and the heart which unites all theological language.

Second, the Word of God for Moravians has been primarily the person of Christ and less the Word about Christ. This was affirmed in the Consensus Paper of the Dialogue of the Moravian Church and the Evangelical Lutheran Church in America held in North America in 1992-95:

> Moravians and Lutherans affirm the centrality, power, and authority of the Gospel in Jesus Christ. God's revelation in and through the Gospel may be expressed in conceptual terms, yet it is far more than doctrines and formulas. Indeed, the Gospel is not an "it"; the Gospel is a person, Jesus of Nazareth. He is the Word made human, alive and present in, with and through our experiences, dilemmas and hopes. He is God in person, that is, really present in every area and situation of life as well as by personally relating God's grace and acceptance to us.
>
> To believe in the Gospel is to trust with our whole beings and to profess in our words and actions that Jesus is our Savior and Shepherd. Through his incarnation, death, resurrection and exaltation, he seals God's promises to be with his people and to raise them to eternal life. The message of God's presence and assurance of everlasting fellowship is proclaimed as saving good news in the Scripture, heard in preaching and words of reconciliation spoken by believers, and made visible in the sacraments. This message is named Jesus; he is the divine Promise in fully human form.[78]

Ministry

Zinzendorf made use of educated clergy for his new community, such as Johann Andreas Rothe, the pastor of Berthelsdorf, and he also had himself examined and certified as an orthodox minister in the Lutheran Church. However, the development of the mission to the West Indies, together with the desire of the Moravians to revive their clerical orders, caused Zinzendorf in 1735 to secure from Daniel Ernst

---

[78] Evangelical Lutheran Church in America and Moravian Church in America, Northern and Southern Provinces, *Following Our Shepherd to Full Communion. Report of the Lutheran-Moravian Dialogue with Recommendations for Full Communion, Worship, Fellowship and Mission*, ed. Walter Wagner and Arthur J. Freeman (n.p.: Evangelical Lutheran Church in America, 1997), p. 22.

Jablonski, grandson of Comenius, the ordination[79] of David Nitschmann
as the first bishop of the Renewed Moravian Church. Originally
intended to provide ordained persons for the developing mission,
clergy were also ordained for service on the continent, and the power of
the Moravian bishops was extended until the confrontation between
Zinzendorf and the bishops resulted in his taking control after his
return from North America in 1743.

When one thinks of ministry in the eighteenth-century Moravian
congregations, the role of the laity is primary. The developing organization of congregations necessitated extensive use of lay leadership,
both men and women. The role of women was already affirmed in the
community structures initiated by Rothe in 1725. That women held all
the offices in women's bands and choirs, equivalent to men's offices in
their communities, was partially a matter of pastoral care, recognizing
that women better understood women and that to have women cared for
by men involved special dangers. At first, women scarcely spoke in the
gathering of the whole community, and there was concern not to break
the apostolic order of 1 Timothy 2:12 that a woman not be allowed to
teach. Gradually women played a more public role. Especially prominent were such figures as Erdmuthe Dorothea, wife of Zinzendorf,[80] who

[79] The actual certificates for David Nitschmann and later Zinzendorf indicate
ordination. After this time the designation of someone as bishop uses the terminology
of consecration, following Anglican usage because of considerations surrounding the
granting of the 1749 Act of Parliament. In the twentieth century Moravians have
emphasized that there is one ordination, to the office of deacon. Presbyters and bishops
are consecrated. Paragraph 685 of the *Church Order of the Unitas Fratrum* emphasized the
meaning of the deaconal ordination for all orders of ministry: "The ordination of a
Deacon admits him/her to the first order of the ministry. As a Deacon he/she has
authority to serve in the pastoral office and to administer the Sacraments under the
Rules and Regulations of the Church in effect for such an office.The ordination as a
Deacon embodies the understanding of ministry as service, which underlies all the
orders" ([Unity Synod 1995 of the Worldwide Unity of the Moravian Church], *Church
Order of the Unitas Fratrum*, ed. Fred Linyard [London: {Unity Synod 1995 of the
Worldwide Moravian Church}, 1995], paragraph 685).

[80] Here see Peter Zimmerling, *Starke fromme Frauen* (Giessen: Brunnen, 1996). One
chapter is devoted to Erdmuthe Dorothea Zinzendorf. Zimmerling also discusses the
role of women in the Moravian Church in *Nachfolge lernen: Zinzendorf und das Leben der
Brüdergemeine* (Moers: Brendow, 1990), particularly in "Kirchliche Emanzipation der
Frau" (pp. 38ff.). (Citation of this latter work will be abbreviated in subsequent notes
as Zimmerling, *Nachfolge lernen*.) The primary biography of Erdmuthe Dorothea is:
Wilhelm Jannasch, *Erdmuthe Dorothea, Gräfin von Zinzendorf, geborene Gräfin Reuss zu
Plauen: Ihr Leben als Beitrag zur Geschichte des Pietismus und der Brüdergemeine dargestellt*
(Herrnhut: Im Verlag des Vereins für Brüdergeschichte, In Kommission der
Unitätsbuchhandlung in Gnadau, 1915. (This was published in *Zeitschrift für
Brüdergeschichte* in 1914. Note that the date 1915 does appear on the title page in the
issue of *Zeitschrift für Brüdergeschichte* for 1914.) This work includes a discussion of the
roles of Erdmuthe and Anna Nitschmann in the life of the church. (For Anna
Nitschmann, see pp. 309-406.)

became Mama to the church, handled its financial affairs, and functioned as an administrator while he was away; Zinzendorf's daughter Benigna; and Anna Nitschmann, who filled a leadership role from the time that she was fifteen and was named "Mother of the *Gemeine*" in 1746.

As Zinzendorf accepted original sin but understood that it had been cared for in the death of Christ and thus no longer constituted human existence, he saw that Jesus' birth of a woman rendered ineffective whatever responsibility woman had in the Fall:

> My brothers and sisters, we have a Husband and our Husband is Priest: because with regard to the female sex the old order which originated from the Fall (that they can have nothing to do with priestly matters) had already been ignored by one or another important women (for example by the old matron in the Temple); but now has been completely abolished since the Creator (i.e., Christ) was born of a woman, and now the sisters as well belong to the classes of those whom the Savior has declared to his heavenly father as priests just as much as men: therefore there is no question that the whole company of the betrothed, the whole choir of his maidens and brides, are priest-women, and not only priest-women but also priestly women.[81]

Through the Choir Helpers, persons who were mostly unordained, the choirs provided pastoral care, and what today might be called spiritual formation. The pastoral care process which Zinzendorf advocated was truly unique in the eighteenth century. This is extensively discussed in Peter Zimmerling's "Pastoral Care in the Community: Zinzendorf and Pastoral Care":[82]

> Underlying Zinzendorf's pastoral care is the knowledge that all persons are distinguished by a God-given diversity.[83] "Don't believe, brothers, that all people can be cared for in the same way, and

---

[81] Zinzendorf, *Öffentlichen Gemein-Reden, 1747*, pt.1, pp. 88f., quoted in Zimmerling, *Nachfolge lernen*, p. 40. The language used here is that of Christ as the husband of the soul. All souls are feminine, those of men as well as those of women, and so all souls are his brides. Thus women join the company of the betrothed, of whom all are priest-women, but, so that the point is not missed, women are also *priestly women* in themselves.

[82] Zimmerling, "Pastoral Care," pp. 54-56. (See above, n. 41 in this chapter, for full bibliographic information.)

[83] Otto Uttendörfer, *Zinzendorfs Weltbetrachtung: Eine systematische Darstellung der Gedankenwelt des Begründers der Brüdergemeine*, Bücher der Brüder, vol. 6 (Berlin: Furche, 1929), source indicated in Zimmerling, "Pastoral Care," p. 54. (Citation of the Uttendörfer work will be abbreviated in subsequent notes as Uttendörfer, *Zinzendorfs Weltbetrachtung*.)

do a better study of the human character."[84] Christ is embodied in
every person in a different way: "His character looks out of everyone
with a different beauty, always distinguishing itself well, to be sure,
from the person's pure humanity, but with a grace which is his and
other than that inherent in the person."[85] Therefore, following
Zinzendorf, no one must be violated in his inner person. On May
24, 1735, Zinzendorf formulated it in this way: "With the Spirit of
the community one must learn to distinguish souls, each one must
be brought up in a royal fashion so that one can say as of the
councilors in Rome: they are all kings."[86] Since Christ has turned
towards every person in a special way, the human provider of
pastoral care, also must proceed differently with everyone. "The
differences of social position, temperament, life, age make a
difference in the special method used by the Savior."[87] Again and
again Zinzendorf emphasizes the necessary difference of pastoral
methods according to the individuality of persons.

Pastoral care should help a person to act according to his/her
own principles which form character. "The Savior judges every one
according to the principles he has given him and if the person acts
accordingly, it is good."[88] Because of human differences Zinzendorf
warns about counseling a person looking for pastoral care according to one's own ideas. "I have often wondered why a brother and
sister have no scruples about something which I would never dare.
One is inclined to teach people all one's own principles and to
point toward them. But I noticed that that won't do; our dear
Savior doesn't assist you in that, for his ways with souls are different
indeed."[89]

[84] Zinzendorf, *Eventual Testament* (27 Dec. 1738), Herrnhut Archives, R3A5, quoted in Uttendörfer *Zinzendorfs Weltbetrachtung*, p. 22, quoted in Zimmerling, "Pastoral Care," p. 54.
[85] Diarium des Jüngerhauses, 12 Feb. 1757, quoted in Uttendörfer, *Zinzendorfs Weltbetrachtung*, p. 21, quoted in Zimmerling, "Pastoral Care," p. 54.
[86] Diarium des Jüngerhauses, 1757, quoted in Uttendörfer, *Zinzendorfs Weltbetrachtung*, p. 27, quoted in Zimmerling, "Pastoral Care," p. 54.
[87] Zinzendorf, *Inhalt einiger öffentlichen Reden, Welche im Jahr 1738. vom Januario bis zu Ende des Aprilis in Berlin an die Frauens-Personen daselbst gehalten worden.* (Berlin: Christian Ludewig Kunst, n.d.), p. 137 (7 Apr. 1738), quoted in Uttendörfer, *Zinzendorfs Weltbetrachtung*, p. 28, quoted in Zimmerling, "Pastoral Care," p. 54. (A misprint in the footnote of the Zimmerling article lists the source as Diarium des Jüngerhauses.)
[88] Diarium des Jüngerhauses, pp. 275 and 283 (20 Sept. 1753) and p. 568 (25 Sept. 1753), Herrnhut Archives, R2A33b, quoted in Uttendörfer, *Zinzendorfs Weltbetrachtung*, p. 32, quoted in Zimmerling, "Pastoral Care," p. 55.
[89] Diarium des Jüngerhauses, 30 Sept. 1751, quoted in Uttendörfer, *Zinzendorfs Weltbetrachtung*, p. 33, quoted in Zimmerling, "Pastoral Care," p. 55.

The idea of the variety of human individuals is bound to the idea of human development. Zinzendorf recognized the connection between natural development and the development of faith.[90] "Faith is childlike with children, with young men like young men, with grown men like grown men."[91] As a consequence Zinzendorf formulated a maxim for all pastoral work meant for children and young people: "One should follow the course of nature and sanctify it."[92]

The provider of pastoral care, the educator, therefore must not ask too much of the child or the young person. He must do what is suitable for the power of understanding at the time. "A child thinks in his sixth year as intelligently as it is fitting for his age and circumstances; and when he is fifty, he, to be sure, wonders at the thoughts he had then; but they were just as fitting in his head when he was six years old as the ones he has now in his fiftieth year. Everything has its own stage, and a time for each; each stage is always a blessing. The person is always blessed in his lot if he is true to that, if he does not go beyond it, but remains in what is his own measure and degree."[93] It would be wrong to ask of an adolescent something that does not agree with his respective stage of development. Zinzendorf discovered the child as having a personality of its own when he recognized the connection between the stages of human development; at that time a revolutionary discovery, as can be seen from pictures of the eighteenth century where children wear the clothing of grownups as a matter of course. In contrast to the views of his time the Count teaches to love and respect the creativeness of the particular world of the child: "Children are little majesties, baptism is their anointing, and from that moment on they should be treated just as a born king. . . . Such a creature should be treated nicely like a raw egg and like a treasure which you

[90] See Uttendörfer, *Zinzendorfs Weltbetrachtung*, especially pp. 172ff., source indicated in Zimmerling, "Pastoral Care," p. 55.

[91] Zinzendorf, Herrnhut Archives, R2a3a1 (13 June 1740), quoted in Uttendörfer, *Zinzendorfs Weltbetrachtung*, p. 176, quoted in Zimmerling, "Pastoral Care," p. 55.

[92] Zinzendorf, Herrnhut Archives, R2a20a (15 Sept. 1746), quoted in Uttendörfer, *Zinzendorfs Weltbetrachtung*, p. 176, quoted in Zimmerling, "Pastoral Care," p. 55.

[93] Nikolaus Ludwig von Zinzendorf, *Die an den Synodum der Brüder, in Zeyst vom 11. May bis den 21. Junii 1746. gehaltene Reden, Nebst noch einigen andern zu gleicher Zeit in Holland geschehenen Vorträgen* (n.p.: Zu finden in den Brüder-Gemeinen, n.d.), pp. 62f. (5 Feb. 1746), quoted in Uttendörfer, *Zinzendorfs Weltbetrachtung*, pp. 62f., quoted in Zimmerling, "Pastoral Care," p. 56.

are to carry in a brittle vessel across a narrow bridge to hold with fear and trembling."[94]

It is interesting that the Zinzendorfian conviction that infants and children had a spiritual life of their own which reflected the relationship with the Savior disappeared by the late eighteenth century from the memoirs of children who died,[95] and so likely also disappeared from the consciousness of Moravians.

The Sacraments

Regarding what makes valid the administration of sacraments, Zinzendorf believed that this depends not on the one who administers the rite, but rather upon the recipient. He said

> that it was an ancient doctrine and rule about which the children of God did not have to trouble themselves very much: namely, who the people were who administered the liturgical things amongst them. . . .[96]

For 'tis the Intention of the Receiver, not the Minister, which can determine the Grace to be more or less.[97]

The concern of the Donatists was wrong.[98] One should not be so concerned about the mode of administration and the persons administering, but the meaning of the sacrament itself. One receives according to what one understands of and expects of the sacrament as recipient. Here Zinzendorf cites the example of the Lord's Supper, which is primarily intended to form the mystical body of Christ in the closest sense, and to strengthen the inner life by participation in Christ's life. To the nominal Christian (Lutheran or Calvinist) who is not yet a living member of the Savior, God by condescension allows the bread and wine to serve as signs pointing to the redemption wrought in Christ. Zinzendorf

---

[94] Nikolaus Ludwig von Zinzendorf, *Sonderbare Gespräche zwischen Einem Reisenden und Allerhand andern Personen, von Allerley in der Religion vorkommenden Wahrheiten, Zweyte mit Fleis verbesserte Auflage* (Altona: Gebrüder Korte, 1739), pp. 127-28, quoted in Zimmerling, "Pastoral Care," p. 56.

[95] Smaby, *Moravian Bethlehem,* pp. 148, 180.

[96] Zinzendorf, *Ein und zwanzig Discurse* [Title page: *Discurse . . . Auctoris*], p. 317 (2 Mar. 1748).

[97] Nikolaus Ludwig von Zinzendorf, *Maxims, Theological Ideas And Sentences, Out Of The Present Ordinary Of The Brethren's Churches: His Dissertations And Discourses From the Year 1738. till 1747. Extracted by J. Gambold, M.A. With a Letter from the Author annex'd* (London: J. Beecroft, 1751), p. 177. (Abbreviated in subsequent notes as Zinzendorf, *Maxims, Theological Ideas and Sentences.*)

[98] Zinzendorf, *Ein und zwanzig Discurse* [Title page: *Discurse . . . Auctoris*], p. 319 (2 Mar. 1748).

regards this partial apprehension of the significance of the Lord's Supper as worthy of respect, something in which any Christian might join.[99]

The person who administers the sacrament does so because of a call from the church to this office and duty. It is for the sake of order, for God is a God of order.[100] The true administrator of the sacraments is the Holy Spirit, who effects what occurs in Baptism.[101]

He (the Spirit) is to be the dispenser of the degrees of grace, the blessings, perceptions, experiences, and gifts of offices which you should have; he will take from that which is mine, says our Savior. Thus it happens that if one speaks of the Lord's Supper, I hold our dear Mother, the Holy Spirit, to be the true consecrator, the one who makes the real transformation in the sacrament. He prepares for us the corpse of Jesus Christ, the blood which issued from his wounds; he is the *conditor*[maker] of this, otherwise our poor hands and words would not suffice.[102]

The Christian must not regard the sacraments as mere tokens which set off the Christian, nor as a revered ceremony, nor as mere signs of God's will being favorable toward us,

but *à la lettre* [literally] as substantial unions of our poor sinful substance with God, with our bridegroom and husband, with his true corpse and blood, with that true water which flowed from his side, with his true death-sweat, unto a true ablution from our sins, a real bath, unto a blessed preservation of our spirit, soul and body, until we come to the grave.[103]

Though Zinzendorf comments that it had not been settled in the Protestant Church that there are only two sacraments and though one might say that according to the common definition there could be seven or more, "there are but two sacraments κατ' ἐξοχὴν [according to prominence], namely, the sacrament of total ablution and purification, and the sacrament of the bodily union; under and with which we afterwards comprehend all the other middling and ordinary ones, as the *speciale* [special] under the *generali* [general]." Thus foot-washing is the lesser, related to Baptism, which is greater; and all "other outward

[99] Zinzendorf, *Maxims, Theological Ideas and Sentences,* p. 177.
[100] Zinzendorf, *Ein und zwanzig Discurse* [Title page: *Discurse . . . Auctoris*], p. 320 (2 Mar. 1748).
[101] Ibid., p. 84 (17 Dec. 1747).
[102] Ibid., pp. 166-67 (6 Jan. 1748).
[103] Ibid., p. 294 (1 Mar. 1748).

testimonials of grace, by which invisible blessings are also really, but less immediately, communicated to us" are to be subordinated to the Lord's Supper.[104]

Baptism

Baptism never was regeneration itself, but it is the bath or washing of regeneration, τὸ λοῦτρον παλιγενέσιας; it is the water in which the newborn child is bathed.[105]

It is true that the ordinary course of grace is for the Spirit to enter the child at the very moment of Baptism,[106] yet it is the Spirit which effects the new birth and not the water used in Baptism. Baptism is therefore a sign of something and not its cause. It is not Baptism which saves, but that to which Baptism points, and salvation may occur without Baptism.

That salvation may occur outside of Baptism is true not only because Baptism is a sign and not a cause of what happens, but because the problem of original sin no longer exists after the cross. Zinzendorf takes literally Paul's statement on all being made alive in Christ.

As in Adam all die, so all can and necessarily are made alive through the sacrifice of Jesus on the cross. No single human soul must any longer be lost on account of original sin and Adam's fall.

This is the great reality of the *satisfaction*, the *imputation*. The *satisfaction* did not happen for two hundred and forty, not for four and twenty thousand, not for a hundred and forty-four thousand, not for a million persons, but it happened for all souls in the world. Therefore all human souls, who in this human tabernacle did not *deliberato* [deliberately] again become servants of corruption, go from the world to heaven and will be holy through the merit of

[104] Ibid., pp. 295-96 (1 Mar. 1748).

[105] Ibid., p. 84 (17 Dec. 1747).

[106] Ibid., pp. 84-85 (17 Dec. 1747). In the diary of the congregation in Bethlehem, Pennsylvania, the question is asked, "At what age would we want to baptize our children?" The answer is: "Our congregations in Europe have differing customs in this respect. In Marienborn, in the Pilgergemeine, a child is baptized immediately after birth, within the space of several hours. Should it be born in the nighttime, the brethren and sisters are awakened so as to attend. The reason for this is that we should like to have our children experience rebirth too so soon as they are born [sic; better "also, as soon as they are born"]. And in this way, also, it becomes less likely for a child to die without being baptized. The married brethren voted unanimously to have baptism administered to their children immediately after their birth, be it day or night" (Kenneth G. Hamilton, trans. and ed., *The Bethlehem Diary*, vol. 1, 1742-1744 [Bethlehem, Pa.: Archives of the Moravian Church, Northern Province, 1971], pp. 33-34).

Jesus Christ, whether they are baptized or not: this is our doctrine, our Lutheran doctrine.[107]

Baptism is understood to be the "solemnity of regeneration" and the installation and inauguration of the children of the congregation into the right of being children of God. And it points to the importance of the Savior's wounds:

There is in Baptism a divine right, a point, the discussion of which the Savior has kept to himself, to the honor of his wounds; namely, the tacit confession that we could not become holy (be saved) nor be partakers of the Holy Spirit, were it not for his wounds and stripes.[108]

The pointing to the Savior's wounds is more than just a reminder of salvation, but it signifies that the Christian finds his life in the wounds of the Savior.

For to be baptized out of the side of Jesus, and to pour the whole stream of the death-water and heart's blood of Jesus Christ upon a soul, and to make her to swim in the sea of the wounds and to place her whole future life, indeed all that is hers, and all that will occur with her in the future, even until the last day and beyond the last day, under the "bed" of the baptismal waters and in the sea of grace, so that the soul, when she eats, drinks, weeps, laughs, whether she is within or outside of the congregation, when she only enjoys herself or communicates: all of this she does, so to speak, several fathoms under the sea of grace, under the ocean of grace, under the stream from the side, so that the streams of grace go far above her head and cover souls as the sea covers the earth — according to the prophetic description. This indeed is beyond comparison.[109]

Baptism is a sacrament of total ablution and purification,[110] for in it it becomes clear that our Lord is satisfied with us "out of grace." We "are looked upon as astonishingly clean, bright, pure, and happy in the eyes of our parents, and of the *pater familias* [head of the family - Christ], I mean our special house-father (John 13:13). He once and for all knows that he is the Master of our hearts."[111] Yet this is only what we are out of

[107] Zinzendorf, *Ein und zwanzig Discurse* [Title page: *Discurse . . . Auctoris*], pp. 125-26 (26 Dec. 1747). Cf. synodical writing in ibid., p. 12.
[108] Ibid., p. 84 (17 Dec. 1747).
[109] Ibid., p. 296 (1 Mar. 1748).
[110] Ibid., p. 295.
[111] Ibid., p. 276 (25 Feb. 1748).

grace, for it is also a reminder that we carry our treasure in earthen vessels which may again gather dust even though we have previously been cleaned. Thus one is in need of a continual application of Christ's blood and atonement, which is provided for in the other sacramental occasions of the church's life, such as the Lord's Supper and the Foot-washing. One always has at hand the medicine which he needs.[112]

> Therefore there are in the congregation these graces which are so interwoven and follow at such a small distance from one another, especially the feast of the embrace of the Bridegroom (where he does everything at once for us which he can do gradually by the other sacraments and blessings), that it must be a strange heart indeed which could not gain something here and in all which occurs in him be saved; it (such a heart) must be very lazy, negligent, ignorant and ill-equipped; for scarcely can any thing have settled upon us, but it is thus sprinkled again, bedewed and rained upon anew, indeed swallowed up by the cold death sweat on the corpse of the Lamb, which is the *universal-tinctur* [universal medicine].[113]

Baptism is also a proof to which one may appeal in later life. One may remind oneself that at a certain time one was installed and enrolled and thus is "now appointed and privileged to be as happy as Jesus' wounds."[114] Zinzendorf even felt that the person who had been baptized was more sensitive to the gospel so that when he preached he felt that God had already created in their hearts some measure of receptivity and any hardness of heart was somewhat softened.[115] "In baptized Persons there is a certain Tenderness, that they must assent to the Word; and the Divine Faithfulness keeps hold of them by some Corner, as it may be possible."[116]

The baptism of children was no problem to Zinzendorf because he understood what happened in Baptism not as a result of human faith or action, but as a result of what God had done. Moreover, it did not involve the use of the mind primarily, but what happened in Baptism could occur without the mind's reflection or realization — thus it could happen to a child. Jesus and his atonement are communicated to the heart of the child by the Spirit, and the new creature comes into being in the child. Zinzendorf said:

[112] Ibid., pp. 277-79 (25 Feb. 1748).
[113] Ibid., p. 279 (25 Feb. 1748).
[114] Ibid., p. 85 (17 Dec. 1747).
[115] Ibid., pp. 85-86 (17 Dec. 1747).
[116] Zinzendorf, *Maxims, Theological Ideas and Sentences*, p. 12.

To have a Feeling in the Heart, and to believe, is the same thing. Thus little ones may believe, which accounts for Infant-Baptism.[117]

Our little children, who are baptized in the name of the Father, of the Son, and of the Holy Spirit, who grow up where they were hatched (born from his holy side), who know nowhere to go but to him; to whom a thousand *notiones* [notions] prevailing in the world remain hidden; but who day and night live [*umgehen*] with the dear Lamb, and are accustomed to live [*umgehen*] with him and who even at their third and fourth year cleave to him with heart and mind, closer than to their own life, in a way which could not be brought about with ever so much effort and *studio* [study] in fifty years even if it was to be presented continuously, or if one was to bring the matter *mechanismum* [mechanically] into his own mind. These little scholars of the Holy Spirit, I say, doubtless get acquainted with their divine Papa [Does this reflect *Abba* in the teachings of Jesus?] and Mama at the same time, as soon as they are capable of thinking; this is quite natural."[118]

Since Baptism was primarily a sign of regeneration and not its cause, it was to be administered with care, and in the case of adults it was not to be administered unless one was sure of lasting effects.[119] This led Zinzendorf to feel that there was value in using exorcism in the mission fields: "Where there is a real conscious connection of the soul with Satan, there it is appropriate and legitimate."[120] However, in baptism of children he did not insist on the same care that he did with adults, " for in their case we do not have to be concerned as to whether it would have the right and lasting effect, for this is the immediate and special concern of the Holy Spirit."[121] The child, of course, is in the special position of not being under the influence of Satan or having yet surrendered to sin (note Zinzendorf's position on original sin). As also noted before, the Spirit may go forth into the child at the very moment of Baptism,[122] and Baptism benefits the heart, softening it for the future operation of the Spirit.[123]

[117] Ibid., p. 61.

[118] Zinzendorf, *Ein und zwanzig Discurse* [Title page: *Discurse . . . Auctoris*], p. 67 (16 Dec. 1747).

[119] Plitt, *Zinzendorfs Theologie*, 2:512.

[120] Zinzendorf, as quoted in Plitt, *Zinzendorfs Theologie*, 2:512. This may be quoted from *Spangenbergs Apologetische Schluß-Schrift*, p. 615.

[121] Zinzendorf, as quoted in Plitt, *Zinzendorfs Theologie*, 2:512.

[122] Zinzendorf, *Ein und zwanzig Discurse* [Title page: *Discurse . . . Auctoris*], pp. 84-85 (17 Dec. 1747).

[123] Ibid., p. 86.

Confirmation

In the early stages of Herrnhut Zinzendorf seems to have understood Confirmation as the renewal of the Baptismal covenant, somewhat as did Spener. In questions addressed to confirmands at Herrnhut,[124] the meaning of Confirmation is portrayed in the light of a renewal of what the children once had in Baptism. The children had received baptismal grace, but had not remained in it and now were awakened through God's grace to knowledge of their need and the salvation offered in Christ. They were then accepted into the congregation, to which they promised obedience.[125] The close relationship of the congregation at Herrnhut with the Berthelsdorf parish would at first cause the Herrnhuters to continue the practice of Confirmation, and the influence of Pietism on the early period in his life would cause Zinzendorf to feel the need for a conversion experience for the children. However, with his turning away from certain Pietistic emphases and his turning to Luther (1734-35), a different attitude to Confirmation comes into being.

Zinzendorf then later seems to have dropped Confirmation, for he hoped that the children of the congregation would grow up in Christ and would not need a later renewal of grace or the covenant relationship. As Plitt comments: "The idea of the personality developing in God is dominant, which Zinzendorf here follows with certain instincts."[126]

Zinzendorf did come to feel that there was a place for a rite of Confirmation, which would sufficiently solemnize the baptismal covenant for children as they arrived at adulthood:

> I would gladly see that the children, when they arrive at the time of their adulthood, would have a ceremony which to some extent would run parallel to Baptism and solemnize at the present time the covenant on our side. It must be an act which is for the children not less impressive than Baptism and the Lord's Supper, even if at the same time it differs in degree.[127]

As to whether this would rob Baptism of some of its meaning, he answered:

[124] *Büdingische Sammlung Einiger In die Kirchen-Historie Einschlagender Sonderlich neuerer Schrifften. Erster Band. Nebst darzu gehörigen Registern. Sind wir doch sein ererbtes gut.* (Büdingen: Joh. Chr. Stöhr [vol. 1], Korte [vols. 2, 3], 1742-44), 2:25ff.

[125] Plitt, *Zinzendorfs Theologie*, 1:575.

[126] Ibid., 1:576.

[127] Zinzendorf, as reported in *Spangenbergs Apologetische Schluß-Schrift*, p. 597, quoted in Plitt, *Zinzendorfs Theologie*, 2:514.

There is no lack among children of the grace of Baptism, but only in the impression of the covenant on their side. I believe that a child in observing a Baptism gains more of an impression than by reflecting on his own Baptism fifteen or sixteen years ago. Is that not too bad? . . . (In a solemn Confirmation, however,) [words in parentheses are in Plitt but not in Spangenberg] the whole church would know that the child stands now in a new situation, and then every foolish person who has a mind to tempt, who is threatened and troubled with the Devil, will not work on the children. That hinders temptation mightily. But the substance of this is not yet ready.[128]

As to why it was not the proper time to introduce this, Zinzendorf answers, "We do not experience it." Actually such a "solemn confirmation" was introduced into the church only after 1818.[129]

Foot-washing

Foot-washing is a "little baptism," not to take the place of Baptism itself, but to act as a means of grace to the ongoing needs of the Christian. It almost becomes a sacrament: "We believe that it is an act established by the Savior himself for his servants," but it is really to be seen as a sacrament only in the broadest sense and is to be distinguished from Baptism and Communion.[130] It was not held before all Communion services, but before certain festival Communions and served as preparation as did the lovefeast.[131]

Zinzendorf believed that the Savior had commanded it in John 13, taking Jesus' words literally and not understanding them in terms of the conversation with Peter as an illustration of humility.[132] He understood Foot-washing as a rite for and expressive of the special relationships within the community that lived in close relationship to the Savior. He said:

I am against introducing Foot-washing into any *Religion*, for there must be brothers who wish to keep it. Even if one can have people

---

[128] Zinzendorf, as reported in *Spangenbergs Apologetische Schluß-Schrift*, p. 597, quoted in Plitt, *Zinzendorfs Theologie*, 2:514.

[129] Plitt, *Zinzendorfs Theologie*, 2:514.

[130] Zinzendorf, as reported in *Spangenbergs Apologetische Schluß-Schrift*, p. 166, quoted in Plitt, *Zinzendorfs Theologie*, 2:516.

[131] *Spangenbergs Apologetische Schluß-Schrift*, pp. 166, 357, quoted in Plitt, *Zinzendorfs Theologie*, 2:517.

[132] Plitt, *Zinzendorfs Theologie*, 2:518.

who are not brothers at Communion, this is not possible with Foot-washing. For no one's feet can be washed whose heart is not washed.[133]

Foot-washing was one of the many gifts which the Savior prepared for his children. Though it required persons in intimate Christian communion, it had to do primarily with the certainty of the person's relationship with Christ, rather than nurturing human relationships. Like Baptism, it is rooted in what Christ has done to cleanse us from sin. In the Sixteenth Discourse in the *Twenty-One Discourses on the Augsburg Confession*, when dealing with Foot-washing, Zinzendorf made extensive use of the language of the wounds:

> There are the institutions which our Savior has made for the consolation of his children, and especially that washing (which can be compared to the great one) the Foot-washing of which we sing, *Bloody death-sweat, wash our feet! Sweaty hair, dry them!* This has the intent to show that we can actually be helped at all times, and that we ought never to be too perplexed or *confus* [confused], but always believe with certainty, if we once have become a little sheep of the dear Lamb, a participant in the open side and the wounds of the dear Lamb, that we then are appointed to pure blessing. Peace he will create for me, peace he will yet create for me — he who would have that I should become holy.
>
> But the same washing has yet the purpose that we should know we stand in need of such a bath.[134]

Foot-washing cares for the settling of dust and the need for continual cleansing in our lives:

> We ought not so soon forget, but should know that we carry our treasure in an earthen vessel (2 Corinthians 4:7). It is possible not only for us to be broken, but also that we gather dust. It is not only that the pot gets damaged, but that it is its nature when used awhile, to grow dusty, dirty, and moldy, so that it must be wiped clean again, if not scalded out. Now this cannot happen by *speculationes* [speculations], nor by our *ordinaire* [common] methods which we must find out for ourselves, but it always happens through the blood of Christ; and if we would sweep the least corner, we must first sprinkle it with Christ's blood, otherwise such a dust would rise all at once which would stop our breath.[135]

[133] Zinzendorf, as reported in *Spangenbergs Apologetische Schluß-Schrift*, p. 587, quoted in Plitt, *Zinzendorfs Theologie*, 2:518-19.
[134] Zinzendorf, *Ein und zwanzig Discurse* [Title page: *Discurse . . . Auctoris*], p. 274 (25 Feb. 1748).
[135] Ibid., pp. 276-77.

Holy Communion

Holy Communion is a mystery and is so presented in Scripture. We are told what Jesus said, but the full significance of the words is not made clear: how are the bread and wine his body and blood? Since Scripture does not define the meaning of the words further, we must live with what Scripture, and Christ, have given us. In the history of the church various understandings of this sacrament have developed ranging from the elements actually becoming the body and blood of Christ (transubstantiation) to the Lutheran position (consubstantiation) that the body and blood of Christ are present in, with, and among the substance of the elements, to a Reformed position which sees Communion as primarily a memorial of what Christ did. As with any mystery in Scripture (see chapter 3 on Scripture) it is best that we do not try to define what has not been defined for us and allow various interpretations to exist without allowing the differences to prevent us from taking Communion together. However, Zinzendorf was clear that in Communion one must take seriously the "real presence" of Christ and that the sacrament is transformational, though one should not try to define, as binding upon others, how this occurs. In Discourse Eighteen on the *Augsburg Confession* Zinzendorf wrote:

> We demand of our communicants faith in the *reale* [real], substantial presence; the *transubstantiations-idèe* [idea of transubstantiation] is sufficiently removed in that the bread, out of the time of its use, is no Sacrament; this clears away all difficulties arising from that quarter at once.[136]

This sacrament is not merely a token or sign, but should be regarded as transformational because of the transformational reality which it represents

> *à la lettre* [literally] as substantial unions of our poor sinful substance with God, with our true Bridegroom and Husband, with his true corpse and blood, with that true water which flowed out of his side, with his true death-sweat, unto a real ablution from our sins, unto a real bath, unto a holy preservation of our spirit, soul, and body, until it comes to the grave.[137]

Zinzendorf pointed out that Luther in his Catechism replies to the question as to why one goes to the Holy Sacrament: "Because he has flesh and blood about him, and has the Devil and sin around him; therefore to be sure, he will go to the Holy Sacrament."[138]

---

[136] Ibid., p. 293 (1 Mar. 1748).
[137] Ibid., p. 294.
[138] Ibid., p. 190 (7 Jan. 1748).

Zinzendorf then commented that though the Communion is a moment of high joy, this being joined with Christ in his death is also essential to mortification of the flesh: "This is not only something to please us, a festival, but our very need demands it, we need that our mind be like the Lamb's mind and our body become like his corpse."[139]

This emphasis upon the mortification of the flesh by being united with Christ in his death does not mean that one ever completes this process of transformation in this life or that in the afterlife one is divinized. Mortification of the flesh enables living with the mind of Christ but never frees one from the need of God's grace or makes one less than human. It also is not a way of attaining union with God, but a way of growing in the union with the Bridegroom already given, which is the starting point (not the end point) of the Christian life.

Plitt comments in his theology of Zinzendorf that this transformational character is the basic significance of Communion to Zinzendorf.[140]

Because of the way one comes into contact with the effects of Christ and his death in the Communion, Zinzendorf said that it is wise for unsettled persons not to partake of Communion, mentioning Hebrews 6:4 and 1 Corinthians 11:27-32.[141] This is probably the reason Wesley was not admitted to Communion during his visit to Herrnhut.

Reflections

That the church is foundationally *Gemeine* rather than institution is crucial for its life. This keeps the church working at the realities which constitute it, to which it is called to bear witness. *Gemeine* is a relational concept which expresses the way the church lives out of its relationship with God and lives in and even from the relationship between persons, whose relationship is constituted by the relationship with God. It makes sense of the Trinity, for God in God's self is relationship; and it sees biblical history in terms of the attempts of God to create relationship with God's creation. The two primary paradigms for Zinzendorf, the Luke 1:39-56 story of the *in utero* communication of Jesus and John the Baptist and the John 19:26-27 story of Mary and the beloved disciple gathered around Jesus on the cross, have implications on which one can meditate for a long time. That the church is the "*Gemeine* in the Spirit,"

---

[139] Ibid., pp. 190-91.

[140] Plitt, *Zinzendorfs Theologie*, 2:519ff.

[141] Zinzendorf, *Ein und zwanzig Discurse* [Title page: *Discurse . . . Auctoris*], p. 299 (1 Mar. 1748).

a terminology which Zinzendorf used more broadly than the attempts to create it in Pennsylvania, living in but transcending the lines drawn by church history and geography, challenges us to ecumenical relationship and endeavor. Though the Moravian Church is no longer ecumenical in its inner structure, intentionally preserving within it the various traditions of its members,[142] it does remain intentionally ecumenical and as an international Unity is organized internationally — which also has ecumenical ramifications. The international nature of the Moravian Church is a special treasure which brings together persons around the world with many cultural differences. How fortunate that we do not have to create organizationally that which has been given to us as a gift out of our history! Because of our international nature, as a Unity we are related to the religious communities to which the varied provinces of the Moravian Church are related. Thus the ecumenical church comes to us not only through involvement in national councils and the World Council of Churches, but through the many ecumenical friendships our provinces have with other traditions.

How pure the church

The Moravian attempts to be church for the first hundred years of the Renewed Moravian Church recognized the character of *Religionen* as retaining valued traditions and providing a place for those with heart *religion*, but also containing many whose membership was nominal. Thus the *Religion* could bear witness to the realities of Gospel and Christ only in a limited way. The Moravian concern, like that of other reforming movements of its time, was to manifest all that the church was, in a sense, to be pure church. This it tried to do by the formation of intentional societies (*Diaspora* work) within the state churches and by planting congregations wherever it went in mission, so that the Christian reality could be observed. It tried to maintain a discipline which would help its members control their humanity and keep them from the world's influence.

That the church could somehow be really what God intends it to be, a pure community expressing Christian life for all to see, not too much affected by the humanity of its members, has always been an ideal. Usually the Jerusalem church and the early church as presented in Acts

[142] In Europe some of the Moravian churches still maintain something akin to the Tropus concept. For example, parts of the Moravian Church are closely related to Reformed, Lutheran or United churches dependent on their location. For more information on this see *TMDK: Transatlantic Moravian Dialogue-Correspondence*, English[-language] edition (Bethlehem, Pa.), issue 12 (July, 1997), where the theme is "The Moravian Church and Other Churches in Europe and Great Britain."

are seen as some sort of ideal utopian stage, and it is believed that since the church was once just what it should have been, so it could be again. However, when one examines the stories of the humanity and mistakes of Jesus' disciples and then explores the problems of such early Christian communities as the church at Corinth, one really begins to question the naive idealism of Luke in Acts. Luke's lack of understanding of the implications of Jesus' crucifixion is also part of this. His paradigm for Christian experience in Acts is the resurrection and the power of the Spirit. One can make a case that in the last revision of his Gospel (the one in our New Testament) he does come to terms with the cross as part of his model for the realities and limitations of Christian existence, but Acts remains triumphalist, without much of the cross.[143]

The real church is not a community where everything is just right and the humanity of its members is adequately repressed, controlled, or eliminated, but where members, aware of their humanity, are living with their humanity in responsible ways and as "humans" (or "sinners") are living from God's grace and the relationship which God offers in Christ. This would mean that in the true church there is no perfection (pretended or otherwise) because perfection is not possible within the human condition. Any expectation of perfection denies the role of God's grace. *The true church consists of a community that takes seriously both grace and responsibility.* This would mean making a critical judgment even upon biblical materials which advocate otherwise (such as the kind of perfection demanded in Matthew and the purity demanded in Revelation). Perhaps it is when the church is truly human (but not irresponsible) that the presence of God can be seen, for "we have this treasure in earthen vessels, to show that the transcendent power belongs to God and not to us" (2 Corinthians 4:17). God's "power is made perfect in weakness" (2 Corinthians 12:9). What could be seen in our perfection (if such were possible) other than *our* perfection? Zinzendorf really knew all of this with his emphasis on the human need for grace, even in the afterlife. He also knew this in the compassion he showed for human

---

[143] The history within Acts ends with Paul's release from Rome, about 62 c.e., before the terrible suffering and the wars between the Jews and the Romans. But the present form of the Gospel knows of the destruction of Jerusalem (70 c.e.) and adopts a different perspective. The suffering of Jesus is important in the resurrection narratives, where Jesus interprets to his disciples from scripture his sufferings and resurrection. In the Gospel even God seems to suffer. This seems to be a legitimate way to understand the Father in the parable of the prodigal in Luke 15 and to understand 11:13, where the heavenly Father does more than give good gifts: God gives the Spirit which is God's self. Thus the Gospel includes suffering in its paradigm of life, while in Acts the power of the Spirit seems to overcome all obstacles.

failure. And yet one still comes away with the expectation that the humanity of the Christian community can be managed if one only sets up the right structures. In no way does this deny the need for structure to help humans manage life and the strange world they experience within and without which is part of life.

If one wants the Christian community (or communities) to be a foundational witness to the lived Christian dynamics, one must come to terms with what Christians, Christianity, and the church are. If one does not wish to become depressed with the realities of life within Christian communities, one must know what to expect. Then amidst the earthiness of the church shine those true jewels of the possibilities which God creates, and one discovers the true heroism of those who live with real human struggle and difficulty, yet live with God. For when the realities of our earthen vessels are faced, the presence of the One who is with us, but beyond us, becomes more visible. Just so Paul, in 1 Corinthians, insists that the love, the ethical life to which we are called, the love which is from God and is God, is seen as in a mirror dimly.[144]

We might then characterize *Gemeinen* as "intentional Christian communities" which take seriously the need to live from fellowship with the Father, Son, and Spirit (Mother), who in their interrelationship provide the original model.   Yet we recognize that most of such intentional churchly communities today belong to *Religionen,* and the American denominations now have traditions as old as were those of the great confessions in Zinzendorf's time. We need appreciation for the treasures and accomplishments of our traditions. Within the *Religionen* there will be intentional congregations or fellowships (more aware of what they are called to be), but also the mixture of more intentional persons and those who are unsure why they are there. It may be that secularization and pluralism will diminish the social pressures to belong to a religious community and thus diminish the number of nominal members, but membership will always be mixed, and may be so even within strongly intentional religious communities — something which could be recognized as related to the very nature of being church. *In fact, to seek to be a pure community may neglect the way the church itself should model what it is to be human and what it is to be Christian.* If there are enough of those who are willing to be intentional, then the church can engage within itself those whose lives are in the process of moving towards God without feeling that there must be a clear line of demarcation between

---

[144] 1 Cor. 13:12. Some mystical traditions advise polishing the mirror to get a better reflection, until the God reflected in the mirror of our lives is hardly to be distinguished from our mirror, for mirror and God become one. This is not Paul's approach.

the fully intentional and those on journey. And perhaps the intentional will also find that they are still on journey and will be challenged by the spiritual movements in the lives of others less sure of their commitments.

Following Christ in the church

If the church lives in response to and from the reality of its true Head and Chief Elder, then somehow this must be expressed in the decision-making processes of the church.   Seeking his guidance in no way diminishes the importance of our own wisdom and insight, but it is a recognition that our wise plans may not be his and that he does intend some things for us. In chapter 1 I discussed Zinzendorf's leadership in the church and his assumption of control at various points.   His presentation of the need to assume control was not because he doubted the presence of Christ and his willingness to be Chief Elder, but because there were problems in the church and he did not want Christ to be identified with the church's mistakes. He felt that the church was again ready for Christ to resume as Chief Elder in 1751, the tenth anniversary of the recognition of Christ in this position and after the conclusion of the Sifting Period. However, it must be remembered that many of the problems of the Sifting Period were related to a naive and simple reliance on Christ in all matters. If we are to take seriously the need to follow Christ's direction in our time, we need to consider what went wrong in the 1740s. For example, the difficulties in Bethlehem in 1748-51 were partially related to the removal of Spangenberg, ending the position of General Elder which Spangenberg held, and restructuring the North American Moravian Church around the governance of Christ as Chief Elder.

If Christ cannot to some extent give us guidance and does not participate in the life of our churches, then we may have to recognize that he is not there after all and we are only dealing with him as a figure of past history, a once-great religious leader who has left for us traditions which shape our present faith. If we cannot take seriously his involvement in the contemporary life of the church, we cannot in all honesty preach his resurrection. Even to put Christ in heaven and remove him from earth cannot disengage him from the life of his church, for he could still function in some way even at this cosmic distance. There is a sense in which the denial of the engagement of Christ with the life of the church also denies the reality of the Spirit through whom the early church felt he was communicated. And soon we are not left with much.

For the recognition of Christ as Chief Elder in 1741 Zinzendorf
wrote a hymn, from which the following is excerpted, expressing his
understanding and hopes for the relationship of Christ to the life of the
church:

> Welcome among your flock,
> and that with thousand joys,
> you, who here is and was,
> come, in your people delight
> who for your Cross's meaning
> surrender all other teaching;
> receive from us everywhere
> holy honor due the Elder.
>
> . . . .
>
> The Elders, your image
> in your church choirs,
> prepare for yourself, as you will,
> to the honor of your house.
>
> . . . .
>
> Be nigh our bishop's office;
> spirit of the open door
> help them Philadelphia
> to adorn with strong pillars.[145]
>
> . . . .
>
> You Lord of the church of God,
> reconciler of all the world,
> chief of pilgrims,
> direct the Council of your servants,[146]
> who now meet for you everywhere,
> at times in conferences,
> to the joy of your heart;
> let your wounds shine for it.
>
> . . . .
>
> Tell your plan in the ear of your people
> Let them be taught aright;
> direct the conduct of your congregations;
> care for your pilgrim flock;

[145] In Rev. 3:7ff. Philadelphia is presented as a faithful church before whom Christ
sets an open door and its members will be a "pillar in the temple of my God." There was
a Philadelphian movement in Zinzendorf's time which sought to restore the church to
the Philadelphian state.

[146] "Council" (German *Rath*) refers to a governing body in the church.

give to each his particular role;
represent us on judgment day;
kiss the children, heal the sick;
ease the business of the churches!
. . . .
Beloved Lamb, dear Husband,[147]
you our every joy,
of whom we truly say,
"He shepherds his little flock";
what more to say? We know
not to empty the heart.
Who can sufficiently praise you,
Jesus Jehovah,[148] love, honor you?[149]

If we take the involvement of Christ seriously, how then do we
determine what he wishes? Both in the New Testament and in the
experience of the centuries the church has developed procedures for
"discernment," for seeking to understand the will of God and the
leading of Christ. This involves a basic theological understanding of the
nature of God's participation in life and then some principles by which
discernment is facilitated.

Discernment: The nature of God's participation

Whereas the Old Testament understood God as a God of great and
unopposable power, who influenced the forces of nature and history
and rewarded and punished as he would, both intertestamental Judaism

[147] Zinzendorf often used the language of mystical experience which spoke of the
relationship of the Savior with the soul as a marriage to him as husband. All souls are
feminine and Jesus is their true husband. See the discussion of mystical marriage in
chapter 4.

[148] Zinzendorf saw Jesus as the God experienced in the Old Testament and the
Creator of the world. The Father of Jesus, the transcendent God of mystery, was only
known through Jesus.

[149] August Gottlieb Spangenberg, *Leben des Herrn Nicolaus Ludwig Grafen und Herrn
von Zinzendorf und Pottendorf. Beschrieben von August Gottlieb Spangenberg* ([Barby]: Zu
finden in den Brüder-Gemeinen, 1773-75), pp. 1354-55. In the translation of the hymn
I have tried to retain the meaning and structure of the original, not to create a new hymn
in English or to place words in the best English word order. Hymn 854 in the British
Moravian hymnal of 1869 is derived from Zinzendorf's hymn, but it deals more with the
personal relationship with Christ and neglects Zinzendorf's presentation of Christ's
involvement with the government of the church. In the present-day *Moravian Book of
Worship,* two verses from this hymn appear in a communion liturgy, but the verses
dealing with the relationship of the Savior to the decision-making processes of the
church are not included (Moravian Church in America, *Moravian Book of Worship*
[Bethlehem, Pa. and Winston-Salem, N.C.: Moravian Church in America, 1995], p.
200).

and early Christianity modified this. They came to see life as more complex. In life there was not only God and us, but Satan and his evil powers, the powers of the stars (which many believed in), the powers of nature, and the powers of political systems often represented with patron gods and goddesses. Thus much of life in New Testament times was seen as a struggle between God and Satan, with principalities and powers, and exorcism was a primary aspect of the ministry of Jesus and his disciples.

Life is not only presented as complex, but it is affirmed that God enters this complexity and God subjects God's self to its conditions. For example, the New Testament affirms in various ways that God was in Jesus: God's Spirit came on Jesus in his birth, baptism, (where God declares him "Son") and ministry; in John, the Word/Wisdom which was with God in the beginning, participated in creation and history, became flesh in Jesus. Although Jesus healed many persons, there is no record of his using his powers to remove himself from the complexities and predicaments of life. He lived life subject to the forces of his day, and because of them he suffered and died.

Many Christians are quick to indicate that all of this was overcome in his resurrection, which immediately placed him above the conditions of human existence. He came into the world for a short time, but quickly escaped. But Zinzendorf has pointed us to John 20, where the resurrected and ascended Jesus comes back from heaven to appear to his disciples *with his wounds.* This meant he had his wounds with him in heaven and he will carry them, and his humanity, with him into the future.

Christians were faced with the same struggle regarding the nature of the Spirit that they had with Jesus' humanity. When the Spirit came upon the church, Luke, who tells the story in Acts, regards this as an experience of great power which will irresistibly drive the church forward on its mission. But others discovered that to have the Spirit does not mean to be saved from the conditions of life and humanity. The Spirit came into a world filled with life's complexity; the Spirit did not dissolve life's conditions. Thus if one takes the incarnation of Christ as indicating God's entry into and sharing of the conditions of human existence, then one may describe the Spirit as God's continuing incarnation.

This can best be illustrated by Paul, who fully recognized the continuing impact of life in its complexity upon those who have committed themselves to Christ and to whom God has given the Spirit. When he thought about all that can happen in life, in Romans 8 he listed tribulation, distress, persecution, famine, nakedness, peril, sword (8:35) and concludes the chapter with a listing of all the spiritual powers that can affect one: death, life, angels, principalities, things present, things to come, powers, height, depth (some of which are astrological terms). In 2 Corinthians he also listed what had happened to him: labors, imprisonments, beatings, often near death, shipwrecked, adrift at sea, danger from rivers, robbers, my own people, Gentiles, danger in the city, the wilderness, at sea, toil and hardship, sleepless nights, hunger and thirst, cold and exposure, and besides this, daily pressure of my anxiety for all the churches (11:23-29).

But it is in the realities of life that he found God present. In Romans 8 he affirmed that nothing in creation "will be able to separate us from the love of God in Christ Jesus our Lord." In 2 Corinthians 12:1-10 he listed revelations of the Lord and an experience of being caught up into heaven, after having recounted his difficult experiences in chapter 11, and then discussed his thorn in the flesh (his struggles with his own humanity) as a messenger of Satan. The theme of human weakness due to the conditions of life is prevalent here. He asked God three times to remove his thorn in the flesh, and God said to him, "My grace is sufficient for you, for my power is made perfect in weakness." Paul then concluded:

> I will all the more gladly boast of my weaknesses, that the power of Christ may rest upon me. For the sake of Christ, then, I am content with weaknesses, insults, hardships, persecutions, and calamities, for when I am weak, then I am strong. (12:9b-10)

Paul has come to realize that when life remains what life is, the added factor of God in life can be more clearly seen, for one cannot understand what emerges in life without recognizing that something (Someone) more is there.

> For it is the God who said, "Let light shine out of darkness," who has shone in our hearts to give the light of the knowledge of the glory of God in the face of Christ. But we have this treasure in earthen vessels, to show that the transcendent power belongs to God and not to us. We are afflicted in every way, but not crushed; perplexed, but not driven to despair; persecuted, but not forsaken; struck down, but not destroyed; always carrying in the body the death of Jesus, so that the life of Jesus may also be manifested in our bodies (2 Corinthians 4:6-10).

Of course there are other models in the New Testament. Luke in Acts is triumphalist and does not show much understanding of what Paul is saying. It is not unusual for two friends to disagree theologically. Revelation presents a powerful Christ who will soon destroy all opposition, though suffering in the present is handled rather realistically. In Revelation it was acknowledged that Christ was slain, but by no means is he the still wounded One (Revelation 5:6ff).

The hardest question of all is whether we want this wounded Savior/ Creator with all that he implies. Most of us would rather have a more triumphant God who identified a bit less with our human predicament.

If God has provided us with the model of God's incarnation into life, of God's sharing with us life and its conditions, of working within human limitations and possibilities, then when we seek to discern God's, Christ's, actions and purposes within individuals, religious communities, and historical process, we must keep this model in mind. The New Testament, with its incarnational model, also tells us that God's primary working is in and through persons. And yet we also must be willing to be surprised by experiences and events which transcend the model.

I believe that the Moravian Church in the Sifting Time of the 1740s had all the right theology by which the excesses could have been avoided, but their enthusiasm, vision, and hope caused them to overlook their own understanding of the limitations of humans, human community, and the nature of Christ's presence in history. And yet we learn by our mistakes. There was much in this time that was good and is now receiving new appreciation.

But it is all right to make mistakes. That is part of being human. I am saddened when I hear the pain which this caused the Moravian Church and its leaders, the pain that this caused Zinzendorf and the pain this caused his son, Christian Renatus, who was deeply involved and died a few years afterwards.[150] But out of such times comes new wisdom by which to understand God and life. The Johannine community (represented especially in the Gospel of John and 1 John) struggled over discernment of the Spirit's purpose and teaching. Belief in the Spirit caused some to develop theology which did not take seriously Jesus'

---

[150] It is unclear as to how the perception of failure by this frail young man during the Sifting Period contributed to his death. He had lung problems, was recalled from Wetteravia to the damp climate of England, often overworked and engaged in hourslong meditations and developed a longing for death. Weinlick indicates that in spite of the close relationship of Christian Renatus and his father in the last two years of his life, the "sensitive young man never ceased brooding over what he felt had been his betrayal of a trust" (John R. Weinlick, *Count Zinzendorf* [Nashville: Abingdon, 1956; reprint, Bethlehem, Pa., and Winston-Salem, N.C.: Moravian Church in America, 1989], p. 210).

humanity or the atonement, and they then broke away from the community. Though the Johannine community then developed principles for discernment (see 1 John 4), it never denied the role of the Spirit because to emphasize the Spirit (a type of subjectivity) could lead people astray. It refused to lose the treasure of the Spirit of God through anxiety about outcomes. For this I am profoundly thankful. At the heart of excesses of the Sifting Period was belief in Christ's leadership of the church. How could we afford to lose this treasure?

Discernment: Principles

The principles for discernment which follow are divided into principles presented in the New Testament (which therefore have a special authority) and other principles. Working with intent on issues of discernment gradually develops skills, as with anything else.

Principles presented in the New Testament

1. *The role of the Spirit must be recognized.* Jesus struggled with his contemporaries to avoid tying God's activity and revelation only to the written word, the Law, what was given in the past. God remains active and wishes to provide guidance and direction not just out of the past but in the present. (1 Corinthians 14, John 16:12-15)

2. *One must stand within the available tradition of the Christ event, recognizing Jesus as Lord and listening to what he taught.* There seems to be some recognition in the New Testament that the tradition about Jesus himself was varied so that some "critical" decisions were probably necessary to know what Jesus wished, taught, and did (e.g., the Evangelists' critical use of the tradition about Jesus before the Gospels). Moreover, to recognize the authority of Jesus as Lord (1 Corinthians 12:3) did not mean that all of the answers were to be found in the Jesus tradition, but that the answers found now through the living Christ and the Spirit were to be *in continuity with* the Jesus tradition. One of the clearest statements of this is in John 16:13-15. The Spirit

> will not speak on his own authority, but whatever he hears he will speak, and he will declare to you the things that are to come. He will glorify me, for he will take what is mine and declare it to you. All that the Father has is mine; therefore I said that he will take what is mine and declare it to you.

3. *A quality of life (particularly love) should be manifested* if one claims to be acted upon by God's Spirit and to experience God's or Christ's guidance. (1 Corinthians 13, 1 John 4:7ff.)

4. *Discernment of God's and Christ's will and truth are to be done in community.* (1 Corinthians 14:26ff.) One needs the help, wisdom, and spiritual gifts of others to be able to understand. To discern in community is an important safeguard against being carried off by one's own subjectivities. To stand in community is an important recognition of the nature of Christian faith as communal and truth, which is ultimately resident in God, as more fully resident in communal experience than individual experience.

5. Especially in the authentic Pauline materials there is *a recognition of the limited nature of all human perception* (1 Corinthians 13:8-13) *and the danger of the ego-centered use of knowledge* (1 Corinthians 8:1-3).

6. *Prayer.* Prayer is not merely praying for solutions or answers. It is a way of carrying on a dialogical relationship with God in which we share with God our life and concerns, seek direction, and express desire to be open to God's presence and leading. It is a living with God sufficient to make us sensitive to God's purposes. In Jesus' ministry, particularly in the Gospel of Luke, there is a rhythm of retreat for extended prayer and then engagement in ministry and action which can present a paradigm for us.

Other principles [151]

7. *Explore the patterns of life* which seem to be guiding you *and that which seems to be indications of God's or Christ's directions to you.* It is very difficult to discern God's will from a single experience. However, when patterns of experience appear over a time, it is more likely that the direction you should follow has been perceived.

8. *Consider your personal needs* and how much the decision you feel led to make will satisfy your personal needs. If you seem to be led to make a choice by your personal needs, this raises a question which you must examine: "Am I doing this because God or Christ want me to, or because I have need to?" If your needs are influential, this does not mean that God may not be calling you through them, but you must raise the question.

9. To process information from your life and God's guidance takes time. Things are not usually immediately clear. Thus you will need *time and patience.* As you go through the process of discernment you will

---

[151] See also the Ignatian Exercises, which include "Rules for the Discernment of Spirits" (*The Spiritual Exercises of St. Ignatius,* trans. Anthony Mottola [New York: Image Books, Doubleday, 1964], pp. 129ff.). For discussion of Ignatius' rules for discernment, see Mariam Cowan and John Carroll Futrell, *The Spiritual Exercises of St. Ignatius of Loyola: A Handbook for Directors* (New York: Le Jacq Publishing, 1982), pp. 139ff.

begin to get a sense of what works best for you and the amount of time you must allow for the process. This will be helpful for the next time that you do this.

10. When it is important to make a decision and there is no clarity about what decision should be made, it may be possible to gain help from . This was extensively used in the eighteenth-century Moravian Church (see the discussion of this in chapter 5 on Christian Life and Ethics). There are various forms of this. One form is to take three slips of paper, one with NO on it, one with YES, and one blank. You may wish to place Bible verses on the NO and YES slips which indicate a positive and a negative response. It is important to have one blank, which would indicate that there is no answer at this time. Pray about what you wish to discern and then, mixing the papers, select one. This should not take the place of the above methods, nor should one understand the answer given to infallibly present the will of God or Christ for you. It merely provides an additional source of information on the basis of which you must ultimately decide.

When seeking to discern what God/Christ wishes, one must be willing to take the risk of discerning it wrongly. That is just in the nature of things. Life is full of choices of which we are not sure. As Jesus went with his disciples in their mistaken choices, so will he go with us. Paul was wrong in Romans 9-11 in his understanding that his mission to the Gentiles would result in the conversion of Judaism and the end of the world. The Jews did not become jealous and become converted. The end of the world did not come. But the Gospel was carried into Asia Minor, Greece, and then to Rome, and we have our Christian faith as a consequence of Paul's discernment and choice.

Forms of church

The first thirty years of the Renewed Moravian Church gave birth to many forms of church. After Zinzendorf's death the church moved into a conservative period, needing to handle matters of structure, theology, and finance without the presence of its leader's charism and authority. The Moravian Church had explored creating societies within state churches, engagement in foreign mission, creation of various forms of communal settlement, and the significance of small groups of persons similar in age and status for spiritual awakening and growth. Its leadership often carried with it a mobile church which carried on a full church life wherever it went. And "sea congregations" were organized among the several groups which came from Europe to North America.

It is interesting how soon an adventuresome movement can become traditional. One sees this even today in such reform movements as charismatics and Pentecostals. The church needs constantly to remind itself that its forms are convenient ways to be for Christ in various contexts, that these ways of being embody insights and treasures, but that to respond to how and where Christ would lead the churches to minister we also need to be adventuresome.

And the church exists in heaven with God as it exists here with God. We cannot forget the great cloud of witnesses to which the eighteenth-century Moravian Church understood it sent representatives at the occasion of every death and which it joined in every occasion of worship. To know this keeps us aware of the tenuous nature of our world and its forms, and the reality of that other dimension to our existence which life's realities tend to obscure.

And ecumenism

Without ecumenical concerns and vision the church is not the church. We are always called to oneness, because our origin is in Oneness. We are called upon to consider not only our oneness with those who confess Jesus as Lord, but with other religious traditions. In recent years dialogue has been discussed as a more appropriate approach to non-Christian traditions than conversion. Zinzendorf solved this by seeing all religions and religious experience as rooted in the experience of Christ as Creator; thus there was a Oneness in what all religious people experienced. The task of the church was then to define the Savior for many who already knew of or experienced the Creator. But this is difficult to do today, as discussed in chapter 2, The Knowledge of God. Sometimes oneness cannot be "worked out," even between Christians. Oneness must start in openness to each other and to that which is central to the religious experience of each other. Our oneness is not merely what we structure, but more often lies in what arises if we are open:

> Unity arises
> where we discover
> that we are touched by the same God
> and that life which flows within us
> has a common origin.

As we speak of this
we draw further apart,
each in the direction of our own description:
a necessary, exciting, but at times
painful and alienating, task.

And so
over the distance of our descriptions
we shout: REMEMBER!
We are brothers, we are sisters.
Lest we forget.

And while we describe,
we frequently stop
to draw from the well
of our common existence
to be reminded

of the One
from Whom all live.[152]

---

[152] By the author.

Conclusion

Zinzendorf had a significant role in the transmission and reshaping of the Moravian tradition. Though one many understand him in the context of the Enlightenment, his own life experience, his family's Lutheran Pietism, and the theological currents of his time, one cannot ignore the significance of the band of Moravians on his estate. They brought with them their tradition, their historic ministry was restored, and they participated extensively in the world mission of the Moravian Church. There are striking similarities between Zinzendorf's theology, with its relational emphasis, and the Ancient Church's understanding of the Essential for salvation. In a very real sense Zinzendorf is part of the stream of theological reflection and formulation which began in the Ancient Moravian Church.

Zinzendorf's comments on the translation of Comenius's *Ratio Disciplinae* in his memorial for Christian David are interesting, for they indicate the role of his conscious awareness of the history of the Ancient Church from 1727 and his concern for its restoration, insofar as the Moravians wished it, though he also resisted the Moravians' desire to take over the Herrnhut developments:

> He (Christian David) was a practical person. And although he himself did not fully digest and absorb everything he heard, he was eager to pass it on. Thus he also stirred up the Moravian Church affair. For in the year 1727 at the place of *Baron Gersdorff at Hartmannsdorf* he found *Comenius's* history of the Brethren's Church with Dr. Buddaeus's preface. This I had to translate into German. Then they gave me no rest. According to them the Brethren's Church Order had to be put into practice immediately, and the Moravian Church had to be restored. Now I have never been willing to permit a people whom the Savior has set free to be put under a yoke if they themselves did not wish it. Also, it was my concern to have all their church heritage restored to them which

they would think of themselves without their having to be reminded of it. For tears came into my eyes, and my whole heart was
affected when I read in the closing paragraphs of the late Comenius's
church history, from Lamentations V:19,20,21, "Lord, bring us
back to thee, that we may come home again. Renew our days as of
old." And certainly, whoever can read those lamentations without
emotion can not have a merciful heart.[1]

The heritage of the past should inform the present and future, but
not in a rigid way. Zinzendorf sought to bring the Moravian heritage into
the Renewed Church as appropriate, but also sought a critical appropriation of Pietism, Luther, Reformed tradition (Synod of Bern), and
mysticism. He stood on the shoulders of several traditions, integrating
them in his thought and person.

There is a piece of African sculpture which I was able to secure while
in Tanzania during the summer of 1995. It is a carving of a person
standing upon the ancestors, evidently a traditional subject. No life is
really a solitary life, even for those who would reject their tradition. The
hands of one are over the eyes of another. The hand of another seems
to poke into the eye of one. One near the bottom is bowed under the
weight of someone who stands on his head. Some seem to have no idea
they are being used to support others, but one breaks into a broad smile.
Their interrelationships are approached with appreciation, but also
humor. I do think a "lightness" is crucial in approaching the ancestors
so that through them one gives birth to new and living forms. The
pyramid of ancestors in the sculpture reaches up until one stands at the
pinnacle who someday will provide the shoulders on which the next
generation may stand; only he does not yet know that. He only glances
slightly down to see from whence he came.

I would hope that the Moravian Church and others might hear the
contributions of Zinzendorf and allow them to become part of the
creative process of present and future theological reflection. The
Moravian Church also needs more extensive exploration of the theology
of the Ancient Moravian Church. Our Czech Moravians rightfully make
the point that the Moravian Church did not start in the eighteenth
century. If North American Moravians discover that they have a theological tradition, this book will have accomplished its purpose. If others find

[1] Nikolaus Ludwig von Zinzendorf and others, *Christian David, Servant of the Lord,
Being a Translation of the Memoir of Christian David as Written by Zinzendorf and Translations
of Selected Letters and Reports Written by Christian David or Pertaining to Him*, trans. Carl John
Fliegel and ed. Vernon H. Nelson, publication no. 2 (Bethlehem, Pa.: Archives of the
Moravian Church, Northern Province, n.d.), section 27.

something of relevance in this *Ecumenical Theology of the Heart* and find it suggesting ways to answers for contemporary questions, it will have accomplished its purpose.

In each chapter I have tried to suggest some directions through my own reflection on issues, but it would be very unnatural if all would agree with me. To reflect theologically as a church, and ecumenically, is to creatively draw near the One upon whom we reflect, and the drawing near may be of more value than our tentative formulations and hopeful conclusions. For it is at the heart of Moravian theology that we live from relationship with God as a matter of the "heart," though we also know the value of intellect, as well as its limitations.

I write this conclusion with a strange feeling that something has come to an end. This is the culmination of a process which began with my doctoral dissertation at Princeton long ago and has been a part of my life for more than forty years. For thirty years I have taught a course on Zinzendorf's theology at Moravian Theological Seminary; and in the last few years I have been privileged to participate in the development of *Transatlantic Moravian Dialogue Correspondence (TMDK)*, a journal for Moravian international theological dialogue. The questions asked by students over the years and the engagement in international theological dialogue have helped to shape this book, and appreciation is due all those whose thought and questions have contributed.

Now seems to be the right time for the birth of this book, after forty years of gestation, for in the year 2000 we will celebrate the 300th anniversary of the birth of the one whom Karl Barth called "a church father who is important and fruitful for the whole church." Perhaps something has come to an end. But also perhaps something is beginning.

> Whether?
> Whither?
> This is
> God's choice,
> and yours.
> Gifts
> received
> gratefully
> I return,
> perhaps with
> something new.
> But how exciting

to have engaged
the thought of
many
years,
and to have felt
the pulse
of their life
— and
the beat of
their heart.
Whether?
Whither?
This is
God's choice,
and yours.[2]

---

[2] By the author.

Appendix A

Outline of Zinzendorf's Life

[Zinzendorf's Publications are listed, with German titles translated into English.]

Childhood and Education   1700-1722

May 26, 1700   Nikolaus Ludwig von Zinzendorf born, Dresden, Saxony
July 9, 1700   Zinzendorf's father dies
Fall, 1700   Mother and child return to home of maternal grandparents at Gross-Hennersdorf, Upper Lusatia
1700-10   Zinzendorf raised by grandmother, Henrietta Katharina von Gersdorf at Gross-Hennersdorf
1702   Grandfather, Nicol Baron von Gersdorf, dies
1704   Mother marries Fieldmarshal von Natzmer and moves away
1710-16   Educated in this center of Pietism, Halle Paedagogium
1716-19   Studies law at orthodox Lutheran University of Wittenberg
1719-21   Educational trip
May 22, 1719   Visit to Düsseldorf art gallery, where affected by the Ecce Homo painting
1719-20   Holland – studies at University of Utrecht; France – resides in Paris, conversations with Cardinal Noailles; Switzerland

Public Service in Dresden   1721-27

1721   Takes office in Dresden as King's Councillor in Saxon Court in October
1722   Buys Berthelsdorf; marries Erdmuthe Dorthea Reuss September 7
1722   First Moravians come to Berthelsdorf estate; first house built at site of Herrnhut, from which location the renewed Moravian Church will develop
1724   First son, Christian Ernst, born and dies

(They had twelve children Only four lived to maturity, and only three outlived their parents.)
1725   Henrietta Benigna Justina born
1726   Grandmother, Henrietta Katharina von Gersdorf, dies

Publications:
1722   *The Last Hours of Our Lord*
1723   *Thoughts on Language and the Use of Words*
1723   First Catechism, *"Pure Milk"* – simple 78 questions and answers to be used by parents in teaching small children
1723   Causes Johann Arndt's *True Christianity* to be translated into French and dedicated to Cardinal Noailles
1725   Catechism – *Certain Ground of Christian Teaching* according to Luther's Short Catechism – for older children, used by Moravian congregations
1725   *The Last Discourses of our Lord* (John 14-16)
1725-26   *The German Socrates* – a periodical published in Dresden

Building up of Herrnhut   1726-36

1727   Returns to his estate, settles in Herrnhut, though not completely released from obligations in Dresden
Christian Renatus born
Manorial Prohibitions and Injunctions May 12
Brotherly Agreement July 4
Spiritual experience of August 13 at Communion service in Berthelsdorf.
Beginning of the Diaspora (establishment of societies among members of the state church)
(In these experiences of 1727 the church at Herrnhut is renewed, and the settlers, of various backgrounds, discover the source of their unity.)
1731   Trip to Copenhagen for coronation of Christian IV
Meets Anthony, a native of the West Indies, and the stage is set for Moravian missions
1732   Beginning of Moravian Missions: Leonhard Dober and David Nitschmann sent to St. Thomas
1734   Zinzendorf examined by Universities of Stralsund and Tübingen for certification as orthodox Lutheran and assumes status of ordained in 1735
1735   First Moravians come to North America (Georgia)

Publications:
In the period 1725-34 Zinzendorf does several shorter New Testament translations: e.g., John 14-17, Revelation 1-4, Jude, Matthew 5-7, and

1 Timothy. Some are paraphrases in popular language, and some
are the work of a Collegium Biblicum at Herrnhut in 1733-34

1727   *Ebersdorf Bible* with Summaries by Zinzendorf, Luther's text used

1727   A. H. Francke's *Thoughts on Simplicity*, with a Preface by Zinzendorf

1727   *Catholic-Christian Hymn and Prayer Book*

1731   First printing of the *Daily Texts* for devotional use. Practice
begun in 1728 with the text announced daily

1735   *German Poetry* – poetry of Zinzendorf

1735f   *Spontaneous Supplements* – a monthly
First edition of the Moravian hymnal *Collection of Ancient and Modern
Hymns*, revised in 1735 with the first Supplement added. A total of
twelve Supplements were later added.

The Pilgrim Count 1736-55

During this period Zinzendorf travels extensively, often accompanied
by the "Pilgrim Congregation." This period begins with his banishment from Saxony in 1736, an order not rescinded until 1747,
though he occasionally visits Herrnhut. His travels take him to
various parts of Germany, Switzerland, Holland, the Baltic Countries. Especially notable during this period are a trip to the West
Indies (1738-39), a trip to North America (1741-43), and several
visits to England, the longest of which was 1752-55. During the
American trip he helps to initiate the Pennsylvania Synods as an
attempt to unify Christians in Pennsylvania and makes three exploratory trips among the Indians.

1736   Property leased in Wetteravia for Moravian settlements

1737   Consecrated a Moravian bishop

1738   Building of Herrnhaag in Wetteravia, which for a time becomes
the headquarters of the Moravian Church during the exile from
Saxony

1743-50   The Sifting Period – a time when some of Zinzendorf's views
on the relationship of Christ and his sufferings to the Christian life
are carried to excess in some sections of the church. These are later
corrected by Zinzendorf and the church. This period is often
understood as a transition to maturer views in the 1750s.

1749   Moravians granted full freedom in Saxony and recognized by the
English Parliament

1752   Son Christian Renatus dies at age twenty-five

Publications:

1738   *Berlin Sermons.* Those to the men on Luther's Explanation of the
second article of the Creed are regarded as containing some of the
best expression of his views. Those to the women are partly on the
Lord's Prayer.

1739   *Another Attempt to Translate the New Testament* – first edition of his translation of the New Testament (separate vols. for the historical books and the doctrinal and prophetical books), hastily done on his trip to the Indies and later rejected by him

1739   *Remarkable Conversations Between a Traveler and other Persons Concerning all sorts of Religious Truths*

1740   *Jeremias, A Preacher of Righteousness* – a commentary designed as a handbook for ministers

1740   *An Attempt at a Little Doctrinal Book for the Brethren's Church* – a catechism where Zinzendorf departs from Luther's arrangement

1740   *Sermon on the Mystery of Religion*

1740   *Catechism for the Heathen* – an interesting approach to a catechism through Christology alone

1740-45   *Büdingen Collection of Several Significant and Recent Writings in Church History* – eighteen parts and a supplement

1741   *Recollections on the Translation of the New Testament*

1741   *Sermon on the Conversion-Struggle*

1741   *Seven Last Sermons Before Departure for America* (West Indies)

1742   *Shorter Catechism for Several Reformed Churches,* based on the *Declaration of Faith and Practice* adopted by the Synod of Berne, 1532

1742   *Pennsylvania Sermons*

1742   *Authentic Relation* – materials from the Pennsylvania Synods

1742   *Pennsylvania News*

1743   *Every Man's Right to Live* – a sermon on Ezekiel 33:2 preached in Philadelphia

1744-46   *New Testament Translation,* 2nd ed. (some Catholic Epistles not translated, Gospel of John placed first as key to the New Testament and the rest of the books arranged in historical order) – a free rendering of the text to express its thought to the uneducated

1744-46   *Thirty-two Homilies or Congregational Sermons*

1744   *The Little Catechism of Luther* with foreword by Zinzendorf

1745   *The Cross-Kingdom of Jesus* – an apologetic writing

1746   *Natural Reflections on All Sorts of Matters* – a weekly collected into a volume containing personal reflections in defense of himself

1746   *Zeist Synodical Sermons*

1746   *Nine Public Lectures on Important Subjects in Religion, Preached in Fetter Lane Chapel in London in the Year 1746*

1747   *Forty-three Homilies on the Litany of the Wounds* delivered at Herrnhaag

1747   *New Collection of German Poetry* of Zinzendorf

1747   *Public Congregational Sermons*

1747-48   *Twenty-one Discourses on the Augsburg Confession*

1749   *Acts of the Unitas Fratrum in England* – materials related to the recognition of the Moravian Church by Pariament in England

1749 *Account of the Doctrine, Manners, Liturgy and Idiom of the Unitas Fratrum* – taken from the Acts of the Unity in England, the Supplement of the Vouchers to the Report of the Committee of the House of Commons concerning the Unitas Fratrum: overview of the Augsburg Confession, text of the Augsburg Confession, extract from the Bern Synod, Church Litany of the Moravians, extracts from General Synods, rationale of the Moravian Liturgies, text of the Enchiridion from the Church Fathers in English and Latin, postscript of the editor

1749 *Bibliotheoria Catholica* – paraphrases of and comments on select verses of Paul's Epistles

1751-55 *London Sermons*

1752 *Enchiridion, i.e., Major Portions of Holy Scripture Made Into a Handbook* (Genesis only) – leaving out geneologies and repetitions and shortening material not relevant for Christians

The Return to Herrnhut 1755-60

June 19, 1756 Wife Erdmuthe Dorothea dies
June 27, 1757 Zinzendorf marries Anna Nitschmann
May 9, 1760 Zinzendorf dies

Publications:

1755 *Sermons to the Married Choir* from 1744 to 1747

1755 *An Exposition, or True State, of the Matters objected in England to the People known by the Name of Unitas Fratrum*

1756 *Several Sermons Preached by Zinzendorf on His Return to Berthelsdorf in 1756*

1755-57 *Children's Sermons*

1757 *Sermons on the Travels of 1757*

1755-59 *Several of Zinzendorf's Last Sermons*

1757 *Story of the Days of the Son of Man Out of the Four Gospels* – a harmony of the Gospels, first ed. 1757, second ed. 1759

1760 *Barby Collection*

1760 *Last Bible Work in the Old Testament* – an improvement and expansion (to Exodus 31) of the Enchiridion of 1752

Selections from Zinzendorf's Sermons, Printed and Unprinted, On Biblical Texts (published after his death) – three on the five books of Moses (Genesis-Deuteronomy), three on Matthew, two on Mark and Luke, one on John. These sermons come from various periods between 1738 and 1760.

Appendix B

The Ground of the Unity

The development of the Unitas Fratrum in the twentieth century has brought significant change. What was once a church of four home provinces with many mission fields is now a church which consists of many provinces which all share in the decision-making processes and international witness.

Patterns of congregational life, provincial administration, and worship vary greatly, and there cannot be said to be any one Moravian way. Yet all provinces subscribe to the basic doctrinal statement prepared by the 1957 General Synod and revised by subsequent synods. (The version below has been altered slightly at the directive of the Provincial Elders' Conferences of the Northern and Southern Provinces, Moravian Church in America, to make language regarding human beings inclusive and to use American spelling.)

The Ground of the Unity

The Lord Jesus Christ calls His Church into being so that it may serve Him on earth until He comes. The Unitas Fratrum is, therefore, aware of its calling in faith to serve humanity by proclaiming the Gospel of Jesus Christ. It recognizes this call to be the source of its being and the inspiration of its service. As is the source, so is the aim and end of its being based upon the will of its Lord.

The Belief of the Church

With the whole of Christendom we share faith in God the Father, the Son, and the Holy Spirit. We believe and confess that God has revealed Himself once and for all in His Son Jesus Christ; that our Lord has redeemed us with the whole of humanity by His death and His resurrection; and that there is no salvation apart from Him. We believe that He is present with us in the Word and the Sacrament; that He directs and unites us through His Spirit and thus forms us into a Church. We hear Him summoning us to follow Him, and pray Him to use us in His service. He joins us together mutually, so that knowing ourselves to be members of His body we become willing to serve each other.

In the light of divine grace, we recognize ourselves to be a Church of sinners. We require forgiveness daily, and live only through the mercy of God in Christ Jesus our Lord. He redeems us from our isolation and unites us into a living Church of Jesus Christ.

Personal Belief

The belief of the Church is effected and preserved through the testimony of Jesus Christ and through the work of the Holy Spirit. This testimony calls each individual personally, and leads each one to the recognition of sin and to the acceptance of the redemption achieved by Christ. In fellowship with Him the love of Christ becomes more and more the power of the new life, power which penetrates and shapes the entire person. As God's Spirit so effects living belief in the hearts of individuals, He grants them the privilege to share in the fruits of Christ's salvation and membership in His body.

God's Word and Doctrine

The Triune God as revealed in the Holy Scriptures of the Old and New Testaments is the only source of our life and salvation; and this Scripture is the sole standard of the doctrine and faith of the Unitas Fratrum and therefore shapes our lives.

The Unitas Fratrum recognizes the Word of the Cross as the center of Holy Scripture and of all preaching of the Gospel and it sees its primary mission, and its reason for being, to consist in bearing witness to this joyful message. We ask our Lord for power never to stray from this.

The Unitas Fratrum takes part in the continual search for sound doctrine. In interpreting Scripture and in the communication of doctrine in the Church, we look to two millennia of ecumenical Christian tradition and the wisdom of our Moravian forebears in the faith to guide us as we pray for fuller understanding and ever clearer proclamation of the Gospel of Jesus Christ. But just as the Holy Scripture does not contain any doctrinal system, so the Unitas Fratrum also has not developed any of its own because it knows that the mystery of Jesus Christ, which is attested to in the Bible, cannot be comprehended completely by any human mind or expressed completely in any human statement. Also it is true that through the Holy Spirit the recognition of God's will for salvation in the Bible is revealed completely and clearly.

Creeds and Confessions

The Unitas Fratrum recognizes in the creeds of the Church the thankful acclaim of the Body of Christ. These creeds aid the Church in formulating a Scriptural confession, in marking the boundary of heresies, and in exhorting believers to an obedient and fearless testimony in every age. The Unitas Fratrum maintains that all creeds formulated by the Christian Church stand in need of constant testing in the light of the Holy Scriptures. It acknowledges as such true professions of faith the early Christian witness: "Jesus Christ is Lord!" and also especially the ancient Christian creeds and the fundamental creeds of the Reformation.*

The Unitas Fratrum as a Unity

We believe in and confess the Unity of the Church given in the one Lord Jesus Christ as God and Savior. He died that He might unite the scattered children of God. As the living Lord and Shepherd, He is leading His flock toward such unity.

The Unitas Fratrum espoused such unity when it took over the name of the Old Bohemian Brethren's Church, Unitas Fratrum" (Unity of Brethren). Nor can we ever forget the powerful unifying experience granted by the crucified and risen Lord to our ancestors in Herrnhut on the occasion of the Holy Communion of August 13, 1727, in Berthelsdorf.

*Note: In the various Provinces of the Renewed Unitas Fratrum the following creeds in particular gained special importance, because in them the main doctrines of the Christian faith find clear and simple expression:

    The Apostles' Creed
    The Athanasian Creed
    The Nicene Creed
    The Confession of the Unity of the Bohemian Brethren of 1662
    The Twenty-One Articles of the unaltered Augsburg Confession
    The Shorter Catechism of Martin Luther
    The Synod of Berne of 1532
    The Thirty-Nine Articles of the Church of England
    The Theological Declaration of Barmen of 1934
    The Heidelberg Catechism

It is the Lord's will that Christendom should give evidence of and seek unity in Him with zeal and love. In our own midst we see how such unity has been promised us and laid upon us as a charge. We recognize that through the grace of Christ the different churches have received many gifts. It is our desire that we may learn from each other and rejoice together in the riches of the love of Christ and the manifold wisdom of God.

We confess our share in the guilt which is manifest in the severed and divided state of Christendom. By means of such divisions we ourselves hinder the message and power of the Gospel. We recognize the danger of self-righteousness and judging others without love.

Since we together with all Christendom are pilgrims on the way to meet our coming Lord, we welcome every step that brings us nearer the goal of unity in Him. He himself invites us to communion in His supper. Through it He leads the Church toward that union which He has promised. By means of His presence in the Holy Communion He makes our unity in Him evident and certain even today.

The Church as a Brotherhood

The Church of Jesus Christ, despite all the distinctions between male and female, poor and rich, and people of different ethnic origin, is one in the Lord. The Unitas Fratrum recognizes no distinction between those who are one in the Lord Jesus. We are called to testify that God in Jesus Christ brings His people out of every ethnic origin and language into one body, pardons sinners beneath the Cross, and brings them together. We oppose any discrimination in our midst because of ethnic origin, sex, or social standing, and we regard it as a commandment of our Lord to bear public witness to this and to demonstrate by word and deed that we are brothers and sisters in Christ.

The Church as a Community of Service

Jesus Christ came not to be served but to serve. From this, His Church receives its mission and its power for its service, to which each of its members is called. We believe that the Lord has called us particularly to mission service among the peoples of the world. In this, and in all other forms of service both at home and abroad, to which the Lord commits us, He expects us to confess Him and witness to His love in unselfish service.

318 An Ecumenical Theology of the Heart

Serving Our Neighbor

Our Lord Jesus entered into this world's misery to bear it and to overcome it. We seek to follow Him in serving His people. Like the love of Jesus, this service knows no bounds. Therefore we pray the Lord ever anew to point out to us the way to reach our neighbors, opening our heart and hand to them in their need.

Serving the World

Jesus Christ maintains in love and faithfulness His commitment to this fallen world. Therefore we must remain concerned for this world. We may not withdraw from it through indifference, pride or fear. Together with the universal Christian Church, the Unitas Fratrum challenges all with the message of the love of God, striving to promote the peace of the world and seeking to attain what is best for all people. For the sake of this world, the Unitas Fratrum hopes for and looks to the day when the victory of Christ will be manifest over sin and death and the new world will appear.

Conclusion

Jesus Christ is the one Lord and Head of His body, the Church. Because of this, the Church owes no allegiance to any authority whatsoever which opposes His dominion. The Unitas Fratrum treasures in its history the vital experience of the Headship of Christ of September 16 and November 13, 1741.

The Unitas Fratrum recognizes that it is called into being and has been sustained hitherto only by the incomprehensible grace of God. Thanksgiving and praise for this grace remain the keynote of its life and ministry.

In this spirit it awaits the appearing of Jesus Christ, goes forward to meet its Lord with joy, and prays to be found ready when He comes.

Bibliography

This is a bibliography pertaining to Zinzendorf and his theology only. It does not include all of the books and articles referred to in the footnotes. Many articles and pamphlets pertaining to Zinzendorf are not included. The bibliography is intended to provide awareness of basic resources for Zinzendorf research and some sense of the scope of the materials. Those wishing more extensive bibliography may consult Dietrich Meyer's *Bibliographisches Handbuch zur Zinzendorf-Forschung*, Düsseldorf, 1987. The reader who does not know German may also consult Appendix A, "Outline of Zinzendorf's Life," which includes translations of the titles of most of the primary sources.

An asterisk next to a bibliographical entry indicates that this item has been reprinted in whole or in part in the twentieth-century reprints edited by Erich Beyreuther and Gerhard Meyer. Parentheses around an asterisk indicate that an edition other than the first one listed has been reprinted. Look for another asterisk within the listing.

In capitalization of words in eighteenth-century German titles I have followed the practice expressed in the title, which is often influenced by the way words are arranged, with the first word in a title line usually being capitalized. Also, some words in titles are totally in capitals, and here I have followed the practice of capitalizing only the first letter of the word. In the German of the eighteenth century there were spellings which differ from modern German; for example "y" at times is used where "i" would be expected and occasionally "th" is used where now one sees only "t."

A. PRIMARY SOURCES

1. Bibliographies of Primary Materials.

Malin, William Gunn. *Catalogue of Books Relating to, or Illustrating the History of the Unitas Fratrum, or United Brethren.* Philadelphia: Collins, 1881.

Meyer, Dietrich, comp. *Bibliographisches Handbuch zur Zinzendorf-Forschung.* Düsseldorf: published by the compiler, 1987. Has notes on contents and various editions.

Meyer, Henry H. *Child Nature and Nurture according to Nicolaus Ludwig von Zinzendorf.* New York: Abingdon, 1928. A chapter on "The Educational Writings of Zinzendorf" discusses many of the materials.

*Spangenberg, August Gottlieb. *Leben des Herrn Nicolaus Ludwig Grafen und Herrn von Zinzendorf und Pottendorf. Beschrieben von August Gottlieb Spangenberg.* 8 pts. [Theile] in 3 vols. [Barby]: Zu finden in den Brüder-Gemeinen, 1773-75. All Zinzendorf's works are listed in the register and reference is made to their historical context. Spangenberg's biography has been reprinted in volumes 1-8 of series 2 of *Materialien und Dokumente,* ed. Erich Beyreuther, Gerhard Meyer, and Amedeo Molnár (Hildesheim: Georg Olms,

1971–). (Citation of the latter has been abbreviated in subsequent bibliographical entries as *Materialien und Dokumente*.)

Lepel, Wilhelm Heinrich Ferdinand Karl, Graf von, comp. *Verzeichnis der Schriften des Grafen Ludwig von Zinzendorf.* Stettin: Struck, 1824.

2. Twentieth-Century Reprints of Primary Sources.

Hauptschriften in sechs Bänden. [6 vols.] Edited by Erich Beyreuther and Gerhard Meyer. Hildesheim: Georg Olms, 1962-63. (Abbreviated in subsequent bibliographical entries as *Hauptschriften*.)

I Schriften des Jüngeren Zinzendorf: Der Teutsche Sokrates; Berlinische Reden; Sonderbare Gespräche.

II Reden in und von Amerika: Sieben letzte Reden; Pennsylvanische Nachrichten; Pennsylvanische Reden.

III Reden während der Sichtungszeit in der Wetterau und in Holland: Homilien über die Wundenlitanei; Zeister Reden.

IV Gemeinreden: Gemeinreden, Teil 1 und 2.

V Londoner Predigten: Londoner Predigten, Teil 1 und 2; Londoner Gesangbuch: Vorwort und Elenchus zu Teil 1 und 2.

VI Verschiedene Schriften: Neun Londoner Reden; Ein und zwanzig Diskurse über die Augspurgische Confession; Zuverlässige Nachricht; Vom Gebrauch der Worte; Berthelsdorfer Reden; Erinnerungen wegen seiner ersten Probe der Übersetzung 1741; Probetestament.

Ergänzungsbände zu den Hauptschriften. 14 vols. Edited by Erich Beyreuther and Gerhard Meyer. Hildesheim: Georg Olms, 1964-85. (Abbreviated in subsequent bibliographical entries as *Ergänzungsbände*.)

I Gerhard Meyer, Nikolaus Ludwig Reichsgraf zu Zinzendorf und Pottendorf: Eine genealogische Studie mit Ahnen- und Nachfahrenliste; Emil von Rajakovicz, Kurze Adelgeschichte im Hinblick auf Zinzendorfs Vorfahren.

II Teutscher Gedichte, XII Anhang zum Herrnhuter Gesangbuch, Zugaben I-IV zum XII. Anhang des Herrnhuter Gesangbuches, Ausgabe 1743.

III A. G. Spangenberg, Apologetische Schlußschrift.

IV Theologische und dahin einschlagende Bedenken; Naturelle Reflexionen.

V Die gegenwärtige Gestalt des Creutz-Reichs Jesu in seiner Unschuld; Spangenbergs Deklaration; Spangenbergs Darlegung richtiger Antworten.

VI Jeremias, ein Prediger der Gerechtigkeit; Zeremonienbüchlein; Reden an die Kinder.

VII-IX Büdingische Sammlung.

X Gerhard Meyer, Zinzendorf und der Katholizismus; Christ-Catholisches Singe- und Bet-Büchlein; Zwey und Dreyßig einzelne Homilien; Briefwechsel zwischen Zinzendorf und Noailles.

XI-XII Freywillige Nachlese I-XIII.

XIII Eines abermaligen Versuchs zur Übersetzung der Historischen Bücher Neuen Testaments aus dem Original Erste Probe, Zweyte Auflage.

XIV Zinzendorfs Berliner Reden, für die Manns-Personen und die Frauens-Personen.

Materialien und Dokumente. 47 vols., to date, in 4 series. Edited by Erich Beyreuther, Gerhard Meyer, and Amedeo Molnár. Hildesheim: Georg Olms, 1971–. (Abbreviated in subsequent bibliographical entries as *Materialien und Dokumente*.)

Reihe 1. Quellen und Darstellungen zur Geschichte der böhmischen Brüder-Unität. Herausgegeben von Amedeo Molnár.
I Matthias Janov.
II Jan Hus.
III Bekenntnisse der Böhmischen Brüder.
IV Quellen zur Geschichtsschreibung der Böhmischen Brüder: Comenius und Camerarius.
V Peter Cheltschizki.

Ergänzungsbände zur Reihe 1.
I Deutsche Katechismen der Bömischen Brüder.
II Zacharias Theobald, Hussiten-Krieg.

Reihe 2. Nikolaus Ludwig Graf von Zinzendorf. Leben und Werk in Quellen und Darstellungen, Herausgegeben von Erich Beyreuther und Gerhard Meyer.
I-VIII A. G. Spangenberg, Leben des Herrn Nikolaus Ludwig Grafen von Zinzendorf und Pottendorf.
IX L. C. Freiherr von Schrautenbach, Der Graf von Zinzendorf und die Brüdergemeine seiner Zeit.
X Johann Albrecht Bengel, Abriß der so genannten Brüder-gemeine.
XI David Cranz, Alte- und Neue Brüder-Historie oder kurzgefaßte Geschichte der Evangelischen Brüder-Unität.
XII Erster Sammelband über Zinzendorf.
XIII Zweiter Sammelband über Zinzendorf.
XIV-XX Antizinzendorfiana.
XXI G. H. Loskiel, Geschichte der Mission der evangelischen Brüder unter den Indianern in Nordamerika.
XXII Schlesien und Herrnhut. G. Meyer, Gnadenfrei; O. Uttendörfer, Alt-Herrnhut, Teil 1 und 2.
XXIII G. Meyer, Zinzendorf als Organisator der Herrnhuter Brüdergemeine; Das Litaneyen-Büchlein, Der 2. Anhang; T. Bechler, 200 Jahre ätzliche Missionsarbeit der Herrnhuter Brüdergemeine.
XXIV Christian David, Beschreibung und Zuverläßige Nachricht von Herrnhut; J.G. Seidel, Haupt-Schlüssel zum Herrnhutischen Ehe-Sacrament; Ideen, im Geist des wahren Herrnhuthianism.
XXV Sammlung der Losungs- und Textbüchlein der Brüdergemeine von 1731 bis 1761.
XXVI D. Cranz, Historie von Grönland.
XXVII C. G. A. Oldendorp, Geschichte der Mission der evangelischen Brüder auf den caraibischen Inseln.
XXVIII F. Staehelin, Die Mission der Brüdergemeine in Suriname und Berbice.
XXIX W. Bettermann, Theologie und Sprache bei Zinzendorf; O. Uttendörfer, Zinzendorf und die Mystik; G. Reichel, Die Anfänge Herrnhuts.
XXX Authentische Relation von dem Anlass, Fortgang und Schlusse der am 1sten und 2ten Januarii Anno 1741/2 in Germantown gehaltenen Versammlung einiger Arbeiter derer meisten christlichen Religionen und vieler vor sich selbst Gott-dienenden Christen-Menschen in Pennsylvania. Herausgegeben von Peter Vogt.

Reihe 3. Herausgegeben von E. Beyreuther und Gerhard Meyer.
I-IV Zeitschrift für Brüdergeschichte 1907-1920.

Reihe 4. Gesangbücher der Brüdergemeine und hymnologische Untersuchungen.
I Berthelsdorfer Gesangbuch.
II Marchesches Gesangbuch.
III Herrnhuter Gesangbuch.
IV Londoner Gesangbuch.
V Kleines Brüdergesangbuch; Hirten-Lieder von Bethlehem; Der Gesang des Reigens zu Saron; des kleinen Brüder-Gesang-Buchs Anderer Theil.
VI J. T. Müller, Hymnologisches Handbuch zum Gesangbuch der Brüdergemeine.

3. Catechisms.

* *Lautere Milch der Lehre von Jesu Christo.* Löbau: Ehlerdt Henning Reimers, 1723. Published in *Der Freywilligen Nachlese, Bey den bißherigen Gelehrten und erbaulichen Monaths-Schrifften, 1. Sammlung. Etiam inter manipulos colligat, et pudore non afficiatis eam. Ruth. C. II. v. 15.* Collection 10. (Frankfurt and Leipzig: M. Christ. Gottfried Marche, n.d.), pp. 1070-89. (Abbreviated in subsequent bibliographical entries as *Freywilligen Nachlese*). The second edition of this latter work has been reprinted in *Ergänzungsbände*, vols. 11 and 12.

Ludwig Grafens u. Herrn v. Zintzendorff Gewisser Grund Christlicher Lehre, Nach Anleitung des einfältigen Catechismi seel. Herrn D. Luthers. Leipzig: Samuel Benjamin Walther, 1725.

* *Heiden-Catechismus.* 1740. Published in *Büdingische Sammlung Einiger In die Kirchen-Historie Einschlagener Sonderlich neuerer Schrifften. Erster Band. Nebst darzu gehörigen Registern. Sind wir doch sein ererbtes gut.* Vol. 3 (Büdingen: Korte, 1744), pp. 402ff. (Abbreviated in subsequent bibliographical entries as *Büdingische Sammlung.*) This latter work has been reprinted in *Ergänzungsbände*, vols. 7-9.

Probe Eines Lehr-Büchelgens Vor Die sogenannten Brüder-Gemeinen Zu Mehrerer Deutlichkeit Und Gründlichern Verstande Unsrer heiligen Wahrheit In diese Form gebracht. Büdingen: Joh. Chr. Stöhr, 1740. Revised edition in 1740. *Die Andere Probe, So wohl Die Grund-Lehren Der Evangelischen Gemeinen, Die man seit 300. Jahren Die Brüder nennt, Als Ihren übrigen Verstand von der Heil. Schrifft, In Frage und Antwort zu fassen: Mit ernstem Vorbehalt Der abermahligen Aenderung und Verbesserung an allen Orten, wo solche nöthig gefunden wird: entworffen Von dem Verfasser Der Ersten Probe.* Büdingen: Joh. Christoph Stöhr, 1742. Translated under the title *A Manual of Doctrine: Or, A Second Essay To bring into the Form of Question and Answer As well the Fundamental Doctrines, as the other Scripture-Knowledge, of the Protestant Congregations who for 300 Years past have been call'd The Brethren. (Reserving a Liberty to alter and amend again, what at any Time shall be found needful.) Written in High-Dutch, by the Author of the first Essay; and now translated into English. With an introduction* (London: James Hutton, 1742). This work was also translated into Dutch and French.

Kurzer Catechismus Vor etliche Gemeinen Jesu Aus der Reformirten Religion In Pennsylvania, Die sich zum alten Berner Synodo halten: Herausgegeben von Johannes Bechteln, Diener des Worts Gottes. Philadelphia: Benjamin Franklin, 1742. (Also another printing in 1742.) A Swedish-language translation was printed by Franklin in 1743.

Der kleine Catechismus D. Martin Luthers. Mit Erläuterungen herausgegeben zum Gebrauch der Lutherische Gemeinen in Pensylvanien. Germantown: Christoph Saur, 1744.

4. Biblical Works, Listed Chronologically.

Die Letzten Reden Unsers Herrn und Heylandes Jesu Christi vor Seinem Creuzes-Tode. Frankfurt and Leipzig: Georg. Marc. Knoche, 1725. John 14-17.

Die gantze Göttliche Heilige Schrifft Altes und Neues Testaments, nach der teutschen Übersetzung D. Martin Luthers. Mit vielen richtigen Parallelen, denen gewöhnlichen, und an einigen Orten vollständigern Summarien. Ebersdorf im Voigtlande: Abraham Gottlieb Ludewig, 1726.

* *Probe der H. Offenbahrung in stilo relatorio. c. 1.2.3.4.* 1734. Published in *Freywilligen Nachlese,* collection 2, pp. 144ff. The second edition of the latter has been reprinted in *Ergänzungsbände,* vols. 11 and 12.

* *Probe einer genauen Erzählung der Heiligen Schrifft – Erzählung des allgemeinen Briefes Judä.* 1734. Published in *Freywilligen Nachlese,* collection 1, pp. 68ff. The second edition of the latter has been reprinted in *Ergänzungsbände,* vols. 11 and 12.

* *Die sogenannte Berg-Predigt des Herrn Jesu Matth. v. vi. vii.* 1734. Published in *Freywilligen Nachlese,* collection 1, pp. 75ff. The second edition of the latter has been reprinted in *Ergänzungsbände,* vols. 11 and 12.

* *Wohlgemeinter Versuch einer Übersetzung des ersten Briefs Pauli an den Timotheum aus dem Griechischen.* 1734. Published in *Freywilligen Nachlese,* collection 1, pp. 1ff. The second editon of the latter has been reprinted in *Ergänzungsbände,* vols. 11 and 12.

(*) *Eines abermahligen Versuchs zur Übersetzung der Historischen Bücher Neuen Testaments Unsers Herrn Jesu Christi aus dem Original Erste Probe.* Büdingen: Joh. Christoph Stöhr, 1739; *Eines Abermaligen Versuchs zur Übersetzung Der Historischen Bücher Neuen Testaments Unsers Herrn Jesu Christi aus dem Original Erste Probe Zweyte Edition Von den vorigen Schreib- Druck- und andern Fehlern gebessert.* Büdingen: Joh. Christoph Stöhr, 1744. Pages 1-59 and 86-97 of the 1744 edition have been reprinted in *Hauptschriften,* vol. 6.

(*) *Eines Abermahligen Versuchs Zur Übersetzung Der Lehr- und Prophetischen Bücher Neuen Testaments Unsers Herrn Jesu Christi aus dem Original. Erste Probe.* Büdingen: Joh. Christoph Stöhr, 1739; *Eines Abermahligen Versuchs zur Übersetzung Der Lehr- und Prophetischen Bücher Neuen Testaments unsers Herrn Jesu Christi aus dem Original Erste Probe zweyte Edition Worinnen die meisten besagter Lehr-Bücher befindlich sind, Von den vorigen Schreib- Druck- und andern Fehlern gebessert.* Büdingen: Joh. Christoph Stöhr, 1746. The 1746 edition has been reprinted in *Ergänzungsbände,* vol. 13.

(*) *Jeremias Ein Prediger der Gerechtigkeit, Allen redlichen Predigern In der Evangelischen Religion, einfältig und als ein Exempel, wie man in seinem Amt Mit Gott mit der Obrigkeit Mit den Lehrern Mit seinen Zuhören überhaupt, und Mit seinen Brüdern insonderheit wandeln könne, vor Augen gestellet.* Frankfurt and Basel: Johann Brandmüller, Jünger, 1740. *A second edition was published in 1741, and a third edition in 1796. Reprints were published in 1830 and 1863. The 1830 reprint of the second edition (1741) has been cited in this book: *Jeremias, ein Prediger der Gerechtigkeit, allen redlichen Predigern in der evangelischen Kirche einfältig und als ein Exempel vorgestellt, wie man in seinem Amte mit Gott, mit der Obrigkeit, mit den Lehrern, mit seinen Zuhörern überhaupt, und mit seinen Brüdern insonderheit wandeln könne. Von Nicolaus Ludwig, Grafen von Zinzendorff. Nach der zweiten verbesserten Auflage wieder abgedruckt.* Berlin: Franklin and Comp., 1830. The revised edition of 1741, in the printing of Stöhr and Brandmüller, has been reprinted in *Ergänzungsbände,* vol. 6.

* *Erinnerungen Des Hrn. Gr. v. Z. Wegen seiner Ersten Probe Der Übersetzung Des Neuen Testaments An seine Herren Gegener.* Büdingen: Johann Christoph Stöhr, 1741; also, with a minor change in the title, Leipzig: D. Korte, 1741. Reprinted in *Hauptschriften,* vol. 6.

Bibliotheoria Catholica Ordinario Frr. Anagnoste, Sectio Prima Demonstrationem Evangelicam Paulo Creditam Decem Et Sex Lectionibus Exhibet. [London]: n.p., [1750].

Enchiridion das ist, Haupt-Summa Der ganzen Heil. Schrift, in ein Hand-Büchlein gebracht, mit möglichster Beybehaltung der Worte des Buchs. [London]: n.p., 1752. Enlarged edition:*Des Seligen Ordinarii Fratrum letzte Bibel-Arbeit im Alten Testamente.* N.p., [1760]. This edition goes beyond Genesis, up through Exodus, chapter 31.

Gemein-Tags-Lectionen. N.p., [1753].

Die Geschichte der Tage des Menschen-Sohnes auf erden, aus den vier Evangelisten zusammen gezogen. N.p., [1757]. The second edition, Barby: n.p., 1759, incorporates into the text some of Zinzendorf's recollections.

Gemein-Tags-Psalmen. N.p., [1760].

* *Eines gelehrten Theologi Summarischer Inhalt der zusammenhangenden Rede des Predigers Salomo.* N.p., n.d. Published in *Freywilligen Nachlese,* collection 3, pp. 73ff. The second edition of the latter has been reprinted in *Ergänzungsbände,* vols. 11 and 12.

* *Kindliche Einfälle über denigen Zusammenhang des Hoheliedes Salomonis.* N.p, n.d. Published in *Freywilligen Nachlese,* collection 4, pp. 440ff. The the second edition of the latter has been reprinted in *Ergänzungsbände,* vols. 11 and 12.

5. Sermons.

Berliner Reden (Berlin Speeches).

* *Inhalt einiger öffentlichen Reden, Welche im Jahr 1738. vom Januario bis zu Ende des Aprilis in Berlin an die Frauens-Personen daselbst gehalten worden.* Berlin: Christian Ludewig Kunst, n.d. Reprinted in *Ergänzungsbände,* vol. 14.

* *Inhalt dererjenigen Reden, Welche zu Berlin vom 1ten Januarii 1738. bis 27ten Aprilis in denen Abend-Stunden sonderlich für die Manns-Personen gehalten worden.* Berlin: Christian Ludewig Kunst, n.d. Reprinted in *Ergänzungsbände,* vol. 14.

Other editions with the two collections published in one volume: second edition, Berlin and Altona: Gebrüder Korte, 1740; third edition, see next paragraph; fourth edition, Leipzig and Altona: Gebrüder Korte, 1749. Many other editions of the Berlin sermons to the men were published, including one in Czech in 1743, one in French in 1744, and two in English (see *Sixteen Discourses* ... just below). There were a few additional editions of the berlin sermons to the women.

The third edition, cited frequently in this book, is a complex of materials all bound together. The first title page lists *Des Grafens von Zinzendorff Inhalt dererjenigen Reden, Welche zu Berlin vom 1ten Januar. 1738. bis 27ten Aprilis in denen Abend-Stunden sonderlich für die Manns-Personen gehalten worden. Dritte Auflage.* Flensburg and Altona: Gebrüder Korte, 1743. Bound with this is the third edition of the sermons to the women, with a separate title page, *Des Grafens von Zinzendorff Inhalt einiger öffentlichen Reden, welche im Jahr 1738. vom Januario bis zu Ende des Aprils in Berlin an die Frauens-Personen daselbst gehalten worden. Dritte Auflage.* Leipzig und Altona: Gebrüder Korte, 1743. In addition there are attachments, without title pages, to both volumes: *Inhalt der übrigen allgemeinen und für die Männer gehalten Reden* following the sermons to the men and *Der Inhalt noch zehn anderer Reden* following the sermons to the women.

The fourth edition of sermons to the women has also been cited: *Des Herrn Grafen von Zinzendorff Inhalt einiger öffentlichen Reden, welche im Jahr 1738. vom Januario bis zu Ende des Aprils in Berlin an die Frauens-Personen daselbst gehalten worden. Vierte Auflage.* Leipzig and Altona: Gebrüder Korte, 1749.

Revised edition of the sermons to the men, 1758:* *Des Ordinarii Fratrum Berlinische Reden, nach dem vollständigen und von ihm selbst eigenhändig revidirten Exemplar, in Druk gegeben von Gottfried Clemens, des Seminarii Theol. Decano und Schloß Prediger zu Barby. Tom. 1.* London and Barby: Zu finden bey dem Seminario Theologico, 1758. Reprinted in *Hauptschriften*, vol. 1.

Sixteen Discourses On The Redemption of Man By the Death of Christ. Preached at Berlin, By the Right Reverend and most Illustrious Count Zinzendorf, Bishop of the Ancient Moravian Church. Translated from the High Dutch. With A Dedication to the Archbishops, Bishops, and Clergy, giving some Account of the Moravian Brethren. London: James Hutton, 1740. Second edition: London: J. Beecroft, 1751. The Berlin sermons to the men.

* *Eine Predigt Vom Geheimniß der Religion, uber die Worte Es geschah, daß er mit dem Tode rang, und betete hefftiger. Es war aber sein Schwieß wie Bluts-Tropffen die fielen auf die Erde. Luc 22, 44. Aus erheblichen Ursachen dem Druck überlassen.* Flensburg and Altona: Gebrüder Korte, 1740; also Frankfurt and Basel: Johann Brandmüller, Jünger, 1740. Translated under the title *Sermon Sur Le Grand Mystere De La Religion* (Altona: Ches les Freres Korte, 1743). The German-language version of this sermon has been added to the *Berliner Reden* of 1740 and to *Sieben Letzte Reden*, and has been reprinted with *Sieben Letzte Reden* in *Hauptschriften*, volume 2.

* *Eine Predigt Von dem Buß-Kampffe Für uns, Gehalten am andern Sonntag in der Fasten 1741.* N.p.: Joh. Christoph Stöhr, n.d. Included in the 1743 edition of *Sieben Letzte Reden*. Translated under the title *Sermon Sur L'Agonie Ou Le Combat que le Sauveur soutint pour nous dans le Jardin de Gethsemane: Prononce en 1741. a Guehlenhausen, Ville Imperiale, Par Louis de Zinzendorf, Eveque des Freres. Traduit De L'Allemand.* Altona: Ches les Freres Korte, 1743. The German-language version of this sermon has been reprinted with *Sieben Letzte Reden* in *Hauptschriften*, volume 2.

(*) *Des Herrn Grafen Ludwig von Zinzendorff Sieben Letzte Reden So Er In der Gemeine, Vor seiner am 7. Aug. erfolgten abermahligen Abreise nach Amerika, gehalten.* Büdingen: Johann Christoph Stöhr, 1742. Edition of 1743: * *Des Herrn Grafen Ludwig von Zinzendorff Sieben Letzte Reden So Er In der Gemeine, Vor seiner am 7. Aug. erfolgten abermahligen Abreise nach America, gehalten. Denen noch beygefügt sind zwey in Gelnhausen von demselben gehaltene und ehmals einzeln gedruckte Predigten.* Büdingen: Johann Christoph Stöhr, 1743. The 1743 edition, which includes *Eine Predigt Vom Geheimniß der Religion* and *Eine Predigt Von dem Buß-Kampffe*, has been reprinted in *Hauptschriften*, vol. 2. Translated under the title *Seven Sermons On The Godhead of the Lamb; Or The Divinity of Jesus Christ. By the Right Reverend and most Illustrious Count Zinzendorf, Bishop of the Moravian Church. Preached in the Congregation, just before his second Voyage to the West-Indies: And translated from the German Manuscript* (London: James Hutton, 1742).

Every Man's Right to Live. A Sermon On Ezek. 33.2. Why will ye die? Preached In Philadelphia, The 10th Day of January 1741, 2. By the Reverend Lewis of Thurenstein, Deacon Κατα ταξιν και ευσχημοσυνην of the ancient Moravian Church, and, for the Time, Pastor of the Lutheran Congregation at Philadelphia. Translated from the German by O. Malander. Philadelphia: n.p., 1743.

(*) *Eine Sammlung Offentlicher Reden, Von Dem Herrn der unsere Seligkeit ist, und über die Materie von seiner Marter. In dem Jahr 1742. Mahrentheils In dem Nordlichen Theil von America der* *das Englische Canada ausmachet vor allerley Christlichen Religions-Meetings gehalten, Von Dem damaligen Evangelischen Lutherischen Inspectore und Past. zu Philadelphia. Erster Theil.* [*Zweyter Theil.*] Büdingen: Johann Christoph Stöhr, 1744. Second edition: *Eine Sammlung Offentlicher Reden, Von Dem Herrn der unsere Seligkeit ist, und über die Materie von seiner Marter. In dem Jahr 1742. Mehrentheils In den Nordlichen Theil von America der das Englische Canada ausmachet vor allerley Christlichen Religions-Meetings gehalten, von Dem damaligen Evangelischen Lutherischen Inspectore und Past. zu Philadelphia. Erster Theil.* [*Zweyter Theil.*] *Zweyte Edition.* Büdingen: Johann Christoph Stöhr, 1746. Third edition: *Des Ordinarii Fratrum, Öffentliche Reden, von dem Herrn, der Unsere Seligkeit ist. und über die Materie Von Seiner Marter, die Derselbe als vocirter Pastor bey der einzigen damals zu Philadelphia in Pennsylvanien bekanten Evangelisch-Lutherischen Gemeine in ihrer Kirche daselbst Im Jahr 1742. gehalten hat, Nebst einem Anhang zweyer andern dergleichen Predigten, und einiger Lieder Von Ihm selbst revidirt und ausgefertigt. Herausgegeben von Gottfried Clemens, des Seminarii Theol. Decano und Schloß-Prediger zu Barby. Dritte Edition.* London And Barby: Zu finden bey dem Seminario Theologico, 1760. In revising this collection for the third edition, Zinzendorf deleted a number of sermons. This was reworked by Zinzendorf before his death. A number of sermons were eliminated from this edition, and the sermons were renumbered. Seven of the sermons were translated into Dutch under the title *N Predicatien Gedaan in Pensylvanien, Door Den Ordinarius Fratrum. Uit het Hoogduitsch vertaald.* Amsterdam: Jacobus Wilhelmus Pruys, n.d. This collection is often called the Pennsylvania Sermons. The second German-language edition, 1746, has been reprinted in *Hauptschriften,* vol. 2.

* *Zwey und Dreyßig einzele Homiliae Oder Gemein-Reden in denen Jahren 1744. 1745. 1746. Daß ich euch immer einerley sage, verdrüßt mich nicht, und macht euch desto gewißer.* N.p.: Zu finden in den Brüder-Gemeinen, n.d. There were two printings. Reprinted in *Ergänzungbände,* vol. 10.

* *Neun Oeffentliche Reden über wichtige in die Religion einschlagende Materien, Gehalten zu London in Fetterlane-Capelle Anno 1746.* N.p.: Zu finden in den Brüder-Gemeinen, n.d. A further edition was issued, with title page notation, "Zu finden in den Brüder-Gemeinen, und Leipzig und Görlitz, in der Marcheschen Buchhandlung 1748." The undated edition listed first has been reprinted in *Hauptschriften,* vol. 6. Translated under the title *Nine Publick Discourses Upon Important Subjects in Religion, Preached in Fetter-Lane-Chapel at London, in the Year 1746. Translated from the German* (London: James Hutton, 1748). Also translated by George W. Forell under the title *Nine Public Lectures on Important Subjects in Religion Preached in Fetter Lane Chapel in London in the Year 1746* (Iowa City: University of Iowa Press, 1973).

* *Die an den Synodum der Brüder, in Zeyst vom 11. May bis den 21. Junii 1746. gehaltene Reden, Nebst noch einigen andern zu gleicher Zeit in Holland geschehenen Vorträgen.* N.p.: Zu finden in den Brüder-Gemeinen, n.d. Revised as *Des Ordinarii Fratrum auf dem Synodo der Brüder zu Zeyst vom 11 Maj bis 21 Jun. 1746. geäusserte Haupt-Ideen und bey jedes Tages verlesenen Schrift-Texte gethane Erinnerungen, Von Ihm selbst revidirt und ausgefertiget. Herausgegeben von Gottfried Clemens, des Seminarii Theol. Decano und Schloß-Prediger zu Barby.* London and Barby: Zu finden bey dem Seminario Theologico, 1759. The first edition has been reprinted in *Hauptschriften,* vol. 3.

* *Der Öffentlichen Gemein-Reden im Jahr 1747. Erster Theil* [pt. 1]. *Mit einem Anhang einiger zu Ende des Jahres 1746. gehaltenen Homilien.* N.p.: Zu finden in den Brüder-Gemeinen, 1748. Reprinted in *Hauptschriften,* vol. 4.

* *Der Öffentlichen Gemein-Reden im Jahr 1747. Zweyter Theil* [pt. 2]. N.p.: Zu finden in den Brüder-Gemeinen, 1749. Reprinted in *Hauptschriften*, vol. 4.

* *Vier und Dreyßig Homiliae über die Wunden-Litaney der Brüder, Gehalten auf dem Herrnhaag in den Sommer-Monathen 1747. von dem Ordinario Fratrum.* N.p.: Zu finden in den Brüder-Gemeinen, n.d. Second edition: *Des Ordinarii Fratrum Reden über die Litaney Des Lebens, Leidens und der Wunden Unsers Herrn Jesu Christi, gehalten vom ende April. bis in den August. 1747. Zweyte Edition.* Barby: Zu finden bey dem Seminario Theologico, 1759. The first edition has been reprinted in *Hauptschriften*, vol. 3.

(*) *Ein und zwanzig Discourse über die Augspurgische Confession gehalten vom 15. Dec. 1747. bis zum 3. Mart. 1748. denen Seminariis Theologicis Fratrum zum Besten aufgefaßt und bis zur nochmaligen Revision des Autoris einstweilen privatim mitgetheilet.* N.p., n.d. *An additional printing: *Ein und zwanzig Discurse über die Augspurgische Confession gehalten vom 15. Dec. 1747. bis zum 3. Mart. 1748. denen Seminariis Theologicis Fratrum zum Besten aufgefaßt und bis zur nochmaligen Revision des Auctoris einstweilen mitgetheilet.* N.p., n.d. These two printings have quite different pagination schemes. To differentiate between the printings, give attention to how *Discourse/Discurse* and *Autoris/Auctoris* are spelled (and to whether *privitim* is included as the second last word). All citations in this book are from the printing listed second, above, (*Discurse . . . Auctoris*, no *privitim*). This work has been translated under the title *Twenty One Discourses Or Dissertations Upon The Augsburg Confession, Which is also the Brethren's Confession of Faith: Deliver'd by the Ordinary Of the Brethren's Churches before the Seminary. To which is prefixed, A Synodal Writing Relating to the same Subject. Translated from the High Dutch, By F. Okeley, B.A.* (London: J. Beecroft, 1753). The German-language printing listed second, above, has been reprinted in *Hauptschriften*, vol. 6.

* *Einiger seit 1751. von dem Ordinario Fratrum zu London gehaltenen Predigten in Dreyen Haupt-Abtheilungen edirter Erster Band.* London and Barby: Zu finden bey dem Seminario Theologico, 1756. See note following next listing. Reprinted in *Hauptschriften*, vol. 5.

* *Der Predigten die der Ordinarius Fratrum von Anno 1751. bis 1755. zu London gehalten hat, Zweyter Band, Nebst Einem Anhange einiger an Englische Brüder-Gemeinen gehaltenen Homilien.* London and Barby: Zu finden bey dem Seminario Theologico, 1757. Reprinted in *Hauptschriften*, vol. 5. This work, and the previous one, are considered the *Londoner Predigten*, the first volume containing sections [Abtheilungen] 1-3, and the second containing sections 4-6.

(*) *Einige Reden des Ordinarii Fratrum die Er vornehmlich Anno 1756. zur zeit seiner retraite in Bethel, an die gesamte Bertholdsdorfische Kirchfahrt gehalten hat.* Barby: Zu finden bey dem Seminario Theologico, 1758. *There was a second and enlarged edition of 1766, and a third edition of 1776, each published at Barby. There was a fourth, unchanged, edition published at Gnadau in 1848. Thirteen of the sermons were translated into French and published at Neuwied in 1762. The German-language edition of 1766 has been reprinted in *Hauptschriften*, vol. 6.

(*) *Sammlung Einiger von dem Ordinario Fratrum während seines Aufenthalts in den Teutschen Gemeinden von Anno 1755 bis 1757 gehaltenen Kinder-Reden.* Barby: Zu finden bey dem Seminario Theologico, 1758. *Second and revised edition: Barby, 1761. The revised edition, 1761, has been reprinted in *Ergänungsbände*, vol. 6.

6. Materials on the Pennsylvania Synods.

* *Avthentische Relation Von dem Anlass, Fortgang und Schlusse Der am 1 sten und 2 ten Januarii Anno 1741/2 In Germantown gehaltenen Versammlung Einiger Arbeiter Derer meisten Christlichen Religionen Und Vieler vor sich selbst Gott-dienenden Christen-Menschen in Pennsylvania; Aufgesetzt In Germantown am Abend des 2 ten obigen Monats.* Philadelphia: B. Franklin, n.d. Reprinted in *Materialien und Dokumente*, ser. 2, vol. 30, along with an English-language translation of the same, based on an eighteenth-century manuscript translation held by the Moravian Archives, Bethlehem, Pa., and with an introduction, notes and bibliography by Peter Vogt.

Avthentische Nachricht Von der Verhandlung und dem Verlass Der am 14den und 15den Januarii Anno 1741/2 Im sogenannten Falckner-Schwamm An Georg Hübners Hause gehaltenen Zweyten Versammlung Sowol Einiger Teutschen Arbeiter Der Evangelischen Religion Als Verschiedener einzelen treuen Gezeugen und Gottsfürchtiger Nachbarn. Nebst einigen Beylagen. Philadelphia: B. Franklin, n.d.

Zuverlässige Beschreibung Der Dritten Conferenz Der Evangelischen Religionen Teutscher Nation In Pennsylvania, Welche am 9. 10. und 11.ten [F]ebruarii 1741/2 In Oley an Johann De Turcks Hause gehalten worden; Samt Denen dieses mahl verfassten Gemein-Schlüssen. Philadelphia: B. Franklin, n.d.

Vierte General-Versammlung Der Kirche Gottes Aus allen Evangelischen Religionen In Pennsylvania, Deutscher Nation; Gehalten zu Germantown am 10. 11. 12ten Martii im jahr 1741/2 An Mr. Ashmeads Hause. N.p., n.d.

Grundliche An- und aufforderung An Die Ehmalig erweckte hier und dar zerstreuete Seelen dieses Landes, In Oder Ausser Partheyen, Zur Neuen Umfassung, Und Gebets-Gemeinschaft; Dargelegt aus dringendem Herzen Eines um Heilung der Brücke Zions ängstlich bekümmerten Gemüths, im jahr 1736. Philadelphia: B. Franklin, 1742.

Extract Aus Unsers Conferenz-Schreibers Johann Jacob Müllers Geführten Protocoll Bey Der Gemeine Gottes im Geist, Gehalten in Germantown 1742. den 6ten April und folgende Tage: Nebst einer Vorrede an die ehrwürdige Conferenz aller Arbeiter bey der Kirche Jesu Christi in Pennsylvania. Philadelphia: B. Franklin, n.d.

Extract Aus Des Conferenz-Schreibers Johann Jacob Müllers Registratur Von Der Sechsten Versammlung Der Evangelischen Arbeiter In Pennsylvania. Und Der Gemeine Gottes im Geist Siebender General-Synodus Zu Philadelphia am 2. und 3ten Junii 1742 st. v. [Philadelphia]: B. Franklin, n.d.

B. Ludewigs Wahrer Bericht De dato Germantown den 20sten Febr. 1741/2, An seine liebe Teutsche, Und Wem es sonst nützlich zu wissen ist, Wegen Sein und seiner Brüder Zusammenhanges Mit Pennsylvania, Zu Prüfung der Zeit und Umstände ausgefertiget; Nebst einem P.S. de dato Philadelphia den 5ten Martii; Und einigen Unsre Lehre überhaupt und dieses Schriftgen insonderheit Erläuternden Beylagen. Philadelphia: Benjamin Franklin, n.d.

* *Pennsylvanische Nachrichten Von dem Reiche Christi, Anno 1742.* N.p., n.d. Contains *Ludwigs Bericht*, supplements, minutes or descriptions of the first four conferences and J. A. Gruber's *An- und Aufforderung zu Gliedlicher Vereinigung.* Reprinted in *Hauptschriften*, vol. 2.

7. Other Works, Listed Chronologically.

Apologetic works, which constitute a large body of literature, are not in the main included here. The titles can be examined on pp. 267-499 of Dietrich Meyer's *Bibliographisches Handbuch.* Hymnals and liturgical materials also are not included.

* *Des Graffen von Zintzendorffs Gedancken vom Reden und Gebrauch der Worte.* [1723]. Reprinted in *Freywilligen Nachlese,* pp. 714-37, and in *Hauptschriften,* vol. 6. See also the reprint of the second edition of *Freywilligen Nachlese* in *Ergänzungsbände,* volumes 11 and 12, and Leiv Aalen's introduction to this little work in volume 11 of the same, page 116.

* *Der Teutsche Socrates. Das ist: Aufrichtige Anzeige verschiedener nicht so wohl unbekannter als vielmehr in Abfall gerathener Haupt-Wahrheiten, in den Jahren 1725 und 1726. Anfänglich in der Königl. Residentz-Stadt Dreßden, Hernach aber dem gesamten lieben Vaterland teutscher Nation zu einer guten Nachricht nach und nach ausgefertiget, und von dem Autore selbst mit einem kurtzen Inhalt jedes Stücks, nunmehro auch mit verschiedenen Erläuterungen, die sich in der ersten Auflage nicht befinden, und einem Anhange versehen.* Leipzig: Samuel Benjamin Walther, 1732. Previous to this edition, individual issues of this periodical had been bound together into an unpaginated assemblage of thirty-two issues (150 pages), 2 Nov. 1725-Dec. 1726, with a title page, a one page preface and a five page descriptive table of contents. The title page of the earliest *single* issue reads: *Le Socrate de Dresde. D. i. Bescheidene Gedancken eines Christlichen Philosoph Uber allerley Gutes und Böses in der Welt Seinen lieben Mit-Bürgern wöchentlich mitgetheilt. Freytags am 2. Nov. als am Tage Aller Heiligen.* The 1732 edition of the collection of the same thirty-two issues has been reprinted in *Hauptschriften,* vol. 1.

(*) *Sonderbare Gespräche zwischen Einem Reisenden und Allerhand andern Personen, von Allen in der Religion vorkommenden Wahrheiten. . . .* Altona, Gebrüder Korte, 1739. Second edition: **Sonderbare Gespräche zwischen Einem Reisenden und Allerhand andern Personen, von Allerley in der Religion vorkommenden Wahrheiten. . . . Zweite mit Fleis verbesserte Auflage.* Altona: Gebrüder Korte, 1739. Third edition, 1769. Two revised editions, 1796. New editions, 1850 and 1869. The second edition has been reprinted in *Hauptschriften,* vol. 1.

* *Teil 1-4 Theologische und dahin einschlagende Bedencken Welche Ludwig Graf von Zinzendorff, Zeitheriger Bischoff Der Böhmisch- und Mährisch-Evangelischen Brüder, Seit 20. Jahren entworffen. Mit des Autoris Zuschrifft An alle Hohe Obrigkeiten Und einer Vorrede Polycarpi Müllers, Ehemahligen Professoris zu Leipzig und Directoris des Gymnasii zu Zittau, nunmehrigen Episcopi Fratrum.* Büdingen: Johann Christoph Stöhr, 1742. There were various earlier publications of parts of this, some under a title which included *Bedencken und besondere Send-Schreiben.* The 1742 edition was reprinted in *Ergänzungsbände,* vol. 4.

My dear Fellow-Traveller, here hast Thou a Letter, Which I have wrote to Thee out of the Fulness of my Heart, and with many Tears for Thy Salvation's Sake; and The Lamb of God hath sprinkled it with His Blood, that it will be profitable for Thee, if Thou abidest by thy Heart, or now findest thy Heart. London: n.p., 1742. Also published as *The Traveller's Present: Or, A Letter Giving a Short History of Religion.* London: James Hutton, 1742. Translated under the titles *Mein lieber Mit-Pilger! Da hast du einen Brief* and *Lettre D'Un Voiageur Pour L'Eternite,* n.p., 1743.

* *Ludwigs von Zinzendorf Peri Eautou. Das ist: Naturelle Reflexiones über allerhand Materien, Nach der Art, wie Er bey sich selbst zu denken gewohnt ist: Denenjenigen Verständigen Lesern, Welche sind nicht entbrechen können, über Ihn zu denken, in einigen Send-Schreiben, bescheidentlich dargelegt.* N.p., n.d. A weekly published Dec. 1746–Dec. 1748, and gathered into various collections. There were three editions of *Naturelle Reflexiones*, which were not dated. The one quoted in this book is the largest of these editions and is the edition reprinted in *Ergänzungsbände*, vol. 4. It consists of twelve issues and nine supplements.

Christian David, Servant of the Lord, Being a Translation of the Memoir of Christian David as Written by Zinzendorf and Translations of Selected Letters and Reports Written by Christian David or Pertaining to Him. Translated by Carl John Fliegel and edited by Vernon H. Nelson. Publication 2. Bethlehem, Pa.: Archives of the Moravian Church, Northern Province, n.d.

8. Collections and Other Works from the Time of Zinzendorf.

Barbysche Samlungen Alter und Neuer, Lehr-Principia, Sitten-Lehren, und den vorigen und itzigen Gang der Öconomie Gottes und ihrer Diener illustrirender Stükke, wie auch theils gedrukter, theils ungedrukter Kleinerer Schriften des dermaligen Ordinarii der Brüder. Erste Samlung. [Zweyte Samlung]. Barby, Zu finden bey dem Seminario Thelogico, 1760.

* *Büdingische Sammlung Einiger In die Kirchen-Historie Einschlagender Sonderlich neuerer Schrifften. Erster Band. Nebst darzu gehörigen Registern. Sind wir doch sein ererbtes gut.* 3 vols. Büdingen: Joh. Chr. Stöhr (vol. 1), Korte (vols. 2, 3), 1742-44. Reprinted in *Ergänzungsbände*, vols. 7-9.

(*) *Der Freywilligen Nachlese, Bey den bißherigen Gelehrten und erbaulichen Monaths-Schrifften, 1. Sammlung. Etiam inter manipulos colligat, et pudore non afficiatis eam. Ruth. C. II. v. 15.* 13 collections. Frankfurt and Leipzig: M. Christ. Gottfried Marche, n.d. The whole appeared in 1740 with the changed title: **Des Grafen von Zinzendorff und Pottendorf Der Böhmischen und Mährischen Brüder Hochwürdigen Bischoffs Kleine Schrifften, Gesammlet In verschiedenen Nachlesen Bey den bisherigen gelehrten und erbaulichen Monaths-Schrifften, Nebst einigen andern erbaulichen Blättern.* Frankfurt, 1740. The latter was reprinted in *Ergänzungsbände*, vols. 11 and 12. (Abbreviated in subsequent bibliographical entries as the second edition of *Freywilligen Nachlese*.)

(*) *Graf Ludwigs von Zinzendorff Teutscher Gedichte Erster Theil.* Herrnhut: Zu finden im Waisenhause, 1735. The planned parts 2 and 3 did not appear. New edition: **Graf Ludwigs von Zinzendorf Teutscher Gedichte Neue Auflage.* Barby: Heinrich Detlef Ebers, 1766. The 1766 edition has been reprinted in *Ergänzungsbände*, vol. 2.

* *M. Aug. Gottl. Spangenbergs Darlegung richtiger Antworten auf mehr als dreyhundert Beschuldigungen gegen den Ordinarivm Fratrvm nebst verschiedenen wichtigen Beylagen.* Leipzig and Görlitz: In der Marcheschen Buchhandlung, 1751. Reprinted in *Ergänzungsbände*, vol. 5.

* *M. Avgust. Gottl. Spangenbergs Apologetische Schluß-Schrift, Worinn über tausend Beschuldigungen gegen die Brüder-Gemeinen und Ihren zeitherigen Ordinarium nach der Wahrheit beantwortet werden, Nebst einigen wichtigen Beylagen.* Leipzig and Görlitz: In der Marcheschen Buchhandlung, 1752. Reprinted in *Ergänzungsbände*, vol. 3.

Maxims, Theological Ideas And Sentences, Out Of The Present Ordinary Of The Brethren's Churches His Dissertations And Discourses From the Year 1738. till 1747. Extracted by J. Gambold, M.A. With a Letter from the Author annex'd. London: J. Beecroft, 1751.

Eine Neue Sammlung zu dem Ersten Theil Teutscher Gedichte, Anstatt des verlegten oder gar verlornen Zweyten, auch halb und halb versprochenen Dritten Theils derselben: Zum Dienst derer, die solche niedliche Elegantien in ihrer ersten Form gerne lesen und verwahren. N.p., n.d. Ten occasional poems from 1745 and 1746, and some poems from the years following.

9. Collections after the Time of Zinzendorf

Auszüge aus des Seligen Ordinarii der Evangelischen Brüder-Kirche sowol ungedruckten als gedruckten Reden über biblische Texte, nach Ordnung der Bücher heiliger Schrift gefertiget und herausgegeben von Gottfried Clemens [Drei Bände über die Bücher Mose]. Barby: n.p., 1763-65.

Auszüge aus des Seligen Ordinarii der Evangelischen Brüder-Kirche Herrn Nicolaus Ludwig Grafens und Herrn von Zinzendorf und Pottendorf sowol ungedrukten als gedrukten Reden über die vier Evangelisten, gefertiget und herausgegeben von Gottfried Clemens. 6 vols. Barby: Gottfried Clemens, 1766-90. Volumes 5 and 6 have the notation: H[eraus] g[egeben] von J[akob] C[hristoph] Düvernoy, 1781 and 1790, respectively.

Einige der letzten Reden des seligen Grafen Nicolaus Ludwig von Zinzendorf. Barby: Zu finden in den Brüdergemeinen, 1784. Further editions in 1824 and 1875, published at Gnadau.

Einige Reden des Seligen Ordinarii Fratrum Herrn Nicolaus Ludwig Grafens und Herrn von Zinzendorf und Pottendorf, mehrentheils auf seinen Reisen im Jahr 1757 gehalten. Barby: Heinrich Detlef Ebers, 1768.

Geistliche Gedichte des Grafen von Zinzendorf gesammelt und gesichtet von Albert Knapp. Mit einer Lebensskizze und des Verfassers Bildniß. Stuttgart and Tübingen: J. G. Cotta, 1845.

Geistliche Gedichte des Grafen von Zinzendorf. Eine Auswahl zur Erinnerung an den Tag seiner Geburt vor zweihundert Jahren. H[eraus] g[egeben] v[on] H[ermann] Bauer and G[uido] Burkhardt. Leipzig: Friedrich Jansa, 1900.

Hagen, F. F. *Old Landmarks: or Faith and Practice of the Moravian Church at the Time of Its Revival and Restoration in 1727, and Twenty Years After.* Bethlehem, Pa.: Hagen, 1886.

Memorials of the Moravian Church. Vol. 1. Edited by William C. Reichel. Philadelphia, 1870. Contains translations of Zinzendorf materials especially related to the mission to the Indians.

Nikolaus Ludwig Graf von Zinzendorf: Evangelische Gedanken: Gewißheit, Freude, Kraft. Edited by Otto Uttendörfer. Hilfe für's Amt, vol. 14. Berlin: Christlicher Zeitschriftenverlag, 1948.

Des seligen Grafen Nicolaus Ludwig von Zinzendorf Gedanken über verschiedene evangelische Wahrheiten, aus dessen Schriften zusammengezogen. Barby: Zu finden in den Brüdergemeinen; und in Leipzig in Commission bey Paul Gotthelf Kummer, 1800. Four more editions were published from Gnadau: 1820, 1840, 1852 and 1861, the last under the title *Traktate aus der Brüdergemeine.*

Zinzendorf: Über Glauben und Leben Aus Zinzendorfs Worten ausgewählt, zusammengestellt und mit Nachwort und Anmerkungen versehen von Otto Herpel, mit einer Einführung von Gerhard Reichel. [Edited by Otto Herpel.] Innenschau-Bücherei, vol. 1. Schlüchtern, 1920. Second edition: *Zinzendorf: Über Glauben und Leben. Ausgewählt und zusammengestellt von Otto Herpel.* Quellen. Lebensbücherei christlicher Zeugnisse aller Jahrhunderte, vol. 7. Sannerz and Leipzig, 1925; also Berlin: Hochweg, 1925.

Zinzendorf und die Herrnhuter Brüder: Quellen zur Geschichte der Brüder-Unität von 1722 bis 1760. Edited by Hans-Christoph Hahn and Hellmut Reichel. Hamburg: Friedrich Wittig, 1977.

9. Manuscript Sources.

Archiv der Brüder-Unität, Herrnhut, Germany: Rubriken der Akten. Unpublished sermons and letters of Zinzendorf and synodal reports. in the notes referred to as Herrnhut Archives, followed by an alpha-numeric designation for the series and/or document referred to.

Diarium des Jüngerhauses. 1747-1760. Herrnhut Archives. This diary recorded the activities of Zinzendorf and those who worked with him. During 1747 and 1748 it was called *Gemein Diarium*; from 1748 through 1753, *Diarium der Hütten*; and from 1754 through 1760, *Diarium des Jüngerhauses*. In the notes the entire diary, 1747-60, has been referred to as Diarium des Jüngerhauses.

Ehechor-Reden. 1747ff. Herrnhut Archives. Sermons of Zinzendorf to the Choir of the Married People. A typescript, evidently never published, with corrections by Zinzendorf written in.

There is much manuscript material for those who wish to pursue this, including Zinzendorf's diaries and correspondence. There are also the diaries of other major Moravian settlements around the world. The second volume of the Bethlehem Diary will soon be published. The major archives are those of the Northern Province in Bethlehem, Pa.; the Southern Province in Winston-Salem, N.C.; the Continental Province and the Unity in Herrnhut, Germany; and the British Province in London. In the eighteenth century many materials were hand-copied and distributed throughout the Moravian Church, and thus the two archives in North America really have materials relevant for understanding the whole Unitas Fratrum.

B. SECONDARY SOURCES

Only a few articles and pamphlets are included. For a listing of articles published in periodicals and collections of articles up to 1987, see *Bibliographisches Handbuch zur Zinzendorf-Forschung* compiled by Dietrich Meyer.

1. Moravian Communal Life and Sociological Studies.

* Erbe, Hellmuth. *Bethlehem, Pa.: Eine kommunistische Herrnhuter Kolonie des 18. Jahrhunderts.* Schriften des Deutschen Ausland-Instituts, Stuttgart. A. Kulturhistorische Reihe [series]. Vol. 24, 1929. Reprinted in *Materialien und Dokumente*, ser. 2, vol. 13.

Gollin, Gillian Lindt. *Moravians in Two Worlds: A Study of Changing Communities.* New York: Columbia University Press, 1967.

Meyer, Gerhard. *Gnadenfrei: Eine Herrnhuter Siedlung des schlesischen Pietismus im 18. Jahrhundert.* Hamburg: L. Appel, 1950.

Myers, Elizabeth Lehman. *A Century of Moravian Sisters: A Record of Community Life.* New York: Fleming H. Revell Co., 1918.

* Reichel, Gerhard. *Die Anfänge Herrnhuts: Ein Buch vom Werden der Brüdergemeine.* Herrnhut: Verlag der Missionsbuchhandlung, 1922. Reprinted in *Materialien und Dokumente*, ser. 2, vol. 29.

Reichel, Levin T. *The Early History of the Church of the United Brethren (Unitas Fratrum) Commonly Called Moravians, in North America, A.D. 1734-1748.* In *Transactions of the Moravian Historical Society* (Nazareth, Pa.) 3 (1888).

Sessler, Jacob John. *Communal Pietism among Early American Moravians.* Studies in Religion and Culture. American Religion Series 8. New York: H. Holt and Company, 1933.

Smaby, Beverly Prior. *The Transformation of Moravian Bethlehem: From Communal Mission to Family Economy.* Philadelphia: University of Pennsylvania Press, 1988.

* Uttendörfer, Otto. *Alt-Herrnhut: Wirtschaftsgeschichte und Religions-soziologie Herrnhuts während seiner ersten zwanzig Jahre (1722-1742).* Herrnhut: Verlag der Missionsbuchhandlung, 1925. Reprinted in *Materialien und Dokumente,* ser. 2, vol. 22.

Wollstadt, Hanns-Joachim. *Geordnetes Dienen in der christlichen Gemeinde: Dargestellt an den Lebensformen der Herrnhuter Brüdergemeine in ihren Anfängen.* Arbeiten zur Pastoraltheologie, vol. 4. Göttingen: Vandenhoeck and Ruprecht, 1966.

Unpublished Theses.

Bemmann, Herbert. "Die soziologische Struktur des Herrnhutertums." Ph.D. diss., Heidelberg University, 1922.

Binoeder, Carl. "Zur soziologischen Bedeutung der Herrnhuter Brüdergemeine." Phil. diss., Erlangen University, 1956.

Brückner, Hedwig. E. "Religiöse Einstellung der frühen Herrnhuter und Wirken ihrer ersten Missionare in Labrador: Dargestellt und kommentiert auf Grund ihrer Aufzeichnungen aus dem späten achtzehnten Jahrhundert." Masters thesis, Memorial University of Newfoundland, 1975.

Nelson, James David. "Herrnhut: Friedrich Schleiermacher's Spiritual Homeland." 2 vols. Ph.D. diss., University of Chicago, 1963. A study of Herrnhut at the end of the eighteenth century.

Sommer, Elisabeth Watkins. "Serving Two Masters: Authority, Faith, and Community among the Moravian Brethren in Germany and North Carolina in the 18th Century." Ph.D. diss., University of Virginia, 1991.

Stead, Geoffrey. "The Moravian Experience on the English Mission, with Reference to the Settlement at Mirfield, 1755 to 1800." Masters thesis, University of Leeds, 1988.

Surratt, Jerry Lee. "From Theocracy to Voluntary Church and Secularized Community: A Study of the Moravians in Salem, North Carolina 1772-1860." Ph.D. diss., Emory University, 1968.

2. General – Books and Theses.

Aalen, Leiv. *Den unge Zinzendorfs Teologi.* Oslo: Lutherstiftelsens Forlag, 1952. Translated from the Norwegian under the title *Die Theologie des jungen Zinzendorf.* Arbeiten zur Geschichte und Theologie des Luthertums, vol. 16 (Berlin and Hamburg: Lutherisches Verlagshaus, 1966).

Atwood, Craig D. "Blood, Sex, and Death: Life and Liturgy in Zinzendorf's Bethlehem." Ph.D. diss., Princeton Theological Seminary, 1995.

Baudert, Samuel. *Gotteswirklichkeit und Religion: Zinzendorfs Gedanken über Mission in ihrer Bedeutung für die Gegenwart.* Gütersloh: Bertelsmann, 1932.

Beck, Hartmut. *Brüder in vielen Völkern: 250 Jahre Mission der Brüdergemeine.* Erlangen: Verlag der Ev. Luth. Mission, 1981.

Becker, Bernhard. *Zinzendorf im Verhältnis zu Philosophie und Kirchentum seiner Zeit: Geschichtliche Studien.* Leipzig: Hinrich, 1886.

* Bengel, Johann Albrecht. *Abriß der so genannten Brüdergemeine, in welchem die Lehre und die ganze Sache geprüfet, das Gute und Böse dabey unterschieden, und insonderheit die Spangenbergische Declaration erlautert wird durch Johann Albrecht Bengel. Erster Theil.* Stuttgart: Johann Benedict Metzler, 1751. Reprinted in *Materialien und Dokumente,* ser. 2, vol. 10.

* ———. "Anmerckungen von der sogenannten Brüder-Gemeine [with responses by Nikolaus Ludwig von zinzendorf]." In *Büdingische Sammlung Einiger In die Kirchen-Historie Einschlagender Sonderlich neuerer Schrifften.* Vol. 3. Büdingen: Korte, 1744. The latter has been reprinted in *Ergänzungungsbände,* vol. 9.

Benz, Ernst, and Heinz Renkewitz, eds. *Zinzendorf-Gedenkbuch.* Stuttgart: Evangelisches Verlagswerk, 1951.

Bernewitz, Hans. "Der Sendungsauftrag der Kirche in den Gesangbüchern der Brüdergemeine von 1927 und 1967 und im Evangelischen Kirchengesangbuch von 1950." Diss., Halle, 1968.

* Bettermann, Wilhelm. *Theologie und Sprache bei Zinzendorf.* Gotha: Klots, 1935. Reprinted in *Materialien und Dokumente,* ser. 2, vol. 29.

Beyreuther, Erich. *Der junge Zinzendorf.* Marburg: Francke, 1957.

———. *Zinzendorf und die sich allhier beisammen finden.* Marburg: Francke, 1959.

———. *Zinzendorf und die Christenheit.* Marburg: Francke, 1961.

———. *Die große Zinzendorf Trilogie.* Marburg: Francke, 1988. The three previous volumes published as one.

———. *Studien zur Theologie Zinzendorfs: Gesammelte Aufsätze.* Neukirchen-Vluyn: Kreis Moers, 1962.

———. *Zinzendorf: L'apôtre de l'unité.* Geneva, 1967.

———. *Zinzendorf und Pierre Bayle: Ein Beitrag zur Frage des Verhältnisses Zinzendorf zur Aufklärung.* Herrnhuter Hefte 8. Hamburg: L. Appel, 1955.

Bintz, Helmut. *Nikolaus Ludwig Graf von Zinzendorf: Dichter der christlichen Gemeinde.* Stuttgart, 1979.

Bintz, Helmut, ed. *Nikolaus Ludwig von Zinzendorf: Texte zur Mission. Mit einer Einführung in die Missionstheologie Zinzendorfs.* Hamburg, 1979. (2nd suppl. [2. Beiheft] to *Unitas Fratrum.*)

Buijtenen, Mari P., Cornelius Dekker, and Huib Leeuwenberg. *Unitas Fratrum. Herrnhuter Studien. Moravian Studies.* Utrecht: Rijksarchyief, 1975.

Church of England and Moravian Church in Great Britain and Ireland. *Anglican-Moravian Conversations: The Fetter Lane Common Statement with Essays in Moravian and Anglican History.* Occasional Paper No. 5. London: The Council for Christian Unity of the General Synod of the Church of England, 1996.

* Cranz, David. *Alte und Neue Brüder-Historie oder kurz gefaßte Geschichte der Evangelischen Brüder-Unität in den älteren Zeiten und insonderheit in dem gegenwärtigen Jahrhundert.* Barby, 1771. Reprinted in *Materialien und Dokumente,* ser. 2, vol. 11. Translated under the title *The ancient and modern History of the Brethren: or, a succinct narrative of the protestant church of the United Brethren, or, Unitas Fratrum, In the remoter Ages, and particularly in the present Century: written in German by David Cranz, Author of the History of Greenland; Now translated into English with Emmendations; and published, with some additional Notes, by Benjamin la Trobe* (London: W. and A. Strahan, 1780).

Cröger, Ernst Wilhelm. *Geschichte der erneuerten Brüderkirche.* 3 pts. Gnadau: Verlag der Buchhandlung der evang. Brüder-Unität bei H. L. Menz, 1852-54.

Deghaye, Pierre. *La Doctrine Ésotérique de Zinzendorf (1700-1760).* [Paris, 1969].

De Schweinitz, Edmund Alexander. *A History of the Unitas Fratrum, from Its Overthrow in Bohemia and Moravia to Its Renewal at Herrnhut, 1627-1722: Based upon Sources Not Heretofore Drawn from, and Showing That the Time of the Hidden Seed Must Be Reduced to Less Than a Quarter of a Century.* Bethlehem, Pa.: Moravian Publication Office, 1877.

Dose, Kai. "Die Bedeutung der Schrift für Zinzendorfs Denken und Handeln." Diss., Bonn, 1971.

Eberhard, Samuel. *Kreuzes-Theologie: Das reformatorische Anliegen in Zinzendorfs Verkündigung.* Munich: Kaiser, 1937.

* Erbe, Hans-Walter. *Herrnhaag: Eine religiöse Kommunität im 18. Jahr-hundert.* In *Unitas Fratrum* (Hamburg: Friedrich Wittig), nos. 23/24 (1988). A book-length study.

———. *Zinzendorf und der fromme hohe Adel seiner Zeit.* Leipzig: M. Heinssius, 1928. Reprinted in *Materialien und Dokumente,* ser. 2, vol. 12.

Evangelical Lutheran Church in America and Moravian Church in America, Northern and Southern Provinces, *Following Our Shepherd to Full Communion: Report of the Lutheran-Moravian Dialogue with Recommendations for Full Communion, Worship, Fellowship and Mission.* Evangelical Lutheran Church in America, 1997.

Freeman, Arthur James. "The Hermeneutics of Count Nicolaus Lud-wig von Zinzendorf." Th.D. diss., Princeton Theological Seminary, 1962.

Gärtner, Friedrich. "Karl Barth und Zinzendorf: Die bleibende Bedeutung Zinzendorfs auf Grund der Beurteilung des Pietismus durch Karl Barth." *Theologische Existenz heute* (Munich: Kaiser), no. 40 (1953).

Glaubrecht, Otto. *Zinzendorf in der Wetterau: Ein Bild aus der Geschichte der Brüdergemeinde.* Revised and edited by Hermann Knodt. Giessen and Basel: Brunnen-Verlag, 1925. First edition was published in 1852-53.

Gloege, Gerhard. *Zinzendorf und das Luthertum.* Jena, [1950].

Hamilton, J. Taylor, and Kenneth G. Hamilton. *History of the Moravian Church: The Renewed Unitas Fratrum 1722-1957.* Bethlehem, Pa., and Winston-Salem, N.C.: Interprovincial Board of Christian Education, Moravian Church in America, 1967.

Hamilton, Kenneth G., trans. and ed. *The Bethlehem Diary.* Vol. 1. 1742-1744. Bethlehem, Pa.: Archives of the Moravian Church, Northern Province, 1971.

336 An Ecumenical Theology of the Heart

Havens, Mary B. "Zinzendorf and the Augsburg Confession: An Ecumenical Vision?" Ph.D. diss., Princeton Theological Seminary, Princeton, N.J., 1989.

Hennig, Liemar. *Kirche und Offenbarung bei Zinzendorf: Ein Beitrag zum Verhältnis von Pietismus und Aufklärung.* Zürich, 1939.

Hirzel, Stephan. *Der Graf und die Brüder: Die Geschichte einer Gemeinschaft.* Gotha: Leopold Klotz, 1935.

Hök, Gösta. *Zinzendorfs Begriff der Religion.* Uppsala and Leipzig, 1948.

Huober, Hans-Günther. *Zinzendorfs Kirchenliederdichtung: Untersuchung über das Verhältnis von Erlebnis und Sprachform.* Germanistiche Studien, no. 150. Berlin, 1934. Reprint, Nendeln/Liechtenstein: Kraus Reprint, 1967.

Hutton, Joseph Edmund. *A History of the Moravian Missions.* London: Moravian Publication Office, 1922.

Jannasch, Wilhelm. *Erdmuthe Dorothea, Gräfin von Zinzendorf, geborene Gräfin Reuss zu Plauen: Ihr Leben als Beitrag zur Geschichte des Pietismus und der Brüdergemeine dargestellt.* Herrnhut: Im Verlag des Vereins für Brüdergeschichte, In Kommission der Unitätsbuchhandlung in Gnadau, 1915. This was published in *Zeitschrift für Brüdergeschichte,* 1914. Note that the date 1915 does appear on the title page of the book in the issue of *Zeitschrift für Brüdergeschichte* for 1914.

Jung, Willhelm Friedrich. *Der in dem Grafen von Zinzendorf noch Lebende und Lehrende wie auch Leidende und Siegende Doctor Luther, Allen verständigen und redlichen Leuten Der beyden Evangelischen Religionen vor Augen geleget Von Willhelm Friedrich Jung, Pastore der Evangelisch-Lutherischen Gemeine zu Hayngen in der Wetterau.* Frankfurt and Leipzig: , 1752.

Kinkel, Gary S. *Our Dear Mother The Spirit: An Investigation of Count Zinzendorf's Theology and Praxis.* Lanham, Md.: University Press of America, 1990.

Lehmann, Hugo. *Zinzendorfs Religiosität.* Leipzig: F. Jansa, 1903.

Levering, Joseph Mortimer. *A History of Bethlehem, Pennsylvania, 1741-1892, with Some Account of Its Founders and Their Early Activity in America.* Bethlehem, Pa.: Times Publishing Co., 1903.

Lewis, Arthur James. *Zinzendorf, the Ecumenical Pioneer: A Study in the Moravian Contribution to Christian Mission and Unity.* Philadelphia: Westminster Press, 1962. Reprint, Bethlehem, Pa., and Winston-Salem, N.C.: Moravian Church in America, 1998.

Loretz, Johann. *Ratio disciplinae Unitatis Fratrum A.C., oder Grund der Verfassung der Evangelischen Brüder-Unität Augsburgischer Confession.* Barby, 1789.

* Loskiel, Georg Heinrich. *Geschichte der Mission der evangelischen Brüder unter den Indianern in Nordamerika.* Barby: Zu finden in den Brüdergemeinen, 1789. Reprinted in *Materialien und Dokumente,* ser. 2, vol. 21. Translated under the title *The History of the Moravian Mission Among the Indians in North America from Its Commencement to the Present Time, with a Preliminary Account of the Indians* (London: T. Allman, 1838).

Lutjeharms, Wilhelm. *Het philadelphisch-oecumenisch streven der Hernhutters in de Nederlanden in de achttiende eeuw.* Zeist, 1935.

Mälzer, Gottfried. *Bengel und Zinzendorf: Zur Biographie und Theologie Johann Albrecht Bengels.* Arbeiten zur Geschichte des Pietismus, vol. 3. Witten, 1968.

Meyer, Dieter. *Der Christozentrismus des späten Zinzendorf: Eine Studie zu dem Begriff "täglicher Umgang mit dem Heiland."* Europäische Hochschulschriften, ser. 23, theology vol. 25. Bern: Herbert Lang; Frankfurt: Peter Lang, 1973.

Meyer, Dietich. *Festschrift für Erich Beyreuther.* Cologne, 1982.

* Meyer, Gerhard. *Die Epoche der Wetterau im Rückblick Zinzendorfs und des Herrnhutertums: Ein nicht bewältiges Generationsproblem der Herrnhuter.* In *Materialien und Dokumente*, ser. 4, vol. 4, pp. 1-77 (In *Londoner Gesangbuch*, pt. 2, pp. 1*-77*).

Meyer, Henry H. *Child Nature and Nurture according to Nicolaus Ludwig von Zinzendorf.* New York: Abingdon, 1928.

Meyer, Matthias. *Feuerbach und Zinzendorf: Lutherus redivivus und die Selbstauflösung der Religionskritik.* Hildesheim: Georg Olms, 1992.

Motel, Heinz. *Zinzendorf als ökumenischer Theologe.* Herrnhut, 1942.

Müller, Johann Georg. *Über Zinzendorfs Leben und Charakter: Meistens nach seinen eigenen Worten.* In *Bekenntnisse merkwürdiger Männer von sich selbst*, edited by Johann Georg Müller. Winterthur, 1795, pp. 1-302.

* Müller, Joseph Theodor. *Zinzendorf als Erneuerer der alten Brüderkirche: Festschrift des theologischen Seminariums der Brüdergemeine in Gnadenfeld zum Gedächtnis der Geburt Zinzendorfs am 26. Mai 1700.* Leipzig: Friedrich Jansa, 1900. Reprinted in *Materialien und Dokumente*, ser. 2, vol. 12.

Müller, Karl. *Gottesworklichkeit und Religion: Zinzendorfs Gedanken über Mission in ihrer Bedeutung für die Gegenwart.* Gütersloh: C. Bertelsmann, 1932. Pamphlet.

Natzmer, Gneomar Ernst von. *Die Jugend Zinzendorfs im Lichte ganz neuer Quellen.* Eisenach: M. Wilekens, 1894.

Nielsen, Sigurd. *Intoleranz und Toleranz bei Zinzendorf,* Vols. 2, 3, of *Der Toleranzgedanke bei Zinzendorf* by Sigurd Nielsen. Hamburg: Appel, 1952-60.

* Pfister, Oskar. *Die Frömmigkeit des Grafen Ludwig von Zinzendorf: Ein psychoanalytischer Beitrag zur Kenntnis der religiösen Sublimierungsprozesse und zur Erklärung des Pietismus.* Schriften zur angewandten Seelenkunde, vol. 8. Leipzig: Franz Deuticke, 1910. Reprinted in *Materialien und Dokumente*, ser. 2, vol. 13.

Plitt, Hermann. *Die Gemeine Gottes in ihrem Geist und ihren Formen.* Gotha: F. A. Perthes, 1859.

———. *Zinzendorfs Theologie.* 3 vols. Gotha: F. A. Perthes, 1869-74.

Podmore, Colin. *The Moravian Church in England, 1728-1760.* New York: Oxford University Press, 1998.

Ranft, Ruth. *Das Pädagogische im Leben und Werk des Grafen Ludwig von Zinzendorf.* Göttinger Studien zur Pädagogik, n.s., no. 3. Weinheim, 1958.

* Reichel, Gerhard. *Der "Senfkornordern" Zinzendorfs. Ein Beitrag zur Kenntnis seiner Jugendentwicklung und seines Charakters. T. 1: Bis zu Zinzendorfs Austritt aus dem Pädagogium zu Halle 1716.* Berichte des theologischen Seminars der Brüdergemeine in Gnadenfeld, no. 9. Leipzig: F. Jansa, 1914. Reprinted in *Materialien und Dokumente*, ser. 2, vol. 12.

———. *Zinzendorfs Frömmigkeit im Licht der Psychoanalyse: Eine Kritische Prüfung des Buchs von Dr. Oskar Pfister: "Die Frömmigkeit des Grafen Ludwig von Zinzendorf" und ein Beitrag zum*

Verständnis der extravaganten Lehrweise Zinzendorfs. Tübingen: J.C.B. Mohr, 1911. Reprinted in *Materialien und Dokumente,* ser. 2, vol. 13.

Reichel, Jörn. *Dichtungstheorie und Sprache bei Zinzendorf. Der 12. Anhang zum Herrnhuter Gesangbuch.* Bad Homburg, 1969.

Renkewitz, Heinz. *Im Gespräch mit Zinzendorfs Theologie: Vorträge aus dem Nachlaß.* Hamburg, 1980.

——. *Zinzendorf.* 2nd rev. ed. Herrnhut, Missionsbuchhandlung, 1939.

Říčan, Rudolf. *The History of the Unity of the Brethren.* Translated by C. Daniel Crews, Bethlehem, Pa., and Winston-Salem, N.C.: Moravian Church in America, 1992.

Ruh, Hans. *Die christologische Begründung des ersten Artikels bei Zinzendorf.* Basler Studien zur Historischen und Systematischen Theologie, vol. 7. Zurich, 1967.

* Salomon, Alice. *La Catholicité du monde chrétien d'après la correspondance inédite du comte Louis de Zinzendorf avec le cardinal de Noailles et les évêques appelants 1719-1728.* Paris: Librairie Félix Alcan, 1929. Reprinted in *Ergänzungsbände,* vol. 10.

Salomon, Gustav. *Gustav Salomons Dresdner Bücher-Auction, Bibliotheca Gersdorfio-Zinzendorfiana: Verzeichhniss der Bibliotheken der verstorbenen Herren Grafen Friedrich Caspar von Gersdorf, Grafen Ludwig von Zinzendorf, Gründer der Brüdergemeinde [sic] zu Herrnhut, Herrn von Schrautenbach, sowie der Herren Syndiken D. Nitschmann und Fr. Köber: 1 Abtheilung, Theologie und Nebe-Wissenschaften, welche am 7. Januar 1880 und folgende Tage . . . durch Gustav Solomon . . . gegen baare Zahlung versteigert werden.* [Dresden]: Ferdinand Thomass, printer, 1879.

Sawyer, Edwin A. *The Religious Experience of the Colonial American Moravians.* In *Transactions of the Moravian Historical Society* (Nazareth, Pa.: Moravian Historical Society) 18, pt. 1 (1961).

Schattschneider, David Allen. "'Souls for the Lamb': A Theology for the Christian Mission according to Count Nicolaus Ludwig von Zinzendorf and Bishop Augustus Gottlieb Spangenberg." Ph.D. diss., University of Chicago, 1975.

Schmidt, H., H. Bintz, and W. Günther, eds. "Protokoll des Gesprächs zwischen Professor Dr. Karl Barth und Vertretern der Brüdergemeine am 12. Oktober 1960 in Basel." *Civitas Praesens* (Königsfeld), no. 13, special issue (May 1961). Translated by Henning Schlimm and Arthur Nehring under the title "Minutes of a Discussion between Karl Barth and Representatives of the Moravian Church," *The Bulletin of Moravian Theological Seminary* (Bethlehem, Pa.) (fall 1961), pp. 57ff.

Schmidt, Theodor Edmund. *Zinzendorfs soziale Stellung und ihr Einfluß auf seinen Charakter und sein Lebenswerk.* Basel: Adolf Goering, 1900.

* Schrautenbach, Ludwig Carl Freiherr von. *Der Graf von Zinzendorf und die Brüdergemeine seiner Zeit.* Edited by Friedrich Wilhelm Kölbing. Gnadau: H. L. Menz, 1851. Written in 1782. Reprinted in *Materialien und Dokumente,* ser. 2, vol. 9.

Schulze, Adolf. *Abriß einer Geschichte der Brüdermission: Mit einem Anhang, enthaltend eine ausführliche Bibliographie zur Geschichte der Brüdermission.* Herrnhut: Verlag der Missionsbuchhandlung der Missionanstalt der Evangelischen Brüderunität, 1901. Translated by S. H. Gapp under the title *World-Wide Moravian Missions in Picture and Story: A Bi-Centenary Publication 1732-1932* (Bethlehem, Pa.: Comenius Press, 1926).

———. "Samuel Lieberkühns Leben und Wirken." In *Zinzendorf und Lieberkühn: Studien zur Geschichte der Judenmission*, by Gustav Dalman and Adolf Schulze, pp. 50-102. Schriften des Institutum Judaicum in Berlin 32. Leipzig, 1903.

Schuster, Kurt. "Gruppe, Gemeinschaft, Kirche: Gruppenbildung bei Zinzendorf." *Theologische Existenz heute* (Munich: Kaiser) n.s., no. 85 (1960).

Sigourney, L. H. *Zinzendorff, and Other Poets*. New York: Leavitt, Lord & Co., 1936.

* Spangenberg, August Gottlieb. *Leben des Herrn Nicolaus Ludwig Grafen und Herrn von Zinzendorf und Pottendorf. Beschrieben von August Gottlieb Spangenberg*. 8 pts. [Theile] in 3 vols. [Barby]: Zu finden in den Brüder-Gemeinen, 1773-75. Reprinted in *Materialien und Dokumente*, ser. 2, vols. 1-8. Abbreviated and translated by Samuel Jackson under the title *The Life of Nicholas Lewis Count Zinzendorf* (London: Samuel Holdsworth, 1838).

Steinberg, H. G., H. L. C. Schütz, W. Lutjeharms, and J. M. Van der Linde. *Zinzendorf.* Boeken der Broeders 1. Nijkerk: G.F. Callenboek, 1960.

Steinecke, Otto. *Zinzendorfs Bildungsreise: An der Hand des Reisetagebuches Zinzendorfs dargestellt von Otto Steinecke*. Halle: Richard Mühlmann, 1900.

———. *Zinzendorf und der Katholicismus: Ein Beitrag zum Verständnis Zinzendorfs*. Halle: Richard Mühlmann, 1902.

Stempel, Hermann-Ad. *Zinzendorfs Kinderreden: Über die Vorbereitung einer kritischen Augabe der 1. Auflage*. In *Unitas Fratrum* (Hamburg: Friedrich Wittig), no. 5 (1979).

Strupl, Miloš. "Confessional Theology of the Unitas Fratrum." Ph.D. diss., Vanderbilt University, 1964.

Tietzen, Hermann. *Die menschliche Persönlichkeit in Anlehnung an Zinzendorfsche Gedanken.* Stuttgart: Steinkopf, 1922.

———. *Zinzendorf: Hier ist wer, der weiß nicht mehr, als daß sein Schöpfer der Heiland ist*. Gütersloh: C. Bertelsmann, 1888.

Uttendörfer, Otto. *Das Erziehungswesen Zinzendorfs und der Brüdergemeine in seinen Anfängen.* Monumenta Germaniae Paedagogica, vol. 51. Berlin: Weidmannsche Buchhandlung, 1912.

———. *Zinzendorfs christliches Lebensideal*. Gnadau: Unitätsbuchhandlung, 1940.

———. *Zinzendorfs Gedanken über den Gottesdienst*. Herrnhut: Gustav Winter, 1931.

———. *Zinzendorfs religiöse Grundgedanken: Seine Religionsphilosophie und -psychologie*. Herrnhut: Missionsbuchhandlung, 1935.

———. *Zinzendorfs Weltbetrachtung: Eine systematische Darstellung der Gedankenwelt des Begründers der Brüdergemeine*. Bücher der Brüder, vol. 6. Berlin: Furche, 1929.

———. *Zinzendorf und die Frauen: Kirchliche Frauenrechte vor 200 Jahren*. Herrnhut: Verlag der Missions-buchhandlung, 1919.

———. *Zinzendorf und die Jugend: Die Erziehungsgrundsätze Zinzendorfs und der Brüdergemeine.* Bücher der Brüder, vol. 2. Berlin: Furche, 1923. This is an abbreviation of *Das Erziehungswesen Zinzendorfs und der Brüdergemeine in seinen Anfängen*.

* ———. *Zinzendorf und die Mystik.* Berlin: Christlicher Zeitschriften Verlag, [1952]. Reprinted in *Materialien und Dokumente,* ser. 2, vol. 19.

Vogt, Peter. "Zinzendorf and the 'Pennsylvania Synods' of 1742: The First Ecumenical Conferences on the North American Continent." Honors paper in religion, Moravian College, Bethlehem, Pa., May, 1992.

Wauer, Gerhard Adolf. *The Beginnings of the Brethren's Church ("Moravians") in England: A Chapter of the Commerce of Thought between Germany and England.* Translated by J. Elliot. Baildon: Moravian House, 1901.

Weinlick, John R. *Count Zinzendorf.* Nashville: Abingdon, 1956. Reprint, Bethlehem, Pa., and Winston-Salem, N.C.: Moravian Church in America, 1989.

Wellenreuther, Hermann, and Carola Wessel. *Herrnhuter Indianermission in der Amerikanischen Revolution; Die Tagebücher von David Zeisberger 1772-1781.* Selbstzeugenisse der Neuzeit: Quelen und Darstellungen zur Social- und Erfahrungsgeschichte. Berlin: Akademie Verlag, 1995.

Westmeier, Karl-Wilhelm. *The Evacuation of Shekomeko and the Early Moravian Missions to Native North Americans.* Studies in the History of Missions, vol. 12. Lewiston, N.Y.: Edwin Mellen Press, 1994.

Wettach, Theodor. *Kirche bei Zinzendorf.* Wuppertal, 1971.

Zeman, Jarold K. *The Hussite Movement and the Reformation in Bohemia, Moravia and Slovakia (1350-1650): A Bibliographical Study Guide with Particular Reference to Resources in North America.* Reformation in Europe, no. 1. Ann Arbor: Published under the auspices of the Center for Reformation Research by Michigan Slavic Publications, 1977.

Zimmerling, Peter. *Gott in Gemeinschaft: Zinzendorfs Trinitätslehre.* Giessen and Basel: Brunnen, 1991.

———. *Nachfolge lernen: Zinzendorf und das Leben der Brüdergemeine.* Moers: Brendow, 1990.

———. *Starke fromme Frauen.* Giessen: Brunnen, 1996.

Zinzendorf-Gedenkjahr 1960. Eine Sammlung von Vorträgen. Herrnhuter Hefte 16. Hamburg: Appel, 1961.

C. JOURNALS FOCUSED ON MORAVIAN HISTORY

Civitas Praesens: Ein Gespräch in der Brüdergemeine. Königsfeld, 1956-1964.

TMDK: Transatlantic Moravian Dialogue-Correspondence. English-language edition. Bethlehem, Pa./ *Transatlanticsche Moravische Dialog-Korrespondenz.* European [German-language] edition. Karlsruhe, 1993–.

Transactions of the Moravian Historical Society. Nazareth, Pa., 1859–.

Unitas Fratrum: Zeitschrift für Geschichte und Gegenwartsfragen der Brüdergemeine. Hamburg: Friedrich Wittig, 1977–.

* *Zeitschrift für Brüdergeschichte.* Herrnhut, 1907-1920. Reprinted in *Materialien und Dokumente,* ser. 3, vols. 1-4.

Index

R

Reformed Church   3, 5, 7, 13, 16, 18, 24, 27, 33, 73, 95, 244, 245, 246, 247, 248, 249, 266, 267, 268, 269, 270, 289, 291, 306
Religion   4, 65, 66, 246-251, 287, 291
Roh, John   16
Rothe, Johann Andreas   28, 226, 257, 259, 275, 276
Russia   23, 35, 255, 265

S

Saxony   3, 30, 32, 35, 226
Scheffler, Johann   55
Schlatter, Michael   270
Schleiermacher, Friedrich   18
Schrautenbach, Ludwig von   21, 22, 57
Schwenkfelders   266
Sekte   246, 250
Sendomir Consensus   16
Sifting Period   13, 28, 29, 36, 51, 104, 113, 114, 195, 227, 267, 271, 294, 299, 300
Simon, Richard   47, 142, 240
Spangenberg, Augustus Gottlieb   7, 8, 18, 23, 34, 38, 50, 52, 53, 54, 57, 58, 89, 144, 225, 255, 267, 270, 271, 272, 287, 294, 296, 304
Spinoza, Benedict de   40, 47, 48

T

Taborsky, John   15
Teresa of Avila   59, 72, 117, 199

theodicy   40, 45, 46
Thirty Years War   3, 13, 17, 31, 46, 230
tropus, tropi   3, 95, 248, 270, 291

U

Umgang mit Christus   58, 221, 222, 254
Utrecht   32, 79

V

Voltaire   42, 45, 46

W

Weiser, Conrad   23, 24
Wernsdorf, Gottlieb   52, 53
Wesley, John   24, 25, 34, 188, 189, 211, 290
West Indies   34, 35, 255, 269, 275
Wetteravia   113, 271, 299
Whitefield, George   270
Wittenberg   32, 52, 53, 63, 65, 178
wounds   13, 29, 36, 56, 58, 63, 68, 89, 93, 97, 100, 104, 110, 113, 117, 120, 121, 127, 129, 131, 136, 142, 145, 146, 178, 186, 194, 209, 210, 214, 216, 218, 239, 241, 252, 281, 283, 284, 288, 295, 297

Z

Zinzendorf, Benigna von   32, 276
Zinzendorf, Christian Renatus   36, 299
Zinzendorf, Erdmuthe Dorothea   32, 33, 37, 276
Zinzendorf, Georg von   31, 62, 63

Writings of Zinzendorf Quoted

Numbers are pages on which footnotes citing the quoted works appear. Works are listed approximately in the order in which they were written. Unless otherwise noted, translations from the German used in this book are by Arthur J. Freeman.

Der Teutsche Socrates. Das ist: Aufrichtige Anzeige verschiedener nicht so wohl unbekannter als vielmehr in Abfall gerathener Haupt-Wahrheiten, in den Jahren 1725 und 1726. Anfänglich in der Konigl. Residentz-Stadt Dreßden, Hernach aber dem gesamten lieben Vaterland teutscher Nation zu einer guten Nachricht nach und nach ausgefertiget, und von dem Autore selbst mit einem kurtzen Inhalt jedes Stücks, nunmehro auch mit verschiedenen Erläuterungen, die sich in der ersten Auflage nicht befinden, und einem Anhange versehen. (Leipzig: Samuel Benjamin Walthern, 1732). 98

Graf Ludwigs von Zinzendorff Teutscher Gedichte Erster Theil (Herrnhut: Zu finden in Waisenhause, 1735). 33, 80, 81, 82, 91

Des Herrn Grafen von Zinzendorff Inhalt einiger öffentlichen Reden, welche im Jahr 1738. vom Januario bis zu Ende des Aprils in Berlin an die Frauens-Personen daselbst gehalten worden. Vierte Auflage (Leipzig and Altona: Gebrüder Korte, 1749). 173

Inhalt einiger öffentlichen Reden, Welche im Jahr 1738. vom Januario bis zu Ende des Aprilis in Berlin an die Frauens-Personen daselbst gehalten worden. (Berlin: Christian Ludewig Kunst, n.d.). 278

Des Grafens von Zinzendorff Inhalt dererjenigen Reden, Welche zu Berlin vom

1ten Januar. 1738. bis 27ten Aprilis in denen Abend-Stunden sonderlich für die Manns-Personen gehalten worden. Dritte Auflage [3rd ed.] (Flensburg and Altona: Gebrüdern Korte, 1743). 87, 88, 125, 180, 208, 225

Sonderbare Gespräche zwischen Einem Reisenden und Allerhand andern Personen, von Allerley in der Religion vorkommenden Wahrheiten, Zweyte mit Fleis verbesserte Auflage (Altona: Gebrüder Korte, 1739). 280

Eines Abermahligen Versuchs zur Ubersetzung Der Lehr- und Prophetischen Bücher Neuen Testaments unsers Herrn Jesu Christi aus dem Original Erste Probe zweyte Edition Worinnen die meisten besagter Lehr-Bücher befindlich sind, Von den vorigen Schreib- Druck- und andern Fehlern gebessert (Büdingen: Joh. Christoph Stöhr, 1746). 46

Der Freywilligen Nachlese, Bey den bißherigen Gelehrten und erbaulichen Monaths-Schrifften, 1. Sammlung. Etiam inter manipulos colligat, et pudore non afficiatis eam. Ruth. C. II. v. 15. collection 13 (Frankfurt and Leipzig: M. Christ. Gottfried Marche, n.d.). 247, 250

Eine Predigt Vom Geheimniß der Religion, Über die Worte Es geschah, daß er mit dem Tode rang, und betete hefftiger. Es war sein Schweiß wie Bluts-Tropffen die fielen auf die Erde. Luc 22,44. Aus erheblichen

Ursachen dem Druck überlassen (Frankfurt and Basel: Johann Brandmüller,
Jünger, 1740). 147

*Jeremias, ein Prediger der Gerechtigkeit, allen
redlichen Predigern in der evangelischen
Kirche einfältig und als ein Exempel
vorgestellt, wie man in seinem Amte mit
Gott, mit der Obrigkeit, mit den Lehrern,
mit seinen Zuhörern überhaupt, und mit
seinen Brüdern insonderheit wandeln
könne. Von Nicolaus Ludwig, Grafen
von Zinzendorff. Nach der zweiten
verbesserten Auflage wieder abgedruckt*
(Berlin: Franklin und Comp., 1830).
248, 249

*Des Herrn Grafen Ludwig von Zinzendorff
Sieben Letzte Reden So Er In der Gemeine,
Vor seiner am 7. Aug. erfolgten
abermahligen Abreise nach America,
gehalten. Denen noch beygefügt sind zwey
in Gelnhausen von demselben gehaltene
und ehmals einzeln gedruckte Predigten*
(Büdingen: Johann Christoph Stöhr,
1743). 84, 150, 216, 217

*Teil 1-4 Theologische und dahin einschlagende
Bedencken Welche Ludwig Graf von
Zinzendorff, Zeitheriger Bischoff Der
Böhmisch- und Mährisch- Evangelischen
Brüder, Seit 20. Jahren entworffen. Mit
des Autoris Zuschrifft An alle Hohe
Obrigkeiten Und einer Vorrede Polycarpi
Müllers, Ehemahligen Professoris zu
Leipzig und Directoris des Gymnasii zu
Zittau, nunmehrigen Episcopi Fratrum*
(Büdingen: Johann Christoph Stöhr,
1742). 259, 266

*Büdingische Sammlung Einiger In die Kirchen-
Historie Einschlagender Sonderlich
neuerer Schrifften. Erster Band. Nebst
darzu gehörigen Registern. Sind wir doch
sein ererbtes gut* (Büdingen: Joh. Chr.
Stöhr [vol. 1], Korte [vols. 2, 3],
1742-44). 52, 53, 76, 190, 224

*Eine Sammlung Offentlicher Reden, Von Dem
Herrn der unsere Seligkeit ist, und über
die Materie von seiner Marter. In dem
Jahr 1742. Mehrentheils In den
Nordlichen Theil von America der das
Englische Canada ausmachet vor allerley
Christlichen Religions-Meetings gehalten,
von Dem damaligen Evangelischen*

*Lutherischen Inspectore und Past. zu
Philadelphia Erster Theil. [Zweyter
Theil.] Zweyte Edition* [2nd ed.]
(Büdingen: Johann Christoph Stöhr,
1746). 107, 140, 141, 142, 246

*Zwey und Dreyßig einzele Homiliae Oder
Gemein-Reden in denen Jahren 1744.
1745. 1746. Daß ich euch immer einerley
sage, verdrüßt mich nicht, und macht
euch desto gewißer* (n.p.: Zu finden in
den Brüder-Gemeinen, n.d.). 260

*Die gegenwärtige Gestalt Des Creutz-Reichs Jesu
in seiner Unschuld d. i. Verschiedene
deutliche Wahrheiten denen unzehligen
Unwahrheiten gegen eine bekante
Evangelische Gemeine In Dreyen
Abtheilungen entgegen, Und allen
unpartheyischen Gemüthern vor Augen
gestellet, Dem aber der die Hertzen kennet
und lencket, und nicht nach dem Ansehen
richtet, sondern ein recht Gerichte. Zu
selbst eigener Symmartyria einfältig
überlassen.* (Frankfurt and Leipzig:
Zu finden bey Johann Christoph
Stöhr, 1745). 224

*Die an den Synodum der Brüder, in Zeyst vom
11. May bis den 21. Junii 1746.
gehaltene Reden, Nebst noch einigen
andern zu gleicher Zeit in Holland
geschehenen Vorträgen* (n.p.: Zu finden
in den Brüder-Gemeinen, n.d.). 195,
279

*Nine Public Lectures on Important Subjects in
Religion Preached in Fetter Lane Chapel
in London in the Year 1746,* trans. and
ed. George W. Forell (Iowa City:
University of Iowa Press, 1973). 91,
139, 171, 172, 176, 177, 182, 183, 184,
185, 186, 190, 193, 194, 195, 220, 247

*Vier und Dreßig Homiliae über die Wunden-
Litaney der Brüder, Gehalten auf dem
Herrnhaag in den Sommer-Monathen
1747. von dem Ordinario Fratrum* (n.p.:
Zu finden in den Brüder-Gemeinen,
n.d.). 96, 100, 105, 130, 144, 146

*Der Öffentlichen Gemein-Reden im Jahr 1747.
Erster Theil. Mit einem Anhang einiger
zu Ende des Jahres 1746. gehaltenen
Homilien* (n.p.: Zu finden in den
Brüder-Gemeinen, 1748). 85, 87, 91,
112, 222, 251, 253, 277